Do No Harm

Do No Harm

A Festschrift in Honor of Charles Fensham

Edited by
Ernest van Eck
and George R. Hunsberger

◖PICKWICK *Publications* • Eugene, Oregon

DO NO HARM
A Festschrift in Honor of Charles Fensham

Copyright © 2025 Wipf and Stock Publishers. All rights reserved. Except for brief quotations in critical publications or reviews, no part of this book may be reproduced in any manner without prior written permission from the publisher. Write: Permissions, Wipf and Stock Publishers, 199 W. 8th Ave., Suite 3, Eugene, OR 97401.

Pickwick Publications
An Imprint of Wipf and Stock Publishers
199 W. 8th Ave., Suite 3
Eugene, OR 97401

www.wipfandstock.com

PAPERBACK ISBN: 979-8-3852-2149-3
HARDCOVER ISBN: 979-8-3852-2150-9
EBOOK ISBN: 979-8-3852-2151-6

Cataloguing-in-Publication data:

Names: van Eck, Ernest, editor. | Hunsberger, George R., editor.

Title: Do no harm : a festschrift in honor of Charles Fensham / edited by Ernest van Eck and George R. Hunsberger.

Description: Eugene, OR: Pickwick Publications, 2025. | Includes bibliographical references.

Identifiers: ISBN 979-8-3852-2149-3 (paperback). | ISBN 979-8-3852-2150-9 (hardcover). | ISBN 979-8-3852-2151-6 (ebook).

Subjects: LCSH: Fensham, Charles, 1956–. | Theology. | Missiology. | Theology—Study and teaching.

Classification: BV4020 2025 (print). | BV4020 (ebook).

04/14/25

Contents

Preface | vii
Ernest van Eck and George R. Hunsberger

List of Contributors | xxvii

List of Abbreviations | xxix

Introduction | xxxi
George R. Hunsberger

1 On a Cultured Christianity | 1
   Ernst M. Conradie

2 A Multi-Voice Conversation Seeking Greater Inclusivity in Theological Education | 16
   Dorcas Gordon

3 In Search of a Theology of the Cross for Korea, a Nation Transitioning into a Multicultural and Multiracial Society: A Critique on Anselm's Cur Deus Homo and Moltmann's Social Trinitarian Understanding of the Cross | 38
   Hye Kyung Heo

4 Emerging Pentecostal Ecclesiology Through the Lens of Missiological Method | 59
   Issac Hong

5 Christian Mission in an Age of Contested Identities | 81
   Robert Hunt

6 Fensham's Theology in a Dialogue with a Theology of Han | 93
   Bong-Chan Ko

Contents

7   Charles Fensham: Missiologist as Poet | 110
    Gregory P. Leffel

8   A Different Kind of Congress: The Congress of Concern, 1968 | 129
    Stuart Macdonald

9   The Inner Mission: Trauma, Extraversion, and Missiology | 149
    Glenn McCullough

10 Radicalizing Women: The Abuse of Women by Radicals in the Reformation | 171
    David Neelands

11 Intercultural Theology as Ecumenical Theology | 181
    Hendrik R. Pieterse

12 Sinister Soldiers and Single Women | 202
    Billie Anne Robinson

13 Naming Human and Divine: Expansive and Inclusive Liturgy in The Presbyterian Church in Canada | 222
    Sarah Travis

14 A Prophet of Old: Jesus the "Public Theologian" | 237
    Ernest van Eck

15 The Threefold Office of Christ (Munus Triplex) in Canadian Presbyterian Theology | 270
    John A. Vissers

Preface

Ernest van Eck and George R. Hunsberger

A Short Biography

CHARLES JAMES FENSHAM WAS born in Stellenbosch, South Africa, on September 4, 1956. His mother, Yvonne Theron, was a librarian and his father, F. Charles Fensham, was Professor of Semitic Languages at the University of Stellenbosch.

Charles's family were committed Dutch Reformed *Moederkerk* (Mother Church) members in Stellenbosch. However, his father was also a regular volunteer preacher at the local Rhenish church whose membership consisted of descendants from slaves brought from Indonesia and Malaysia. In the South African apartheid system, the members of this church were classified as Colored People. Some of Charles's fondest memories of the church were enjoying the services at the Rhenish church with its enthusiastic singing and the warm welcome always received as the family sat in the front pew. Later these memories would encourage ethical reflection as he became aware of the apartheid system and its systemic discrimination and harm directed at racialized people.

The first memory of awareness of racial injustice came when the apartheid government decided to forcefully relocate members of the Rhenish church from their small vegetable farms to an area inappropriate for farming. Charles's parents became deeply involved in advocacy against this

Preface

displacement, and Charles overheard the heated discussions in meetings in their living room as members from the church came to ask for help. Eventually, he observed the quiet tears shed when his parents could not influence the process in any way.

As a teenager and young adult in a middle-class family, Charles experienced the privilege of being white in South Africa. He went to a racially separated high school at Paul Roos Gymnasium in Stellenbosch where education was conducted in both Afrikaans and English. Teachers would teach speaking one sentence in Afrikaans and the next in English. In grade twelve, Charles became a confessing member of the Dutch Reformed church after a catechism class under the mentorship of Professor Nico Smit, who would later become one of the major white Afrikaner anti-apartheid activists in South Africa. As Charles benefited from white privilege in South Africa, his decision to study architecture at the University of Cape Town was easily realized. There he became increasingly aware of the apartheid system and its impact on racialized people. After two years of architectural studies, he felt a call to ministry and decided to study theology.

As a result of his experience of the racism and a spirituality that seemed devoid of passion and ethics in the Dutch Reformed Church and an inability as a young member of the church to bring change towards racial justice, he decided to join the Presbyterian Church of Southern Africa and became a candidate for ministry in that denomination. After completing a theology degree at the University of South Africa, Charles was called to Kokstad Presbyterian Church in Natal Province. Charles married Marina Lombaard, and they proceeded to this first charge where he was ordained after a year of internship.

In 1982, Charles and Marina decided to work with the French youth mission organization *Jeunesse en Mission* and moved to Paris, France, where they engaged in language studies to become fluent in French. After they received training in Lausanne Switzerland, they were sent to the French Polynesian islands in the Pacific. This ministry was by invitation of the Polynesian church, *Eglise Evangelique*, a denomination of Presbyterian and French Reformed missionary heritage. During this time, Charles also completed an honours degree in religious studies at the University of South Africa, specializing in Hinduism and Islam, and then proceeded to start work on a ThM on the dialogue between Roman Catholics and Evangelicals on the nature of salvation.

Preface

When the economic system in South Africa declined and financial support for their work became impossible, Charles and Marina returned to South Africa where Charles was called to St. Francis Presbyterian Church in Pretoria. St. Frances was a joint Anglican-Presbyterian community that shared services monthly. Having completed his ThM degree, Charles was also appointed to a part-time position as a junior lecturer in mission studies at the University of South Africa.

After completing his ThM degree, Charles proceeded to doctoral studies under the joint supervision of David J. Bosch and Tom Sine. During this time at St. Francis and the University of South Africa, Charles's activities and anti-apartheid sentiments became a matter of concern for the authorities. He was informed by a friend who worked in the security industry that his telephone was tapped; later, his office was raided, books confiscated, and he received harassing visits from the security police that threatened his parents and sisters.

Charles and Marina decided to respond by quietly moving to Canada. In 1988, Charles received a call from Kirkwall Presbyterian Church in Canada, and he started his ministry in The Presbyterian Church in Canada in January 1989. In 1992, Charles graduated with a ThD degree with the title *Missiology for the Future: A Missiology in the Light of the Emerging Systemic Paradigm* at the University of South Africa. In 1994, Charles accepted a call to Eastmount Presbyterian Church in Hamilton, Ontario. After completing his doctoral degree, Charles felt a need to focus his pastoral care skills and completed a ThM in Pastoral Care at Waterloo Lutheran Seminary, which was focused on the practice of Narrative Therapy. As part of that training, he also completed the supervised clinical work to be certified as a teaching supervisor in pastoral counselling in the Canadian Association of Pastoral Practice Education (currently known as CASC, i.e., the Canadian Association of Spiritual Care) and he was also certified as a clinical member of the American Association of Marriage and Family Therapy. Charles and Marina had two sons, Alexander Fensham (1993) and Andrew Fensham (1996). During the 1990s, Charles was nominated by his presbytery to serve on the Committee on Church Doctrine of the General Assembly of The Presbyterian Church in Canada.

In 2002, Charles was called to the position of Professor of Systematic Theology at Knox College in Toronto. He soon achieved tenure and was promoted to Associate Professor in 2007. In 2012, he was further promoted to Full Professor. His greatest pleasure was being in the classroom, interacting

Preface

with students and mentoring students in the graduate programs of the Toronto School of Theology. Being committed to theology in context, Charles focused his research on the challenge of the decline of Christianity and The Presbyterian Church in Canada and responded to this challenge in his first book, *Emerging from the Dark Age Ahead: The Future of the North American Church* (2008), which was published by St. Paul's University, Novalis Press. This was followed by *To the Nations for the Earth A Missional Spirituality* (2013), published by Clements Academic, which was focused on developing a missional spirituality in light of the challenges to the Christian faith in contemporary Canada.

During the period leading up to the publication of his second book, Charles and Marina started facing up to their growing awareness and acknowledgement of their sexual orientations. For Charles, this was further highlighted by the debates and controversies within The Presbyterian Church in Canada on the rejection or affirmation of people who are LGBTQI2+. Eventually, this led to Charles and Marina agreeing to an amicable separation and later divorce. As a theologian who was always in some way aware of his sublimated gay sexual orientation, Charles engaged in a research project on the history of homophobia in Christianity, the so-called biblical arguments against LGBTQI2+ people, and the history of harm and abuse suffered at the hand of Christians throughout the existence of Christianity as a religious movement. This research led to the publication of his book *Misguided Love: Christians and the Rupture of LGBTQI2+ People* (2019), published by the Journal of Pastoral Care Publications after a peer review process.

Since his appointment to the Committee on Church Doctrine of The Presbyterian Church in Canada and his subsequent ex-officio appointment to that committee as Professor of Systematic Theology, Charles actively participated in the production of documents of this committee, including the key document "Confessing the Faith Today" on the meaning of ordination in the Presbyterian church, the document "Living in God's Mission Today," the drafts on the proposed new preamble to ordination vows, and one of the study documents on the Bible and LGBTQI2+ people. Charles has also been an active participant in his academic guild, "The American Society of Missiology," where he served on its Board of Governors. Since his doctoral studies, Charles was also committed to highlighting the relationship between the global ecological crisis and faith and became involved in the global working group on ecology and faith, "Christian Faith and the Earth."

Preface

During his final years at Knox College, Charles collected some of his journal publications and some new material into a book focused on highlighting the major themes of his work in Theology of Mission. This book, *Mission as Penance: Essays on the Theology of Mission from a Canadian Context* (2023), was published by Pickwick Publications.

Today, as Professor Emeritus of Knox College, Charles and his partner Charles Chuck Wah Ho live in Toronto; Marina and her wife Michelle Kamerling live in Ancaster, Ontario; and their children and partners live in Toronto and Hamilton. As an extended and blended family, they enjoy and are thankful for many blessings as they gather for special occasions and seasonal celebrations.

It is almost hard to believe that Charles retired on December 31, 2023, as Professor of Systematic Theology after serving Knox College with distinction for 21 years. He served the College and The Presbyterian Church in Canada with great devotion and enthusiasm. He often mentioned how proud he was to be a minister in The Presbyterian Church in Canada. The students at Knox have the utmost respect for the quality of Professor Fensham's teaching, his supervision, how he supported students as their advisor, as well as his general support to students. His kindness, uprightness, thoughtfulness, and authenticity will be remembered, and his sermons and prophetic voice will be missed. Professor Fensham's faith and witness at Knox, on campus and in the broader church, have made a tremendous difference in the lives of his students and colleagues. With this Festschrift, Knox College gives recognition to his contribution as a faculty member at Knox, his remarkable contributions to the fields of missiology and systematic theology, and especially his advocacy for the rights of the LGBTQI2+ community. We thank God for his remarkable career, his dedicated service to the church, and his contributions to creating a just society. We are forever in his debt.[1]

---

1. The College held a farewell function for Charles Fensham on Wednesday, December 13, 2023. In preparation for this event, I, as Principal, invited Faculty members and staff to share a few reflections on their experiences working with Charles, which he could incorporate into his farewell speech. The comments received beautifully captured the significant contributions Charles made during his time at Knox College. For the record, I list some of these remarks:

"You are already missed."

"It has been a pleasure to work with you."

"Your kindness, uprightness, thoughtfulness and authenticity will always be remembered."

"You have made an undeniable difference at Knox. It will not be the same at Knox without you."

Preface

A Conversation with Professor Fensham

The Editors believed that it would be useful to provide a more intimate portrait of the person whose life's work is being celebrated in this volume. They consulted with him about a set of questions that would allow him to tell his own story. Let us listen in.

1. You have been teaching theology at Knox College (University of Toronto) since 2002, and before that, you also taught at McMaster Divinity College and the University of South Africa for a total of thirty-eight years. What do you consider to be the most important roles in being a professor of theology?

My hope is always that the most successful outcome of theological education is to form leaders who are deeply human, self-aware, faithful, and humble. This posture, combined with faithfulness and integrity, can weather the doubts and painful wounds that come with ministry. For that reason, I believe it should be the core goal of theological education. This does not in any way mean attaining perfection, rather, it means being truly human embracing frailty and inevitable failures as part of being creatures of God.

You would notice that I go with this first before I talk about the content and knowledge of theological education. That is because the things we teach and believe have no meaning if they are not held in a deeply human and faithful way in our lives. A minister who can lead worship from a position of vulnerability, compassion, and love is more minister than one with a golden tongue that can wow audiences with snappy quotes and public performance.

A hymn that expresses this beautifully is Thomas Troeger's ordination hymn "As a Chalice Cast of Gold." When I taught students about the ordination vows, I always started with this hymn. In fact, I tried to use hymns

---

"Thank you for years of Gospel witness; I will cherish our conversations. Thank you for being you!"

"A *mensch* is leaving the building."

"Thank you for your kindness and welcoming. I will miss your sermons and our conversations."

"Thank you for inspiring students to think critically and creatively."

"Thank you for being an advocate for Qu(e)ering Religion. I will miss your rainbow lanyard!"

"Your legacy at Knox will not be forgotten."

"Your presence and voice have always been both prophetic and challenging, but also deeply compassionate."

"Your faith and witness at Knox, on campus, and in the broader church, have made a tremendous difference in the lives of so many."

in all my core courses as a way to bring worship and theology together, because hymns and theology should never be divorced. After all, the Pauline literature in the New Testament is peppered with hymns. Troeger writes in this hymn, "When I bend upon my knees, clasp my hands or bow my head, let my spoken public pleas, be directly, simply said, free of entangled words that mask, what my soul would plainly ask."

Those who go into Christian leadership in Canada today go into an uncertain world, with little security, much opposition, and lots of harms done by Christians in the past hanging over their heads. In addition, such leaders face false forms of Christianity tainted by money, power, and sometimes greed. They need a humble grit that can face these things and see God's love through it all.

2. Your work in theology has always borne a close relationship with missiology. How has your work positioned itself within that discipline's trends and debates?

In 1991, David Bosch defined mission as participation in the liberating mission of Jesus. I would largely agree with this, except that I would add that mission is first of all born of God in our understanding of the theology of creation (as I believe Bosch would agree). Creation itself is a Divine act of mission, and the coming of Jesus to the world is God's self-giving act of mission for the healing and wholeness of creation. In all this, the church plays an important role to continue mission. Mission is first of all an act of a loving and gracious God.

In 1970, Ivan Illich defined mission as "the birth of the church beyond its boundaries, beyond the linguistic barriers in which she feels at home, beyond the poetic images it taught its children—the church as surprise."

In the 1990s, Darrell Guder, George Hunsberger, Craig van Gelder, Inagrace Dietterich, Alan Roxburgh, and Lois Barrett published the book *Missional Church*. To their chagrin, the idea became a meme embraced for all kinds of simplistic self-help menus focused on growing churches bigger to make more money and claim more power. Rather, what they meant was that the church is by its nature missional, and, where it is not, it is leaving its meaning for existence behind. They conceived mission in the wider way I described in the definitions above. It is perhaps reminiscent of Brunner's famous quote, that the church exists by mission as a flame exists by burning.

Today, much of what goes under the title mission is not mission at all, but attempts at perpetuating a triumphalistic, self-congratulatory form of religion which tries to impose itself on others and grow its power base. Hence my response in my book *Mission as Penance*.

3. One of your interests focused strongly on public theology, that is, the relevance of theology for society. What would you describe as the relevance of your research for society today?

One of my key involvements in the American Society of Missiology has been in participating in a working group of scholars from all over Turtle Island to develop a public missiology response to our present context. In this group I work with people like Greg Leffel (One Horizon Foundation), Gregg Okesson (Asbury Theological Seminary), George Hunsberger (Western Theological Seminary), Hendrik Pieterse (Garrett-Evangelical Theological Seminary), Robert Hunt (Perkins School of Theology) and William Kenney (One Horizon Foundation) as we try to respond to the momentous changes in the world—climate change, culture, politics, and Christianity. One of our key concerns is something that the Public Theology movement has neglected: the role of the church. Public Theology constructs brilliant cutting-edge ideas, but there is little to give these ideas legs that actually impact and change cultures and the world. This led to a debate that I engaged with Sebastian Kim, the founding editor of the International Journal of Public Theology. Our main concern is how do the churches and representatives of the Christian faith engage the world today in relevant and responsible ways that reflect the best of the Jesus traditions we find in the Bible. How can our theology help transform churches into healing social movements in the world?

However, it is important to qualify *church* and *churches*. The church is to be a movement of God's grace and love in the world. Christian churches are institutions. Religious institutions are vital and critically important, but they also hold the danger of becoming harmful. There is overwhelming evidence from the history of the Christian church of this dark side of the church as institution. We see this in the development of so-called "just war theory," the Inquisition and the torture and murder arising from it, and the persecution of so-called witches and people on the LGBTQI2+ spectrum. This is true for both Catholicism and Protestant churches who literally killed children in the name of God . . . We see this in the treatment of the Indigenous peoples in Canada, and we see it now in the US racist Christian nationalism that has captured the evangelical movement in the US. For all these reasons, institutions are important: they give meaning to society and are part of the imaginaries that create our cultures and behaviour. Thus, I have been consistently focused on calling the institutional church, my church, to faithfulness to the Gospel. In my book *Emerging from the Dark Age Ahead*, I outlined some of these arguments, and in my book *To the Nations for the Earth*, I developed a missional spirituality for our time. In *Misdirected Love*, I called the church to account for its treatment of LGBTQI2+ people, and in *Mission as Penance*, I tried to chart a course towards a form of Christianity that is faithful to the best of what we have in the Jesus traditions in the New Testament.

4. From your publications, it is clear that you firmly believe in the power of the biblical message for social formation and positive change (e.g., issues related to LGBTQI2+). Please reflect academically on the hermeneutical restrictions and possibilities of applying the ancient text of the Bible to modern situations.

I remember how eye-opening it was for me to engage in biblical studies at the University of South Africa. I remember one of my professors stressing that critical biblical scholarship is about respecting the Bible for how it came into being and, therefore, what it is meant to be. The deconstruction of biblical fundamentalism is about a faithful respect for the intention and meaning of the text. I mean *faithful* in capitals here. *It is an act of faith and trust in God.* When we engage the Bible in this way, it makes sense. The Bible speaks through the structures of culture and history and prompts us to think creatively about the traditions handed down to us through this book and its history of interpretation. Such an approach has the potential for persuasive integrity. As someone who is not trained as a biblical scholar, I realise just how complicated this is. It is complicated for students who come to seminary with a naive form of faith formed by a lack of education and understanding in their own faith journey. It is perhaps even more complicated for theologians, including some very famous ones. In his book *Experiences in Theology*, Jürgen Moltmann writes that he tried to make sense of biblical studies as he encountered it in the university setting and gave up!

My thesis supervisor, David Bosch, who himself studied New Testament studies with Oscar Cullman, responded to this question in a way that has carried my own faith, arguing that our task is to creatively extend the logic we find in the Jesus traditions contained in the Bible. How to engage the Bible both critically and faithfully is one of the most important things we can help students prepare for ministry to learn. Although I did not teach

Preface

the Introduction to Theology course for many years, I think it needs to start there with sources and methods and some real-life examples that fit in that kind of course. I tried to pick up on this in my second-level course, "Church, Ministry and Sacraments." To do that, I had my students read David Bosch's famous paper on the so-called "great commission" in Matthew 28. In that paper, Bosch suggests that the role this text has played in nineteenth and twentieth-century mission thinking does not do justice to the text. One of the things he does is to address whether Matthew 28:16–20 necessarily reports the actual words of Jesus. I guess this was his way of weighing in on the Jesus Seminar! He concluded that these words were most likely not uttered by Jesus as recorded. However, he goes on to suggest that what happens in these kinds of texts in the Gospels is early Christianity working to creatively and faithfully extend the logic of the Jesus stories that they have heard handed down orally. He argues that this text is a key to understanding the whole Gospel of Matthew. This text also depends heavily on all that comes before it. The instruction to "teach them to obey all," he argues, means taking seriously the Jesus traditions recorded in the Gospel and bringing its logic to their contemporary situation. A faithful reading of the Gospel means considering, and thinking through, how these ancient creative conclusions of early Christianity can inform our own work at making sense of the tradition, thus letting it shape our own actions and faith journey in our own time. Many of my students over the years have shared how much this has helped them in making sense of biblical scholarship.

Of course, there is not one "biblical message"; the Bible is not univocal: it speaks from many different times and in many different cultural shapes. Our task is to study, discern the best understanding of the original texts, grasp the cultural clothing it wears, and then seek to creatively extend its logic shaped always by a constant reference to the several Jesus traditions captured in the New Testament. In the history of Christianity, this is what Christian people did in relation to slavery and racism, what they did in relation to the role of women in the church and society, what we finally acknowledged in our apologies to Indigenous peoples, and what a large part of the Christian faith is now doing in relation to LGBTQI2+ people. I agree with the British sociologist and Anglican priest, David Martin, that these Jesus traditions can serve as seeds within the cultures of the world for love and justice. When these seeds start to flower in cultures, they transform the world into a place of healing and wholeness. Sometimes the institutional church, as David Bosch claimed, is just a fragment of the Gospel while the

Preface

Spirit is at work in a much deeper and wider way. Our reading of the Bible in the present context must have integrity; it cannot become simplistic, or, as Karl Barth called it, "a paper pope." Only then can it inspire social movements of healing, love, and justice.

5. Over the time of your teaching ministry, the church and its place in the world has changed dramatically in Canada and the larger world. What do you believe is the most important thing for the Christian churches to consider given our changed context and role in the world?

My answers above provide some hints. I believe Christians and their institutions should stop seeking money, power, influence, and prestige. We are, as Miroslav Volf pointed out, no longer *the* chair at the table of the world; we occupy but one chair in God's amazing diverse creation. Douglas Hall has called Canadian churches to account in this way for decades now. Fundamentally, beyond ceasing to seek money, power, and influence, our posture in the world must faithfully reflect our faith. Our posture should be one of repentant humility in the face of the evils done by Christian institutions in the past and still being perpetrated today. To give some examples of the ongoing harm done by Christian institutions, we can think of forms of evangelicalism in Canada that keep attacking transgender youth and other LGBTQI2+ people and continue to try to assert political power over a small and vulnerable group of people. Churches, including our own beloved Presbyterian Church in Canada, still let it happen in our own midst. We can point to the Orthodox church in Russia that supports the violent invasion of Ukraine, and the role of churches in countries such and Uganda and Ghana in creating draconian laws against LGBTQI2+ people, claiming God's command in these evil actions. Therefore—mission as penance is where we as Christians and our institutions need to begin.

6. A theology professor is also a human being with feelings, experiences, and challenges, how would you describe the major challenges you faced personally as a professor, and what have you learned from those experiences?

One of the most surprising things in my twenty-two years as professor of systematic theology at Knox College has been the ridicule I have observed and experienced within The Presbyterian Church in Canada in relation to a commitment to deep theological thinking. Since 1998, I have served on the Committee of Church Doctrine of the church, and I would say, initially,

Preface

there was a spirit of real debate and respectful disagreements. Then, slowly, the nomination process became political. People worked behind the scenes to try and control the agenda, and some of those appointed to this committee did not come to do the hard work of study, reflection, and careful dialogue but rather to block considered dialogical discussions. Prooftexts and simplistic readings of the Scripture became more common. I also experienced this on several occasions when I was invited to preach. I would get introduced as if I were from another planet, and no one would understand what I will say because I am the professor of systematic theology. In fact, one minister, who must have somehow graduated from Knox College, in introducing me to his congregation, claimed that he did not know what systematic theology was and claimed that this ignorance was a badge of honour. I was also surprised by the lack of theological dialogue among the faculty of colleges of the church as, more and more, the colleges seemed to move into adversarial relationships with each other and seemed to try to ignore or trump one another.

Of course, it was personally quite painful to face the lies, the un-invitations, and the way many successfully worked to silence me during our debates on the place of LGBTQI2+ people. For me, this journey had a profound impact on my mental health to the point of seriously considering suicide. It was not the church that provided spiritual care at that time; on the contrary, it was a kind and gentle family doctor.

The Assembly where the two compromise remits, re: marriage and the ordination of LGBTQI2+ people, were approved stands out as particularly nasty, including one minister claiming on the floor of the Assembly that Jesus Christ was not about love! Of course, people can say strange things, but not calling out a minister of the Gospel who publicly makes such a claim in an official church meeting is a failure in the integrity of the Gospel.

What have I learned from this? Most of all, that God calls me to repentance and humility. I must ask to what extent I contribute to the rising tide of nastiness within the institution. I learned to refrain from engaging people with ill intent on social media. I learned to refrain from fighting the person but to keep my eye on the message of the Gospel. I also learned to pray, particularly for those who seek to attack and harm me and for The Presbyterian Church in Canada itself and its well-being. Through these experiences, my daily prayer life became focused on praying for the world, my community, my enemies, and, of course, my friends. These experiences also taught me to be thankful for the wonderful blessings in my life. I have seen

Preface

the amazing healing power of the church turning around and embracing grace and love. This is most dramatically demonstrated when I march with Presbyterians in the Toronto Pride Parade. Every year, as I march in my clergy collar, I have young people reaching out to touch my hand with tears streaming down their faces as they hear that God actually loves them . . .

7. As a professor of systematic theology, your task was to teach the major themes of Christian faith as we read the Bible for today. What would you see as the most important theological idea or insight for our time and context?

Perhaps my earlier comments on the Bible begin to respond to these questions. I believe that the message of the Jesus traditions and the logic of their meaning needs to be creatively extended and made known in ways that can be grasped in our culture and our time with integrity and clarity. Systematic theology is not about impossibly long German sentences. It is about what makes sense for the healing and wholeness of all creation. The most important thing is captured in a course I taught throughout my twenty-two years at Knox College—"Doctrines of Reconciliation." In that course, we explored the simple questions: What does the consistent Christian claim that Jesus died for my sins mean for us today? Why did he die? What is wrong with this world, and how does God heal it? How does this make sense in our present culture and world? How does this event bring healing and wholeness? What is our role in the light of this?

Personally, and I shared this with my students every year, I find Jürgen Moltmann's response to these questions most helpful and meaningful. Theology is never the final answer; it is always love and faith seeking to understand in bumbling human ways. However, this quest can bring deep peace and wholeness to us in our love for God, God's world, and God's people. For me then, Moltmann's imagination, built on solid Christian and Jewish traditions, provides a very helpful and healing way to understand something so profound that we can only grasp it imperfectly.

I ask my students to imagine what is before the act of creation. In the "time before time began," as Adrianus van Selms so beautifully put it in his commentary on Genesis. Imagine there is only God and nothing that is different from or other than God. Then the God-being chooses to create something beyond Godself. Moltmann takes this moment and builds on the insight of the Kabbalistic scholar Issaac Luria to argue that to make this altruistic, loving act of God possible, God must make space for something

Preface

different from God to come into being. The only way to do this is for God to withdraw to make room for creation. It is in this altruistic act of love that God goes beyond Godself. God makes room, creates hospitality, and in fact, makes Godself vulnerable to what is being created. Yet, also, of necessity, when God withdraws, that space in which creation is ordered is disordered because it is a space empty of God's presence. All evil, sin, suffering, and pain in creation originate in this Godlessness that surrounds creation and impinges on it. Godlessness is the very definition of hell. Godless space is a state of non-being. It is a state of nothingness, as early Christianity claimed. Karl Barth called it sin as the impossible possibility.

But, creation is a process rooted in God loving God's creation. Therefore, God cannot leave it to be harmed and to suffer. Therefore, God, in God's love, comes to the world and keeps coming to the world to become present to the nothingness and its evil. The story of the coming of Jesus is the sign of this divine response. God enters creation to become present to Godlessness to heal the sin, imperfection, pain, and suffering of creation. "The Logos became flesh and dwelt among us full of grace and truth." The cross and the death of Christ begin the process of God becoming present to Godless space and its disruption of the love and justice of God's presence. The cross exposes sin—Godlessness—on different levels. The crucifixion of Jesus exposes the evil of hatred, scapegoating, killing, oppression, and abuse of political power and the powers behind it. But, the crucifixion also allows God to become present to the Godlessness, the source of evil and sin. In the death of Jesus, the Son enters separation from the presence of the fullness of God to make God present. Thus, Godself is broken open in agonizing love as God as Creator grieves the pain of the Son, and the Son grieves the absence of the Creator, and the Spirit suffers with the Creator and the Son in redeeming Godlessness. Jesus enters the God-less nothingness and, painfully, makes God present. God's love thus creates a painful rift in the trinitarian bonds of love.

The implication of the cross is not just political: even though it surely is political on earth, yet it is also cosmic. Both God and God's cosmic creation are changed as God starts to become present to a yet imperfect creation through the Spirit that now flows to the world from the life of Christ that emerges out of the evil of Godlessness. Our task is to surrender to this flow of God's presence in justice, grace, and love brought by the Spirit and to participate in its healing power.

Preface

8. You were not teaching worship and preaching, yet the content of worship and preaching is intimately related to the content of our faith. How do you see worship within The Presbyterian Church in Canada in our time and what are your thoughts about worship and preaching?

Because of what I said about the meaning of the crucifixion of Christ, I believe that the corporate worship of God is of profound importance. It is because Jesus came to make God present with us. After all, he came to make profound communion between creation, people, and God possible, and the expression of that communion in thanksgiving, praise, and prayer is critical for the healing of the world. Gathering for worship is the way we express and experience the amazing gift of God with us. Our institutional approach to worship has often become focused on relaying moral lessons and, in the wealthier congregations, on music performance. Of course, any form of communion and communication is performative in some way, but worship is not performance for others; it is about participation in communion with God. I pray that our worship may become more of that, more of experiencing God present with us, more silence to listen, more openness to hear, and more praise for God's sake. I dream of such worship and from time to time I get a glimpse of it, and when I do, I know that God's healing has come to me.

9. One of the courses you taught at Knox College was on our Christian understanding of our relationship with other religions. In Canada we live in a very religiously diverse reality today, so how should we as Presbyterian Christians respond to and engage our neighbors of other religions?

I remember a General Assembly where a Muslim Imam was invited to bring greetings. In protest, several commissioners walked out as the Imam was stepping onto the stage. To me, such behaviour communicates a profound misunderstanding of our faith as Presbyterians. In fact, it also communicates a rebuttal of Jesus himself, who admonished us to love our neighbours as ourselves. Yet, I would say that this kind of unfriendly behaviour is also a result of a failure of leaders in The Presbyterian Church in Canada and the colleges to provide clarity of leadership on how we understand our relationship with other faiths. I believe our denomination has a deeply thoughtful theological understanding of what is called the "theology of religions." We have a beautiful section in our subordinate standard, *Living Faith*, that makes clear that our neighbours of other faiths may have devotion, reverence, truth, and goodness in their midst and that the Holy Spirit is thus at work through such qualities in people's lives. It goes on to say that we should not have arrogance but should witness to our faith in humility as beggars telling others where food is to be found. Our role is one of humble witness, pointing to God. That sentiment was again affirmed by the General Assembly in 2017 by approving the document "Living in God's Mission Today," a document close to my heart. Nevertheless, through my time at Knox College, I encountered students who were taught by their Presbyterian ministers that people of other faiths are evil, harbour evil, and are to be aggressively approached. Of course, The Presbyterian Church in Canada does not teach that everyone is perfect, and that includes us and others, no matter what their faith! What it does teach is to treat those different from ourselves with the respect of a creature of God that might very well have God's Spirit already present in their lives.

10. Who do you consider the most influential in shaping your Christian journey and what have you learned from them?

I do not doubt that my father had the greatest influence on me. He was an example of faith and humility as well as an example of how to be a holy troublemaker when Christian institutions became too rigid. In my teenage years, I would make coffee and join my dad in his office where he would often work until midnight or beyond, and we would have long theological conversations that were profoundly formative for my understanding of the Bible. He would read me a text he was translating from Arabic and ask me what religion it represented. I would say undoubtedly Christian, and he would laugh and say, no, it is an Islamic text! He taught me critical thinking and his friendship with the Jewish community and the local Rabbi demonstrated respectful interfaith friendship.

My students, on the other hand, would joke that they only have to say "David Bosch" and that would get them an A for any assignment because I refer to David so often in class! Of course, David had a profound influence on my thinking as I was shaped by his writing and personal friendship and guidance which we sadly lost due to his untimely death in a car accident in 1992. While writing his magisterial book *Transforming Mission*, he would send me chapters to read and provide feedback. Not that I had much to offer!

Nico Smit had a profound influence on me as well, first as my catechism teacher and my dad's dear friend. When he publicly came out against

Preface

apartheid and was fired from his position as professor of Missiology at the Seminary in Stellenbosch, he set an example of courage and faith and "coming out." His influence continued when he defied apartheid laws to move into a black township to live amid his parish. At that time, we shared an office at the University of South Africa, and I was able to see firsthand the way his black parishioners were treated in the Mamelodi Township in Pretoria. His courage, love, care, and personal support meant the world to me.

The fourth person is Willem Saayman, who supervised my master's thesis on the dialogue between Protestants and Catholics on the nature of salvation. Willem acted as an engaged mentor; later he and his family attended the Presbyterian Congregation, St Francis Waterkloof, where I was a minister in Pretoria, and I had the joy of confirming their daughter in their faith in that congregation. Willem taught me that the outcome of true Christian redemption should be manifested in becoming deeply and truly human.

Finally, after I moved to Canada, I met Father Albert Nolan, the famed author of "Jesus Before Christianity," and somehow, we hit it off. Albert was not someone to be manipulated. When he was elected to be Master of the Order of Preachers in the Dominican order in 1983, one of the most important positions in the Roman Catholic hierarchy, he declined, wishing to stay as an ordinary priest in the townships near Johannesburg. Every time I returned to South Africa on sabbatical, we would spend a day in retreat together. When he received his honorary doctorate from Regis College, he called me and said, "I don't want to stay with the Catholics, can I stay with you when I come to Toronto?" And so, he did. I took him around to Catholic events and Catholic schools as he did the rounds, and we had tons of fun together. His passing in 2022 at age eighty-eight was a very sad moment for me. As a liberation theologian, a critical biblical scholar, and mostly as a pastor whose faith was profoundly woven in all parts of his action and thinking, he was an example that kept reminding me what true Christian humility looked like.

Publication List

Books

Fensham, Charles. *Emerging from the Dark Age Ahead: The Future of the North American Church*. Ottawa: Novalis/St. Paul's University Press, 2008. Reissued, Toronto: Clements Academic, 2011.

Preface

Fensham, Charles. *To the Nations for the Earth: A Missional Spirituality*. Toronto: Clements Academic, 2013.

Fensham, Charles. *Misguided Love: Christians and the Rupture of LGBTQI2+ People*. Decatur, GA: Journal of Pastoral Care Publications, 2019. (Peer-reviewed).

Fensham, Charles J. *Mission as Penance: Essays on the Theology of Mission from a Canadian Context*. Eugene, OR: Pickwick Publications, Wipf & Stock, 2023.

Peer-Reviewed Articles

Fensham, C.J. "An Evaluation of the Nature of Mission and the Gospel of Salvation in the Evangelical-Roman Catholic Dialogue on Mission." *Missionalia* 16, no. 1 (1988) 25–39.

Fensham, C.J. "The Glory of God Gives Life: Unmasking Subjugation for a Post-Colonial Missionary Ecclesiology in Canada." *Toronto Journal of Theology* 22, no. 1 (2006) 55–69.

Fensham, C.J. "Wake Up Call: Towards Churches in Solidarity and Resistance Against 'Future Forecasting.'" *The Ecumenist* 44, no. 3 (2007) 6–11.

Fensham, C.J. "Measuring the Unmeasurable: Learning Outcomes in a Canadian Theological College." *Toronto Journal of Theology* Supplement 1 (2009) 77–89.

Fensham, Charles J. "Sin and Ecology: A Conversation with Jürgen Moltmann and the School of René Girard." *Journal of Reformed Theology* 6 (2012) 234–50.

Fensham, C.J. "The Sacrament of the First Child of God: A Renewed Christian Eco-Imaginary." *Scriptura: International Journal of Bible, Religion and Theology in South Africa* 111, no. 3 (2012) 323–32.

Fensham, C.J. "Faith Matters: Towards a Public Missiology in the Midst of the Ecological Crisis." *Toronto Journal of Theology*, Supplement 1 (2015) 17–28.

Fensham, C.J. "The Transformative Vision: Public Witness and the *Poiesis* of Christian Social Transformation." *Missiology: An International Review* 44, no. 2 (2016) 155–66.

Fensham, C.J. "The Conversation Between Public Theology and Missiology: A Response to Sebastian Kim." *Missiology* 45, no. 4 (2017) 396–406.

Fensham, C.J. "Douglas Hall's Theology of the Cross as Contextual Theology in the Postcolonial Context." *Toronto Journal of Theology* 34, no. 1 (2018): 111–123.

Fensham, C.J. "The Methodology of Missiology in the Context of Turtle Island." *Missiology: An International Review* 47, no. 3 (July 2019) 300–314.

Fensham, C.J. "Considering Spiritual Care for Religiously Involved LGBTQI Migrants and Refugees: A Tentative Map." *Religions* 12 (2021) 1113. https://doi.org/10.3390/rel12121113.

Fensham, C.J. "Misguided Love: How Christian Denominations Keep Doing Harm to Sexual and Gender Minority People." *The Canadian Journal of Theology, Mental Health and Disability* 1, no. 2 (2021) 122–5.

Fensham, C.J. "Mission and Principalities and Powers Reconsidered." *Missiology: An International Review* 50, no. 2 (2022) 125–37.

Leffel, G.P., C.J. Fensham, G.R. Hunsberger, G.A. Okesson, R.A. Hunt, W. N. Kenney and H.R. Pieterse. "What We Mean by Public Missiology." *Missiology: An International Review* (May 2023 online edition).

Preface

Chapters in Multi-Author Volumes

Fensham, C.J. "Culture." In *The Encyclopedia of Protestantism, Volume 1*, 544–547. New York: Routledge, 2004.

Fensham, C.J. "The Lausanne Committee for Evangelism." In *The Encyclopedia of Protestantism, Volume 3*, 1073–1074. New York: Routledge, 2004.

Fensham, C.J. "Mass Media." In *The Encyclopedia of Protestantism, Volume 3*, 1176–9. New York: Routledge, 2004.

Fensham, C.J. "Emerging from the Dark Age Ahead: The Canadian Church in the Third Millennium." In *Walking Humbly with God: Church and Mission Engaging Plurality*, edited by V. Mortensen and A. Osterland, 113–34. Grand Rapids: Eerdmans, 2011.

Fensham, C.J. Foreword. In *Celebrating God's Cosmic Perichoresis: The Eschatological Panentheism of Jürgen Moltmann as a Resource for an Ecological Christian Worship*, by B.J. Lee, ix–xii. Eugene: Pickwick Publications, 2011.

Fensham, C.J. "Imagine a Sacramental Tree Planting Conspiracy." In *Living Eco Justice*, 69–75. Ottawa: Citizens for Public Justice, 2013.

Fensham, C.J., and S. Travis. "What on Earth is Liturgy?" In *The Church in the Household of God*, edited by C. Ayre and E. Conradie, 10–30. Pietermaritzburg: Cluster Publications, 2016.

Fensham, C.J. "Towards a Faithful Christian Community in Canada: A Missiological Response to Religious Change." In *The Decline of Established Christianity in the Western World*, edited by Paul S. Peterson, 145–55. New York: Routledge, 2018.

Contributors

ERNST M. CONRADIE, Senior Professor, Department of Religion and Theology at the University of the Western Cape, Cape Town, South Africa.

REV. DR. J. DORCAS GORDON, Principal Emerita at Knox College, Toronto School of Theology, University of Toronto.

REV. DR. HYE KYUNG HEO, pastor in the English Ministry of the Korean Evangelical Church of the Word. Taught Christian Ethics at Knox College, Toronto School of Theology, University of Toronto.

ISSAC HONG, PhD student, Knox College, Toronto School of Theology, University of Toronto.

REV. DR. GEORGE R. HUNSBERGER, member of the Public Missiology Working Group and Professor Emeritus of Missiology at Western Theological Seminary, Holland, Michigan, USA.

ROBERT HUNT, Professor of Christian Mission and Interreligious Relations, Director of Global Theological Education, Perkins School of Theology, Southern Methodist University

REV. DR. BONG-CHAN PAUL KO, St. Paul's Presbyterian Church, Burlington, Ontario.

GREGORY P. LEFFEL, PhD, President and Co-director of One Horizon Institute, Lexington, Kentucky, USA

REV. DR. STUART MACDONALD, Professor of Church and Society at Knox College, Toronto School of Theology, University of Toronto.

REV. DR. GLENN MCCULLOUGH, Assistant Professor of Practical Theology and Spiritual Care at Emmanuel and Knox Colleges, University of Toronto.

Contributors

REV. CANON DAVID NEELANDS, Dean Emeritus of the Faculty of Divinity at Trinity College, Toronto.

HENDRIK R. PIETERSE, Associate Professor of Global Christianity and Intercultural Theology at Garrett-Evangelical Theological Seminary, Evanston, Illinois, USA.

DR. BILLIE ANNE ROBINSON, Faculty of Divinity at Trinity College, University of Toronto.

REV. DR. SARAH TRAVIS, Associate Professor, Ewart Chair in the Practice of Ministry and Faith Formation, Knox College, Toronto School of Theology, University of Toronto

REV. DR. ERNEST VAN ECK, Principal and Professor of New Testament at Knox College, Toronto School of Theology, University of Toronto.

REV. DR. JOHN A. VISSERS, Professor of Systematic Theology at Knox College, Toronto School of Theology, University of Toronto.

Abbreviations

Old Testament

Gen	Genesis	Prov	Proverbs
Exod	Exodus	Qoh (Eccl)	Qoheleth
Lev	Leviticus	Isa	Isaiah
Deut	Deuteronomy	Ezek	Ezekiel
Josh	Joshua	Dan	Daniel
Judg	Judges	Hos	Hosea
1–2 Kgs	1–2 Kings	Joel	Joel
1–2 Chr	1–2 Chronicles	Amos	Amos
Ps/Pss	Psalm/Psalms	Mic	Micah

New Testament

Matt	Matthew	Gal	Galatians
Mark	Mark	1–2 Tim	1–2 Timothy
Luke	Luke	Heb	Hebrews
John	John	1–2 Pet	1–2 Peter
Acts	Acts	1–2–3 John	1–2–3 John
Rom	Romans	Rev	Revelation
1–2 Cor	1–2 Corinthians		

Abbreviations

Other

Gos. Thom.   *Gospel of Thomas*

Introduction

George R. Hunsberger

Do No Harm

I AM STRUCK BY an undercurrent in the opening chapters of Professor Charles Fensham's most recent book, *Mission as Penance*. The title itself anticipates it. Words like *harm, harmed, and harmful* flow unceasingly and meaningfully beneath the surface as he makes the case for Penance as the essential missional posture for the churches of the West, especially those in North America, for whom it appears to have been absent. It is as though he is forging a new Hippocratic Oath for the church-as-missionary, whether among neighbours near or far away: "First, do no harm."

This accent was neither accidental nor new for Fensham. The rest of the book, drawing materials from his previous published work, shows the marks of one for whom noticing harm done to peoples, nations, and the earth itself had become deeply situated in his theological and missiological method. Even in the most well-meaning and benevolent of missionary strategies and practices, he noticed, harm was being done to people and lands in the process. That it went largely unnoticed by the churches and their various missions has been Fensham's constant motive to undo harm, call for its cessation, and live, himself, in proper penance.

This is Fensham's claim: harm we have done. Harm we are doing. And apart from a posture of penance, harm we will continue to do. He touches

Introduction

the nerve, the sore nerve, of memories now awakened to see how often in the church's traditions of life and mission there has been harm done to peoples, tribes, nations, persons, and the earth itself. All in the name of caring concern.

I had already encountered this deep recognition of harm in Fensham's previous book, *Misguided Love*. After reading it together in a small community of "Jesus Apprentices," the theme that stood out as having pervaded the whole was harm. In his first chapter, the invitation to the reader had said it clearly: "Here I bring evidence of the history of harm and the infliction of harm on sexual and gender minority Christians." He positions that discussion alongside others of like kind:

> My own adoptive country, Canada, has undergone a process of "truth and reconciliation" with its aboriginal peoples over the past years, and key to the harm done here was the teaching and abusive role of Christian churches both Protestant and Roman Catholic. In South Africa, my country of origin, I lived through the apartheid era and experienced first-hand how "biblical teaching" can be used in pious ways to exploit, discriminate, and kill people. Presently and in the past, similar things happen to sexual and gender minority Christians. When we discover that we do harm, we must stop.[1]

Even more emphatic is the subtitle of *Misguided Love*: *Christians and the Rupture of LGBTQI2+ People*! His own personal story and those of others make his point poignant throughout.

In *Mission as Penance*, he makes specific reference to a number of issues where his hermeneutic of harm (as I would call it) is at work. Within the wider horizon of the history of missions, he notes, there are "many ways in which Christian mission in Christendom caused harm." The rivulets of harm flowing out from the Colonialism era of mission are legion, including ways that "people with different cultures were harmed, exploited, subdued, and even tortured and killed." Amongst them, Fensham insists that "it is our task to oppose injustice, selfish exploitation, and practices that harm God's earth and our neighbor."[2] The penance for which Fensham calls is "a corporate and systemic concept that recognizes harms done in the past and harm still being done . . . Penance, conceived in this way, is not so much a goal of mission . . . as an individual and corporate posture."[3] It is certainly

---

1. Fensham, *Misguided Love*, 5.
2. Fensham, *Mission as Penance*, 15.
3. Fensham, *Mission as Penance*, 18.

Introduction

not a strategy, nor program, although it must characterize both. It is not merely a theological affirmation, nor a celebration of the affirmation, as well, but it touches the character of every interaction. At its best, the church in its mission "seeks to enter the world with repentant humility."[4]

The language of penance had its origins for Fensham in the lives of key mentors, among whom he names Nico Smit, Willem Saayman, and Albert Nolan. They created for him "examples of humble Christian penitential engagement in mission. Christian triumphalism simply was not an option in their engagement with the world."[5] But the primary catalyst for his lifelong fascination with the notion of *penance* came from his mentor, thesis director, and senior colleague in the missiology department at the University of South Africa, David Bosch. In the final sentences of his first book, *Witness to the World* (1980 ET), Bosch quoted and embraced the idea of penance which he had found in the final pages of an earlier work by the Reformed missiologist J. H. Bavinck, *An Introduction to the Science of Missions* (1960). Bosch puts it this way:

> Out of the ruins of the *corpus Christianum* the *corpus Christi*, the Body of Christ, arises, stripped of her earlier self-assurance, of her self-confidence and megalomania. Precisely in her mission the Church confesses her guilt about the way in which she has always attempted to dominate the world. "Mission is . . . the penance of the church, which is ashamed before God and man." Mission is the Church-crossing-frontiers-in-the-form-of-a-servant.[6]

It would be instructive to read this alongside the way Bavinck framed this assertion in the concluding pages of his earlier book:

> The idea has been expressed in more than one quarter that the missionary enterprise is a form of penance . . . We have approached other peoples in their primitive tribal relationships and mercilessly involved them in our world's economic and political game, without taking into account the immeasurable damage we were doing to their hearts. For this reason the missionary enterprise is actually doing penance when it enters this deeply wounded world in humility and love. Missions is thus the penance of the church, which is ashamed before God and man.[7]

---

4. Fensham, *Mission as Penance*, 92.
5. Fensham, *Mission as Penance*, 3–5.
6. Bosch, *Witness*, 248. He cites Bavinck, *Introduction*, 303.
7. Bavinck, *Introduction*, 303.

Introduction

Two things are to be noticed in a comparison of the two. First, Bavinck comes to the notion of penance because he is aware that there are others at the time (in the mid-1950s) who were expressing the notion. It was not original to him, as though it simply grew directly out of his book's argument. However, it cannot be doubted that he was willing to bring the notion on board and saw it to be congruent with his own perspective. This is indicated by his repetition of the claim a few pages later, in the final paragraph of the book:

> The only thing that is fit for us to do is to go calmly forward now, and in the future, in the power of the Lord. For in ourselves we are more powerless than ever before. We are also ashamed, and we feel guilty. We are indeed doing a sort of penance in our mission work. We learn more and more to understand that God alone can accomplish what needs to be done.[8]

That being the case, Bosch nonetheless takes it up and receives it for his own purposes.

A second observation is that the point of reference shifts from Bavinck to Bosch. Bavinck says it this way: "Missions is thus the penance of the church." Bosch (and subsequently Fensham) says it this way: "Mission is . . . the penance of the church." The dropped letter (*s*) in Bosch's quotation from Bavinck is not accidental (though perhaps inadvertent). Bavinck's book, and interest, is about the missions: those specific ventures of mission sent around the world by churches or other agencies. He locates the penance he speaks about within that "missionary enterprise," the collective history and patterns of such ventures. Bosch's omission of the final *s* moves within the sensibilities of the mid to late twentieth century shifts in focus toward understanding that mission is first about the purposing actions of God and then as something in which the church participates. For Bosch, mission is about ecclesiology, a fundamentally missional ecclesiology. "Our entire life in the world is life-in-mission. The Church in the world is only Church insofar as she has a missionary dimension."[9] That is where he locates the necessary penance, in the church's life of humility and repentance.

Bavinck and Bosch concur that humility, love, and a spirit of repentance are the qualities that must characterize mission. It is especially Bosch's rendering of it that first captured Fensham's attention and, as he says, "has fascinated me all my adult life." It was enough to make him perpetually on

8. Bavinck, *Introduction*, 309.
9. Bosch, *Witness*, 245.

Introduction

alert, attentive to the harms that litter the trail of the church's teachings and its mission efforts. His book, *Mission as Penance,* gathers together his own lifetime of engagement with the world in the posture of penance.

Essays in Celebration

The authors of this volume offer a festival of celebration of the life and work of a colleague, friend, and mentor. From him, we have learned to "do no harm." In subtle ways, as well as overt ones, our written work here expresses our debt of gratitude for the faithful example, the careful scholarship, and the genuine friendship by which we have been enriched in our own lives and vocations. These essays are attempts to continue the veins of work we have shared with him in one way or another. We seek to extend his arguments, to focus paths of thought and practice that open up in response to his challenges, and to join him in faithfulness to the Jesus whom we also have endeavored to follow. We count Micah, the Hebrew poet-prophet, as a companion among us: with him we seek to do justice, love kindness, and walk humbly with our God.

Here then is a taste of the essays which follow. We begin by noting one contributed by a childhood friend who shared the neighbourhood in which Fensham grew up in South Africa. Only several years apart in age, they together roamed the streets of Stellenbosch in the Western Cape—the area where Ernst Conradie remains. They had common experiences of schooling, catechesis in church life, and the realities of an apartheid society. In the years since, they have shared many common interests, including, especially, ecotheology. In his contribution to this volume, "On a Cultured Christianity," Conradie interacts with Fensham's work in critique of a "cultured Christianity" to conduct a thought experiment on "Afrikaner civil religion." While an erudite treatment of the issues raised, the essay nonetheless displays a winsome dialogical character, with refrains here and there: "Do you agree? I wondered if this is what you were thinking? And you?" The kindly schoolmate banter of old remains alive!

Some of the essays that follow are written by former students of Fensham for whom he was their academic supervisor, guiding especially their thesis work. First there is Bong-Chan Ko, who studied under Fensham for a combined eleven years in his MDiv and PhD studies. He takes the occasion of this volume to review and synthesize Fensham's academic legacy as he has experienced it. His essay is entitled "Fensham's Theology in a Dialogue

Introduction

with the Theology of *Han*." In it he highlights at the core of Fensham's theology his "strong orientation toward love and justice," and brings that theme into conversation with a Korean theology of *Han*.

Also engaging in that sort of contextual interplay that Fensham had taught and encouraged is the essay by Hye Kyung Heo, entitled "In Search of a Theology of the Cross for Korea, a Nation Transitioning into a Multicultural and Multiracial Society: A Critique on Anselm's *Cur Deus Homo* and Moltmann's Social Trinitarian Understanding of the Cross." Growing out of her doctoral dissertation, Heo proposes that "Moltmann's social trinitarian understanding of the cross" provides a better fit for the newly multicultural, multiracial society that Korea is becoming. A critical read of Anselmian notions of cross and atonement and then of Moltmann's social trinitarian interpretations leads Heo to commend the latter as most useful for "envisioning and building an inclusive society" in contemporary Korea.

Isaac Hong expresses gratitude that Professor Fensham (a Presbyterian) was the first to introduce him to his own theological tradition—Pentecostalism. In his essay, "Emerging Pentecostal Ecclesiology Through the Lens of Missiological Method," he makes use of key elements in Bosch's missiological method to help mature in Pentecostalism "a more nuanced definition of charismatic experience . . . a doxological missional nature . . . and the relational identity of human, socially-embedded believers who encounter the Holy Spirit."

Another former student, Billie Anne Robertson, did her doctoral work in Hebrew Bible literature, in particular the book of Judges. Her dissertation engaged the interplay of violence and humour in the Judges narratives, and this essay draws from that approach to provide a pregnant sample. The essay is entitled "Sinister Soldiers and Single Women," and it opens to view the intrusion of humour into the telling of a particular, otherwise violent, pair of deaths.

The volume includes several essays supplied by Fensham's colleagues on the faculty of Knox College. They represent a variety of academic fields, including New Testament, church and society, practical theology, systematic theology, and the practice of ministry. What is on display is the bandwidth of concerns that touch, and are touched by, the kind of missiology that Fensham has espoused and practiced. The principal of the college, Ernest van Eck, takes up themes resonant with Fensham's work by exploring the assertion, "A Prophet of Old: Jesus the 'Public Theologian.'" Doing so is to enter a thicket of issues and debates in New Testament studies (the

Introduction

thickest of which are reserved for the footnotes!). His careful studies of the parables of Jesus leads to the conclusion that they "painted a different and new kingdom with a Ruler who is compassionate and inclusive, a kingdom in which there was no place for exploitation and systemic injustice."

Van Eck's predecessor as Principal, Dorcas Gordon, presents an essay on "A Multi-Voice Conversation Seeking Greater Inclusivity in Theological Education." In light of her own experience as a theological student and finally principal of a theological college, and her work seeking to encourage and strengthen theological education in Asia and the Pacific, she seeks "to identify elements [she] believes to be essential to a more integrated and inclusive model of theological education."

A pair of colleague essays included in this volume have particular relevance to Fensham's themes of harm and penance. His colleague at Trinity College, University of Toronto, David Neelands extends these concerns (and those of Gordon's essay) with "Radicalizing Women: The Abuse of Women by Radicals in the Reformation." In it, he surveys the Reformation era rhetoric that on the face of it posits the "weakness of women" especially as found in the writings of Richard Hooker, and in his comments attributing the same to Calvin (although basing that mostly on Theodore Beza's account of Calvin's life). Neeland concludes that "Hooker (like Calvin) is criticizing not the weakness of women but the deceitfulness of those who abuse them."

Even more to the point of Fensham's concerns, though at some distance into the field of psychology and pastoral care, Glenn McCullough addresses the issue of "The Inner Mission: Trauma, Extraversion, and Missiology." He seeks to consider "the balance between these two concerns: the activist approach to social justice, and the contemplative approach to mental and spiritual health." This he does in the context of "two related topics: the seeing and healing of trauma . . . and the extraverted tendency in Christianity."

Several colleagues took up issues having to do with the life of The Presbyterian Church in Canada (PCC). Since Fensham first arrived in Canada in the late 1980s, he was actively involved as a minister and professor of theology in that denomination and a member of its Committee on Church Doctrine. John Vissers' essay "The Threefold Office of Christ (*Munus Triplex*) in Canadian Presbyterian Theology" examines how this doctrine was applied to the church's doctrine of ministry in the 1960s, and the role played by Fensham's predecessor at Knox College, David W. Hay.

Introduction

The harm done to sexual and gender minority people by the church's teachings and attitudes was a long-term concern of Fensham's. He and others sought a change. Finally, "the 2022 General Assembly adopted a Confession to God and LGBTQI2+ people, confessing the harm caused by homophobia, transphobia, heterosexism, and hypocrisy in The Presbyterian Church in Canada, and committing the church to a true change of heart and behaviour."[10] In the interest of encouraging the ongoing transformation it was calling for, Sarah Travis provides the essay, "Naming Human and Divine: Expansive and Inclusive Liturgy in The Presbyterian Church in Canada." The language used in the community's life and worship is a crucial place to embody what has been confessed.

Akin to recent issues, and responses to them, there have been historic seasons in the life of the PCC from which lessons may be learned for today. Stuart MacDonald chronicles one such season in his essay, "A Different Kind of Congress: The Congress of Concern, 1968." The concerns were varied and far-reaching, mostly focused on finding new patterns for doing business in the meetings of the General Assembly. The essay probes the dynamics that unfolded during and following the Congress.

Finally, three essays in the volume were written by collegial colleagues in the Public Missiology Working Group, in which Professor Fensham has been an intimate participant.[11] All three live in the United States of America, so the broader context of North America is their purview. The one most directly engaging Fensham's work is the essay by Gregory Leffel,[12] "Charles Fensham: Missiologist as Poet." Leffel is drawn to Fensham's (and Bosch's before him) frequent use of the notion of *poiesis* regarding the meaning and function of mission. He seeks to weave it into his own framework of understanding and hone its contributions for public missiology. In the process, he engages Fensham's four major books.

In Robert Hunt's[13] essay, "Christian Mission in an Age of Contested Identities," he provides a critical reflection on two concepts essential to it: incarnation and culture. He moves from a supposedly normative sense of human nature as unchanging essences toward a sense of "narrated identity,"

---

10. PCC, "Gender, Sexuality."

11. The formal statement of the group, "Public Missiology," is republished in Fensham, *Mission as Penance*, 219–29.

12. Leffel is the co-director of One Horizon Institute in Lexington, Kentucky.

13. Hunt is on the faculty of the Perkins School of Theology, Southern Methodist University, Dallas, Texas.

Introduction

seeing culture as that which is, in the shared social space, what "creates the possibilities and limits to our life story." This leads Hunt to affirm that multiculturalism is the way of incarnation and mission.

The same recognition of the multiplicity of human cultures undergirds the essay by Hendrik Pieterse.[14] In "Intercultural Theology as Ecumenical Theology," Pieterse joins others who perceive the "current ecumenical stagnation" and call for a shift from the older ecumenical guilt paradigm to a plurality paradigm which embraces the world's diversity of peoples and cultures as "God-intended and God-willed." The recently developing field of intercultural theology and the realities of a diverse world of Christianity hold promise for bringing that shift forward.

All the authors of the essays in this volume express in a variety of ways their deep appreciation for Charles Fensham and his extraordinary gifts in thought, life, and action. Some ferret out gems of his wisdom from his writings, some push his ideas forward in new ways, and some bring alongside developments in corollary fields to enhance the values of his work. All, either explicitly or implicitly, show deep affection for him and gratitude for the kind of person he has shown himself to be. The essays are an expression of love for Charles and praise to God.

Bibliography

Bavinck, J. H. 1960. *An Introduction to the Science of Missions*. Phillipsburg, NJ: Presbyterian & Reformed Publishing.
Bosch, David J. 1980. *Witness to the World: The Christian Mission in Theological Perspective*. Atlanta: John Knox.
Fensham, Charles J. 2019. *Misguided Love: Christians and the Rupture of LGBTQI2+ People*. Atlanta: Journal of Pastoral Care Publications.
———. 2023. *Mission as Penance: Essays on the Theology of Mission in a Canadian Context*. Eugene, OR: Pickwick Publications.
The Presbyterian Church in Canada (PCC). "Gender, Sexuality & LGBTQI2+ Inclusion." https://presbyterian.ca/justice/social-action/gender-sexuality-inclusion/.

---

14. Pieterse is on the faculty of Garrett-Evangelical Theological Seminary in Evanston, Illinois.

1

On a Cultured Christianity

Ernst M. Conradie[1]

Dear Charles,

Greetings from Stellenbosch, the town where you grew up. We had a week of scorching summer heat here (no doubt exacerbated by El Nino), while I note that it is snowing in Toronto. Are you longing to come back sometime? I guess that you have ambiguous feelings in this regard. There is the splendid beauty of Stellenbosch but also its economic inequality in a country riddled with social tensions, load-shedding, collapsing infrastructure, corruption, and the like. The underlying problem remains the long-lasting impact of colonialism and apartheid. Not that Canada can escape from any of that, as you also comment in your latest *Mission as Penance* (2023).[2] Congratulations with that publication: it seems to be the exactly appropriate angle to take in talking about mission from within the global North.

Charles, may I ask you to join me in something like a thought experiment? I see you as an eloquent exponent of the critique against a cultured Christianity, seeking a form of discipleship that no longer assumes

---

1. Ernst M. Conradie is senior professor in the Department of Religion and Theology at the University of the Western Cape. He is currently the series editor of *An Earthed Faith: Telling the Story Amid the "Anthropocene,"* published by AOSIS and Wipf & Stock.

2. Fensham, *Mission as Penance*.

Christian hegemony. Allow me to unpack this under the following rubrics (with footnotes for your scholarly interest).

Resistance Against the Cultured Christianity of Our Youth

One thing that we have in common is a gut-level resistance against the cultured Christianity of our youth. Although you were a few years ahead of me, we both grew up in Stellenbosch in the late 1960s and early 1970s. At the time, the town was a classic example of the dominance of Christendom, given the close alignment between the power of the National Party government, the economic power of Anton Rupert and the Rembrandt company (new money), the old money associated with wine estates, the Dutch Reformed church, Afrikaner culture, and the elitism of Stellenbosch University. David Bosch (we have a common affinity for his missiology) and others rightly described that as Afrikaner civil religion.[3]

One would need to add that this was also a time of the enforcement of the Group Areas Act, forced removals, for example around "Colored" parts of the town in Roesdorp and "Die Vlakte,"[4] military conscription, the escalating anger among Black students that erupted in Soweto in 1976, and the brutal suppression of such resistance that shaped South African politics in the name of state security until 1994. Cultured Christianity served (in Peter Berger's terminology) as a "sacred canopy"[5] that provided religious legitimation for the constellation of power at the time. It undermined the authenticity of the Christian gospel in every possible way. One is reminded of the critique of such cultured Christianity as found already with Tertullian but also Søren Kierkegaard and the young Karl Barth.

On a more personal level, let me add a few footnotes. Both of us lived in the now very affluent former white part of Stellenbosch, not too far from Anton Rupert's house in Thibault street. I need to add that my grandfather bought us a house in 1967 after my father died—for just R12,000! We both studied at Paul Roos Gimnasium which served as a breeding ground for rugby heroes (a dominant "feel good" part of the town culture). We both belonged to the conservative Voortrekker youth movement where your father (Charles Fensham senior) even served as the Commandant. Your

---

3. Bosch, "Roots and Fruits."

4. A moving account from within is edited by Hilton Biscombe, *In Ons Bloed* ("In our blood").

5. Berger, *Sacred Canopy.*

dad and my mom were both employees of Stellenbosch University while our mothers were both students at the Huis ten Bosch residence on campus and moved in similar circles. We both went to Sunday school in the *Moederkerk* ("Mother Church"). Its tower still dominates the town's almost medieval landscape. And we both later picked up scruples with military conscription, although you had the courage to take that much further as a conscientious objector.

From there, our lives followed different trajectories as students at the University of Cape Town and Stellenbosch University, respectively. For the last few decades, we were based worlds apart in Toronto and at the University of the Western Cape. Nevertheless, we share an interest in missiology, and we both teach systematic theology, engage in Christian ecotheology, and maintain an alignment with the Reformed tradition, broadly understood. Despite your earlier charismatic interests, you served The Presbyterian Church in Canada and taught for many years at Knox College. As I have often observed, I do not self-consciously seek to be Reformed: it is when I engage critically with Catholic, Orthodox, and Anglican scholars that I realize that I am more Reformed than I may have thought.[6] I fondly remember your participation in conferences and workshops hosted by the University of the Western Cape, not least because that enabled you to visit your mom at a time when she was aging. She was immensely grateful to me. I frequently reference your essay in *Scriptura* following the Christian Faith and the Earth conference in August 2012.[7]

Niebuhr's Typology Revisited

The critique of a cultured Christianity will surely remind you of H. Richard Niebuhr's famous typology on *Christ and Culture*, notably the "Christ of culture" type.[8] What do you make of his typology? My sense is that it remains remarkably lucid and is therefore an excellent teaching tool to invite reflection on church and society among students. Do you agree?

There are criticisms, of course. Let me mention these: Ian Barbour, a student of Niebuhr, adapted Niebuhr's typology for an almost equally famous typology of his own but changed the point comparison to the relation

---

6. See Conradie, "Placing Reform."
7. See Fensham, "Sacrament."
8. Niebuhr, *Christ and Culture*.

between science and religion.⁹ This does raise the question whether a clear distinction between nature and culture can be maintained. No longer in the so-called Anthropocene, I would think.¹⁰ In fact, for Niebuhr *culture* was shorthand for civilization while *Christ* was shorthand for the power and attraction that Jesus exercises.¹¹ Then there is the problem of the relation between nature and grace, which Niebuhr in a way evades, but is perhaps the real issue underlying confessional divides.¹² Glen Stassen observes that, despite Niebuhr's title, Christ tends to disappear from his analysis so that a more Christocentric approach is needed.¹³ Following John Howard Yoder, Craig Carter (do you know him? I see he is based in Toronto as well) argues that Niebuhr's typology and his emphasis on Christ transforming culture assumes and legitimizes the Christendom paradigm of his day and has therefore become outdated.¹⁴ Stephen Long offers a guide to the contemporary discussion on theology and culture where he mentions the influence of postliberal theology (in Niebuhr's own backyard), the Anabaptist witness, and radical Orthodoxy.¹⁵ Perhaps the most significant challenge is that culture is no longer as monolithic as Niebuhr could assume in the 1950s. There is still the new hegemony of a consumerist culture, but otherwise the cultural experience of many is more one of hybridity, paradox, and contradiction. This applies to any Western cosmopolitan city but even more so to cities such as Sydney, Cape Town or Kingston, Jamaica.¹⁶

These are what I could find on my shelves. There are surely more. Do you have other critical voices to add?

To be fair to Niebuhr, although he clearly favored "Christ transforming culture," he did recognize some legitimacy in each of these types. As

---

9. See Barbour, *Religion and Science*. I recently compared Niebuhr's and Barbour's typologies in "Models for Intertwining God's Story and the Universe Story."

10. The clearest argument for me remains that of Dipesh Chakrabarty, "Climate of History."

11. Niebuhr, *Christ and Culture*, 24, 32.

12. I would add the problem of the relationship between God's work of creation and of salvation which has long intrigued me. See especially my *Earth in God's Economy*.

13. Stassen, "Take Jesus Back."

14. Carter, *Rethinking Christ*. Carter argues that Niebuhr's program is as a result deficient in two ways: it loses touch with the gospel, undermining authentic Christian witness, and it confirms the world and does not actually transform it through repentance and conversion (30).

15. Long, *Theology and Culture*.

16. See the analysis by Hewitt in *Church and Culture*.

Dirk Smit pointed out in a paper read at the Theological Society of South Africa in 1989, assuming the validity of "Christ transforming culture" is not self-explanatory as apartheid was exactly such a Calvinist attempt to transform the South African society according to God's will. He traces Niebuhr's own sources to show that such transformation (better: conversion) requires reflection, in the light of God's revelation, on the prior questions: What is happening? And: What is God doing?[17]

At times, at least, there is a need for stating that Christ is against culture (e.g., in the context of consumerism[18])—for the sake of culture.[19] When confronted with reductionism of various stripes it may help to say that Christ is "above" culture; although this is, for me, rather hard to swallow. The Lutheran emphasis on paradox is helpful to guard against any aggressive neo-Calvinist idea that every square inch of society belongs to Christ. But is there some legitimacy also in the Christ of culture type? That is the direction toward which this thought experiment is leading me.

African and Other Indigenous Voices

As you know, African inculturation theology is one of the primary forms of African Christian theology. The same debates may be found across the world where there is a need to retrieve indigenous cultures; also in Canada, of course, given the predicament of First Nations. It is a different ballgame where culture is in flux and where hybrid identity is the name of the game. In such cases it is not clear what inculturation and indigenization could mean.[20]

The word *inculturation* is perhaps especially at home in the Roman Catholic context, given debates on the inculturation of the liturgy (and the use of Latin!). In Protestant circles, the same debates are found around inculturation, indigenization, or contextualization, whatever term you wish to work with. There are of course many methodological debates, and I typically go back to David Bosch's discussion in *Transforming Mission* for guidance.[21] Of course, it is the same underlying question that is at stake,

17. See Smit, "Theology."
18. For my engagement with UWC students in this regard, see Conradie, *Christianity and a Critique*.
19. Carter, *Rethinking Christ*, 25.
20. See again the discussion of such terms by Hewitt in *Church and Culture*.
21. See Bosch, *Transforming Mission*, 447–57.

namely on the relation between "Christ and culture." Or, if you like, Christian identity and cultural identity.[22]

May I offer you two observations that are derived mainly from working with postgraduate students at UWC who grapple with such issues.[23] The first is on rhetoric. It is striking to me that the students are obviously keen to find a closer alignment between their Christian faith and traditional African culture. This is obviously a critique of the way in which much of African culture (and much wisdom) was denigrated in missionary praxis. So, there is a retrieval and even a celebration of culture in the name of Christian theology. Such rhetoric is obviously different from my own resistance against cultured Christianity, also in the form of consumerist Christianity.[24] I guess there is something worse than adopting a cultured Christianity, and that is being forced to adopt someone else's cultured Christianity! I am thinking here of the westernization of consciousness, the global propagation of the American way of life, and decolonial critique of all of that. Such differences in rhetoric also surface in conversations around justice and human rights: while some are rightly concerned about their own rights, my own concern is typically about the rights of others. And you?

The second observation is on method. The deductive logic of "translating" the gospel into an African idiom does not work because the gospel is always already encultured. It seldom succeeds in doing justice to culture. The opposite logic of starting with (African) culture is often too uncritical (as pointed out especially in African women's theology) in not allowing the power of the gospel to challenge aspects of culture. That includes issues of patriarchy. The issue is one of hermeneutics, understanding the relationship between text and context.[25] There are dangers here of a lack of Christian authenticity (if the text is underplayed) and of irrelevance (if the context is underplayed), but the truth does not lie somewhere in the middle. I think the debate remains unresolved because of an uncritical hermeneutics. Or perhaps because a hermeneutics of suspicion (against missionary Christianity) dominates the discussion. This allows for what Bosch called an

---

22. For me, the most perceptive exploration of such issues in African Christian theology remains Kwame Bediako's *Christianity in Africa*.

23. For a perceptive analysis, see Sakuba, "Critical Assessment."

24. See again my *Christianity and a Critique*.

25. At UWC there has been a long-standing interest in issues of hermeneutics, precisely because something clearly has gone awry in interpreting the gospel. See, for example, the textbook *Fishing for Jonah* (UWC, 1995) that we developed, also my *Angling for Interpretation*.

"inverse hermeneutics," where the question is no longer about the meaning of the gospel, for us, today, but the implications of the contemporary context for reinterpreting the gospel.[26]

I am reminded here of Leslie Newbigin's reflections on returning to England from India, where such debates on gospel and culture were rife. The worry from a missionary perspective in the Indian context was one of accommodating to culture so that the gospel is compromised. Newbigin was shocked to see how the gospel was being compromised in England because of the form of cultured Christianity that he encountered upon his return.[27] It is this crucial insight that underlies any adequate form of missional theology.[28] Missionaries have become the recipients of their own message that challenges their accommodation to the hegemonic culture of Britain and the United States of America—as imperial powers. I learned a lot in this regard from George Hunsberger—who I am pleased to see is involved in editing this Festschrift in your honor. We had long conversations on this at the Center of Theological Inquiry in Princeton in 2008.

What do you make of this given your own teaching experience in the Canadian context, Charles? I must confess that I do not have a copy of your *To the Nations for the Earth: A Missional Spirituality* (2013)[29] but wondered whether this is also how you understand missional theology?

A Journey to Tuvalu

Let me tell you about my visit to Tuvalu in September 2023. You will soon see where this is going and how this is relevant to the critique of cultured Christianity. The visit was part of a longer trip to discuss an ongoing collaborative project on "An Earthed Faith: Telling the Story amid the 'Anthropocene,'" with participants based in Suva, Sydney, Auckland, and Tuvalu. My host in Tuvalu was Maina Talia. He contributed a superbly crafted essay to the second volume in the series, namely on method in ecotheology.[30]

---

26. Bosch, *Transforming Mission*, 320–32.
27. See Newbigin, *Gospel*; Foolishness.
28. You may know that there is considerable interest in missional theology in South Africa, especially in the Dutch Reformed context. I am not convinced that this core insight, the critique of "our culture" is taken seriously. This surfaces especially around issues of whiteness, as Johannes Mouton, one of my current PhD students, points out.
29. Fensham.
30. Talia, "Fakalofa."

I also served as external examiner for his doctoral thesis at Charles Sturt University. The thesis was on theological responses to climate change, in which he offered a reading of the parable of the Good Samaritan to ask where good neighbors can be found.[31] That is another story.

Just a bit of basic background from a traveler's impressions: Tuvalu is a small island state consisting of nine small islands with a total population of around twelve thousand people. I visited only the capital of Funafuti, which consists of a narrow strip of land between twenty and four hundred meters wide, partially encircling a lagoon. The total land area of this coral atoll is two hundred and forty hectares where no natural point is higher than three meters above sea level. The human population is just over six thousand people. Alongside Kiribati (one may add the Maldives and the Seychelles), it is the place in the world that is most vulnerable to sea level rise, given the impact of cyclones and king tides. Not surprisingly, climate change is at the top of any nationwide agenda. They are currently building a sea wall of seven hundred meters long that will protect one part of one side of the island from sea level rise of up to one meter. I guess you would ask: What about the other parts, the other side (towards the open sea), and the other islands? Nevertheless, the spirit in Tuvalu is one of "We are not drowning; we are fighting."[32]

Incidentally, Tuvalu was part of the so-called Gilbert and Ellice Island Colony, a British protectorate from 1892 to 1916, and then a British colony until 1976. This was, if you like, colonization by request in order to protect the citizens from other colonial powers, including Germany. Tuvalu became independent in 1978 but remains part of the British Commonwealth. A picture of King Charles III as monarch hangs in the office of the Governor-General. Kiribati was under Japanese occupancy during World War II, while the US Marine Corps occupied what is now Tuvalu in 1942 in order to use Funafuti as a base for subsequent seaborne attacks.

Besides the natural beauty and the tropical heat, I was struck by the fondness with which the Tuvaluan language is spoken (there are only around fourteen thousand native speakers), the vibrancy of its culture, the reliance on fossil fuels especially for driving around the island on the ubiquitous motorcycles, the energetic dances and poetry (fatele),[33] the abundance of seafood, the relative economic equality, and the culture of sharing

---

31. Talia, "Am I Not Your *Tuakoi*?"
32. See, alongside Talia's work, also Lusama, *Vaa Fesokotaki*.
33. See Talia, "*Kauafua Fatele.*"

and caring. Maina Talia claims that "there is no poverty in Tuvalu."[34] Did you hear that? He would be right. I certainly saw no deprivation in walking around the island.

Some 95 percent of the Tuvaluan population are Christians, with only a few others belonging to the Baha'i faith or with no religious adherence. The Congregational Christian Church of Tuvalu (in Tuvaluan, Te Ekalesia Kelisiano Tuvalu or EKT), commonly the Church of Tuvalu, is officially the state church of Tuvalu. No less than 86 percent of the population in Tuvalu belongs to this church. That percentage was even higher a few decades ago. Being the state church means the right to officiate during major national events while the Constitution of Tuvalu guarantees freedom of religion. There is no doubt, however, about the cultural influence of the church. Twice a day a period of silence (marked by a siren) is observed throughout the islands for devotion. The current governor-general is a former pastor of the EKT.

The Church of Tuvalu is Reformed, basically Calvinist, in its orientation. Christianity came to Tuvalu through the work of the London Missionary Society in the 1860s and is very warmly embraced. Missionary Christianity is widely questioned for its devaluation of traditional Tuvaluan culture, but the Christian faith itself forms part of the cultural assumptions of the Tuvaluan population, by now for several generations. You will see where this is going: What about such a close association between Christianity and culture? There is again no doubt that the Church of Tuvalu is one of the main sources for the protection of the Tuvaluan language, traditions, and culture. This applies also and especially to migrant communities of Tuvaluans, for example in Aotearoa, Australia, and Fiji. Although English is one of two official languages, the medium of instruction in schools, and widely understood, the Tuvaluans simply love their own language as a rich source of wisdom, stories, poetry, and dancing. Here Christ is still the Christ of culture, one would think. And who would want to question that from the outside; certainly not as a white South African.

Nevertheless, this may not be the full truth. The Church of Tuvalu has its own internal struggles with forms of fundamentalism and some Adventist and/or Pentecostal influences. At one stage, the default response to rising sea levels was to refer to God's covenant with Noah. Accordingly, God promised never to destroy the world again through water.[35] Some would therefore conclude that God will keep God's promises to protect us

---

34. Talia, "Fakalofa," 185.
35. See again the PhD theses by Lusama and Talia.

(Tuvaluans) from the impact of climate change. The EKT's telling statement on climate follows a different route that is closely aligned with national politics.[36] If the world will not be destroyed through water, could it perhaps be destroyed through fire? There are some Adventist influences also among some pastors in the EKT. The hosts asked me to address this issue. I did so through a public lecture with the provocative title, "Is the Advent of the Anthropocene a Tell-tale Sign that Jesus Is Coming Again Soon?" The answer may be a vehement "Nein!" but this does raise the question how Christian hope, especially the Parousia of Christ, is to be understood. And that, I realized, is not such an easy question . . .

The conference that I attended in Tuvalu to revise the EKT's theological statement on climate change had sessions on climate change of course, but also on labor, mental health, artificial intelligence, drug trafficking, gender-based violence and, you will be pleased to note (given your work on *Misguided Love*, tested out at UWC),[37] inclusivity in terms of sexual orientation (which did raise some eyebrows). Incidentally, the EKT allows for women's ordination—unlike some other Reformed churches in the region—but there are currently no women who actually serve as pastors in the EKT. So, there is some debate and ongoing fermentation with a few young Turks who are challenging the prevailing Christ of culture paradigm.

Let me conclude with a comment about percentages, cognizant of your argument in *Mission as Penance* that the church should be liberated from power games and numerical growth. It seems to me that Reformed churches operate in very different ways depending on whether their members constitute 80 percent or 60 percent or 20 percent or 2 percent or 0.2 percent of the population in a particular town or country. The critique against Christendom makes sense where the church forms a minority, but what if this is not the case? Here is what I said at a conference on the future of Reformed theology at the Faculty of Theology, Stellenbosch University in October 2022:

> Reformed forms of Christianity at times constitute a majority in a particular country, region, town or institution . . . Reformed

---

36. The Ekalesia Kelisiano Tuvalu concluded in an unpublished but widely circulated statement, entitled "Dancing with God in the Rainbow," dated September 2016, that "At this point in time the EKT supports the government's position that migration and relocation is not an option." It explains: "The proposal on migration avoids the radical call to change the economic practices that destroy the land and people. The need is to save the earth from destruction and not to save a few selected individuals from the drowning land." I received this document in the form of a handout.

37. See Fensham, *Misguided Love*.

Christianity easily becomes hegemonic (e.g., the Dutch Reformed Church under apartheid) or follow a sectarian option, depending on its sphere of influence. It is possible to withdraw from society but still be hegemonic within a particular institution (e.g., in a Reformed theological seminary). As is the case elsewhere, power can easily corrupt. It seems to me that Reformed Christianity functions best when it is *not* in a majority, when it actively engages in attempts to reform something else from within as an influential minority! If true, this assessment is rather unbearable for Reformed office bearers who have been elected by a majority (presumably guided by Word and Spirit).[38]

Christ Transforming Culture Revisited

Charles, you may know that I have some admiration and affinity with Arnold van Ruler.[39] I presume that your version of being Reformed is shaped less by Dutch sources than mine, although I noted that you do draw on Johan H. Bavinck's notion of mission as penance. Let me draw a bit on Van Ruler to suggest a way forward.

Van Ruler's first book was titled *Kuyper's Idee Eener Christelijke Cultuur* (1940). It is a rather densely written text, and I would not recommend that for your reading. Maybe first books are like that. Van Ruler was interested in Abraham Kuyper and Herman Bavinck's conviction that the sphere of influence of the Christian faith should not be restricted to the individual life of the soul, family matters, or the church. It should extend to every square inch of society.[40] This is relevant for an adequate understanding of catholicity (not only in the church but also in society)[41] but especially for the sanctification of all of life. It may start with regeneration (palingenesis) but should extend everywhere.[42] Fair enough, I think you would agree: the whole earth is to be filled with God's glory. For Kuyper this also implies a Christianizing of culture. This is not just about Christian culture in the sense of Christian music, Christian art, or devotional literature. It could

---

38. Conradie, "Placing Reform," 6.
39. See van Ruler, *This Earthly Life*.
40. In his inaugural speech at the VU University Amsterdam (1880), Kuyper stated: "There is not a square inch in the whole domain of our human existence over which Christ, who is Sovereign over all, does not cry, Mine!" See Bratt, Abraham Kuyper, 488.
41. See especially Bavinck's "Catholicity of Christianity."
42. See Kuyper's *Work of the Holy Spirit*.

also include (in the Dutch society of the time) Christian labor unions and political parties. Culture is something comprehensive. Culture should not be Christianized in the sense of Christian window dressing: all ordinary aspects of life—from sexuality to politics—should be sanctified, be made whole through the healing power of the gospel. Kuyper himself was involved in journalism and politics and established the Vrije Universiteit in Amsterdam. But should this also lead to a Christian culture? Is there something like that, alongside, let us say, Muslim or Hindu culture? I think Kuyper would say yes; in fact, he would even say there is something like a Reformed culture that is distinct from Catholic, Orthodox, or Anabaptist cultures.[43] But Christianity clearly does not replace other cultures (also not in Tuvalu) while there are obvious cultural differences in terms of language, dress code, food, sport played, and so forth amongst those who otherwise share similar confessional allegiances.

Van Ruler basically argued that Kuyper did not go far enough in his idea of a Christian culture. The point is not to establish a Christian culture or even to Christianize culture, i.e., to make culture more Christian. This would seem to indicate that Christianity is higher than culture, "above culture," Niebuhr may say. Van Ruler's intuition was that, instead, Christianity is there for the sake of culture, to allow culture to flourish. He worked this out in multiple, often anecdotal, ways in his more mature work.[44] This has nothing to do with a legitimation of culture or nationalism. The core insight is that the gospel does not replace culture but is necessary to liberate culture from the impact of evil, for Van Ruler especially, from sin understood as guilt.[45] Put differently, we are not humans in order to become Christians. We have to become Christians in order to be human again. If so, the church is there for the sake of society, the gospel for the fulfilment of the law, Christ for culture, mission for the sake of the world (Van Ruler was an exponent of the Dutch theology of the apostolate[46]), basically because God so loved the world. To press the point, Van Ruler would say that the meal at home is holier than the holy communion—which is necessary in order to enjoy the meal at home.[47] Paying taxes to the government for the sake of a better distribution of wealth is worthier than tithing in the church, because this

---

43. See the logic of Kuyper's *Lectures on Calvinism*.
44. For a discussion, see my "Van Ruler."
45. For references, see the index to van Ruler's *This Earthly Life*.
46. See van Ruler, *Theologie*.
47. See van Ruler, *This Earthly Life*, 173.

is for the sake of God's kingdom.⁴⁸ On this basis, for Van Ruler, salvation is not an aim in itself. It is not about salvation or being saved or even the Savior but about the being of those who are saved.⁴⁹ We are saved in order to be. One should not give soteriological answers to ontological questions.⁵⁰

Let me frame this in the language of debates on inculturation. The gospel is often understood as a foreign seed (coming from Palestine, not Europe) that has to become deeply rooted, for example in Tuvalu. This I think is mistaken. There is nothing wrong with indigenous plants and seeds. They form part of God's good creation. As does culture. The problem is that sin is like a parasite that strangles indigenous plants. Sin has no ontological status, it cannot exist on its own; it is the privation of the good.⁵¹ If so, the gospel operates more like a shovel or pruning scissors that can cut out the parasites, turning that into compost so that indigenous plants can thrive again.

Are you convinced by this argument, Charles? I hope so! But do not you think that this turns Niebuhr's views on Christ transforming culture on its head? If so, *Christ* is not the power of Christendom that is able to transform culture. Instead, it is the ferment of the gospel that allows culture to flourish. Or perhaps the problem is the binary of Christ and culture. I am not suggesting a trinitarian logic because that is already there is the phrase "Christ transforming culture." I am suggesting a more dialectical interplay between God's work of creation, salvation, and re-creation, for the sake of the flourishing of God's creatures.⁵²

What does this have to say for the resistance against the cultured Christianity of our youth? I would think that such resistance needs to be maintained vehemently. But not at all times and in all places. One does need to read the signs of the time, as you also recognize in your *Emerging from the Dark Age Ahead*.⁵³ I often feel called to say what others are not saying. Almost like a spoilsport. And you?

48. On taxation, see van Ruler, *This Earthly Life*, 107.

49. This is how van Ruler puts it: "In fact, the concept 'salvation' itself points in another direction. It suggests that it is not about the Savior, also not about salvation, not even about the being saved of those saved but about the being of those saved. The primary consideration is to be able to be there again, before the face of God, and also, going beyond this, about simply being there." See *This Earthly Life*, 188.

50. Van Ruler, *This Earthly Life*, 98, 182.

51. I have discussed such issues in *Redeeming Sin?*

52. See again my *Earth in God's Economy*.

53. See Fensham, *Emerging*.

Wishing you good years of good health ahead, despite living in such dark and darkening times.

With fondness, even if nowadays we do not see one another all that frequently,

Ernst M. Conradie

Bibliography

Barbour, Ian G. *Religion and Science: Historical and Contemporary Issues*. San Francisco: Harper & Row, 1997.

Bavinck, Herman. "The Catholicity of Christianity and the Church." Translated by John Bolt. *Calvin Theological Journal* 27 (1992) 220–51.

Bediako, Kwame. *Christianity in Africa: The Renewal of a non-Western Religion*. Maryknoll, NY: Orbis, 1995.

Berger, Peter L. *The Sacred Canopy: Elements of a Sociological Theory of Religion*. New York: Doubleday, 1967.

Biscombe, Hilton, ed. *In Ons Bloed*. Stellenbosch: SUN, 2006.

Bosch, David J. "The Roots and Fruits of Afrikaner Civil Religion." In *New Faces of Africa: Essays in Honour of Ben (Barend Jacobus) Marais*, edited by Jan W. Hofmeyr and Willem S. Nicol, 14–35. Pretoria: Unisa, 1984.

———. *Transforming Mission: Paradigm Shifts in Theology of Mission*. Maryknoll, NY: Orbis, 1991.

Bratt, John D. *Abraham Kuyper: A Centennial Reader*. Grand Rapids: Eerdmans, 1998.

Carter, Craig. *Rethinking Christ and Culture: A Post-Christendom Perspective*. Grand Rapids: Brazos, 2006.

Chakrabarty, Dipesh. "The Climate of History: Four Theses." *Critical Inquiry* 35.2 (2009) 197–222.

Conradie, Ernst M. *Angling for Interpretation*. Stellenbosch: Sun, 2008.

———. *Christianity and a Critique of Consumerism: A Survey of Six Points of Entry*. Wellington: Bible Media, 2009. http://www.bmedia.co.za/content/ view/486/353/.

———. *The Earth in God's Economy: Creation, Salvation and Consummation in Ecological Perspective*. Berlin: LIT Verlag, 2015.

———. "Models for Intertwining God's Story and the Universe Story." In *Issues in Science and Theology: Creative Pluralism?* Edited by Michael Fuller et al., 147–57. Heidelberg: Springer, 2022. https://doi.org/10.1007/978-3-031-06277-3_13.

———. "Placing Reform: The Ecumenical Future of Reformed Theology." *Stellenbosch Theological Journal* 9.3 (2023) 1–12. http://dx.doi.org/10.17570/stj.2023.v9n3.a3.

———. *Redeeming Sin? Social Diagnostics amid Ecological Destruction*. Lamham: Lexington, 2017.

———. "Some Theological Reflections on Multi-disciplinary Discourse on the 'Anthropocene.'" *Scriptura* 121 (2022) 1–23. http://dx.doi.org/10.7833/121-1-2076.

———. "Van Ruler as an Early Exponent of Christian Ecotheology?" In *This Earthly Life Matters: The Promise of Arnold van Ruler for Ecotheology* by Arnold van Ruler, edited by Ernst M. Conradie, 32–57. Eugene, OR: Pickwick Publications, 2023.

Conradie, Ernst M., et al. *Fishing for Jonah*. Bellville: University of the Western Cape, 1995.

Ekalesia Kelisiano Tuvalu (EKT). "Dancing with God in the Rainbow." Statement released in September 2016.

Fensham, Charles. *Emerging from the Dark Age Ahead: The Future of the North American Church*. Clements, 2011.

———. *Misguided Love: Christians and the Rupture of LGBTQI2+ People*. Atlanta: Journal of Pastoral Care Publications, 2019.

———. *Mission as Penance: Essays on the Theology of Mission from a Canadian Context*. Eugene, OR: Pickwick Publications, 2023.

———. "The Sacrament of the First Child of God: A Renewed Christian Eco-imaginary." *Scriptura* 111 (2012) 323–32.

———. *To the Nations for the Earth: A Missional Spirituality*. Clements Group, 2013.

Hewitt, Roderick R. *Church and Culture: An Anglo-Caribbean Experience of Hybridity and Contradiction*. Pietermaritzburg: Cluster, 2012.

Kuyper, Abraham. *Lectures on Calvinism*. New York: Cosimo, 2007.

———. *The Work of the Holy Spirit*. Translated by Henri De Vries. New York: Cosimo, 2007.

Long, D. Stephen. *Theology and Culture: A Guide to the Discussion*. Eugene, OR: Cascade Books, 2008.

Lusama, Tafue. *Vaa Fesokotaki: A Mafulifuli Reconstruction of the Theology of te Atua for a New Tuvalu Climate Change Story*. Suva: Pacific Theological College Press, 2022.

Newbigin, Lesslie. *Foolishness to the Greeks: The Gospel and Western Culture*. Grand Rapids: Eerdmans, 1986.

———. *The Gospel in a Pluralist Society*. Geneva: World Council of Churches, 1989.

Niebuhr, H. Richard. *Christ and Culture*. New York: Harper Torch, 1951.

Sakuba, Xolani. "A Critical Assessment of the Concept of Culture in the First Wave of African Christian Theology." PhD thesis, University of the Western Cape, 2013.

Smit, Dirk J. "Theology and the Transformation of Culture—Niebuhr Revisited." *Journal of Theology for Southern Africa* 72 (1990) 9–23.

Stassen, Glen H. "It Is Time to Take Jesus Back: In Celebration of the Fiftieth Anniversary of H. Richard Niebuhr's 'Christ and Culture.'" *Journal of the Society of Christian Ethics* 23.1 (2003) 133–43.

Talia, Maina. "Am I Not Your *Tuakoi*? A Tuvaluan Plea for Survival in Time of Climate Emergency." DPhil thesis, Charles Sturt University, 2023.

———. "The *Fakalofa* Lies Before You: Re-reading Scripture in Tuvalu." In *How Would We Know What God is Up To?*, edited by Ernst M. Conradie and Cynthia D. Moe-Lobeda, 177–90. Durbanville: Aosis, 2022.

———. "*Kauafua Fatele* for Christ' Sake: A Theological Dance for the Changing Climate." In *Theologies from the Pacific*, edited by Jione Havea, 63–76. Cham: Palgrave Macmillan, 2021.

Van Ruler, Arnold A. *Kuyper's Idee Eener Christelijke Cultuur*. Nijkerk: Callenbach, 1940.

———. *Theologie van het Apostolaat*. Nijkerk: Callenbach, 1954.

———. *This Earthly Life Matters: The Promise of Arnold van Ruler for Ecotheology*. Edited by Ernst M. Conradie. Eugene, OR: Pickwick Publications, 2023.

2

A Multi-Voice Conversation Seeking Greater Inclusivity in Theological Education

Dorcas Gordon

I AM GRATEFUL FOR the opportunity to contribute to this volume honoring Professor Charles Fensham.[1] I have known Charles since he accepted the invitation to become Professor of Systematic Theology at Knox College in 2002. Over the years, until my retirement from Knox in 2018, I became increasingly impressed with Charles's passion and commitment to teaching systematic theology from the perspective of inclusivity and justice and to do so in a way that was both academically sound and focused on an integrated ministerial practice.

---

1. This work is a revised version of a chapter in a Festschrift written in 2018 for the Rev. Dr. Henry Wilson whose commitment to developing a contextualized Asian theology spans many decades.

Introduction

Since my retirement from Knox College, I have been deeply involved in the work of the Foundation for Theological Education in Asia and the Pacific (FTEAP), whose mission is to foster excellence in theological education in Asia and, more recently, the Pacific. As part of this commitment, I have participated in numerous consultations and workshops focused on investigating what model of theological education might best serve both church and society in the complex context of Asia. At one consultation held in 2018 in Kota Kinabalu, Malaysia, the present model of education with its fourfold division into departments, Theology, Bible, History, and Pastoral, inherited from the West through the mission movement, was critiqued by several of the participants. Their critique focused on the way in which each department seemed to exist in a silo removed from the others and, even more concerning, existed primarily in the realm of theory rather than life. Many presenters identified the need for a more integrated or interdisciplinary model that began with a context where a significant part of the population suffered from poverty and violence. Of additional concern was the formation of faculty to teach and research within this context especially since so many who were educated in North America or Europe returned home ill-prepared to form students for ministries in the Asian church and society.

As Convenor of the Programme Committee of FTEAP, I am presently involved in several projects, one of which is investigating what is needed for building capacity for inclusivity within institutions, administration, and faculty around gender and sexuality. Still in the preliminary stages, FTEAP has made a three-year commitment to work with college administrators, faculty, and students who are committed to reframe policies and practices, curricula, teaching methods and, of equal importance, to investigate the influence of the hidden curriculum on building capacity for inclusivity.

Although I have much to learn, my exposure to theological education in Asia has convinced me that, not only in Asia but also in Canada, theological educators need to continue to explore what it means in this context to develop more integrated and inclusive models of education. This conviction also arises out of my own social location and experience as a woman who began seminary education in 1969 when women were still looked upon by many as out of place. When I returned in the 1980s to do graduate study, now married with four children, I was unprepared for the ways in which certain prejudices and judgments remained. In attaining a doctoral degree, I may have learned as much about gender and theological education as about my major in biblical studies. Over the years, as I continue to reflect on my experience, I have made a commitment to work with students whom I suspect have experienced marginalization by virtue of their ethnicity, race, sexuality, or ableness, not only because of church polity but perhaps even more because of those policies and often unconscious institutional practices that identify some as acceptable and others as not.

These reflections both personal and arising out of my conversations with colleagues in Asia and the Pacific convince me that in the Canadian context there is more to be done in reconstructing or reframing how we do theological education, a reconstruction or reframing that needs to take place in an ongoing process of deconstruction. Linda Tuhiwai Smith, a New Zealander and Professor of Indigenous Studies would agree, reflecting on her own experience:

> The reach of imperialism into "our heads" challenges those who belong to colonized communities to understand how this occurred, partly because we perceive a need to decolonize our minds, to recover ourselves, to claim a space in which to develop a sense of authentic humanity.[2]

Not surprisingly, this chapter will focus on a multi-voice conversation seeking to identify elements I believe to be essential to a more integrated and inclusive model of theological education.

In a 1996 article, Kwok Pui Lan, an Asia American biblical scholar, writes about the contested narratives describing the handover of Hong Kong to China. Her concern is not focused on what she calls "the grand political narratives of nationalism, sovereignty, democracy, human rights, and civil society." Instead, she fixes her attention on the cultural practices that need to change for the complex process of decolonization to be realized. This process she describes in the following way:

> Hong Kong, referred to as the "Pearl of the Orient," was not built in one day. The colonization process and its internalization by the colonized took a long time. Decolonization of a colony involves not simply a political turn-over but also complicated, controversial and contested changes in cultural practices. Decolonization of the mind and the imagination involves debunking the regimes of truth imposed by the colonizers and the collaborators; dislodging the mind from familiar thinking patterns, disintegrating seemingly coherent discourses, displaying silences and closures of

2. Tuhiwai Smith, *Decolonizing*, 23.

texts, decomposing the garbage that has filled the brain cells for too long, and much more.[3]

Her statement makes clear that, for those who were colonized, decolonizing minds is a complex process.

This, however, situates only one side of the process of decolonizing minds. Equally challenging, or perhaps more challenging, is the process of decolonizing the minds of the colonizer. Pui Lan in an earlier article quotes the French philosopher Michel Foucault, who affirms:

> Each society has its own regime of truth . . . that is, the types of discourse which it accepts and makes function as true; the mechanisms and instances which enable one to distinguish true and false statements; the means by which each is sanctioned; the techniques and procedures accorded value in the acquisition of truth; the status of those who are charged with saying what counts as true.[4]

In other words, both colonized and colonizer are held captive to epistemologies, frameworks of meaning, authoritative scripts legitimated by those we accept as having authority to proclaim truth. These frameworks once established are difficult to question, with the result that they become enculturated, normative, and hence are understood as universal, as true in all circumstances and contexts. For those of us in theological education there is an urgency to examine our heads (and bodies), in order "to recover ourselves, to claim a space in which to develop a sense of authentic humanity."[5]

The Eurocentric Myth and the Colonial Legacy

Decolonization of the mind emerged as part of "the more recent shifts" to frame epistemologically "the colonial intellectual legacy."[6] Ary Fernandez-Alban, a Cuban scholar, speaks of decoloniality as that which seeks to develop "discourses critical of the colonial and imperial practices and the Eurocentric imaginary and epistemology embodied by coloniality/modernity."[7] What this means, in part, is that decolonial theory focuses on exposing the mythic construct of Europe called the Eurocentric

---

3. Kwok, "Response," 211–12.
4. Kwok, "Discovering the Bible," 26.
5. Tuhiwai Smith, *Decolonizing*, 23.
6. Fernandez-Alban, "De-colonial Thought," 1.
7. Fernandez-Alban, "De-colonial Thought," 1.

exceptionalist narrative that emerged in the sixteenth century so that new constructs and practices could emerge. Important for Reformed models of theological education is that this century also saw the development of theological doctrines and practices within the Protestant reformation that continue to inform our theology, our polity, and worship life.

The Eurocentric myth embodies the way Europe set up an ethno-racial hierarchical classification of the European versus the non-European. This meant the imposition of the white/European identity over all dimensions of power: economic, political, social, cultural, and religious.[8] In other words, Europe claimed for itself qualities it understood to have attained through its own superiority not through interaction with others.

> Eurocentric narratives represent Europe as the sole author of modernity and, thus imagine Europe developed the modern ways of knowing the world all by itself. By denying the global scope of modernity, Eurocentric knowledge production denies that colonial violence is the product of modern, liberal political economies but, instead, lays such violence at the feet of deviant persons or theories.[9]

As a result, the narratives of others who were on the underside of this violent myth needed to be suppressed. As "others," they had to be convinced of the truth of Europe's narrative by physical force and/or psychological manipulation that resulted in a dismissal of their values and practices and, in many cases, their humanity.

According to Tuhiwai Smith, referring to the work of Ashis Nandy,[10] the underlying connection to other aspects of this imaginary was the principle of order. It became the "code" or "grammar" of imperialism.[11] Thus, the concept of disorder was applied to those considered "other," resulting in their dismissal through a series of negations: "they were not fully human, they were not civilized enough to have systems, they were not literate, their languages and modes of thought were inadequate."[12] As a result, Europe and European values and practices became a concept that led to a

---

8. Fernandez-Alban, "De-colonial Thought," 4.

9. Gordon, *Eurocentric*, 10.

10. Nandy has published dozens of books and articles on the psychology of politics and culture. These include The Intimate Enemy, in which Nandy turns colonial studies around by examining the impact of imperialism on the colonizing nation itself.

11. Tuhiwai Smith, *Decolonizing*, 28.

12. Tuhiwai Smith, *Decolonizing*, 43.

characterization and classification of the other, which resulted in a system of representation with its criteria for comparison and evaluation.[13] Walter Mignolo puts it this way: "From a detached and neutral point of observation . . . the knowing subject maps the world and its problems, classifies people and projects into what is good for them."[14]

Christianity's role in this worldview was to "order the disorder," that is, to Christianize, to civilize, to redeem the other by transforming bodies and minds to be acceptable within this mythic framework. This resulted in silencing and excluding not only their systems of belief and values but also any alternative narratives they might present. Thus, the Eurocentric narrative remained with its claim that through its institutions and ideas it had created an ordered, that is, less violent and more progressive, world. "Europe and European culture become the standard against which modern societies and institutions can be evaluated."[15]

Settler Colonialism, and Residential Schools

Over the centuries, because of their northern European heritage, that is, their whiteness, this myth migrated to include colonial nations such as Canada, the United States, Australia, New Zealand, South Africa, and, more recently, Israel. Within these countries, the colonialism that developed was one that focused on replacing the Indigenous populations with a dominant settler society. Over time, it developed its distinctive identity and hegemony. From the beginning, these colonial outposts were to represent what civilization or order looked like. To quote Tuhiwai Smith, "colonialism was in part, an image of imperialism, a particular realization of the imperial imagination. It was also, in part, an image of the future nation it would become."[16]

This speaks forcefully to the need for a settler colonial nation like Canada to acknowledge how much the code or grammar of the Eurocentric myth continues to be embedded in the institutional structures and practices of theological education, in the norms by which we judge what is acceptable (properly human/civilized) and what is not. Although my family, part

---

13. Tuhiwai Smith, *Decolonizing*, 43, is referring in this discussion to the work of Hall, "The West and the Rest: Discourse and Power."
14. Mignolo, "Epistemic Disobedience," 1.
15. Gordon, *Eurocentric*, 36, is referring to Dussel, "Beyond Eurocentrism," 3.
16. Tuhiwai Smith, *Decolonizing*, 23.

of a conservative Reformed/Presbyterian mindset, immigrated to Canada long after the original colonial period, I recognize that there are parts of this code that continue to live within me. Thus, I write about the ongoing need to decolonize minds and bodies, reflecting on my mind and body in terms of the institutional structures and practices of theological education.

The work of decolonization has ongoing significance within Canadian society as we accept and respond to the "94 Calls to Action of the National Truth and Reconciliation Commission" published in 2015, challenging government, educational institutions, and the Christian churches to examine their institutional structures and operative practices in terms of how they impacted and continue to impact Canada's First Nations.[17] The catalyst for this report began in the nineteenth century when the Canadian government, assuming responsibility for educating Indigenous peoples, determined that successful enculturation within Canadian society required them to learn English and adopt Christianity and Canadian customs. A policy of "aggressive assimilation" was established to be taught in church-run, government-funded schools called residential (boarding) schools, focused not on adults but on children. In these schools, the children were forbidden to speak their tribal language or practice their tribal culture and spirituality. Within this framework, the "curriculum and its underlying theory of knowledge . . . redefined the world and where the Indigenous peoples were positioned within the world."[18] This residential education sought to ensure that only as white Canadian and Christian could these children define themselves. The "disorder" of their previous life would no longer exist.

The Canadian *Report of the Royal Commission on Aboriginal Peoples* describes the physical and cultural violence of these schools:

> The very language in which the vision [of Residential Schools] was couched revealed what would have to be the essentially violent nature of the school system in its assault on child and culture. The basic premise of resocialization, of the great transformation from "savage" to "civilized" was violent . . . In the end at the point of final assimilation, "all the Indian there is in the race should be dead." This was more than a rhetorical flourish as it took on a traumatic reality in the life of each child separated from parents and community and isolated in a world hostile to identity, traditional

---

17. http://www.trc.ca/websites/trcinstitution/File/2015/Findings/Calls_to_Action_English2.pdf.

18. Tuhiwai Smith, *Decolonizing*, 33.

belief, and language. The system of transformation was suffused with a similar latent savagery—punishment . . . In the vision of residential school education, discipline was the curriculum and punishment an essential pedagogical technique.[19]

In the late 1980s and early 1990s, the churches in Canada that held responsibility for operating Residential Schools began to offer apologies for their part in the abuse of Aboriginal children. Words from The Presbyterian Church in Canada apology speaks to our recognition that the Eurocentric colonial myth was deeply embedded in our actions:

> We acknowledge that the stated policy of the Government of Canada was to assimilate Aboriginal peoples to the dominant culture, and that The Presbyterian Church in Canada co-operated in this policy. We acknowledge that the roots of the harm we have done are found in the attitudes and values of western European colonialism, and the assumption that what was not yet moulded in our image was to be discovered and exploited. As part of that policy we, with other churches, encouraged the government to ban some important spiritual practices through which Aboriginal peoples experienced the presence of the creator God. For the Church's complicity in this policy we ask forgiveness.
> We confess that The Presbyterian Church in Canada presumed to know better than Aboriginal peoples what was needed for life. The Church said of our Aboriginal brothers and sisters, "If they could be like us, if they could think like us, talk like us, worship like us, sing like us, and work like us, they would know God and therefore would have life abundant." In our cultural arrogance we have been blind to the ways in which our own understanding of the Gospel has been culturally conditioned, and because of our insensitivity to Aboriginal cultures, we have demanded more of the Aboriginal people than the Gospel requires and have thus misrepresented Jesus Christ who loves all peoples with compassionate, suffering love that all may come to God through him. For the Church's presumption we ask forgiveness.[20]

---

19. Regan, *Unsettling the Settler*, 100, citing http://www.collectionscanada.gc.ca/webarchives/20071211055821/http://www.ainc-inac.gc.ca/ch/rcap/sg/sg31_e.html.

20. PCC, Confession.

Decolonizing Canadian Theological Education: A Beginning

A brief review of the reports and debates of the General Assembly during the early period of the Residential Schools suggests there were few voices raised decrying our role in this system. A resolution from Principal Caven of Knox College, part of a lengthy statement criticizing the "wrongs that have been perpetrated against those who are wards of the Government," calls for "the cancelling all appointments of agents or instructors who are known to be tyrannical, unjust or immoral." He continues, however, with these words:

> Further, the Presbyterian Church pledges itself to co-operate with the public authorities in promoting the social improvement and the temporal well-being of the Indians, whilst in common with other churches, seeking to bring them under the holy influence of the Christian religion.[21]

In other words, this formal accusation, not of the system, but of those who abused it indicates how many in The Presbyterian Church in Canada and in our theological colleges were held captive to this Eurocentric imaginary framework. Why were there not more voices within the churches' leadership decrying their role in this system? Why were we held captive to this myth, unable within our seminaries and in our teaching and research to recognize the assumptions and biases that existed in our curriculum and practices?

For me, the churches' apologies raise significant questions about the theological and cultural aspects of the exceptionalist myth we continue to accept and practice as truth. Equally critical today is the question: What other assumptions and biases exist throughout the educational system holding us captive to beliefs and practices which deny full humanity to the other? What needs to take place to ensure that we do not teach other theologies or interpretive practices that are equally destructive?

Recognizing the sin of the church's complicity in residential schools provides me with a starting point for a reframed model or epistemology for theological education in the Canadian context, including what remains to be done in responding to Professor Kwok's call to live into the "complicated, controversial and contested changes in cultural practices"[22] that a renewed model of theological education requires. Questions like: How does "what

21. Article Reporting on the General Assembly.
22. Kwok, "Response," 211.

we know and how we know it and the way certain modes become or do not become authorized"[23] direct our work? What might such reframing require us to change in our institutional structures and policies, the curriculum, syllabi, the method of delivery, as well as the theologies and ingrained beliefs of faculty and students?

Fernandez-Alban, along with Kwok and Gordon, agree that coloniality did not end with the so-called end of the colonial period but "mutated into a complex web of power relations at the level of the economy, politics and culture [including religion] that constitutes a global coloniality."[24] They insist that coloniality is not just a political-economic project with its "juridical control of a given population by a different entity, it also includes the profound interconnection of cultural and social factors, deep ideological Eurocentric epistemic forces, and ethno-national identities."[25] Gordon's work on archival studies is significant in its clarity about the control archives have over faculty research, given the way in which archives not only privilege written over oral records but also decide what is relevant and made available to researchers and what is not, as well as determining how that material is organized and profiled.[26]

The challenging work for theological educators to decolonize minds and bodies means a commitment to use what Fernandez, building on the work of Walter Mignolo,[27] calls epistemological disruption or epistemic disobedience at all levels of institutional life. This means, considering the power and all-encompassing framework of the Eurocentric myth, that we ask disturbing questions about the structure of knowledge that we claim and teach as truth. For Fernandez-Alban it means nothing less than an examination of "the construction, acquisition and production of theological knowledge."[28] Here again Gordon is helpful in his work on European exceptionalism and archival studies when he states: "There is no one fatal flaw within settler nationalism that can be exploited that will decolonize the settler nation. It requires new frameworks."[29]

---

23. Gordon, *Eurocentric*, 3.
24. Fernandez-Alban, "De-colonial Thought," 5.
25. Fernandez-Alban, "De-colonial Thought," 4.
26. Gordon, *Eurocentric*, 5, quoting Joan Schwartz, "Having New Eyes."
27. Mignolo, "Epistemic Disobedience," 1–23.
28. Fernandez-Alban, "De-colonial Thought," 43.
29. Gordon, *Eurocentric*, 15.

It is not difficult to find examples of how such disruption or disobedience might work in different areas. A simple question asks how the various parts of the world are named, for example, the Near East, Middle East, Far East. Epistemological disruption asks, "middle of where," "near or far from what."[30] The answer: Europe. As Edward Said describes it, the way that Orientalism assigns "one space that is 'ours' and an unfamiliar space beyond 'ours' which is 'theirs' is a way of making geographical distinctions that can be entirely arbitrary" yet "in this imaginary geography their space is 'out there' and inside 'ours' is crowned with suppositions, associations and fictions."[31] Epistemological disruption asks how Europe and a coloniality of power with the right to name reality/truth remains at the center of a more diverse and complex world.

In the political realm we can see examples of the mythic paradigm of European exceptionalism in the United States' appropriation of the Eurocentric paradigm as American exceptionalism. Eric Cheyfitz, a Professor of American Studies at Cornell University, focuses his research on the way in which the Puritan sects "imagined themselves in their writings as repeating the sacred journey of the Jews, as being God's chosen people." The continuation of this myth allows the US, called by God to promote democracy and decency in the global context, to be the "good guy" in all circumstances. Whatever bad happens, it is the fault of the other. As exceptional, the US speaks of responsibilities and rights, of bearing a special burden.[32] However, also as an exceptional nation, the US understands that it should enjoy exceptional freedom to behave as it sees fit and make its own rules because of its deep-seated democratic traditions and inherent morality.[33] Epistemic disobedience asks about the truth of claims of morality considering its ongoing political and economic practices.

In Christian Zionism circles, this colonial epistemology continues to promote violence and exclusion. The Bible is interpreted in terms of the identification of modern Israel with ancient Israel. This theology then proceeds to assert that modern day Israel has been given ownership of the whole land of Palestine, so-called ancient Israel. It is interpreted as an eternal promise that calls for the destruction of its Indigenous people (Deut

---

30. This example is found in Raheb, *Faith*, 43.
31. Said, *Orientalism*, 54.
32. Cheyfitz, "Exceptionalist Narratives," 114–15.
33. Beinart, "Iran Deal."

20:16–18; Josh 11: 10–14). Epistemic disobedience asks: is the God we worship an ethnic cleansing God?

A consideration of these examples asks: What model of theological education can contribute to the process of fostering epistemological disruption or epistemic disobedience thus disrupting the aspects of this exceptionalist myth that continue to be lived out within theological education?

Habitus, Social Imaginary, and Decolonizing Minds

A starting point may be found in the work of Pierre Bourdieu on habitus and reflexive sociology and Charles Taylor on social imaginary. Pierre Bourdieu sees "power as culturally and symbolically created and constantly re-legitimized through an interplay of agency and structure."[34] Habitus is the way persons are conditioned into society. Bourdieu speaks of dispositions, shaped by past events and structures that shape current practices and structures, and, importantly, that condition our very perceptions of these.[35] However, habitus "is not fixed or permanent, and can be changed under unexpected situations or over a long historical period."[36] His development of what he calls a "reflexive sociology" is also helpful to the conversation about more integrated and inclusive models of theological education. Reflexive sociology recognizes that one's biases, beliefs, and assumptions are central in the act of sense-making. This self-critical knowledge discloses the "sources of power" and reveals the reasons that explain social asymmetries and hierarchies, thus becoming "a powerful tool to enhance social emancipation."[37]

Charles Taylor's concept of social imaginary is described as underpinning "the way people imagine their social existence, how they fit together with others, how things go on between them and their fellows, the expectations that are normally met, and the deeper normative notions and images that underlie these expectations."[38] He continues:

> I adopt the term imaginary (i) because my focus is on the way ordinary people "imagine" their social surroundings, and this is

---

34. Powercube, "Bourdieu and 'Habitus.'"
35. Bourdieu, *Distinction*, 170.
36. Powercube, "Bourdieu and 'Habitus.'"
37. Navarro, "In Search," 15–16.
38. Taylor, *Modern Social Imaginaries*, 23.

often not expressed in theoretical terms, but is carried in images, stories, and legends. It is also the case that (ii) theory is often the possession of a small minority, whereas what is interesting in the social imaginary is that it is shared by large groups of people, if not the whole society which leads to a third difference: (iii) the social imaginary is that common understanding that makes possible common practices and a widely shared sense of legitimacy.[39]

For Taylor, theory may transform a social imaginary; but even more can a social imaginary transform theory.

Taylor's theory of the social imaginary with its emphasis on images, stories, and legends and its power for transformation has potential for a reframing of theological education. So also does Bourdieu's theory of reflexive sociology, which recognizes that one's biases, beliefs, and assumptions are central in the act of sense-making in their potential to disclose sources of power and reveal explanations for social asymmetries and hierarchies. When given more prominence might personal agency (formation) become a tool to challenge hierarchies and might habitus or a social imaginary (worldview) result in changed patterns of enculturation? If so, what might such a model of theological education look like?

Three Voices and Their Possibilities for a Model of Inclusive Theological Education

In this multi-voice conversation, I have chosen to highlight three representative voices removed from each other in time, geography, and culture. These voices, one from Brazil, one from South Korea, and another from the United States, I believe have the potential to encourage educators to engage in epistemic disobedience with the possibility of disrupting the exceptionalist narrative that continues to affect institutions, theories, and practices within theological education. I say this with caution mindful of Smith's timely warning that "the organization of school knowledge, the hidden curriculum and the representation of difference in texts and school practices all contain discourses which have serious implications" for all minority groups within theological education.[40]

In a seminal volume, *Pedagogy of the Oppressed*, published in 1968 (first translated into English in 1970), Brazilian educator Paolo Freire

---

39. Taylor, *Modern Social Imaginaries*, 23.
40. Tuhiwai Smith, *Decolonizing*, 11.

called for the development of a critical consciousness in his students to tackle what he considered humankind's central problem. Written in the context of Brazil, the question's focus is quite specific: How do those who are oppressed affirm their identity as human beings and in the process be empowered to bring about social change? Central to this system is the development of a model of education that does not result in the internalization of oppression.[41]

To answer such questions and to avoid an internalizing of oppression, Freire's model seeks to break down what he calls a banking model of education, a system in which teachers have the knowledge, which they "deposit" into the minds of the students who memorize and recall what they have been taught and continue to make "withdrawals" throughout their lives. His alternative, a "problem posing model," sought to teach students how to view the world critically, how to raise questions and to analyze why certain problems exist. For Freire, education requires a model of praxis, that is, a dialogue between teachers and students consisting equally of abstract theory and concrete action. In the present day understanding of inclusivity in education, one of the most important critiques of Freire's work concerns the fact that he does not view oppression from a contemporary understanding of intersectionality but from the perspective of a singular oppressed class.[42]

A second voice, Hyun Sook Kim of Yonsei University in South Korea, in proposing a way forward examines the changing paradigms in theological education. His analysis begins by identifying the pressing need for theological education to move away from its enlightenment (Eurocentric) framework to embrace the pluralism of the contemporary situation. From his perspective, this means a refocusing away from religious questions that address primarily personal, subjective needs. The focus instead, he argues, should be on embracing the public sphere with its human need and suffering.[43] This immediately raises the question as to what is the public sphere? Who defines it? His response is captured in what follows.

He maintains that what is required is a conversation model, which, like Bourdieu's reflexive sociology, begins by a self-acknowledgement of the power of ideologies to distort and invite absolutist thinking. Recognizing there is no such thing as pure objectivity, this model requires all in the conversation (faculty, administrators, and students alike) to identify their

---

41. Gomes, *Review*, 21.
42. Gomes, *Review*.
43. Kim, "Changing Paradigms," 425.

social location, which contains the biases, beliefs, and assumptions that directs their learning, teaching, research, administrative, or strategic decisions. Early in my doctoral work I came across this quote which I think has great wisdom for theological education: objectivity is subjectivity aware of itself. In other words, all participants need to identify the social location from which they speak and recognize that they must be open to attending intentionally to the social location of each participant in the conversation. No social location is normative.

This model also requires mutual understanding in which common goals that include all in the process are established. Kim, aware of the limitations of the clerical and theory-to-practice paradigms, as well as the discipline-based structure of theological education, is committed to a conversation conducted along the lines of analogical imagination. Such a conversation welcomes alternative ways of knowing, such as Taylor's focus on images, stories, and legends, as well as an acceptance of a plurality of worldviews and a pathway to lead those participating into new understandings of what has remained hidden, seen as deficient or even heretical.

To structure theological education in this way would call upon Canadian educators to enter an institutional wide conversation to imagine how theological education might be reconstructed. According to Kim such a conversation demands an intentional focus on the interrelationship and interdependency of curriculum, pedagogy, and the environment.[44] It requires a refocusing, a process of letting go of previous concepts and patterns, and here I would add practices, a decision that Shoki Coe, when he was President at Tainan Theological College and Seminary in Taiwan, described as "not throwing the baby out with the bath water" yet fully aware that keeping "the baby in cold, soiled water" compromises its life.[45] This model is an interested, deliberately ideological model in which there is a shared commitment to the transformation both of participants in the conversation and of the context, local and global, in which they live. Here the warning of Tuhiwai Smith becomes important: "The organization of school knowledge, the hidden curriculum, and the representation of difference in texts and school practices all contain discourses which have serious implications for Indigenous students as well as for other minority ethnic groups."[46]

---

44. Kim, "Changing Paradigms," 431.
45. Coe, "Theological Education," 7.
46. Tuhiwai Smith, *Decolonizing,* 11.

The third voice is that of Mark Taylor, a professor at Princeton seminary. His work focuses on the difference between what he calls Theology with a capital *T* and the theological. He views Theology as distinct from the theological in two senses. First, Theology, especially in theological institutions in the West,

> tends to focus on doctrinal loci, traditional topics of God, creation, sin, Christology, Holy Spirit, church, eschatology, and so on, all of which provide an ordering function, its parts drawn from established church formulae, creeds, and the biblical narrative's view of history. Strictly observed, arrangements of these loci structure a sense of "orthodoxy."[47]

Although he would agree that today's theologians hold the notion of orthodoxy more loosely, he argues that these traditional topics still operate as a web of symbols in which theological education grounds its work.[48]

Distinct from this is the language of the theological, that is, the artful image in song, poetry, story, literature, and painting. What Charles Taylor refers to as the social imaginary, these he identifies as the primary form of discourse of the theological, "insofar as they convey and constitute the haunting power of peoples bearing the weight of the world." Taylor views the theological as tracing and theorizing the way this haunting power forms into "specters and forces both threatening and promising alternative patterns and lifeways."[49] His contention is that "in terms of liberatory and transformative potential, Theology's doctrinal language is no rival to the symbolic language of such an art-force."[50]

The second difference he identifies between Theology and the theological is the binary relationship in which Theology situates transcendence and immanence. Instead, Taylor uses the term *transimmanence*, which he defines "as a practice or reflection that steps *into* and moves *within* the political."[51] It is "existence thus refusing to be locked in place 'locked down' in systems that resist continual opening and closing." Taylor continues:

> Transimmanence, then, while pervading the entire human condition, abides in and flashes forth along the agonistic boundaries of

---

47. Taylor, *Theological*, 12.
48. Taylor, *Theological*, 12.
49. Taylor, *Theological*, 9.
50. Taylor, *Theological*, 14.
51. Taylor, *Theological*, 15.

being, especially as agonistic tension shifts from a fruitful balance of power into a more concentrated and onerous exercise of power over others. The theological addresses this concentration, grates against it, engages and deflects it.[52]

I interpret this in terms of the incarnation, where in the person of Jesus Christ transcendence and immanence meet at the crossroads of where life is lived with both joy and suffering. Taylor claims that "tracing the transimmanental will offer us a way to discern the powers that sustain and liberate the world." In other words, this attribute of the theological offers both to personal formation and to the structure of theological education a way to identify what has the potential to contribute to human flourishing in all its aspects—spiritual, political, economic, and social.

Conclusion

Let me conclude with what is but a beginning, hoping that in some way it honors Charles Fensham's commitments to the reframing of theological education in mission studies and in broadening the understanding and acceptance of diversity in the definition and practices of gender and sexuality.

As a lifelong feminist whose primary field is biblical interpretation, I am aware of the ways that the Bible has been and continues to be used in violent and oppressive ways to marginalize and demonize and in extreme cases destroy the other. As a woman I have experienced that oppression and violence in the ways I have been dismissed and discounted simply by virtue of being something I could not change or disguise—my identity as a woman. I recognize that more extreme forms of that violence and oppression continue to be perpetrated against others who have been othered,[53] including those who do not embody the binary gender/sex divide.

As a teacher of New Testament interpretation my priority has been the investigation of those larger, often invisible, frameworks of meaning, which control how we interpret the biblical story. As a teacher of homiletics my concern is to probe and understand how such narratives impact the way in which these stories become truth in the hearts and minds of modern listeners. Following earlier interpreters, I did not use the term *decolonizing*

---

52. Taylor, *Theological*, 16.

53. The recent dehumanization and marginalization of the Palestinian people by Israel and Western governments is a prime example. Called "human animals" by an Israeli military official, it was accepted that they could be left to suffer starvation.

but rather saw my work as that of a resistant reader, which meant asking multiple questions from multiple perspectives, a kind of epistemic disobedience, looking for new or previously dismissed ways to frame text and context. Increasingly central to this work is a critical analysis of the intersection of gender and sexuality, race, and class.

This paper intentionally accessed representative global voices who name the destructive power of the mutated Eurocentric based model and seek alternatives. Given what Pui Lan described as the complex process needed for decolonizing minds,[54] theological education must commit to examine not only how it constructs, acquires, and produces theological knowledge but also must display a willingness to allow new frameworks to emerge.

At this stage in my life, now as principal emerita of Knox College, I find hope in many areas. I affirm the work of Kwok, Tuhiwai Smith, Fernandez, and Gordon and emerging educational models of which those of Freire, Kim, and Taylor are only examples. All such have the power to continue to motivate Canadian theological educators to acknowledge what went wrong in the past and to rethink and renew the critical work of theological education so that it strengthens the Canadian church and nation in such a way as to ensure the flourishing of all. I also have learned so much—still underdeveloped—about the diversity of contexts, institutions, and hopes of theological educators in Asia to be part of building a society where, as I dream of for the Canadian context, all can flourish. Let me end by briefly summarizing four areas that I think are critical, recognizing it could easily become a much longer list.

First, the need to emphasize critical thinking and the solving of "real life" problems as key goals for an integrated approach to the formation of students.

Included within this is a formation that privileges questions of self-reflection aimed at a transformation in student and faculty understanding not only of their minds but as important if not more so questions as to where their hearts are focused and what they commit to with their hands. This would also include greater emphasis on art forms that are critical in opening imagination, which is a precursor to bringing innovative ideas and approaches into reality. To move beyond the theory to practice, doctrinally-focused curriculum of theological education requires trust that a multi-voice plurality can move theological education toward a model that the feminist

---

54. Kwok, *Response*, 211–12.

Elisabeth Schüssler Fiorenza names "an emancipatory educational space"[55] or what Mark Taylor calls transimmanence, with its focus on a ministry that is incarnate, vitally alive, and committed to fullness of life for all.

Second, I believe that in theological education we need to pay greater attention to what many call the "hidden curriculum."

Increasingly, educators affirm that the hidden curriculum is a greater danger to learning than the authorized curriculum because, through it, students learn from what takes place throughout the institution outside formal learning about the lived values of trust, respect, inclusion, and fairness. Central to this is an examination of the structures of power that exist within theological institutions, including the way the faculty and administrators relate to each other and to students: who does what and in what circumstances, who has authority to speak on behalf of the school, and so much more. This came home to me in profound ways when I recognized that I was the only woman present in so many decision-making meetings; or when our Korean students, over 35 percent of the student body, continued to view themselves as guests in *our* house and not as equal participants with us in the Knox family. Educators would affirm that this hidden curriculum has the potential to undo all that we seek to accomplish in the formation of students for ministry and as faculty. It is really about what we in Canada call "walking the walk and not just talking the talk."

Third: Key to a model of theological education that ensures the flourishing of both church and society is the contextual formation of the faculty and with it the need to recognize the limitations of the fourfold discipline model of theological education.

Models aimed at transformation challenge faculty to an integration, an interdisciplinarity, in teaching and in their interactions with students for which many are unprepared. The words of Tuhiwai Smith about the fourfold discipline-based educational approach are helpful in situating what I mean. She writes: "Insularity protects a discipline from the 'outside' enabling communities of scholars to distance themselves from others and, in more extreme forms, to absolve themselves of responsibility for what occurs in other branches of their discipline, in the academy and in the world."[56]

---

55. Schüssler Fiorenza, *Democratizing*, 14. She argues to create such a space requires a fourfold change: "a change of interpretive assumptions and goals, a change of methodology and epistemology, a change of individual and collective consciousness, and a change of social-religious institutions and cultural-religious formations."

56. Tuhiwai Smith, *Decolonizing*, 67.

I have learned from my decade on the FTEAP Board how much the assumptions, structure, and organization of this Western model of education lives on in Asia despite numerous efforts to deconstruct it. Faculty research in a particular discipline is the road to tenure not interdisciplinary work; Western publications are considered of greater quality than Asian works.

The Sabah consultation raised a central question: are theological institutions in the religious pluralism of Asia providing suitable formation for individuals to develop so that they can bring about change in both church and society? The response from the Sabah Listeners' Group was to affirm that for theological schools and the church to play a role in nation-building in the context of massive poverty and marginalization, globalization and migration, human trafficking, LGBTIQ+ gender complexity, climate justice, and the urban/rural divide—a daunting list—new curricula and pedagogies were of the upmost urgency,[57] both of which require a faculty deeply formed in the realities of the Asian context.

Fourth, the buy in of administrators and principals.

The buy in of administrators and principals is essential for transformation to occur, for such changes require challenging reflection on institutional context, budget principles, hiring of faculty, philosophies of learning, and curriculum integrity, which from my experience can quickly become a battleground if a dean or principal were to ask a faculty member to relinquish a required course in their particular discipline or moved to change a cherished line in the budget.

In the context of Canadian theological education, I concur with other voices that a process of decolonization continues to be essential before new possibilities in theological education will emerge. I also maintain that a reconstructed theological education is well placed to face the ongoing power of the Eurocentric myth because of its emphasis on the formation of students to think critically and engage ecclesial and societal problems as central to preparation for ministry. The challenge is to risk exploring new paradigms beyond the present discipline-based, theory to practice, doctrinally-focused curriculum of theological education, paradigms which are open to a conversational model like that presented by Kim or to embrace the reality of life as presented in the arts. It bears repetition that trust is central to this process of moving theological education toward Schüssler Fiorenza's emancipatory educational space, as is the courage to think deeply about what continues to be life-giving in what African American feminist

---

57. Wilson and Longchar, *Diversity*, 348.

Audre Lorde calls "the master's house"[58] and to explore what new tools are generative for its urgent reconstruction. The question before us all is one of will.

Bibliography

Article Reporting on the General Assembly. *The Presbyterian Witness and Evangelical Advocate*, June 26, 1886 (Vol. XXXIX, No. 26). In *Doctrine of Discovery Report for Justice Ministries* by Bob Anger, rev. ed. February 2019.

Beinart, Peter. "The Iran Deal and the Dark Side of American Exceptionalism." In *The Atlantic*, May 9, 2018. http://www.theatlantic.com/international/archive/2018/05/iran-deal-trump-american-exceptionalism/560063.

Bourdieu, P. *Distinction: A Social Critique of the Judgement of Taste*. London: Routledge, 1984; https://www.powercube.net/other-forms-of-power/bourdieu-and-habitus/.

Cheyfitz, Eric. "The Force of Exceptionalist Narratives in the Israeli-Palestinian Conflict." *Norte American Indian Studies* 1.2 (2016) 114–15.

Coe, Shoki. "Theological Education: A Worldwide Perspective." *Theological Education*, Autumn (1974) 5–12.

Dussel, Enrique. "Beyond Eurocentrism: The World System and the Limits of Modernity." Translated by E. Mendieta, in *The Cultures of Globalization*, edited by Jameson and M. Miyoshi, 3. Durham: Duke University Press, 1998.

Fernandez-Alban, Ary. "De-colonial Thought: An Exploration of its Developments and Implications for Latin American Liberation Theologies." Unpublished paper. Toronto: Emmanuel College, 2012.

Schüssler Fiorenza, Elisabeth. *Democratizing Biblical Studies: Toward an Emancipatory Educational Space*. Louisville: Westminster John Knox, 2000.

Foucault, Michel. *Power and Knowledge: Selected Interviews and Other Writings, 1972–1977*. Edited by Colin Gordon, 131. New York: Pantheon, 1980. Quoted in "Discovering the Bible in a Non-Biblical World" by Pui Lan Kwok. *Semeia* 47 (1989) 25–42.

Gomes, André. "Paulo Freire: Review of 'The Pedagogy of the Oppressed.'" *Harm Reduction Journal* 29:21 (2022).

Gordon, Aaron. *Eurocentric Archival Knowledge Production and Decolonizing Archival Theory*. PhD diss., York University, Toronto, 2014.

Hall, S. "The West and the Rest: Discourse and Power." In *Formations of Modernity*, edited by S. Hall and B. Gielban, 276–320. Cambridge: Polity and Open University, 1992.

Kim, Hyun Sook. "Changing Paradigms in Theological Education: Dreams and Visions of Christian Higher Education." In *Christian Responses to Asian Challenges: A Glocalization View on Christian Higher Education in East Asia*, edited by Philip Yuen Sang Leung and Peter Tze Ming Ng, 421–39. Hong Kong: Chinese University Press, 2007. This work was published as part of the 55th Anniversary of Chung Chi College, Hong Kong.

Kwok, Pui Lan, "Discovering the Bible in a Non-Biblical World." *Semeia* 47 (1989), 25–42.

---

58. Lorde, "Master's Tools," 110–4.

———. "Response to the *Semeia* Volume on Postcolonial Criticism." *Semeia* 75 (1996) 211–7.

Lorde, Audre. "The Master's Tools Will Never Dismantle the Master's House." In *Sister Outsider: Essays and Speeches*. Berkeley: Crossing, 2007.

Mignolo, Walter D. "Epistemic Disobedience, Independent Thought and De-colonial Freedom." *Theory, Culture and Society*, 26.7–8 (2009) 1–23.

Nandy, Ashis. *The Intimate Enemy: Loss and Recovery of Self Under Colonialism*. New Dehli: Oxford India, 2010.

Navarro, Zander. "In Search of a Cultural Interpretation of Power." *IDS Bulletin* 37.6 (2006) 11–22.

Powercube. "Bordieu and 'Habitus'." https://www.powercube.net/other-forms-of-power/bourdieu-and-habitus/.

The Presbyterian Church in Canada (PCC). The Confession of the Presbyterian Church as Adopted by the General Assembly, June 9, 1994. http://presbyterianarchives.ca/wp-content/uploads/2016/10/RS-Confession.pdf.

Raheb, Mitri. *Faith in the Face of Empire: The Bible Through Palestinian Eyes*. New York: Orbis, 2014.

Regan, Paulette. *Unsettling the Settler Within: Indian Residential Schools, Truth Telling and Reconciliation in Canada*. Vancouver: UBC Press, 2010. Citing http://www.collectionscanada.gc.ca/webarchives/20071211055821/http://www.ainc-inac.gc.ca/ch/rcap/sg/sg31_e.html.

Said, Edward. *Orientalism*. New York: Vintage, 1979.

Schüssler Fiorenza, Elisabeth. *Democratizing Biblical Studies: Toward and Emancipatory Educational Space*. Louisville: Westminster John Knox, 2000.

Taylor, Charles. *Modern Social Imaginaries*. Durham: Duke University Press, 2004.

Taylor, Mark Lewis. *The Theological and the Political on the Weight of the World*. Minneapolis: Fortress, 2011.

Tuhiwai Smith, Linda. *Decolonizing Methodologies: Research and Indigenous Peoples*. 9th Impression. London: Zed Books, 2006.

Wilson, H.S., and Wati Longchar. *Diversity of Theological Education in Asia: A Search for Cooperation and Mutual Enrichment*. PTCA Study Series No. 18. Hualien, Taiwan, and Philadelphia: Programme for Theology and Cultures in Asia and Department of Research/SATHRI, 2019.

www.cbc.ca/news/canada/a-history-of-residential-schools.

www.trc.ca/websites/trcinstitution/File/2015/Findings/Calls_to_Action_English2.pdf.

3

In Search of a Theology of the Cross for Korea, a Nation Transitioning into a Multicultural and Multiracial Society

A Critique on Anselm's *Cur Deus Homo* and Moltmann's Social Trinitarian Understanding of the Cross

Hye Kyung Heo

THIS ESSAY AIMS TO answer the question, "What theology of the cross can envision a community which reflects the very nature of the loving God revealed by the crucified Christ?" In so doing, I will first revisit and critique whether Anselm's theory of atonement is able to take account of, illumine, and integrate the currently accessible experience of people facing the fast-changing situation of Korea. Then, I will suggest Moltmann's social trinitarian understanding of the cross as a better rationale to the current situation of Korea, which has been changing to a multicultural, multiracial society.

At the center of the Christian gospel stands the cross of the resurrected Christ Jesus. The cross, according to Moltmann, is the "inner criterion of all theology" and "the key signature of all Christian theology."[1] The fundamental questions are then, What kind of theology of the cross will do justice to the man from Nazareth who was crucified under Pontius Pilate? And is necessary today? Christian believers, therefore, must be able to demonstrate what they really believe about the crucified Christ and what practical consequences they wish to draw from their belief.

Doing theology consequently necessitates the analysis of the *Sitz im Leben* of the theologian. Douglas Hall in his book *Cross in our Context* emphasizes the importance of contextuality by stating, "Entering into the specificity of one's own time and place is *the conditio sine qua non* of real theological work."[2] Contextuality is an essential element in doing theology because it conditions the manner in which the Christian message, centered on Christ and his work, is to be articulated and received. It is a matter of the very viability of the Christian religion for the present and coming generations. In terms of the viability of the Christian religion, Elizabeth A. Johnson, citing Wolfhart Pannenberg, affirms that religions die when they lose the power to interpret the full range of present experience in light of their idea of God:

> The truth of God is tested by the extent to which the idea of God takes account of currently accessible aspects of reality and by the ability of the idea of God to integrate the complexity of present experience into itself. If the idea of a God does not keep pace with developing reality, the power of experience pulls people on, and the God dies fading from memory.[3]

To come up with a theology of the cross which is appropriate and effective to the present and future generations it is necessary to analyze the *Sitz im Leben* of Korea today. Up until the late 1990s, Korea has been one of the world's most ethnically homogeneous nations. Foreigners were often rejected by the Korean society or faced discrimination. However, the word *multiculturalism* is no longer foreign to Korea today. In 2007, Stephen Castles of the International Migration Institute argued:

> Korea no longer has to decide whether it wants to become a multicultural society. It made that decision years ago—perhaps unconsciously—when it decided to be a full participant in the

---

1. Moltmann, *Crucified God*, 2, 72.
2. Hall, *Cross in Our Context*, 47. See also Tillich, *On the Boundary*, 13–16.
3. Johnson, "Incomprehensibility of God," 445. See also Pannenberg, "Toward a Theology," 65–118.

emerging global economy. It confirmed that decision when it decided to actively recruit foreign migrants to meet the economic and demographic needs of a fast-growing society. Korea is faced by a different decision today: what type of multicultural society does it want to be?[4]

Korea once viewed its homogeneity as its greatest strength, establishing a country of shared values and fraternity. Thus, homogeneity was considered a cornerstone, helping Korea survive adversities throughout their tumultuous history. However, today the hottest politico-social issue is what kind of immigration policy the government should establish to meet the economic and demographic needs for maintenance of the country. Another drastic change in the Korean mind is that the people of Korea do not consider themselves oppressed or a minority but as one of the most prominent, economically powerful, and cultured people in the world. Unlike the previous generation who volunteered to join the army to fight the war in Vietnam, or went to Germany as nurse or miner, or went to Saudi Arabia as constructor to earn American dollars, the present generation export high technologies and K-culture to the world and have become employers who hire foreigners to work in their own factories and farms.

Living in this kind of changing social milieu, theologians are challenged to answer the question raised from this generation: What does the Cross of Jesus Christ mean to us and people of different cultures in this world? Definitely, what they need today in the multicultural world is a new understanding of the Cross that would allow them to envision a new human community based on the values of equality, mutuality, and reciprocity between different races and cultures.

Traditionally, Korean men and women needed to seek empowerment from God to overcome their helpless circumstances as well as God's forgiveness of their sins, which they often believed to be the cause of punishment in the form of conflicts, struggles, and illness. They needed the almighty God who would deliver them from their helpless situations. The substitutionary atonement of Christ depicts the almighty God who forgives sins through the death of Jesus Christ. The almighty Father's sacrifice of the Son for humanity has been understood by Koreans as good news. In the early Christian history in Korea, those who had been doubly fettered through frequent invasions by foreign superpowers and oppression within the hierarchical system of their own country understood very well what it

---

4. Castles, "Labour Migration."

meant for a powerful king to sacrifice his only son for the benefits of his subjects. For them, the ones in power were usually exploiters and oppressors, but the almighty God introduced by Christian missionaries was one who sacrificed the only Son for their benefit. Thus, they understood and accepted God's sacrifice as an amazing, immeasurable grace which they could never be able to repay with human efforts. This image of God as the Lord who is responsible for the welfare of his subjects, and who in turn deserves honor, was well accepted by Koreans who had been familiar with the feudal system in Korea. Consequently, Anselm's substitutionary atonement theory was the most popular hermeneutical lens through which Christian Koreans explained the gospel when Christianity was first introduced to Korea.[5]

Given the changing social milieu in Korea today, however, I as a theologian feel obliged to investigate whether Anselm's apologetical explanation of the gospel which depicts the necessity of Jesus' incarnation and death speaks persuasively and effectively to the present generation and society in general.

To critique Anselm's substitutionary atonement of Christ, it is important to set it in the socio-religious context of its time. In the *Cur Deus Homo*, Anselm aims to prove the necessity of the incarnation by reasoning alone, apart from any prior knowledge of Christ (*remoto Christo*). This work of Anselm's is composed of two short books. The first book contains the objections of unbelievers who despise the Christian faith because they regard it as contrary to reason. Leaving Christ out of view (*remoto Christo*), it proves by absolute reasons, the impossibility that any man should be saved without him.[6] The second book demonstrates by equally plain reasoning and fact that "human nature was ordained to enjoy happy immortality both in body and soul; and that it was necessary that this design for which man was made should be fulfilled; but that it could not be fulfilled unless God became man, and unless all things were to take place which we hold with regard to Christ."[7]

The argument of the *Cur Deus Homo* could be summarized like this: God created human beings with certain purpose and established a

---

5. In *Cur Deus Homo* I/VII, Anselm of Canterbury reflected the feudal medieval worldview and presupposed his understandings of law, offense, reparations, and social obligations. God and humans are related like feudal lords and their serfs. Any act of disobedience dishonors the lord, and satisfaction must be given. This part on the analysis of Anselm's *Cur Deus Homo* is partially excerpted from my book *The Liberative Cross*, 76–90.

6. Anselm, *Cur Deus Homo*, 191.

7. Anselm, *Cur Deus Homo*, 191.

particular order in the universe. God's purpose in creating human beings was that they enjoy perfect blessedness or happiness. This blessedness requires the total and voluntary submission of their will to God's will, for it is God's will upon which the beauty and rational harmony of the universe rests. However, human beings fell through disobedience. Sin according to Anselm is not to render God his due. According to Anselm, "He, who does not render this honor, which is due to God, robs God of his own and dishonors him, and this is sin."[8] Human beings caught in a state of sin are no longer able to live as God created them to live. God's order, the way things ought to be according to God's creation, has been disrupted. As a result, human beings are left in a situation of indebtedness to God by not rendering to God what is God's due and, so, condemned to death.

This is a dilemma which human beings face: they ought to render to God what is owed to God, but they cannot. Anselm argues God's justice; the order of justice requires that the debt be paid. The offering for redemption ought to be made by human beings; however, they were unable because they already owed everything to God before they sinned and incurred debt on top of that. An obvious solution would be for God to forgive the debt and to show mercy toward sinful humanity by removing the obligation. However, unconditional forgiveness is not an alternative for Anselm, for it would introduce irregularity into God's universe.

The second phase of Anselm's argument proceeds from the dilemma that human beings have no means to pay the debt. Since they cannot pay the debt, it seems that human beings will suffer forever and God's plan for creation will always remain disrupted. God's order and purposes, however, ought to be fulfilled and human beings saved. Only God is able to make the offering human beings are indebted to make. Therefore, the incarnation was necessary so that the God-man, Jesus Christ, would redeem the disrupted order of justice on behalf of humanity. In this respect, the incarnation is God's action on behalf of humanity and for the sake of straightening the disrupted order of justice.

Continuing his argument, Anselm explains that the incarnate Son of God freely offers up his sinless life in honor of God. The Son is sinless, therefore does not have to die. However, death is to be incurred to pay the debt for human beings. Jesus' death is of infinite worth; therefore, it is able to accomplish the redemption of human beings and set right the order of justice.

---

8. Anselm, *Cur Deus Homo*, 216.

There has been a criticism that Anselm's doctrine of atonement is guilty of a tyrannical and arbitrary use of power and contributes to the culture of abuse. To argue against this criticism, Walter Kasper succinctly contends that "Anselm's satisfaction theory can be understood only against the background of the Germanic and early medieval feudal system."[9] Within this social system we find a mutual dependence between lord and vassal, who promise each other loyalty for loyalty. From the lord, the vassal obtained a fief and protection, and the feudal lord received in return a pledge of allegiance and service. Kasper argues that this system of loyalties not only gives the individual his determined role and rights, but also it secures the social order and peace, unity, and coherence of their political structures.[10] Thus, this system regulates and delineates powers and responsibilities for all parties.

Kasper also points out that the concept of God's honor which Anselm insists to be upheld is about the moral, rational order of justice established in creation. In the *Cur Deus Homo*, Anselm makes clear that God's personal honor is inviolable: "Nothing can be added to or taken from the honor of God. For this honor, which belongs to him, is in no way subject to injury or change."[11] According to Anselm, God is honored "when the human being chooses what he ought . . . not by bestowing anything upon him, but because he brings himself freely under God's will and disposal, and maintains his own condition in the universe, and the beauty of the universe itself."[12] In other words, when humans will what they ought to will, submitting themselves to God's direction, they honor God, and when humans do not will what they ought, they dishonor God. These statements imply that a human's dishonoring of God, according to Anselm, is to be understood as the refusal to recognize God's rightful authority or God's place of rightful honor. Consequently, "the object of offense," Kasper affirms, "is not the lord's personal honor, but his social status by which he is the guarantor of the public peace."[13] Hunter Brown agrees with Kasper's position as he points out that "the focus of *Cur Deus Homo*'s soteriology then is not upon the personal, juridical appeasement of an offended God

---

9. Kasper, *Jesus the Christ*, 220. On this point, Kasper is indebted to Gresake. See Gresake, "Redemption," 63.

10. Kasper, *Jesus the Christ*, 220. See also Gresake, "Redemption," 63.

11. Anselm, *Cur Deus Homo*, 222.

12. Anselm, *Cur Deus Homo*, 222–23.

13. Kasper, *Jesus the Christ*, 220.

but upon redressing the abuse of human fiduciary participation in divine power over the world."[14]

At this point, it is noteworthy that Anselm's theory of satisfaction atonement clearly differs from the penal substitutionary image in which God punishes Jesus as a substitute for punishing sinful humankind. According to Anselm, the restoration of harmony, order, and balance requires payment. He understood Jesus' death as the debt payment that satisfied the honor of God, and thus restored balance and order to the universe. Therefore, Anselm's God seems not so much concerned about Godself as about redressing the disorder and disharmony in the universe produced by human sin. The death of Jesus in this view is not about having Jesus bear punishment merited by human beings, but is about restoring order and harmony in the universe.

Simply put, Anselm's satisfaction atonement differs from Luther's penal substitution. For Anselm, satisfaction is not punishment for sin; rather, it is a substitute for punishment—*aut poena aut satisfaction*. For Luther, satisfaction includes the notion of penal substitution.[15] Jesus' death satisfied the requirement of the divine law that sin be punished. With his death, Jesus bore the punishment that was really due to sinners. Jesus was punished in our place. Jesus substituted himself for us, and died a penal, substitutionary death. Luther states: "Christ . . . who offered himself in place of our sinful nature, who took upon himself all the wrath of God merited by ourselves without works."[16]

Both Anselm's satisfaction atonement and Luther's penal substitution attempt to explain why Jesus died for us. For Anselm, satisfaction atonement satisfies God's honor, while penal substitution satisfies the law of God. Both of them, however, require death, whether it is for God's honor or God's law. Without death, the debt to God's honor remains unsatisfied, or the penalty required by God's law remains unpaid.

Weaver argues how although Anselm uses different language from penal substitution, his motif of Jesus' death as a payment to God's honor still contains within it the assumption of retributive violence and placation of wrath through the sacrifice of a son.[17] With regard to the question, Who ultimately killed Jesus? Weaver explains the dilemma that Anselm's

---

14. Brown, "Anselm's Cur Deus Homo," 194.
15. Tappert, *Book of Concord*, 414. See also Peters, "Atonement," 310.
16. *Luther's Works*, on "Epistle Sermon, New Year's Day," vol. VII, no. 50.
17. Weaver, "Violence," 9.

satisfaction theory and Luther's penal substitution theory face like this: with Satan deleted, it is the sinner who offended God. Sinful human beings cannot save themselves by paying their own debt. Therefore, God is the only one left to orchestrate the death of Jesus in order to pay the debt owed to God's honor. In penal substitution, God is the one who arranged to provide Jesus' death as a means to satisfy the divine law. Weaver here points out within the framework of satisfaction atonement or penal substitution we cannot avoid a dilemma:

> And the evil powers who oppose the reign of God by killing Jesus—whether the devil, the mob or the Romans—are the ones who are actually doing the will of God, by killing or punishing Jesus to provide the payment that God's honor or God's law demands. The strange implication is that both Jesus and those who kill Jesus would be carrying out the will of God.[18]

In removing the devil from the equation of atonement, Weaver argues, the Father arranges the death of God's Son for the benefit of others. The motif of Jesus as the substitute object of punishment, which assumes the principle of retribution, is the image that some feminists have particularly found very offensive. They contend that the Jesus of this motif models passive submission to innocent and unjust suffering for the sake of others.

However, according to Anselm, including the devil into the equation of salvation would mean distorting the issues of power and responsibility. It is human sin which disrupted the order of creation and the right relationship that God intended. If God uses God's power to forgive humanity without requiring satisfaction, then human responsibility will be compromised. The God-human, Jesus Christ, exercises power and responsibility. Therefore, God's power is not arbitrary or absolute because God takes responsibility for the order of the universe and uses power for the sake of that order.

As we look into Anselm's reasoning, we come to ask this question, Why would not God put away sins by compassion alone without any payment of debt? Two reasons are given in *Cur Deus Homo*: first, with such forgiveness, "there will be no difference between the guilty and the not guilty . . . and it makes injustice like God. For as God is subject to no law, so is neither injustice."[19] Second, such forgiveness would do nothing to correct the disturbance of the "order and beauty of the universe" caused by sin. The slightest uncorrected disorder argues a deficiency either in God's justice or

---

18. Weaver, "Violence," 5.
19. Anselm, *Cur Deus Homo*, 216–18.

in his power, which is impossible if we affirm that God is perfect in both ways.[20]

With regard to this problem of mercy and justice, Ted Peters rightly points out that what we have to understand behind Anselm's argument is the neo-platonic structure:[21] God is the final reality for Anselm, and the rational and moral structure of existence issues from the nature of God. The whole universe is an expression of God's intrinsic character and will. Therefore, justice is not reduced to the simple notion of rendering to each person his or her due, but implies doing that which befits the supreme goodness of God.[22] With this background, Peters argues, "mercy cannot finally be seen to work against justice."[23] In the *Proslogium*, Anselm demonstrates that mercy and justice are one insofar as they are expressions of God.[24] Mercy requires that human beings be everlastingly blessed, and justice requires that sin be met on its own terms. Atonement becomes the point at which justice is satisfied and mercy achieves its end. Peters concludes:

> God created man out of love, and it was God's purpose that men find fulfillment in eternal blessedness. And in the final analysis, God's purpose is accomplished. His grace is victorious. But *en route* Anselm wants us to take seriously the gravity of man's sin and the ultimate dimensions of God's historical activity. The legalistic structure of the relationship between God and men is not the last thing to be said about God. It is the means whereby God's mercy is shown to triumph.[25]

Anselm portrays Jesus' crucifixion as self-giving: no person can give himself more fully to God than Jesus does when he surrenders himself to death for God's honor.[26] Jesus Christ as sinless did not owe anything to God, but Jesus gave himself up for us as pure self-offering. Jesus had freedom and choice. He chose to be obedient to meet the requirements of the Father's order and justice. It was of his own accord that Jesus endured death for the salvation of humanity. The father did not compel the Son to suffer death or even allow the Son to be slain against his will.

---

20. Anselm, *Cur Deus Homo*, 222–24.
21. Peters, "Atonement," 305.
22. Peters, "Atonement," 305. See also Anselm, *Proslogium*, 63.
23. Peters, "Atonement," 305.
24. Anselm, *Proslogium*, 60–63.
25. Peters, "Atonement," 305.
26. Peters, "Atonement," 269–74.

Anselm's view of the cross has given Korean Christian men and women a strong sense of spiritual devotion to pay the debt that they individually owe to Jesus. However, salvation for them is defined and accepted in inherently individual terms. The sinner owes a debt, and the debt is personal. Because of this view of individualistic heavenly salvation, the social component is logically an afterthought, something to consider after one has dealt with the prior fundamental and individualistic problem of personal guilt and penalty. Anselm's view of atonement leads to an overemphasis on personal sin and grace and the separation of the spiritual life of individuals from their daily concrete conditions. Consequently, salvation becomes a transformation of an individual's relationship with God from an unredeemed and oppressive position into some mystic communion with God.

Anselm's view of atonement also overlooks the broader view of the work of Christ, which aims at the transformation of a person, not only in his spiritual aspect but also in his total physical context. By positing a transaction outside of history and involving only the death of Jesus, it excludes the life and ministry of Jesus. Consequently, it offers little theological ground upon which one can challenge injustice in the social order. Salvation, according to Anselm, envisions a change in an individual's status outside of or beyond this life. This ahistorical orientation has caused in Christian believers an anti-ethical orientation throughout history. With this ahistorical, anti-ethical approach to the cross, Christian churches have accommodated violent exercises and social injustices like slavery, racism, classism, etc., instead of challenging them. James Cone, founder of the black theology movement, criticized this anti-ethical orientation of the churches. He argues that Anselm's theory dehistoricizes the work of Christ, separating God's liberating act from history, defining atonement in a way which favors the powerful and excludes the interests of the poor.[27] Cone affirms that this abstract, ahistorical character has caused ironies, such as the situation in which slave owners have preached salvation to slaves.

In fact, the *Cur Deus Homo* was written for the purpose of demonstrating why the incarnation was necessary. Anselm, therefore, mentioned nothing about the life or person of Jesus except that he was obedient and chose freely. It was not important to Anselm that Jesus had a life history, except that Jesus exercised his will freely and chose to offer his life. Anselm, in fact, clearly stated in the Preface to the *Cur Deus Homo* that he was "leaving

---

27. Cone, *God of the Oppressed*, 230–32.

Christ out of view" and proceeding "as if nothing were known of Christ."[28] No wonder there is no narrative of Jesus' personhood and actions.

Even though it was not important to Anselm that Jesus had a life history, the lack of Jesus' personhood in his atonement theory limits its ability to empower. By reducing the entire work of Christ on the cross to the forgiveness of sins and guilt, it tends to overlook the liberating and transforming power of Christ's work in sociopolitical conditions. It fails to comprehend the extent of divine involvement in human suffering on behalf of the oppressed, the weak, and the helpless. In this respect, it is important to include in the theology of the cross the person and work of Jesus Christ in order to construct a comprehensive view of salvation, not merely as the salvation of an individual soul but also as the total liberation of humanity from its physical suffering. Anselm's theory of atonement, which focuses primarily on personal regeneration, fails to deal adequately with the complexity of human suffering as well as explain what God's involvement in these sufferings entails for human oppression in the situation of injustice.

This critique makes us go back to the fundamental questions we raised in the beginning: What kind of theology of the cross will do justice to the man from Nazareth who was crucified under Pontius Pilate, and is necessary today? To answer the question, we must include the history, death, and resurrection of Jesus Christ.

Moltmann emphasizes that "not from the cross in isolation but from the cross understood in its context both of Jesus' earthly life and of his resurrection can Jesus be recognized as not just another condemned criminal or another innocent victim but as one who in love became their brother."[29] Jesus' message of God's justifying grace for the godless and his life of fellowship with sinners incited the world against himself. Therefore, the death of Jesus was the result of a life of proclaiming God to be on the side of the godless.

However, Jesus' life and death, Moltmann affirms, must be viewed in the light of his resurrection because "only in the light of his resurrection from the dead does his death gain that special, unique saving significance which it cannot achieve otherwise, even in the light of the life he lived."[30] Only in light of the resurrection is the death of Jesus understood to be the death of the Christ, the Son of God.

28. Anselm, *Cur Deus Homo*, 191.
29. Moltmann, *Crucified God*, 51.
30. Moltmann, *Crucified God*, 182.

This dialectical Christology of Moltmann contrasts the death of the resurrected Jesus with the resurrection of the crucified Christ. Crucified Jesus in his death is identified with all the negative qualities of the present reality such as godlessness, godforsakenness, and transitoriness. However, this same Jesus is raised from the dead to affirm God's promise of new creation for this godforsaken reality. Jesus, who was raised into the glory of the coming God, is in his cross the incarnate God who identifies with godless and godforsaken people so as to bring the new life of the resurrection to them in their situation. The resurrection of the crucified Christ is God's promise and awakening of hope for a different future.[31] God, who raised the crucified Christ, creates anticipation for the future kingdom of God within history and thus becomes the source of hope for transformation. Authentic Christian hope allows people to resist and work to redeem the brokenness of the world.[32]

In his dialectical Christology, Moltmann stresses other aspects of the revelation of God in the cross: in the cross God is revealed as contrary to the false gods of the law, political religion, and theistic religion.[33] Moltmann explains:

> The history of Jesus which led to his crucifixion was rather a theological history in itself, and was dominated by the conflict between God and the gods; that is between the God whom Jesus preached as his Father, and the God of the law as he was understood by the guardians of the law, together with the political gods of the Roman occupying power.[34]

The crucified Christ liberates humanity from enslavement to the false gods of the law, political religion, and theistic religions. First of all, Jesus was crucified as a blasphemer against the law by the guardians of the law. Following Ernst Käsemann, Moltmann sees Jesus' teaching as characterized by the tendency to place himself above the authority of Moses and the Torah.[35]

---

31. Moltmann, *Theology of Hope*, 30.
32. Moltmann, *Theology of Hope*, 22.
33. Moltmann, *Crucified God*, 68–69.
34. Moltmann, *Crucified God*, 127. This part on the conflict between God and the gods; that is, between the God whom Jesus preached as his Father, and the God of the law as he was understood by the guardians of the law, together with the political gods of the Roman occupying power, is partially excerpted from my book, *The Liberative Cross*, from chapter 3, "Moltmann's Theology of the Cross."
35. Käsemann, *Essays*, 37.

In his ministry, Jesus placed himself with sovereign authority above the limits of the contemporary understanding of the law. He also demonstrated God's eschatological law of grace towards those without the law and the transgressors of the law through his forgiveness of sins. In so doing, Jesus sets himself against the law by introducing a new basis of righteousness that abolishes the legal distinctions between the religious and the secular, the righteous and the unrighteous, the devout and the sinful. Jesus also preached the imminence of the kingdom of God, not as judgment but as the gospel of the justification of sinners by grace. For Jesus, the kingdom comes as the unconditional and free grace of God by which the lost are sought out and the unrighteous are accepted.

From this point of view, the life and ministry of Jesus was a theological clash between him and the prevailing understandings of the law. That is why the Gospel of Luke describes Jesus as dying by the law as one who was reckoned with transgressors (Luke 22:37). The Apostle Paul also interprets the death of the crucified Jesus in relation to the law: Since the law had brought Jesus to his death upon the cross, so the risen and exalted Jesus becomes "the end of the law" that everyone who has faith may be justified (Rom 10:4). The crucified God, therefore, liberates us from the idols of legalism. Here, we see Moltmann concur with Luther as he emphasizes that if we want to justify ourselves by works, we idolize our own achievements and become slaves to the idol of justification by works.[36]

Secondly, the crucifixion of Jesus was also caused by the conflict between God and the political gods of the Roman occupying power. According to Moltmann, Jesus was crucified by the Romans not merely for the immediate political reasons of peace and good order in Jerusalem, but also for the glorification of Roman state gods who assured the *Pax Romana*.[37] This is proven by the fact that the Christians of the early church openly rejected emperor worship, and consequently faced martyrdom, which was both a religious and political act.

Moltmann adds a political dimension to the theology of the cross from the fact that Jesus was crucified as a political criminal, who in some respect threatened the *Pax Romana* and yet was raised up and vindicated by God. Accordingly, the theology of the cross is not "pure theology" in a modern non-political sense or in the sense of private religion.[38] The theology of the

36. Moltmann, *Crucified God*, 128–35.
37. Moltmann, *Crucified God*, 136.
38. Moltmann, *Crucified God*, 144–45.

cross bears a public testimony to the freedom of Christ and the law of grace in the face of the political religions of nations, empires, races, and classes. Political religions emerge whenever religion serves to integrate society and to sanctify the existing political and social systems. In other words, religion becomes a kind of political idolatry when it absolutizes rulers or ruling systems, consequently leading to a pattern of domination and enslavement.[39]

Moltmann calls for a new critical political theology. He insists, "Christianity did not arise as a national or a class religion . . . The crucified God is in fact a stateless and classless God. But that does not mean that he is an unpolitical God. God is the God of the poor, the oppressed and the humiliated."[40] For him, "the rule of the Christ who was crucified for political reasons can only be extended through liberation from forms of rule which make men [and women] servile and apathetic, and from the political religions which give them stability."[41]

Thirdly, Moltmann maintains that the cross contradicts and liberates people from the false god of theistic religion. He uses *theism* in the sense of the traditional metaphysical concept of God which defines God's infinity over and against humanity's finiteness. God, according to theism, is indivisible, immutable, impassible, immortal, and omnipotent whereas humanity is finite, mortal, weak, and suffering. In the model of theistic religions, humanity finds support from suffering and the nothingness of death in a divine being that is completely free from suffering and death.[42] According to him, the crucified God contradicts the false god of theistic religion in that while the idolatry of theism seeks freedom from suffering and death through "its projection of childish needs for authoritarian protection in a god who cannot suffer and die,"[43] the crucified God represents liberation from suffering and death through loving solidarity.

Moltmann in this way affirms that God revealed by the cross is a suffering God, which connotes the passibility of God. In early Christianity, the notion of *apatheia* was taken up to designate God's essential incapacity for suffering. It distinguished God from human beings and other non-divine beings subject to suffering, transience, and death. Consequently, salvation

---

39. Moltmann, *Crucified God*, 328.
40. Moltmann, *Crucified God*, 328.
41. Moltmann, *Crucified God*, 329.
42. Moltmann, *Crucified God*, 214.
43. Moltmann, *Crucified God*, 216–19.

confers immortality, non-transience, and impassibility.[44] In contrast, Moltmann insists that to perceive God as either essentially incapable of suffering or as fatefully subject to suffering lacks the notion of the suffering of God's passionate love. According to him, God does not suffer in the exact same way humans suffer. God suffers not because of any deficiency in God's being but because of love.[45] God can go toward suffering and accept it because God is interested in God's creation and people. Therefore, God of love is affected by human actions and suffering.[46]

Moltmann also explains how the cross of Jesus is a trinitarian event between the Son and the Father and the Spirit.[47] According to him, the abandonment of Jesus is God's divine act of solidarity with all people in pain who cry out to God in their abandonment. For him, it is not only Jesus the Son of God who suffers, but also the Father who suffers as the Father of the Son. The cross as a trinitarian event reveals the mutual act of surrendering between the Father and the Son. Moltmann explains it by looking at the use of the Greek word *paradidonai*, which means "delivered up."[48] He points out that the word *paradidonai* was used in the passion narratives with a negative connotation to mean "hand over," "give up," "deliver," "betray," "cast out," and "kill." It also appears in Pauline theology as an expression of the wrath and judgment of God for the lost state of humanity. In the first chapter of Romans, the Apostle Paul uses the word to express God's wrath over the godlessness of humanity. God abandons the heathens to their unrighteousness (Rom 1:23, 25, 28) and idolatry, the Jews to their legalism, and thus all people to their self-willed compulsion to die.[49] However, in light of the resurrection of Jesus Christ, the Apostle Paul completely turns around the sense of the word *paradidonai* to mean how the Father's forsaking the Son was "for us." The God who raised Jesus from the dead is the same God who gave him up to death on the cross. In the forsakenness of the cross itself, out of which Jesus cries "Why?" the apostle Paul already sees the answer to that cry: "He who did not spare his own Son but gave him up for us all, will he not also give all things with Him?" (Rom 8:32). Moltmann insists "the Father 'gave up' the Son so that through Him God

44. Moltmann, *Trinity and the Kingdom*, 23.
45. Moltmann, *Crucified God*, 230.
46. Moltmann, *Crucified God*, 270.
47. Moltmann, *Crucified God*, 246.
48. Moltmann, *Way of Jesus Christ*, 173.
49. Moltmann, *Way of Jesus Christ*, 172–78.

may become the Father of all those who are 'given up' (Rom 1:18ff)."[50] God himself abandoned God's own Son to evil people and to the abyss of destruction. The Son is surrendered to death in order to become the brother and Savior of all people who are condemned (2 Cor 5:21) and accursed (Gal 3:13).[51]

In the historical event of the cross, the apostle Paul sees eschatologically the Son surrendered by the Father for the godless and godforsaken. He stresses that it is God's own Son whom God gives up. However, this act of not sparing the Son affects the Father. When the Father abandons the Son, the Father also abandons himself. When the Father sacrifices the Son, the Father sacrifices himself.

Nevertheless, Moltmann claims that this act is not *patripassionism*,[52] because it is not the Father who was crucified, dead, and buried. The suffering of the Father, he insists, was different from that of the Son. Jesus experiences what it is to die abandoned, but the Father experiences the death of the Son in the infinite suffering of the Father's love. If the Father does not spare the Son but gives him up, then the Father suffers his separation from the Son.

Having said that, Moltmann also warns against understanding the Father's suffering in *theopaschitic* terms. The cross is not the death of God. God did not die. God did not cease to exist or cease to function. We must speak of the death of God in trinitarian terms: "The Son suffers dying, the Father suffers the death of the Son of the Father . . . The Fatherlessness of the Son is matched by the Sonlessness of the Father."[53] Each person of the Trinity suffers, although in different manners. Moltmann insists that though they are most deeply separated in forsakenness, they are most inwardly one in surrendering.

To explain the fact that the cross as a trinitarian event reveals the mutual act of surrendering between the Father and the Son, Moltmann also emphasizes that the event of Godforsakenness on the cross is also *passio activa,* the active surrender of the Son. The suffering and death of Jesus on

---

50. Moltmann, *Way of Jesus Christ*, 173.

51. Moltmann, *Way of Jesus Christ*, 173. Moltmann has provoked considerable feminist critique and concern with respect to his claim that the Father "abandons" the Son in the event of the crucifixion. Sölle's accusation in her *Suffering* is given significant attention in Moltmann-Wendel's *Autobiography* (see 177–80), as well as in Moltmann's *Autobiography* (see 198–200).

52. Moltmann, *Way of Jesus Christ*, 243.

53. Moltmann, *Way of Jesus Christ*, 243.

the cross is a *passio activa*. In the passage of *kenosis* in Philippians 2, we see how Jesus deliberately chose the path of suffering, and by dying on the cross affirmed his passion for the Father. In Galatians 2:20, we find the *paradoken* formula again, but with Christ as the subject: "The Son of God, who loved me and gave himself for me." It is not only that the Father gives up Jesus, but the Son also gives himself. This corresponds to the presentation of the passion of Christ in which Jesus consciously and willingly set out on the road of suffering to Calvary.[54]

Moltmann insists that the suffering and death of the Son was an act of *passio activa* for us through the eternal Spirit (Rom 9:14). Accordingly, the Spirit plays an active role in this mutual act of surrendering between the Father and the Son. The offering of the Son takes place through the Spirit, who is the link joining the bond between the Father and the Son in their separation at the cross.[55] In his *The Crucified God*, Moltmann describes the Spirit as creative love proceeding out of the Father's pain and the Son's self-surrender to justify the ungodly, rescue the forsaken, and raise the dead.[56]

The cross of Jesus is, therefore, the trinitarian event. The nature of God revealed by the cross is love: the Father loves the world through the Son with the very same love which the triune God *is* in eternity. Accordingly, to say "God so loved the world that he gave his only begotten Son" (John 3:16) presupposes that "God is love" (1 John 4:16).[57] By seeing the cross as the revelation of the compassionate God, Moltmann affirms that "Christ's suffering on the cross is human sin transmuted into the atoning suffering of God."[58] On the cross, Moltmann contends, the Son experienced the Godforsakenness and the pain of the divine love for sinners on the basis of the statements made by the Apostle Paul: "For our sake he [God] made him [Jesus] to be sin who knew no sin" (2 Cor 5:21), and Christ "became a curse for us" (Gal 3:13). Likewise, Moltmann sees in the death of Christ more than just Christ's solidarity with the accursed of the earth. He emphasizes the aspect of atonement in the death of Jesus by saying that in the death of Christ is "the divine atonement for sin for injustice and violence on earth. This divine atonement reveals God's pain. But God's pain reveals

---

54. Moltmann, *Way of Jesus Christ*, 173.
55. Moltmann, *Trinity and the Kingdom*, 82.
56. Moltmann, *The Crucified God*, 244.
57. Moltmann, *Spirit of Life*, 137.
58. Moltmann, *Spirit of Life*, 136.

God's faithfulness to those he has created, and his indestructible love which endures a world in opposition to him and overcomes it."[59]

Lastly, the cross as the trinitarian event reveals the perichoretic trinitarian relationship. Moltmann employs the concept perichoresis to portray the tri-unity as the community and fellowship among three equal divine persons. He defines this perichoretic relationship between the Father, the Son, and the Holy Spirit as an "open Trinity."[60] The unity of the Son with the Father is not a closed unity: it is an open union as expressed in the High Priestly prayer (John 17:21). The fellowship of the disciples with God and with one another in God presupposes that "the tri-unity is open in such a way that the whole creation can be united with it and can be one within it."[61] God invites God's creation to enter into the trinitarian fellowship; therefore, Moltmann affirms, "the unity of the Trinity is not merely a theological term; at heart it is a soteriological one as well."[62] In other words, for him, the triune God is not a closed circle of perfect beings in heaven; rather, the triune God is the open Trinity, God who is "open to humanity, open to the world and open to time."[63] We are invited to join the trinitarian fellowship and participate in the trinitarian process of God's history actively and passively by loving, praying, and hoping.[64] In this way, Moltmann argues through the notion of perichoresis that in God's relationship with the world it is not so much lordship as loving fellowship which God seeks, and in God's kingdom it is relationships of free friendship which most adequately reflect and participate in the trinitarian life.[65]

In this essay, I revisited and critiqued whether Anselm's theory of atonement in his *Cur Deus Homo* speaks effectively to people faced with

59. Moltmann, *Spirit of Life*, 136. See Ansell, *Annihilation of Hell*, chap. 4, sec. 2. See also Ansell, "Annihilation of Hell," 436–38. In this essay, Ansell discusses the centrality of the Son in Moltmann's conception of universal salvation. Ansell points out that for Moltmann, the justification of sinners is "more than merely the forgiveness of sins," because, in Moltmann's understanding, the cross addresses and overcomes the conditions that make sin possible. Ansell gives a good discussion on how the conditions of possibility will be transformed in the eschatological perfection of creation and sin will no longer be an "option."

60. Moltmann, *God in Creation*, 242. See also Moltmann, *Crucified God*, 255; and Moltmann, *Trinity and the Kingdom*, 96.

61. Moltmann, *Trinity*, 96. See also Moltmann, *Experiences*, 322.

62. Moltmann, *Trinity*, 96.

63. Moltmann, *Crucified God*, 255. See also Moltmann, *God in Creation*, 242.

64. Moltmann, *Crucified God*, 255.

65. Bauckham, *Theology*, 17.

today's fast changing milieu of Korea to a multicultural, multiracial society. I evaluated it as inadequate because of its unique ahistorical and anti-ethical orientation. Then, I suggested Moltmann's theology of the cross as a better rationale for Korea today. His social trinitarian understanding of the cross reveals God as a suffering God of compassion in solidarity with the godless and the godforsaken. The perichoretic fellowship among the divine persons culminated at the cross invites the humanity to create relationships of free friendship reflecting the very nature of the triune God, which is compassion, equality, mutuality, and reciprocity, and to participate in the trinitarian process of God's history. Accordingly, Korean men and women today are challenged to respond to this invitation by envisioning and building an inclusive society where everyone regardless of gender, race and ethnicity would be equally treated and generously accepted.

A Word of Appreciation to Professor Charles Fensham

I cannot imagine my theological journey at Knox College without Professor Fensham. He taught me how to "do theology." Theology is not just a contemplative exercise but always has to accompany *praxis* in our *Sitz im Leben*; therefore, it is orthopraxis. Professor Fensham has been my great teacher. With an abundance of knowledge, patience, and gentleness, Professor Fensham walked me on my long journey to complete the doctoral program and finally teach at Knox. The imprints you have left on me for more than the last two decades of my life will never be forgotten; I will cherish them always with the hope that our God will bring a renewal and revival in this land.

Bibliography

Ansell, Nik. "Annihilation of Hell and the Perfection of Freedom: Universal Salvation in the Theology of Jürgen Moltmann (1926–)." In *All Shall Be Well: Explorations in Universalism and Christian Theology from Origen to Moltmann*, edited by Gregory MacDonald, 417–39. Eugene, OR: Cascade Books, 2011.
———. *The Annihilation of Hell: Universal Salvation and the Redemption of Time in the Eschatology of Jürgen Moltmann*. Eugene, OR: Cascade Books, 2013.
Anselm, St. *Cur Deus Homo*. In *Basic Writings*, translated by S. W. Deane, 191–302. 2nd ed. La Salle, IL: Open Court, 1962.
———. *Proslogium*. In *Basic Writings*, translated by S. W. Deane, 191–302. 2nd ed. La Salle, IL: Open Court, 1962.

Aulen, Gustaf. *Christus Victor: An Historical Study of the Three Main Types of the Idea of Atonement.* Translated by A. G. Herbert. 1961. Reprint, Eugene, OR: Wipf & Stock, 2003.

Bauckham, Richard. "'Only Suffering of God Can Help': Divine Possibility in Modern Theology." *Themelios* 9 (1984) 6–12.

———. *The Theology of Jürgen Moltmann.* Edinburgh: T. & T. Clark, 1995.

Brown, Hunter. "Anselm's Cur Deus Homo Revisited." *Eglise et Theologie* 25 (1994) 189–204.

Castles, Stephen. "Will Labour Migration Lead to a Multicultural Society in Korea?" Global Human Resources Forum 2007, International Migration Institute.

Cone, James H. *A Black Theology of Liberation.* Philadelphia: Lippincott, 1970.

———. *God of the Oppressed.* Maryknoll, NY: Orbis, 1997.

Gresake, Gilbert. "Redemption and Freedom." *Theology Digest* 25 (1977) 61–5.

Hall, Douglas John. *The Cross in Our Context: Jesus and the Suffering World.* Minneapolis: Fortress, 2003.

Heo, Hye Kyung. *The Liberative Cross: Korean-North American Women and the Self-Giving God.* Eugene, OR: Pickwick Publications, 2015.

Johnson, Elizabeth A. *Consider Jesus: Waves of Renewal in Christology.* New York: Crossroad, 1990.

———. "The Incomprehensibility of God and the Image of God Male and Female." *Theological Studies* 45 (1984) 441–65.

———. *She Who Is: The Mystery of God in Feminist Theological Discourse.* New York: Crossroad, 1999.

Jowers, Dennis W. "The Theology of the Cross as Theology of the Trinity: A Critique of Jürgen Moltmann's Staurocentric Trinitarianism." *Tyndale Bulletin* 52 (2001) 245–66.

Käsemann, Ernst. *Essays on New Testament Themes.* London: SCM, 1964.

Kasper, Walter. *Jesus the Christ.* Translated by V. Green. London: Burns & Oates, 1976.

Luther, Martin. *Luther's Works.* Vol. 7. Edited by Jaroslav Pelikan et al. 55 volumes. American ed. Vols. 1–30: St. Louis: Concordia; Vols. 31–55: Philadelphia: Fortress, 1955–86.

Moltmann, Jürgen. *A Broad Place: An Autobiography.* Translated by Margaret Kohl. Minneapolis: Fortress, 2008.

———. *The Coming of God.* Translated by Margaret Kohl. Minneapolis: Fortress, 1996.

———. *The Crucified God: The Cross of Christ as the Foundation and Criticism of Christian Theology.* Translated by R. A. Wilson and John Bowden. Minneapolis: Fortress, 1993.

———. *Ethics of Hope.* 1st Fortress ed. Translated by Margaret Kohl. Minneapolis: Fortress, 2012.

———. *Experiences in Theology: Ways and Forms of Christian Theology.* Translated by Margaret Kohl. Minneapolis: Fortress, 2000.

———. *God in Creation: A New Theology of Creation and the Spirit of God.* Translated by Margaret Kohl. Gifford Lectures 1984–1985. Minneapolis: Fortress, 1993.

———. "The Social Doctrine of the Trinity." In *The Christian Understanding of God Today*, edited by James Byrne, 104–11. Dublin: Columba, 1993.

———. *Spirit of Life: A Universal Affirmation.* Translated by Margaret Kohl. Twentieth Century Religious Thought. Minneapolis: Fortress, 2001.

———. *Theology of Hope: On the Ground and the Implications of a Christian Eschatology.* Translated by James W. Leitch. New York: Harper & Row, 1967.

———. *The Trinity and the Kingdom: The Doctrine of God*. Translated by Margaret Kohl. San Francisco: HarperCollins, 1991.

———. *The Way of Jesus Christ: Christology in Messianic Dimensions*. Minneapolis: Fortress, 1989.

Moltmann-Wendel, Elisabeth. *Autobiography*. Translated by John Bowden. London: SCM, 1997.

Pannenberg, Wolfhart. "Toward a Theology of the History of Religions." In *Basic Questions in Theology*, 2:65–118. Translated by G. H. Kehm. London: SCM, 1971.

Peters, Ted. "The Atonement in Anselm and Luther: Second Thoughts about Gustaf Aulen's *Christus Victor*." *Lutheran Quarterly* 24 (1972) 301–14.

———. "Jürgen Moltmann's Theology as a Theology of the Cross." *Studies in Religion* 24 (1995) 95–107.

Tappert, Theodore G., ed. *The Book of Concord*. Philadelphia: Fortress, 1959.

Tillich, Paul. *On the Boundary: An Autobiographical Sketch*. New York: Scribner, 1966.

Weaver, J. Denny. "Violence in Christian Theology." *Cross Currents* 51 (2001) 150–76.

4

Emerging Pentecostal Ecclesiology Through the Lens of Missiological Method

Issac Hong[1]

THE TWENTIETH CENTURY SAW many important shifts in ecumenical missional ecclesiological thought: the development of *missio Dei*, the decline of Christendom, the recognition of the whole world—including the West!—as a mission field, the related rise of the status of churches in the Majority World, emphasis on the communion of local churches as the body of Christ, and more. Included among these might be an increased use of pneumatological descriptions for the nature of the church. One might consider this to be closely related to the rise of Pentecostalism, a movement defined by pneumatological encounter. Yet this is not always readily apparent. One reason for this is that Pentecostals were largely absent from ecumenical dialogue, particularly in the first half of the twentieth century. This may be in part due to the newness of the movement, which scholarship typically dates

---

1. Congratulations, Dr. Fensham, on your retirement! I am so grateful for your teaching, supervision, and encouragement. You were the first to introduce me to writers of my own theological tradition, from which my current research interests have emerged. Your compassionate teaching has profoundly shaped how I view the task of theological pedagogy. Your gracious support and constant prayer have uplifted me, especially in recent challenging times. Thank you and many blessings in this next season of your life!

to 1906,[2] while the historic Edinburgh Conference would occur just four years later. But the more pressing reason was an anti-ecumenist attitude in early Pentecostals that stemmed from a disagreeable relationship with other Christian traditions. Furthermore, Pentecostals carried an attitude of suspicion towards the academic study of theology. While this has changed dramatically in the last few decades, early Pentecostals rarely participated in higher education.[3] Thus, the academic discipline of Pentecostal theology is new, and subsequently, a full Pentecostal ecclesiology has yet to be articulated.

Yet articulating ecclesiology will be difficult for Pentecostalism because Pentecostalism itself is difficult to define. Despite gradual historical institutionalizations that have taken place in various forms of the movement, there has never been one single central authority or hierarchy acting towards total unification. Instead, a unified denominational body might be considered as antithetical to the charismatic nature of the movement. Furthermore, early Pentecostalism was the site of many divisions. Despite the belief that the Spirit overcomes social barriers, several factors kept American Pentecostal denominations ethnically segregated. Oneness Pentecostals rejected the trinitarian understanding of God and created their own communities. Global expansion has led to a huge multiplication of the diversity of the movement. Therefore, neither defining Pentecostalism nor articulating its ecclesiology is simple. This is not to claim that theological diversity is exclusive to Pentecostalism. It is simply to recognize that unlike most Christian traditions, Pentecostalism had not organized itself according to an institution or a systematic theology.[4]

Thus, the goal of this essay will not be to articulate a complete ecclesiology for Pentecostalism, but to begin to approach it with the help of an abbreviated use of the missiological method of David Bosch.[5] It would

2. Anderson, *Introduction*, 337.

3. This was due to several factors, some of which will be explored in this essay. Two that will not be developed here are the reticence to higher criticism in Pentecostal biblical interpretation and the emphasis on charismata as a more reliable credential for ministry—both of which continue to exist in various degrees in the Pentecostal tradition today.

4. Furthermore, most of the scholarly discussion and resources regarding Pentecostal ecclesiology has come from a Western scholarly perspective. While it will be an important project for Pentecostalism to consider the development of its diverse global ecclesial expressions, to narrow the scope, this essay will focus on the Classical Pentecostalism of the twentieth century from the North American scholarly perspective as its main subject.

5. As seen in *Transforming Mission*, Bosch uses a distinct missiological method to construct theology. He begins with an expansive analysis of the Bible as a normative text

likewise be impossible to repeat the scope of Bosch's constructive theology in a brief essay. Instead, this essay will attempt to uncover a few modest insights from placing into dialogue a normative reading, a portion of Scripture, a narrow historical focus on the development of Pentecostalism, and some ecclesiological themes that have emerged from modern Pentecostal scholarship. Thus, this essay will begin by engaging the Bible to uncover scriptural norms by which the history of Pentecostalism might be evaluated. This will involve the identification of ecclesiological tensions in the Book of Acts and the early church community, as it is a biblical site of vital importance for Pentecostal identity. This will be followed by a brief survey of some elements of formative history for Classical Pentecostalism, with some reflection on its successes and failures in light of Scripture. Lastly, these will be assessed alongside some recent developments in the field of Pentecostal ecclesiology. Through this process, this paper will argue that Pentecostal ecclesiology might include a more nuanced definition of charismatic experience in continuity with the biblical witness of the Spirit of Christ, a doxological missional nature that uncompromisingly witnesses within a charismatic egalitarian fellowship, and the relational identity of humans, socially embedded believers who encounter the Holy Spirit.

Biblical Sources for Pentecostal Ecclesiology

Making use of biblical sources from the Pentecostal tradition involves more than a selection of passages. Rather, it is to engage a particular hermeneutic. The origin of Classical Pentecostal identity is rooted in its distinct interpretation of Scripture, which many scholars will locate historically with Charles Parham and an interpretive task he gave to students in his Bible school.[6] Following this assignment, a female student of Parham named Agnes Ozman underwent the experience of Baptism in the Holy Spirit and spoke in tongues.[7] While locating the historical roots of Pentecostalism with Parham

---

that evaluates the historical actions of missions. He then offers a descriptive recording and reflection on the history of mission. By putting these in dialogue with one another, a constructive theology of mission emerges.

6. The exercise was to determine, from a close reading of Acts, the initial evidence of baptism in the Holy Spirit, which they had determined to be *glossolalia*. Archer, "Early Interpretation," 48.

7. Thomas, "Pentecostal Interpretation," §1.

has been problematized by recent scholarship,[8] his approach to Scripture exemplifies what would be foundational for Pentecostal interpretation and identity. In the words of Kenneth Archer, "[early] Pentecostals were not like classical Protestants or Fundamentalists when it came to interpreting the Bible. Classical Protestants and Fundamentalists read the Bible as past inspired revelatory document, but Pentecostals read the Bible as a presently inspired story."[9] Thus, they bore the conviction that the scriptural narrative of the early apostolic community was directly analogous to theirs, particularly regarding the pneumatic experience of the Holy Spirit.

Therefore, Pentecostalism was already a situated form of interpretation as early as the beginning of the twentieth century, and largely avoided the definitive argument in the academy between modernists and fundamentalists regarding the method of higher criticism.[10] Early academic criticism aimed towards Pentecostal interpretation, described it as literal, ahistorical, and pietistic.[11] However, while Pentecostal emphasis on subjective experience was at odds with other traditions early on, the criticism of being extrascriptural would be unfair.[12] Early Pentecostals challenged the foundations of modernity by adopting a transhistorical and transcultural perspective that saw the biblical world as analogous to their own.[13] Biblical support for one's belief and practice was of critical importance for Pentecostals, such

---

8. Problems have been identified on two fronts. Firstly, there has been growing recognition of charismatic phenomena occurring outside the traditional Pentecostal narrative. Anderson points to such occurrences all throughout Christian (in the wide sense) tradition—though these experiences often took place on the margins and were not accepted by the majority. Likewise, within three years of the tradition-defining Azusa Street revival, other charismatic revivals had independently taken place in at least three other places worldwide. Secondly, scholars have de-emphasized Parham's role in the development of Pentecostalism in part due to his insistence on *xenolalia* over *glossolalia*, as well as his discriminatory views. Anderson, *Introduction*, 21–25, 35–37.

9. Archer, "Early Interpretation," 37.

10. Pentecostalism did have more affinity with fundamentalists than modernists in their rejection of higher criticism, the social gospel, and ecumenism, but divisions over *glossolalia* and worship experiences would ostracize Pentecostalism from the academic struggle. Payne, "New Voices," 18.

11. These descriptions would have functioned pejoratively in its time, particularly the term *ahistorical* which pointed to an apparent disinterest in understanding the assimilation of the biblical texts within their historical and cultural contexts. Furthermore, a pietism that mixed the internal, subjective religious experience with the objective text was considered uncritical. Archer, "Early Interpretation," 32–41.

12. Mittelstadt, "Scripture," 125.

13. Archer, "Early Interpretation," 39.

that any doctrinal understanding of faith required scriptural evidence on the levels of common-sense grammar and biblical culture.[14] Thus, Pentecostalism developed distinct emphases for interpretation, which one might call their canon-within-the-canon.[15]

Ecclesiological Insights from Pentecostal Interpretation of Luke–Acts

First among these emphases, Pentecostal identity and interpretation of Scripture emerges from their experientially oriented posture towards Luke–Acts. The discussion to this point highlights the critical importance that experience plays in Pentecostal interpretation and identity formation. While other traditions might emphasize the need to read Acts critically or sympathetically, Pentecostals insist on seeking experiences analogous to the lives of the early Christian community as recorded in Luke–Acts.[16] In Acts 2, Luke's narrative describes how the earliest Christian community was born out of an embodied, pneumatological experience. This being filled with the Holy Spirit precedes—and more to the point, enables—Peter's sermon and the subsequent gathered community.[17] That initial divine encounter is described in terms that challenge a purely scientific, rationalistic understanding of reality. Likewise, those that indirectly witness the

---

14. Archer, "Early Interpretation," 52.

15. Mittelstadt argues for this perspective, particularly that Pentecostal interpretation follows traditional Judaic-Catholic hermeneutics. Mittelstadt, "Scripture," 130.

16. This is certainly not to say that critical interpretation is not necessary for Pentecostals. While that might be the case in some popular forms, Pentecostal scholarship is making the case for interpretation that is both critical and experiential. See Keener, *Spirit Hermeneutics*.

17. Holding to this implication for the Pentecostal community requires further argumentation on two fronts. Firstly, it requires an understanding that Luke's prehistorical narrative was intended to set a precedent for the Christian community, or at the very least, set normative expectations. Stronstad argues that placing hermeneutical priority on Pauline epistles does not allow the Lukan narrative to be understood for its own theological merit. See Mittelstadt, "Scripture," 126. Keener argues that the vantage point of Pentecost necessitates experiential readings, because the arrival of the Holy Spirit gives a personal knowledge of the text's divine Author. See Keener, *Spirit Hermeneutics*, 40. Secondly, it would be necessary to understand the narrated reality to correspond with the reader's reality, which was particularly challenging in the culture of Enlightenment rationalism from which Pentecostalism emerged. Keener argues that the advent of the Spirit has epistemological consequences, including a pneumatological posture that is demanded by Scripture itself. Keener, *Spirit Hermeneutics*, 7.

encounter are left bewildered, as empowered speech allows them to hear God's praises in their own languages.

This biblical experience creates a tension for Pentecostal ecclesiology. Luke writes to his audience within a premodern plausibility structure that resonates with Pentecostal experience.[18] This Acts community gathers in response to a "supernatural" pneumatological experience that frames their identity. However, this experience is still embodied and exists within the subjective experience of both the recipients of the pneumatic encounter as well as its witnesses.[19] Somehow, there is a miraculous multi-*xenolalaic* encounter with the Holy Spirit that is still mediated within the field of human experience. It is at once bewildering and yet not irrational. Indeed, while words might limit the description of the event to the analogous,[20] when Peter subsequently provides an interpretation of the encounter, he coherently draws from Joel 2:28–32 and narrates what had occurred from a biblical perspective.

Indeed, a constant tension of Pentecostal ecclesiology will be its grounds in this Lukan encounter that is simultaneously bewildering yet explainable according to the logic of the Spirit. It is that the Holy Spirit is doing both that which is new, and that which is in continuity with what has come before. For while the modes of encounter might not be the same according to the various embodied contexts in which the Spirit is mediated, it is still the Spirit of Christ. Pentecostal theologians point to Acts 2 as evidence of plurivocity as part of the very nature of the ecclesial community.[21]

---

18. The term *plausibility structures*, as used by Hauerwas, is useful as it carries ecclesiastical implications. While Hauerwas is focused on a communally defined canonical tradition, Pentecostals might understand this to be an embodied experience mediated by the Holy Spirit. See Hauerwas, "The Church," 154. This has also led Archer to argue rather than being uncritical, a better description for Pentecostal interpretation would be pre-critical—though it would be difficult to suggest that Pentecostals avoided any of the hermeneutical developments that followed the Enlightenment. Archer, "Early Interpretation," 25.

19. Amos Yong tries to correct the priority that has been placed on hearing and seeing as modes of experiencing God within his argument for a wider understanding of the Body of Christ to center those with disabilities. He asks, might Pentecost not be limited to speaking, hearing, and seeing, but also touching, feeling, and perceiving? Yong, *The Bible*, 72.

20. Luke uses ὥσπερ to describe "what seemed as" a violent wind, and ὡσεί for what was "as" tongues of fire. Acts 2:2–3.

21. This is especially prominent in the writing of Amos Yong, who argues that diverse expressions of the Spirit and "many Pentecostalisms" is reflective of the many tongues and many senses of the event of Pentecost. Yong, "Pentecostal Ecclesiologies," 346.

Part of the task of Pentecostal ecclesiology, then, is to hold the dynamism and continuity of the Spirit in constant tension.

Pentecostal scholars have noted the indiscriminate distribution of spiritual gifts in the Joel pericope of Peter's speech as an essential element in the early apostolic community.[22] Various examples in Luke–Acts point to what might be described as an impetus towards egalitarianism in this community. For example, throughout Luke–Acts, attention is consistently drawn to women of various stations participating in ministry.[23] In Acts 4, the gathered people are described as having no needy among them, because they were sharing in all their possessions. Luke clearly understands the Spirit's activity to empower and include those who would have traditionally been excluded, towards an equitable community.

However, this reveals another tension. For while this group gathered in the Spirit might be idealized, various communal problems quickly arose. The apostolic leadership faced pressure from the Jewish religious leaders (Acts 4). Members of the community were giving false testimony in their offerings, leading to their instantaneous death (Acts 5). Members of the community became marginalized and overlooked in the distribution of food (Acts 6). These concerns give reason to pause and consider why a pneumatologically-encountered community continues to struggle despite its daily signs and wonders.

It would be impossible to claim that an encounter with the Holy Spirit extricates someone from the problems of their location, be they social, religious, cultural, psychological, or otherwise. If the Holy Spirit mediates this encounter through embodied experience, then one should not expect an escape from the nexus of human creaturely existence. The Holy Spirit indwelling within humanity does not erase the human. Thus, pneumatological communities, though transformed by their experience, will inevitably face troubles pertaining to the difficulties of human communal existence.[24]

However, perhaps what the Spirit does enable is discernment to recognize these communal issues, and an empowerment/impetus towards addressing them. It is telling that the Spirit's advent in Acts 2 did not reveal a completely new language, but rather, spoke the wonders of God in languages

---

22. Mittelstadt, "Scripture," 134.

23. Mittelstadt, "Scripture," 134.

24. Or as Mittelstadt argues, Pentecostal communities are not immune to the influence of broader religious and social trajectories. Mittelstadt, "Scripture," 134.

all were able to recognize.[25] Perhaps the role of the Spirit is not to reprogram the human being, but to teach the human community how to speak—and embody—God's praise. In this sense, the pneumatological community is a doxological one through their discernment of the injustices in which they participate and reorientation towards their correction. This touches once again on the theme of pneumatically empowered egalitarianism. What is interesting in Acts 6 is the mode by which a solution to the problem of marginalization was adopted by the community. The apostles, though possibly holding a preferred position because of their ministry, offer a possible solution, to which the community responds in affirmation.[26] This implies that while a hierarchical structure may have existed in this community for the sake of ministerial service, the voice of all in the gathering mattered when it came to its decisions. Likewise, those chosen for the task of serving the marginalized are those who are communally recognized as being filled with the Spirit.[27] Thus, the filling of the Holy Spirit is used for the purpose of serving the community, which may illustrate that egalitarianism as a pneumatological response to marginalization is a feature of this group.

One additional insight from Acts 2 for Pentecostal ecclesiology is in its missiological nature. Acts 1:8 might be seen as a missionary mandate for Pentecostals,[28] but it does not appear that within the Lukan narrative the missional nature of the apostolic community arises from obedience to this mandate.[29] Rather, the encounter with the Holy Spirit and subsequent focus towards communal equity and justice may be the catalyst for the growing numbers in Acts. In the chapters following, the repeating motif of the Lord adding to their number is often accompanied by the persistence of apostolic signs and wonders, as well as a remark of the ecclesial community being held in high regard by those around them.[30] Thus, while the demonstration of spiritual power does appear consistently (and may attribute to

---

25. This is not an argument against *glossolalia*, but simply a theological interpretation local to Acts 2. This argument is indebted to the work of Amos Yong, who argues for tongues to refer to languages in a wider sense, including "the language of science." Yong, *Theology*, 11.

26. Acts 6:5.

27. Acts 6:3.

28. Mittelstadt, "Scripture," 132.

29. Thus, Anderson argues that Pentecostal communities do not function missiologically in the same way as Catholic understanding of *missio Dei* or Protestant understanding of the Great Commission. Anderson, *Introduction*, 199.

30. Acts 2:46–47, 5:13–14, 6:7.

the high standing), Luke draws attention to the importance of how those beyond the ecclesial community are also drawn to God's praise through the actions of the believers. Notably, this does not equate to pandering to those that did not believe. After the death of Ananias and Sapphira, Luke writes of how people were afraid to join the community despite holding it in high regard.[31] This popular standing also fails to prevent the persecution of members of the community, as seen in the martyrdom of Stephen.[32] Thus, the early ecclesial community of Acts does engage in pneumatological witness to the community that results in the declaration of God's wonders among those outside the group. Yet this does not occur through the goal of pleasing those outside, but, rather, through the communal witness of the spiritually empowered believers.

Thus, the early ecclesial community as recorded in the narrative of Acts reveals three tensions that shape pneumatological ecclesiology. First, pneumatological encounter is experience of the Spirit of Christ that is at once surprising yet continuous with the revelation of God. Second, the divine encounter is mediated within embodied experience such that human egalitarian communities engage in a process of demarginalization. Third, the missionary root of the community is pneumatological witness that draws the other into the declaration of God's wonders without compromising the goal of faithful witness. These tensions arising from the Lukan narrative may thus help inform Pentecostal ecclesiology.

Historical Sources for Pentecostal Ecclesiology

The twentieth century saw many developments in the ecumenical Christian tradition, particularly in the areas of ecclesiology and missiology. The 1900s began with missionary optimism, as demonstrated in the gathering of the World Missionary Conference in Edinburgh in 1910. There, participants felt that political, economic, and religious factors were seeming to converge to spread the Gospel to every part of the world.[33] While positive theological shifts began to emerge from this event,[34] missionary confidence was cut

---

31. Acts 5:13.
32. Acts 7:54–58.
33. Stanley, World Missionary Conference, 2.
34. These include growing recognition of culture as opposed to race, a shift away from the direction of "Christendom to Heathendom," and a growing sense of Christian unity, to name a few.

short by the traumatic experiences of both World Wars. Western nations professing to be Christian had engaged in two devastating global conflicts, suppressing the sense of evangelical expectation. Furthermore, the steady rise of Enlightenment Rationalism and the decline of Christendom in the West threatened the traditional understandings of the church.[35] Yet, this has paradoxically led to tremendously fruitful self-reflection on the nature of the church and its mission in every Christian tradition.

Pentecostalism has its own distinct history in navigating these ecclesial developments of the twentieth century, starting from the event commonly described as the birth of its classical form—the Azusa Street Revival in Los Angeles from 1906–1908.[36] William Seymour, the key figure in the revival, was an African American preacher and a former student of Charles Parham.[37] Seymour became persuaded by Parham's teachings, and upon invitation to preach in a small African American Holiness church in Los Angeles in 1906, he delivered a sermon on tongues as sign of Spirit baptism. This offended the pastor responsible for the invitation, leading them to expel Seymour from the congregation. However, members of the church and others continued to meet with Seymour in prayer outside the church, and during one such meeting, participants encountered a pneumatic experience characterized by falling and speaking in tongues. More people began joining these meetings, to the point where houses were no longer adequate for conducting the gathering, and the group moved to a former African Methodist Episcopal Church located at 312 Azusa Street, from which the revival would derive its name.

An incredible feature of these early meetings was the racial integration of both Caucasian Americans and African Americans, in a period where segregation laws continued to be enforced.[38] What is particularly notable is

35. Bosch, *Transforming Mission*, 357.

36. As with every movement, Pentecostalism emerges from a variety of earlier influences, particularly the Wesleyan Holiness tradition. However, the focus of this section will be on the developments of the Pentecostal tradition in the twentieth century. For further reference in its historical roots, see Anderson, *Introduction*.

37. As noted earlier, Parham had a profound influence in the development of classical Pentecostalism but diminished in influence among early Pentecostals partly because of his racist views. Seymour, for example, had only been allowed to listen to Parham's lectures through a half-opened door, in strict observation of segregation of southern states and Parham's own prejudice. Anderson, *Introduction*, 41.

38. Thus, some scholars advocate for a multicultural or polycentric approach to understanding Pentecostal history, particularly in identifying important influences from African American culture of the nineteenth century, as well as the prominence of black

that Charles Parham greatly opposed such racial intermingling and strongly advocated for segregated gatherings.[39] It is a testament to the significance of the shared pneumatological experience of these early Pentecostals that they resisted the influence of one of its most prominent members and continued, for a time, to meet in gatherings without racially defined lines. Some have argued that this has been a neglected aspect of Pentecostal history, that they were professing a "new, deep fundamental unity in the spirit" when they exhibited this communal love that had been generated by their experience.[40] However, this was not to remain the case, as civil societal pressures led the budding Pentecostal community to racially segregate their gatherings. Furthermore, as similar Pentecostal sites began opening across the city and in other states, an element of competition appeared to arise, with various charismatic people attempting to struggle for leadership of the movement. Thus, very early in the movement, a diversity of spiritual expressions becomes apparent, which has led to some scholars describing Pentecostalism as the site of many schisms.[41] Nevertheless, an egalitarian principle was apparent within Pentecostalism early in its history, if no longer racially then in encouraging the participation of women in ministry.[42] This was also unusual for the time, partly emerging from the interpretation of Acts 2 and Joel 2 of the Holy Spirit indiscriminately pouring upon all believers, but more directly was a reflection of their pneumatic experience. Indeed, the first person in the narrative of Pentecostal history to receive the Baptism of the Holy Spirit was Agnes Ozman, a woman. However, the equitable impulse towards gender would become a complicated issue during the development and gradual institutionalization of Pentecostal communities, leading to additional splits within the tradition.[43]

One aspect that these communities often did share was an eschatological and providential perspective towards their own movement. They saw the various forms of spiritual experiences as evidence of the immediate proximity of God's eschatological reign.[44] In particular, they saw in the advent of the Spirit a restoration of vitality to the Christian faith

churches and leadership in the movement. Anderson, *Introduction*, 45.

39. Anderson, *Introduction*, 42.
40. Lord, *Network Church*, 64.
41. Anderson, *Introduction*, 45.
42. Mittelstadt, "Scripture," 133.
43. Mittelstadt, "Scripture," 134.
44. Anderson, *Introduction*, 46.

tradition, over the "routinized environments" of the mainline traditions.[45] The manner in which they participated in this eschatological time was to engage in global evangelism. Pentecostals emphasize prophethood of all believers—rather than the more traditional priesthood—where spiritual manifestations were available for all to be empowered for missionary activity.[46] Thus, Azusa began launching missionaries around the world, as well as establishing churches across North America. This eschatological movement prioritized evangelization over social reform, the time to Christ's return created urgency within an evangelical paradigm for salvation.[47] In some ways, this reflects the missionary character of the broader Christian tradition at the time, particularly when considering the World Missionary Conference of Edinburgh 1910 (WMC). Both Pentecostals and the WMC carried a sense of optimism for missions and emphasis on what might be described as a triumphalist, paternalistic presentation of the Gospel that saw its task as going from Christendom towards heathendom. However, the specific eschatology and charismatic practices of Pentecostalism put it at odds with other church traditions early on in its history. This was in part due to how Pentecostals were perceived, as their insistence on the validity of subjective spiritual experiences was viewed suspiciously by many traditions. Pentecostals, too, contributed towards this antagonism, as they carried sectarian habits and engaged in a non-inclusive rhetoric when it came to other Christian traditions.[48]

However, this perception would begin to change as Western Christianity entered the second half of the twentieth century. Charismatic movements began taking place within mainline Protestantism in the late 1950s, and Roman Catholics felt charismatic influences from within leading to and during the Second Vatican Council.[49] This shift is characterized as a growing sense that mainline ecclesial forms were lacking vitality or were too suppressive in their institutions. Yet, this explanation mirrors initial Pentecostal attitudes towards the institutional church. Early Pentecostals were suspicious of institutional forms and resisted denominational labels, seeing them as lacking spiritual vitality.[50] But if this was always the case in

---

45. Yong, "Pentecostal Ecclesiologies," 337.
46. Yong, "Pentecostal Ecclesiologies," 348.
47. Mittelstadt, "Scripture," 135.
48. Yong, "Pentecostal Ecclesiologies," 338.
49. Mannion, "Pilgrim Church," 129.
50. Yong, "Pentecostal Ecclesiologies," 336.

Pentecostalism, why did a charismatic movement take place in mainline Protestantism fifty years later? Perhaps the missionary pessimism that followed the Second World War, along with the decline of Christendom, created the conditions for the wider Christian tradition to reflect on their fiduciary frameworks.[51] Or perhaps it was the continual growth of Pentecostalism that gained additional influence within other traditions as they confronted the presence of spiritual experiences.[52] But whatever the reason, the result led to the increasing complexity in how the Pentecostal tradition is understood. Some Protestants and Catholics left their churches to join Pentecostal groups. Others remained within their own tradition and attempted to revitalize them from within, becoming designated as Charismatic.[53] Mainline Protestant groups began forming offices to manage, facilitate, or integrate these expressions into denominational and ecclesial life. Others, still, formed independent groups that neither associated directly with classical Pentecostalism nor mainline Protestantism or Catholicism. Thus, an already diverse field of Pentecostal movements becomes multiplied with the charismatic revival beginning in the 1950s.

Ecclesiological Insights from Pentecostal History

This very brief overview of classical Pentecostalism in North America nevertheless provides ecclesial insights for current constructive Pentecostal ecclesiologies. These reflections are organized according to the previously identified scriptural tensions.

Multiplicity and Continuity

Diversity has been clearly inherent within the history of the Pentecostal movement, whether regarding pneumatological experiences, theologies, or even communal modes of organization. But is this a product of schism and socio-historical frictions, or is it inherent for those gathered by pneumatic experiences? Amos Yong argues for the latter and suggests that such an

---

51. That is, to borrow the phrase from Bosch, *Transforming Mission*, 5.

52. Andrew Lord describes how the focus of these charismatic participants was on a personal faith and experience of the Spirit, rather than engagement with questions regarding the nature of the church. Yet, these two explanations are certainly not mutually exclusive and likely both were factors. Lord, *Network Church*, 77.

53. Yong, "Pentecostal Ecclesiologies," 338.

understanding is scripturally warranted,[54] and that it results from Pentecostal ecclesial institutions not being monolithic.[55] Pentecostalism in North America alone represents an incredibly multiplicative range of ecclesial practices. This does not even account for global forms of Pentecostalism, which represent the majority of the movement today. If pneumatic experience is indeed mediated within an embodied culture, then that would imply a pluriform expression of practices according to the various contexts in which these encounters take place. In this way, Yong is appropriately arguing for a widening of the Pentecostal ecclesial body, to include legitimate pneumatological expressions that take place throughout the world.

Yet, should every spiritual experience be counted as legitimate? Yong rightly opens the way for pluriform expressions, but too broad a definition may lack focus on what constitutes a Pentecostal ecclesiology. This is apparent in Anderson's criticism of Pentecostal history, where he interprets the pluralism of the movement to be a result of internal divisiveness and doctrinal haggling.[56] On the one hand, this is likely to be expected, given that "in its beginnings, Pentecostalism in the western world was an ecumenical movement of people claiming a common experience rather than a common doctrine."[57] As Pentecostalism progressed as a movement, doctrinal differences would certainly emerge, especially as early members came from a diverse background of Christian traditions, bringing with them a range of theological intuitions. On the other hand, Pentecostalism has not had the institutional centralization found within other Christian traditions that would allow for an ecclesial discernment of legitimate expressions of spirituality. Within Catholicism, one could argue that the range of theological beliefs of various members would span even greater differences than that of Pentecostalism, yet no one would argue the consistent apostolic unity of the Catholic tradition.

Considering scriptural and historical precedent, one way forward would be to discern the continuity of pneumatological expressions with the biblical revelation of God in Jesus Christ. The early Pentecostals insisted

---

54. In his argument, the outpouring of the Spirit in Acts 2 reveals divine intention towards multiplicity. Thus, "the logic of incarnation and Pentecost together defy the erasure of difference and the reduction of otherness to self-sameness. Rather, both establish difference and otherness, each in its own place within the context of the whole." Yong, *Spirit-Word-Community*, 103.

55. Yong, "Pentecostal Ecclesiologies," 339.

56. Anderson, *Introduction*, 61.

57. Anderson, *Introduction*, 59.

that their understanding of Scripture and the Spirit was in continuity with the witness of Scripture. Applied to the diversity of the Pentecostal church, ecclesial identity would be determined through the discernment of the Spirit of Christ within diverse cultural contexts. Care would have to be taken not to mistake cultural diversity for spiritual digression. It is the question of articulating a clear Pentecostal hermeneutic, both in the sense of interpretation of Scripture as well as the living text of communities.

Surprising Egalitarianism and Institutional Tensions

As in the biblical witness, the immediate aftermath of pneumatological experiences in early Pentecostal history saw a deep communal love formed across prominent social boundaries. These experiences of the Spirit were never limited to preferred groups but were a shared experience across race and gender. Thus, the initial gathered community shared much anticipation for the new workings of the Holy Spirit. Yet, also like the biblical witness, social pressures and cultural instincts threatened this pneumatological unity. A community filled with the Spirit does not render it immune to the pressures of the context in which it is found.

As Pentecostalism developed, these forces increasingly exerted themselves. Seymour began with a community of racial inclusiveness amidst segregation and carried an ecumenical vision. Yet, soon Pentecostal churches would become divided between African Americans and Caucasian American congregations. Furthermore, Pentecostals developed an anti-ecumenical attitude that came from rejection by established churches on account of their focus on spiritual manifestations—particularly towards fundamentalists, with whom they shared sympathetic theologies in all other areas.[58] In the process of institutionalization, hierarchical relationships based on evangelical inequitable rhetoric divided Pentecostal communities.[59] Gatherings that were originally formed in reaction to stale dogmatic institutions later haggled over doctrine.

As with any movement, classic Pentecostalism has had to reckon with the socio-religious forces of its context. Initial excitement for the imminent return of Christ would gradually subside and eschatological interpretation of pneumatological manifestations would be rearticulated.[60] Yet, Pentecos-

---

58. Anderson, *Introduction*, 61.
59. Mittelstadt, "Scripture," 134.
60. And in this way may they share another similarity with the early biblical apostolic

tals would continue to insist that charismatic participation was available for everyone, particularly in the involvement of laity in worship in ecstatic experiences. Collections of churches developed into various forms of governance. Continuing to view hierarchical structures with suspicion, these collections often described themselves as organic fellowships.[61] As such, while the initial thrust of classical Pentecostalism transitioned from movement to institution, there remained an orientation towards egalitarian principles, even as they experienced struggles in several forms.

Missiological Nature

An internal orientation towards missions was present even in the initial stages of the movement. The first Pentecostals interpreted the outpouring of the Spirit as for them to engage in end-time harvest of souls, with the conviction that the Holy Spirit was the motivating power behind all this activity. The initial *xenolalaic* interpretation of these experiences took an interesting turn when early missionaries discovered they did not speak the languages of the people to whom they went.[62] However, they continued in the missionary task with the conviction that of foremost importance was not the tongues, but the encounter of the Holy Spirit.[63]

Today, Pentecostalism's center is no longer located in North America, as it has shifted to a fundamentally Majority World phenomenon.[64] The exact nature of how this came to be has not been fully researched, yet it is safe to say that the missionary focus inherent within Pentecostalism has contributed to its globalization—albeit perhaps not in a directly linear process.[65] Given Pentecostalism's emphasis on the prophethood of all believers, it was likely the effort of "untold thousands of local revivalists" who spread the Pentecostal gospel, rather than a few high-profile charismatic leaders,[66] which may again reflect the equitable impulse of the empowerment of the Holy Spirit. Thus, a critical factor to Pentecostalism's global expansion is its inherent missiological nature in response to the pneumatic activity.

---

community?

    61. Yong, "Pentecostal Ecclesiologies," 337.

    62. Anderson, *Introduction*, 198.

    63. Anderson, *Introduction*, 198.

    64. Kärkkäinen, "Pentecostal Ecclesiology," 249.

    65. Kärkkäinen, "Pentecostal Ecclesiology," 250.

    66. Anderson, *An Introduction*, 210.

Therefore, the historical roots of classical Pentecostalism have a great degree of resonance with a Pentecostal reading of the Acts narrative. In both, there is the surprising development of spiritual manifestation that they claim to be continuous with the wider biblical witness. Likewise, early pneumatic encounters led to profound communal bonds that superseded traditional social barriers. While these communal bonds would be tested and at times broken by contextual pressures against them, there was a repeated sense that the Spirit was orienting these communities towards an egalitarian ministry. Lastly, the pneumatological impulse was one of witness to the world, and the Spirit's empowerment led numerous unnamed Pentecostals to engage in missionary work around the world, contributing to the global nature of the Pentecostal tradition today.

Contemporary Pentecostal Ecclesiologies

The biblical and historical insights that have emerged for approaching Pentecostal ecclesiology will now be considered alongside a brief survey of contemporary ecclesiological emphases from Pentecostal theology.

A Fellowship of the Spirit

One of the recurring themes within the Pentecostal tradition has been the focus on personal faith and experiences of the Spirit, rather than theological reflection regarding the nature of the church.[67] Upon reflection by Pentecostal theologians, what resulted was a shift to seeing the personal experience of Spirit as something that draws people into Christian community, rather than a matter of individualistic piety.[68] Thus, the outpouring of charismatic gifts is for the sake of edifying the community as opposed to a self-centered accumulation of power. Kärkkäinen identifies this with the term *koinonia*, pointing to an ancient biblical and theological concept of fellowship to describe the nature of the Pentecostal community.[69] Thus, he writes, "theologically put, for Pentecostals the Church is a charismatic fellowship, a fellowship of persons, the body of Christ." Indeed, in Pentecostal history, there has been a preference towards self-identification by the term

---

67. Lord, *Network Church*, 77.
68. Lord, *Network Church*, 77.
69. Kärkkäinen, "Pentecostal Ecclesiology," 251.

fellowship rather than *church* because of possible institutionalized connotations.[70] There is a focus on personal relational, rather than structural, sacramental, or ecumenical aspects of *koinonia*, which Kärkkäinen sees as extending from serious engagement of the *koinonia* between the believer and the Son and Holy Spirit.

This ecclesiology of *koinonia* puts earlier insights about egalitarian community into greater perspective. The communal love that overcame social boundaries is a result of the fellowship that the believer encounters with the Spirit of Christ in a charismatic manner. The empowerment of marginalized individuals for service is both for witness to those outside the community, but also edification of those within the community. This Spirit of *koinonia* is made available to all, such that "a real congregational life, wherein each member has his opportunity to contribute to the life of the whole body through gifts with which the Spirit endows him, is as much part of the *esse* of the Church as are ministry and sacraments."[71]

Amos Yong takes up Kärkkäinen's ecclesiological insights in order to describe church as charismatic fellowship.[72] While considering how the diversity of Pentecostalism might affect ecclesiology, he goes back to an often-used expression for him of the many tongues of Pentecost.[73] He asks, "could a mantra for Pentecostal ecclesiology be: many tongues, many ecclesial practices, many ecclesial forms?" That is, for Yong, multiplicity in ecclesiology is inherent to seeing church as charismatic fellowship. Fellowship of the people of God exists in and through the Spirit analogously to the perichoretic fellowship of the Godhead.[74] Indeed, the influence of social trinitarianism is apparent here, as Volf and Moltmann's insights are taken a step further by Yong. He argues that the trinitarian fellowship is formed in and through the Spirit—that is, the perichoretic relationship of God is pneumatologically mediated—in a manner akin to the pneumatologically mediated fellowship within the ecclesial community.[75]

---

70. Kärkkäinen, "Pentecostal Ecclesiology," 252.

71. This is Kärkkäinen quoting Newbigin in describing the need for increased recognition of the personal contribution to the body of Christ, as well as the ministerial and the sacramental. Kärkkäinen, "Pentecostal Ecclesiology," 252.

72. Yong, "Pentecostal Ecclesiologies," 346.

73. Yong's theology advocates for a flourishing diversity that he locates in the multiplicity of languages in the Pentecost narrative. Many of his works refer to this aspect, including his works on hermeneutics, disability theology, and ecclesiology.

74. Yong, "Pentecostal Ecclesiologies," 347.

75. Yong, "Pentecostal Ecclesiologies," 347.

Volf is further helpful for framing earlier perceived tensions regarding the divine-human encounter. It was noted that pneumatological encounter is embodied, and this creates tension between the surprise of the divine and the socio-cultural embeddedness of the human. If Yong is correct in the pneumatological mediation of the community reflecting perichoresis, then Volf's understanding of how identity interacts in perichoresis may be revealing. He suggests that the divine persons are not simply interdependent and influence each other from outside their selves, but are personally interior to one another.[76] Yet, while they indwell and interpenetrate one another, they do not cease to be distinct. Rather, this interpenetration presupposes their distinctiveness, as otherwise it could not be described as interpenetration. But here, Volf's key insight is that their identities overlap, such that "every divine person is and acts as itself and yet the two other persons are present and act in that person."[77] The perichoretic identity is relational—at once non-reducible, yet not self-enclosed.[78]

Volf remains extremely cautious when attempting to translate the perichoretic nature within the Trinity towards ecclesial community. Perhaps what can be understood from this notion of identity is that the Baptism of the Spirit creates a perichoretic encounter of indwelling within the believer such that, while they remain distinct, their identity is now understood in relation to the Spirit. Thus, while the challenges of human social embeddedness remain, so too the Spirit's indwelling allows the believer to negotiate those challenges in their relation to the Spirit of Christ. Volf argues that the negotiation of identity boundaries in perichoresis are described in the narrative of divine self-donation on the cross.[79] He sees the task for the ecclesial community as re-narrating the history of the cross, understood as the triune God's perichoretic engagement with the world, participating in "the divine labor of suffering and risk."[80] The Pentecostal ecclesiological community engages in this task through pneumatic empowerment for service towards creating a charismatic egalitarian fellowship that is inherently missional.

---

76. Volf, "Trinity," 409.
77. Volf, "Trinity," 409.
78. Volf, "Trinity," 410.
79. Volf, "Trinity," 412.
80. Volf, "Trinity," 413–15.

Plurivocity of Ecclesial Forms Part of Its Nature

It was previously noted that Yong sees the diversity of pneumatic expressions as inherent within a charismatic ecclesial community. He argues that Pentecostals have always held to a multiplicity of ways in which encounter with Jesus is experienced,[81] and furthermore, that "this is in itself also consistent with the foundational Pentecostal imagination rooted in the multiplicity of tongues spoken on the Day of Pentecost."[82] Again, as noted earlier, Yong is correct in expanding the field of legitimate pneumatological experience. What may require additional development is describing a process for discerning which experiences are truly pneumatological. This essay has suggested that part of this discernment requires the recognition of the Spirit of Christ that is in continuity with scriptural witness, in a manner that accounts for diversity in cultural applications. This requires the further development of a Pentecostal hermeneutic, particularly one that incorporates intercultural dialogue.

A Missional Ecclesiology

Lastly, Yong emphasizes the need for Pentecostal and pneumatological ecclesiology to clarify the question, "ecclesiology . . . what for?"[83] What is the goal of the gathered community? For Yong, the church is the mission of the Spirit. Believers are sent and empowered by the Spirit to declare Christ for a holistic redemption of creation, to the glory of the Father. The Holy Spirit of Pentecost is a missionary Spirit, such that the church full of the Spirit is missionary by its very nature. Anderson describes the Pentecostal church's witness as the release of this inward dynamic of the filling of the Holy Spirit.[84] Yong's insistence towards the glorification of the Father resonates with the doxological effect the early apostolic community gave rise to among those to whom they witnessed while never compromising the integrity of their pneumatic word. Perhaps this resonates with previously highlighted aspects of Pentecostal history. The early Azusa community testified to an

---

81. His argument pertains to Pentecostalism's fivefold Christology, that these various modes of understanding Christ may be analogous to a multivalent recognition of Spiritual encounter. Yong, "Pentecostal Ecclesiologies," 345.

82. Yong, "Pentecostal Ecclesiologies," 346.

83. Yong, "Pentecostal Ecclesiologies," 347.

84. Anderson, *Introduction*, 199.

egalitarian fellowship in a period of segregation, even while one of its most prominent members attempted to cause disruption. Likewise, Pentecostals gave witness to the importance of relational pneumatic experience despite decades of rejection in other Christian traditions. Now, ecumenical awareness has shifted to the point of consistently describing the nature of the church in pneumatological terms.[85]

In conclusion, some suggestions for the emerging field of Pentecostal ecclesiology might include an interculturally-determined hermeneutic that better defines charismatic experience in continuity with the biblical witness of the Spirit, a doxological missional nature that uncompromisingly witnesses to a charismatic egalitarian fellowship, and a growing appreciation for ways in which Pentecostalism can nuance the relational identity of human believers who encounter the Holy Spirit. All of this necessitates a continued posture of humility and sensitivity towards the direction of the Spirit. Are there current societal or even ecclesiological norms that inhibit equitable justice? Are there currently new ways to express communal love more graciously and bring those outside the believing community to doxology? Might the fellowship of Pentecostalism be called to further widen its embrace towards surprising intercultural expressions of the Spirit? And at the same time, might there be a greater articulation of scriptural resources that help discern the contours of Pentecostal ecclesiologies?

Bibliography

Anderson, Allan Heaton. *An Introduction to Pentecostalism: Global Charismatic Christianity*. 2nd ed. Cambridge: Cambridge University Press, 2013.

Archer, Kenneth J. "Early Pentecostal Biblical Interpretation." *Journal of Pentecostal Theology* 9.1 (2001) 32–70.

Bosch, David J. *Transforming Mission: Paradigm Shifts in Theology of Mission*. Maryknoll, NY: Orbis, 2011.

Hauerwas, Stanley M. "The Church as God's New Language (1986)." In *Hauerwas Reader*, 142–62. Durham: Duke University Press, 2020.

Kärkkäinen, Veli-Matti. "Pentecostal Ecclesiology—Does it Exist?" *International Journal for the Study of the Christian Church* 11.4 (2011) 248–55.

Keener, Craig S. *Spirit Hermeneutics: Reading Scripture in Light of Pentecost*. Grand Rapids: Eerdmans, 2017.

Lord, Andrew. *Network Church: A Pentecostal Ecclesiology Shaped by Mission*. Global Pentecostal and Charismatic Studies 11. Leiden: Brill, 2012.

---

85. This is true for Protestants and Catholics alike. Included, too, would be the Orthodox tradition, but pneumatology has long been a central feature of their theology. Yong, "Pentecostal Ecclesiologies," 338.

Mannion, Gerard. "The Pilgrim Church: An Ongoing Journey of Ecclesial Renewal and Reform." In *The Cambridge Companion to Vatican II*, 115–35. Cambridge Companions to Religion. Cambridge: Cambridge University Press, 2020.

Mittelstadt, Martin. "Scripture in the Pentecostal Tradition: A Contemporary Reading of Luke-Acts." In *Canadian Pentecostalism: Transition and Transformation*, 123–41. Montreal: McGill-Queen's University Press, 2009.

Payne, Leah. "New Voices: Pentecostal Preachers in North America, 1890–1930." In *Scripting Pentecost: A Study of Pentecostals, Worship and Liturgy*, edited by Mark J. Catledge and A. J. Swoboda, 15–31. Explorations in Practical, Pastoral, and Empirical Theology. London: Routledge, 2017.

Stanley, Brian. *The World Missionary Conference, Edinburgh 1910*. Grand Rapids: Eerdmans, 2009.

Thomas, John Christopher. "Pentecostal Interpretation." In *The Oxford Encyclopedia of Biblical Interpretation*. Oxford: Oxford University Press, 2013. https://www.oxfordreference.com/view/10.1093/acref:obso/9780199832262.001.0001/acref-9780199832262-e-32.

Volf, Miroslav. "The Trinity Is Our Social Program: The Doctrine of the Trinity and the Shape of Social Engagement." *Modern Theology* 14.3 (1998) 403–23.

Work, Telford. "Pentecostal and Charismatic Worship." In *The Oxford History of Christian Worship*. Oxford: Oxford University Press, 2006.

Yong, Amos. *The Bible, Disability, and the Church: A New Vision of the People of God*. Grand Rapids: Eerdmans, 2011.

———. "Pentecostal Ecclesiologies." In *The Oxford Handbook of Ecclesiology*, edited by Paul Avis, 335–53. Oxford Handbooks. Oxford: Oxford University Press, 2018.

———. *Spirit-Word-Community: Theological Hermeneutics in Trinitarian Perspective*. Ashgate New Critical Thinking in Religion, Theology & Biblical Studies. Aldershot, UK: Ashgate, 2002.

———. *Theology and Down Syndrome: Reimagining Disability in Late Modernity*. Waco: Baylor University Press, 2007.

5

Christian Mission in an Age of Contested Identities

Robert Hunt

Psalm 87

Glorious things are said of you,
city of God:
4 "I will record Rahab and Babylon
among those who acknowledge me—
Philistia too, and Tyre, along with Cush—
and will say, 'This one was born in Zion.'"
5 Indeed, of Zion it will be said,
"This one and that one were born in her,
and the Most High himself will establish her."
6 The Lord will write in the register of the peoples:
"This one was born in Zion."
7 As they make music they will sing,
"All my fountains are in you."

Do No Harm

Introduction

THIS ESSAY, BASED ON an address to a consultation of the United Methodist General Board of Global Ministries in 2023, will explore the relationship between two concepts critical to Christian mission in an age of contested identities: incarnation and culture. In particular, I will assert that God Incarnate is God encultured. And this helps us better understand the ways in which Christians must realize the gospel.

As contemporary philosophers such as Calvin Schrag, Charles Taylor, and Matthew Crawford and many others have noted, our understanding of what it means to be human in the West has undergone a dramatic shift in the last three hundred years. We no longer necessarily understand ourselves in terms of unchanging essences, but in terms of a narrated identity.[1] As importantly, we are deeply conscious that our humanity is held not only, or even primarily, within ourselves. Our humanity is held in the shared social space that creates the possibilities and limits to our life story, as Crawford and Taylor's explorations of modernity demonstrate.[2] And what about beyond the West? We have become aware, or should be aware, that neither prior to nor after the advent of modernity is a Western understanding of what it means to be human normative for all places and times.

The value of the concept of culture is that it provides the framework for understanding these different concepts of what it means to be human, both modern and non-modern.

Under these circumstances we cannot simply reiterate the same old theological anthropology based on the supposedly unchanging essentials of human nature upon which traditional understandings of Incarnation have been based. If we have new understandings of what it means to be human, then at the very least we need new articulations of what it means to say God has come as a human. If cultures vary in their understanding of what it means to be human, then we must recognize the possibility that there can be multiple understandings of what it means to say that God is incarnate in Jesus Christ. And these, if we are honest, will change in the future. Indeed, I've argued elsewhere that the advent of modern medical technology and the rise in AI are creating a sea-change in human self-understandings as profound as those which occurred in earlier epochs in human history.[3] In

---

1. Schrag, *Self After Postmodernity*.
2. Taylor, *Secular Age*; Crawford, *World Beyond Your Head*.
3. Hunt, "AI."

short, there is no such thing as a normative theological anthropology, not even and perhaps particularly not from scripture. Because scripture itself contains multiple different cultural understandings of what it means to be human.

If that sounds unsettling, then let us look at the positive side. Out of the possibilities arising when we think of incarnation in relation to culture there grow new possibilities for understanding and enacting our mission within God's Mission in Jesus Christ. We gain a tool for reimagining how the Good News emerges within the shared social space in which the church finds itself today in many places across the globe. I lived most of my life in the twentieth century and most of my academic career with twentieth century theology. I do not regret leaving both behind if it will help us better serve the gospel in this century, and in these places and times.

The Inheritance of the Past

One aspect of the old theological anthropology that has been consequential for Christian mission is the idea of *distance* between God and humanity. Mission was built, in part, on the idea of a boundary-crossing God who then sends the church on a boundary-crossing mission. As we used to sing in my youth group, "He came from heaven to earth to show the way, from the earth to the cross our souls to save, from the cross to the grave, from the grave to the skies, Lord we lift your name on high."[4]

But does this do justice to the witness of Scripture that the Word became flesh and dwelled among us? It is my belief that our concept of a boundary crossing God is deeply tied to emerging modernity in the West and the formation of the New International order that was so formative of nineteenth century mission. A boundary crossing God was suited to the self-understanding of boundary crossing missionaries and justified both their work and the emergent political order in which it was taking place.

So powerful was the idea of a boundary crossing God that the spatial imagery of a boundary crossing God has become deeply embedded in the contemporary Christian imagination. Thus, it may be difficult to recognize that whatever its past, this imagery may now be out of touch with the worldview of rising generations raised on not only the Copernican view of the universe, but its vast expansion through a series of astronomical discoveries from the nineteenth century onward and the rise of quantum mechanics

4. Founds, "Lord We Lift Your Name on High."

and relativity. Even taking an Enlightenment approach and mapping the physical journey from Heaven to Earth as a conceptual/metaphysical journey from transcendence to Immanence, spatial language may not speak to those for whom the distinction between transcendence and immanence has no meaning. For many inhabitants of our time, and many in cultures far away and long ago, that distinction never made sense. Such philosophical niceties never became part of their imagined world. In short, between quantum entanglement and the death of transcendence, it is not clear how we can imagine a boundary crossing God.

Another burden for contemporary missiology from its storied past is the idea that in the incarnation God privileges the intersection of Jewish religion, Graeco-Roman culture, and the Roman Empire. As recently as Pope Benedict, and still in textbooks on mission used today, there is an effort to associate God's providence with that particular moment in human history where the political Roman Empire intersected Judaism in the context of Greco Roman culture.[5] Supposedly, just that moment in history made available both the ideas and the means to spread them universally that were necessary to God's mission. The same kind of imperial thinking would be found at the beginning of the twentieth century as well. Those promoting global mission would highlight the system of Roman roads, the brilliance of Greek philosophy, and in the modern world the steamship, telegraph, and railroad.

This privileging of Western culture as God-chosen naturally places it at the center of Christian life, and therefore the cultural and social starting point for Christian mission. If one stands in Wesley's chapel, London, and looks out, one finds etched into the glass William Blake's poem "The New Jerusalem," deliciously looking out on Blake's grave in the church yard opposite. If it tells us little of Wesley, it certainly says a lot about his successors. The English dreamed of building the new Jerusalem on their fair isle, and Americans pursued the same dream in New England and points West. They mapped Jesus' call to his disciples to go from Jerusalem to Judea to Samaria and the ends of the Earth with a call to go from their cultural centers of the gospel to other cultures both more distant and different from their own. *But this is a misleading mapping of reality*, and certainly not shared. China, *chung guo,* can be translated "the Middle Kingdom" but only so long as you understand the *middle* means the middle of human civilization and history. A Persian map will put Persia, not the North

5. Ratzinger, "Non-Stop Venture."

Atlantic, in the center. Older Islamic maps revolve around the Ka'ba, while older Christian maps made Jerusalem the center. It is not surprising that when you visit the church of the Holy Sepulcher you can visit not only Golgotha but the original Garden of Eden.

While our public missional theologies often disavow such privilege, the center-periphery framework remains active in the ethos of most Western churches and their successors. Indeed, many continue to believe that Christians can be unified by a central set of structures and beliefs negotiated, documented, and mandated within ecumenical circles. Even our ideas of inclusion and exclusion are based on a center-periphery model. It is hard to escape, and yet I think we need to try.

God Does Not Need to Cross Boundaries

A more positive understanding of incarnation might begin by observing that *in scripture God does not cross boundaries,* because between God and humanity there are no boundaries to cross. God is present everywhere at all times, in all lives and cultures. We too easily forget that the Ptolemaic system that dominated Graeco-Roman and subsequent Western (including Islamic) cosmologies is not biblical but is built on an entirely different set of cultural presuppositions about the ordering of the cosmos. The Bible identifies high places and even the sky as the domain of God, but even that represents the kind of cultural borrowing of which I'll speak in a moment.

It is only later, particularly in the work of Thomas Aquinas, that Christians adopted as doctrine the Ptolemaic system that places the realm of God beyond a boundary of epicyclical realms of increasing perfection culminating in the crystalline spheres of the stars. In Scripture our help may come from the hills, but God is always as close as the Law written on our hearts and the lifeblood that flows through our bodies. God's image is already written into every human's inmost being.

Revelation is not boundary crossing, it is manifestation, it is emergence, it is an event in the inner person and life of the community of those whom the spirit prompts to sight and understanding. God says to Israel through Moses: "Now what I am commanding you today is not too difficult for you or beyond your reach. It is not up in heaven, so that you have to ask, 'Who will ascend into heaven to get it and proclaim it to us so we may obey it?' Nor is it beyond the sea, so that you have to ask, 'Who will cross the sea to get it and proclaim it to us so we may obey it?' No, the word is very near you; it is in your mouth and in your heart so you may obey it" (Deut 30).

The Word did not *travel* to become flesh any more than God's breath *traveled* to enter the living beings at creation. It simply chose to dwell fully, to be fully manifest in a human person. Consider John 1, although we could as easily work through an exegesis of the birth narratives. The author of the gospel writes:

> The true light that gives light to everyone was coming into the world. He was in the world, and though the world was made through him, the world did not recognize him. He came to that which was his own, but his own did not receive him. Yet to all who did receive him, to those who believed in his name, he gave the right to become children of God—children born not of natural descent, nor of human decision or a husband's will, but born of God. The Word became flesh and made his dwelling among us. We have seen his glory, the glory of the one and only Son, who came from the Father, full of grace and truth. (1 John 9–14, NIV)

The Word is coming *into* the world. The Word *becomes* flesh and then *dwells* among us. This is not so much travel as it is manifestation.

But what does this say about culture? "*Becomes flesh and dwells among us*" of necessity meant becoming historical and cultural as well as physical. Flesh, *sarx* in John's gospel, cannot be merely meat, despite the implications of the word incarnation from the Latin. It more clearly references Genesis 1 and the Hebrew word for what emerges when God breaths God's Spirit into Adam. They are *nephesh*. The Word became a living being and all that this entails, which is a person shaped by history, society, and culture. And so perhaps we do need to remind ourselves of the birth narratives, which so clearly place Jesus in a family located in a specific time, place, culture, and society. This is a critical paradox—That in his uniqueness Jesus becomes universal. By becoming culturally located, he becomes like all of us.

God binds God's self to a social location, a history, culture, and a body. That is what it means to be fully human. Yet this act of God in the context of Scripture is radically inclusive. Scripture teaches that God reveals God's self among the nations in many times and places. Just look at the Genesis narratives, or more explicitly Amos 9, where God recounts to Israel how God has providentially guided many nations, not least Israel's rivals. Or as in Psalm 87, which I read at the beginning, we see that the nations of the earth come to Zion with no need to apply for a visa, or even permanent residence. Their names are already recorded as citizens of the realm. Alfred Lord Tennyson got this right when he recounted in his *Mort d'Arthur* the dying king saying to Bedivere, "The old order changeth, yielding place to new, And God fulfils Himself in many ways, Lest one good custom should corrupt the world."

What Incarnation offers is thus not exclusion, but a necessary opportunity for human participation in God's work. The uniqueness of Incarnation affirms that our full humanity, not least our embodiment as determined by social, cultural, historical, and biological environments, can be fit for God's reign. In Christ we can know ourselves once again as children of God, born of water and the spirit, hearing as if for the first time God's call to care for creation, be fruitful and multiply and cover the face of the earth. We can know that our power to participate in God's mission is restored by Christ's defeat of all those powers that hinder us.

God's Mission is Intercultural

But now let me take this a step further. Because we understand our restoration as embracing us as flesh, as historical, cultural, physical creatures, so we can also grasp that the full scope of God's saving work can only be understood interculturally. As understood in scripture, we are, in the flesh, not merely cultural but intercultural beings.

If we look across the scriptural telling of the history of humanity and Israel, we find that it is invariably intercultural. There is never just a single people's group, a single language or culture making its ways through the natural world. Every key moment in Israel's history is an intercultural moment, and Israel itself, like its worship traditions, is shaped by constant interaction with other peoples. Whenever Israel begins to valorize its own purity, prophets like Amos, Isaiah, and Micah arise to remind it that God has been providentially at work in the histories of its rivals and enemies. As the psalmist says, you cannot escape God even if you go to the ends of the earth (Ps 139)! How fascinating that we sometimes believe we can still take God there. Or better, from Isa 19:23:

> In that day there will be a highway from Egypt to Assyria. The Assyrians will go to Egypt and the Egyptians to Assyria. The Egyptians and Assyrians will worship together. In that day Israel will be the third, along with Egypt and Assyria, a blessing on the earth. The Lord Almighty will bless them, saying, "Blessed be Egypt my

people, Assyria my handiwork, and Israel my inheritance." Israel is
not the only nation that is a blessing on the earth.

This intercultural world is also the world of Jesus, not least in his lineage that is filled with those outside Israel's tribes. Jesus constantly comes into contact with Samaritans and Greeks and affirms that they have genuine insight concerning God's reign. Incarnation becomes the ratification and reiteration of the revelation that God is active and present in all cultures and histories in their interaction with one another. Which is to say, in their history, which is always history of intercultural engagement. Nor is God present in some vague metaphysical way or through some hidden providential hand, but in their visible histories, wisdom, and, indeed, capacity to nurture faith.

But if Israel led an intercultural existence, it is only because that is the nature of humanity. We misconstrue the incident at Babel as an inevitable dividing of humankind. It was simply God's way of sending us on our mission. As soon as humans spread out across the earth, they begin bumping into each other, intermarrying, and, in general, sharing their languages, cultures, and worldviews. Israel, with its founders, its prophets, and its kings is the child of Babel. And in the New Testament? Any idea that God's reign was going to be a monoculture was put to rest by the apostles at the council in Jerusalem. The apostolic church is an intercultural church or it is not apostolic.

The Bible, God's Word, comes to us as an intercultural document: words spoken in various dialects of Hebrew rendered in Greek and read in cultural contexts that may have shared the language but not the basic assumptions of the writers. The Bible was born to be translated and was translated as soon as it was born. The Word emerges incarnate among us from the intersection of constantly changing cultures, not by leaping from one fixed cultural location (as if such a thing even existed) to another.

I spent a fair part of my life working on the translation of the Bible into Malay. It was a fascinating and complex process. But most of all it was revelatory. God's Word is not transmitted from one language into another. It emerges through the continual dialogue and intersection of its original cultures and those of its translators. At every step in the translation of Scripture, not only indigenous Christians but also non-Christians play a role. *Language claims us as its own, not the other way around.* As those of us who speak more than one language know, language shapes our self-understanding even as we speak it. I am not, I cannot be the same person when I speak Malay, German, or English. And because I finally learned to read the Bible in Malay, I cannot be the same person I was when I read it only in English. As Lamin Sanneh so brilliantly demonstrated, God's Word emerges in the process of translation, at the intersection of cultures.

But if language claims us as its own, so does the totality of our embodied, encultured life. And indeed, being embodied and being encultured are inseparable. And this is the reason that in a time of intense cultural change and intercultural engagement our identities are so often contested. Whatever accommodations a culture or subculture may have made to the varieties of embodied human living, they are being challenged by the confluence of resistance to cultural change and the presence of multiple cultural understandings of what it means to live out an embodied life. Going further, and returning to Schrag's analysis, we see how emergent narratives of human identity challenge efforts to maintain a single narrative account of what it means to be human.

We find ourselves once again at Babel, with desperate efforts to shore up the walls that both protect whatever monoculture we desire and also prevent us from engaging in Christian mission.

The Way Forward in Mission

We now live in a time when the illusions of monocultures can be sustained only by voluntary ignorance and political manipulation. The idea that God's Word crosses cultural boundaries, while it was once a revolutionary improvement in mission theology, now seems naive. The Gospel does not travel, it becomes manifest in the process of evangelization—bearing witness to God's reign in constant dialogue with those being invited to take their place in it at the intersections of multiple cultures.

So *kerygma* is not just dogma, and *euangelizomai* is not just talking. They are participation in God's reign in ways that create the opportunity for Incarnation to be recognized and affirmed by faith. The apostles themselves did not know the meaning of Incarnation until they engaged in and were transformed by intercultural mission. *Intercultural dialogue turns out to be the essence of obedient witness: it is not the transmission of the gospel; it is the way we learn the gospel.*

And this makes us all missionaries in our time, because we all live at the intersection of multiple cultures in which God is not yet incarnate. And this, in closing, presents these challenges:

1. We must become self-consciously intercultural people if we are to become an incarnational presence in the world.

2. We will need to broaden our understanding of revelation. We'll need to recognize that God makes Godself known in culture, and with it, religion, as much as in the natural world and the reasoning capacity of the human mind. We need to take on board Georgia Harkness's hymn, "this is my home, the country where my heart is; here are my hopes, my dreams, my holy shrine: but other hearts in other lands are beating, with hopes and dreams as true and high as mine." And those other lands may be as close as our next-door neighbor.

3. We must live for a gospel that is continually emergent rather than merely being passed on. Jesus tells us that new wine needs new wine skins. In Austria, late summer is the beginning of the season for harvesting grapes. When the *trauben saft*, the grape juice, begins to ferment it lets off carbon dioxide. One can find this fermenting wine, called *stürm*, sold on the roadside in half gallon jugs. They are covered with aluminum foil attached by a rubber band, and into the foil, holes are punched to let out the gas. Because otherwise they explode. Some of us are quite fond of the metaphor of holding the treasure of the gospel in earth vessels, as Paul writes to the Corinthians. I'll remind us that even after two thousand and one hundred years what we hold in earthen pots is new wine, still alive and active. If we get broken it's likely because we tried to contain it in our dogma and our ritual and it blew its way out.

4. We need to cultivate the skills for intercultural living:

    i. We need to make cultural intelligence part of every program of Christian preparation for witness.

    ii. We need to adopt an emotional toolkit that helps us see that all emotions are created, as Batja Mequita says, *Between Us*.[6] They do not exist apart from a social, cultural, and situational context. Feelings are dance with different steps in different cultures—and we may need to learn more steps than we know.

---

6. Mesquita, *Between Us*.

    iii. We need to grasp, as James Fowler and others have shown, that faith, just like morals and the intellect, develops as humans mature.[7]

    iv. And finally, we need to recognize that identity is created by the stories we tell with others about ourselves. That it is narrative not essentialist, and that the church in mission must provide the space for many different narratives to unfold.

But these are only a basis for what is most important, a willingness for dialogue and commitment to the emergence of God's incarnate word among us. Dialogue, even in the hardest of conflicts, is the ultimate expression of "hope in things unseen." We carry out dialogue because of our confidence that the gospel will emerge between us in a way that it has never before existed within us.

5. In her brilliant song, *The Joke*, Brandy Carlile sings of those who oppress and exclude: "Let 'em laugh while they can, Let 'em spin, let 'em scatter in the wind, I have been to the movies, I've seen how it ends, And the joke's on them."[8]

Well, it was not in the movies, but we know how it ends (Rev 21:22–26).

> I did not see a temple in the city, because the Lord God Almighty and the Lamb are its temple. The city does not need the sun or the moon to shine on it, for the glory of God gives it light, and the Lamb is its lamp. The nations will walk by its light, and the kings of the earth will bring their splendor into it. On no day will its gates ever be shut, for there will be no night there. The glory and honor of the nations will be brought into it (NIV).

Is it not the task of Christian mission to play our role in affirming that the glory and the honor of the nations of the earth is brought into God's reign?

In the book of Matthew, Jesus gives Peter, the representative of the apostolic church, the keys to the reign of God and tells him that what he binds on earth will be bound in heaven, and what he loses on earth will be loosed in heaven. Given that God's reign is a place where the gates will never be shut, then we who hold the keys must make sure they are always open to everyone.

---

7. Schweitzer and Fowler, *Stages of Faith*.
8. Carlile, "The Joke."

Bibliography

Carlile, Brandi, "The Joke." On *By the Way, I Forgive You*. (e2017e).
Crawford, Matthew. *World Beyond Your Head: On Becoming an Individual in an Age of Distraction*. New York: Farrar, Straus & Giroux, 2015.
Founds, Rick. "Lord We Lift Your Name on High," 1989e.
"AI: Human Authenticity in an AI World." In *Interfaith Encounters* podcast, S9:E8. December 2, 2023.
Mesquita, Batja. *Between Us: How Cultures Create Emotions*. New York: Norton, 2022.
Ratzinger, Joseph A. "Paul: Non-Stop Venture for the Sake of the Gospel." *L'Osservatore Romano*, September 3, 2006.
Schrag, Calvin O. *The Self After Postmodernity*. New Haven: Yale University Press, 1997.
Schweitzer, Friedrich, and James W. Fowler, eds. *Stages of Faith and Religious Development: Implications for Church, Education, and Society*. New York: Crossroad, 1991.
Taylor, Charles. *A Secular Age*. Cambridge, MA: Belknap, 2007.
Tennyson, Alfred Lord. "Morte d'Arthur." In *Poems*, vol. 1, 145–52. London: Moxon, 1842.

6

Fensham's Theology in a Dialogue with a Theology of Han

Bong-Chan Ko

Introduction

NOT HAVING PREVIOUSLY PARTICIPATED in the great academic exercise of writing a Festschrift, I was unsure how to approach the task. Usually, when faced with such uncertainty, one of my first calls is to the person who has been my mentor and professor since I first became involved in the academic arena. However, because Dr. Charles Fensham is the honoree of this magnificent project, it would have been a little strange to ask his advice on how to proceed.[1] So instead I did the work that I have learned from Dr. Fensham over the past eleven years: research. This chapter is the fruit of that research into Fensham's academic achievements from my Korean theological perspective. Yet what follows is not solely an academic review, but also reflects my personal experience with him. Over the past decade, Fensham has greatly shaped my faith and theology. His abiding concern for

---

1. Dr. Charles Fensham was my advisor in the MDiv degree program (2013–2017) and later the supervisor of my PhD (2017–2024). As my program advisor, he offered insightful counselling and guidance as I prepared to become an ordained minister of The Presbyterian Church in Canada. As my doctoral supervisor, he provided me with the precise direction and expert guidance I needed to complete my dissertation successfully.

people who are suffering, and his expert insights, allowed me to pursue my doctoral program with intellectual enthusiasm as well as develop a deep concern for the vulnerable in the world through my pastoral ministry. In this chapter, I explore Fensham's theology, in particular his missiology and contextual theology, in light of his strong orientation toward love and justice. Further, I evaluate Fensham's theology from my Korean perspective, bringing it into a dialogue with a theology of *han* so that I can make the argument that his theology of love and justice has been shaped by his *han*-like experience.

Fensham's Theology of Love and Justice

Mission as Penance

The title of Fensham's latest book, *Misson as Penance*, gives us a glimpse into how he understands mission. For Fensham, Christian mission is the penitential posture of Christian communities toward the world God creates. He points out that the concept of mission as penance originated in Johan Bavinck's claim that "mission is the penance of the church before God and humankind," and that he has long wrestled with the idea of mission as penance in his own context and time.[2] Fensham considers Bavinck's concept of missional penance as a possible direction for missiology. However, he is well aware of both the Eurocentric bias, which is deeply ingrained in Bavinck's work *Introduction to Science of Missions*, and the limitations of Bavinck's approach to theological concepts, such as his use of scriptural passages as proof texts and his understanding of mission history.[3]

Fensham's understanding of mission as penance crystallized and developed through the influences of his four South African mentors: David Bosch, Nico Smit, Willem Saayman, and Albert Nolan. This understanding, he says, "is reflected in David Bosch's 'bold humility,' in Nico Smit's sacrificial self-giving life in the face of apartheid, in Willem Saayman's unflinching commitment to mission as humanization, and in Albert Nolan's humanity and his life engagement with the poor."[4] Of all of the above, David Bosch,

---

2. Fensham, *Mission as Penance*, xv.

3. When comparing Bavinck's theological methods with those of Bosch, Fensham follows Bosch in terms of theological and missiological concepts. See Fensham, *Mission as Penance*, 5–18.

4. Fensham, *Mission as Penance*, 17.

Fensham's thesis director, has had the greatest influence on Fensham's theological development of the idea of mission as penance. According to Fensham, penitential mission is one of the key themes of Bosch's missiology. For Bosch, mission is a "bold engagement with the world in the name and Spirit of Christ" and requires a deep sense of humility and repentance.[5] In fact, Bosch's understanding of mission as "a bold humility—or a humble boldness" is treated as an important evangelical and dialogical aspect of mission in *Transforming Mission*.[6] Bosch uses this concept to convey vulnerability, conviction, and commitment, which are the essential characteristics of Christian mission in the encounter with different religions. He argues, for example, that "true repentance and humility are cleansing experiences which lead to renewal and renewed commitment."[7] Even though the concept of mission as penance can be traced back to Bavinck's missiology, it is believed that Bosch's idea of mission in a bold humility serves as the real theological foundation for Fensham's understanding of mission as penance.[8]

Fensham employs the concept of mission as penance as a lens through which he can examine the unsettling instances of mission gone wrong in the context of the Canadian churches, such as the violent and dark history with the Indigenous people of the nation and the harm done by numerous Christian churches to sexual and gender minorities. For Fensham, penance is not a display of guilt, melancholy, or self-flagellation; rather, it is a concrete and concerted action that always comes after acknowledging harms done in the past and harm still being done. He argues that penance as an act of communal responsibility entails relational accountability to our neighbors and all creation, a daily resistance to indifference and cynical hopelessness, and ultimately an ongoing participation in God's ministry of renewal.[9] As the Christian communities carry out their mission in shame and penance, the world witnesses the transformation of sadness, brokenness, and hopelessness into joy, healing, and reconciliation. Consequently, Fensham's missiology is a theological journey seeking a consistent commitment to mission as penance before God and the world.

---

5. Fensham, *Mission as Penance*, 5.

6. Bosch, *Transforming Mission*, 501.

7. Bosch, *Transforming Mission*, 497.

8. Saayman and Kritzinger also encapsulate the concept of "mission in a bold humility" in the title of their Festschrift dedicated to Bosch: *Mission in Bold Humility*. See Saayman and Kritzinger, *Mission*.

9. Fensham, *Mission as Penance*, 216–18.

Do No Harm
Contextual Theology in Bold Humility

Fensham's theological interest concerns the way the church engages with the world in our time and place, and what the Christian faith can tell us about that. He expresses this interest in his book *Mission as Penance*, saying, "this book seeks to bring together the pieces of my ongoing theological struggle with context, identity, and Christian faith."[10] In this sense, his theology is not only missiology but also contextual theology. Since his move to Canada in 1988, his theological and missiological context has been Canada and the Canadian Protestant churches, particularly his own denomination, The Presbyterian Church in Canada. He has brought various theological approaches—including feminist, liberation, and postcolonial—into his scholarly work for Canadian Christian communities. However, his theological boundary has not been limited to Canada. He has conducted his theological and missiological work with diligence, being mindful of all the churches in North America and, by extension, the churches across the world.

The first fruit of Fensham's theological engagement with his context is the book *Emerging from the Dark Age Ahead: The Future of the North American Church*, published in 2008. In this work, richly informed by extensive and profound scholarship, Fensham undertakes diverse theological and missiological engagements with the society and culture around us in light of the immense social and technological challenges we face. In both his meticulous analysis of North American society and culture and his constructive but creative suggestions for the church he has a prophetic voice, yet he never loses sight of humility. He speaks prophetically about the opportunities and dangers of massive change in our consciousness as the "dark age ahead" approaches.[11] He points out that we, the Christian church, have fundamentally lost "memory, wisdom, meaning, and moral ethics related to the reign of God and the vision of the restoration of God's creation" in the face of the dark age.[12] We need to rethink where we come from, where we are, and ultimately where we are going. Fensham further

---

10. Fensham, "Preface," *Mission as Penance*, xv.

11. Fensham employs the title of Canadian author Jane Jacob's last book, *Dark Age Ahead* (2004), as his theological metaphor for describing the society, culture, and technologies of the twenty-first century in his own book *Emerging*, 7.

12. Fensham, *Emerging*, 8.

emphasizes that as God's self-giving community of love, we should understand the mission of the church in light of the dialogue of *poiesis* with God through the other.[13]

Fensham's contextual and missiological theology is conducted with the bold humility that his mentor David Bosch greatly stressed. For example, when he analyzes the past of the church, asking where we come from, Fensham emphasizes that we should listen to the Bible attentively and humbly. He points out that there are various ways of reading and interpreting the Bible; that the Bible tells us about diverse communities of interpretation where Christians built memory and meaning and gained hope in life. He thus suggests Bosch's hermeneutic as one way of interpreting the Bible so that the church might grasp a missional understanding of God. Even though he seems to lean on his mentor's missional hermeneutic, he never says that is the only way to grapple with the hermeneutical problem. Instead, Fensham attempts to evaluate Bosch's theological and missiological approach to the interpretation of the Bible critically and thoroughly with respect and humility. Moreover, he fair-mindedly addresses some of the criticisms levelled at Bosch's ideas and emphasizes that Christian communities in North America would benefit from using Bosch's missional hermeneutic to better understand the shifting multicultural context, the numerous marginalities living within that context, and the radicalized culture that modernity has produced. In sum, it is evident that Fensham demonstrates bold humility in his theological practice through his thoughtful evaluation of, and balanced approach to his mentor's theology.

Theology of Love and Justice

Fensham is one of a few systematic theologians to focus profoundly on Christian mission.[14] His enthusiasm for ecclesiology, which subsequently intersects with missiology and ecology, was fostered and shared during his years at Knox College, Toronto.[15] How then might we describe Fensham's theology? What words can best characterize it? What is the primary orientation of his theology? It is difficult to fully answer these questions, even to define what his theology is like, because his theology is not yet complete

---

13. Fensham, *Emerging*, 192–93.
14. Seitz, "Mission as Penance," 462.
15. Effa, "Foreword," xii.

and is still evolving. Nevertheless, we can discern the themes of love and justice that run through his work.

Love and justice are the two pillars of Fensham's theology. These two words are inseparable in his works. Love in Fensham's theology is deeply rooted in the self-giving love of God and is toward neighbors, the church, and the world God creates. Justice in his theology is not about making people feel guilty or about individual repentance. Instead, his concept, which is closely associated with God's liberating and restorative justice, aims at the full awareness and transformation of the social, political, and cultural systems that destroy God's people and creation. Therefore, for Fensham, love and justice have to do with Christian integrity.[16] His abiding theological and missiological concern for those who are marginalized, suffering, and facing discrimination results from his compassionate love and justice.

Love, for Fensham, is not just a sentiment but something expressed in concrete action. His understanding of love has developed concretely and thoroughly over numerous theological works. It seems clear to me, at least, that Fensham holds that Christian love is and should be deeply grounded in the self-giving love of the triune God. He understands Christian mission as God's gracious and loving mission for humankind and all creation.[17] He then argues that the church and its leadership (ecclesiology), its mission to the world (missiology), and its responsibility for the whole creation (ecology) should be accessible to God's self-giving love, which binds us in a profound unity of the community of healing, reconciliation, and transformation.

Moreover, according to Fensham, God's self-giving love reminds us that pain and suffering are part of our task. Fensham's theological and missional focus is on the poor, the marginalized, the discriminated against, and the oppressed. One of his greatest theological contributions to those who are suffering is the book *Misguided Love: Christians and the Rupture of LGBTQI2+ People*, published in 2019. In this book, Fensham traces the tragic history of harm done to sexual and gender minorities by Christian communities and examines the Christian teachings that have caused damage through a particular Protestant Reformed perspective. The book stems not only from his theological concern for sexual and gender minorities, who have been subjected to a wide range of discriminatory and hateful words and deeds in Christian communities, but also from his compassionate love

---

16. Fensham, *Mission as Penance*, 38–44.
17. Fensham, *Emerging*, 17.

for those minorities and all Christian communities, even non-affirming ones. In the introduction to the book, Fensham makes this clear:

> Non-affirming Christian teaching and behavior has caused and still causes great harm to sexual and gender minority people. There is no unambiguous Christian scriptural base for maintaining Christian non-affirming attitudes and teaching. This . . . is particularly important in the light of the Gospel witness to Jesus' teaching about the central interpretive principle of the scriptures—love God and neighbor.[18]

His theology is therefore profoundly directed by compassionate love, which is grounded in God's self-giving love. As mentioned previously, for Fensham love is not just an emotion. Love should be demonstrated in concrete and practical action, which is closely related to his understanding of justice. Since his theology is centered on Canada and Canadian Christian communities, Fensham focuses on the Eurocentric cultural arrogance and Christian sense of superiority over other religions which are deeply embedded in Canadian Christian mission and theology. In particular, Fensham sees the long and tragic history of harm and abuse directed at the Indigenous peoples of Canada by Christian communities and the government of Canada as a systematic process of injustice. He emphasizes that Christian mission needs to be conducted by doing penance before God and the Canadian Indigenous peoples.[19] He analyzes how the harmful, exploitative events between the Western colonizers and Canadian Indigenous communities were supported by the Christian churches. He thoroughly evaluates important Christian doctrines and concepts, such as the "doctrine of discovery" and the idea of *terra nullius*, which justified Western colonization and led to cultural misunderstandings and exploitation of the Indigenous peoples in Canada.[20] Fensham stresses that Canadian Christian communities should pursue truth and reconciliation before God and Indigenous peoples, not only by repenting of the past and doing penance, but also by learning from and sharing with Indigenous peoples their love of the Creator and their spirituality.[21]

---

18. Fensham, *Misguided Love*, 6.

19. Fensham, *Mission as Penance*, 20.

20. Fensham conducts research on the history of Canadian Indigenous peoples under the title "The Church Doing Penance on Turtle Island." See Fensham, *Mission as Penance*, 19–34.

21. Fensham, *Mission as Penance*, 34.

Returning to *Misguided Love*, it is important to see this book not only as a fruit of Fensham's compassionate love but also as an expression of justice for LGBTQI2+ people. This is because Christian teachings and attitudes that harm fellow human beings because of their sexual orientation or gender identity are not a theological difference of opinion but a matter of justice.[22] It is an act of love and justice to abandon such teachings and attitudes and instead welcome and recognize LGBTQI2+ people as beloved children of God in the body of Christ. This is God's call for a penitential response, and therefore "the penance involves political action both inside the church and in society at large."[23]

Doing justice and loving those who are suffering is not only Fensham's theological focus but also his way of life. He was involved in the struggle for the rights of black South African colleagues who suffered in the face of white supremacy and apartheid. He has demonstrated his compassionate love for Canadian Indigenous peoples and his ongoing concern for their reconciliation through his teachings at Knox College. This was also reflected in his presence at the 1994 General Assembly of The Presbyterian Church in Canada, where a formal apology was presented to Indigenous representatives. He has also stood with those who are harmed and suffering due to their sexual orientation and gender identity, and he has dedicated his life to restoring their rights both inside and outside of the church.

Fensham's theology of love and justice is deeply rooted in his *han*-like experiences. Although *han* is a foreign feeling to Fensham, as a white South African and North American theologian, he grasps *han* theologically and conceptually through his extensive engagements with Korean theology. Thus, his theology of justice and love can be read through the lens of the theology of *han*, which I briefly articulate in the following section.

Fensham in a Dialogue with a Theology of Han

A Theology of Han

It is necessary to briefly explain the concept of *han* and how it has been conceptualized as a method of theological reflection by Korean *minjung* theologians.[24] In the Korean context, *han* is broadly described as

---

22. Fensham, *Mission as Penance*, 37.
23. Fensham, *Mission as Penance*, 43.
24. The word *minjung* can be translated to mean "masses" or "people." However, many

> an accumulation of . . . unresolved resentment against injustices, a sense of helplessness because of the overwhelming odds against one, a feeling of acute pain in one's guts and bowels, making the whole body writhe and squirm, and an obstinate urge to take revenge and to right the wrong.[25]

In practice, the word is often considered untranslatable and is best viewed as an emotional state that combines grief, anger, and resentment at injustice. Likewise, *han* is understood culturally, philosophically, and theologically as a unique concept, one which plays a pivotal role in explaining *minjung* suffering in Korea. The concept has been shaped as a unique phenomenon in traditional and modern Korean thought and is developed in many pieces of Korean literature. Korean *minjung* theologians, including Suh Nam-Dong, Suh Kwang-sun, and Kim Jung-Jun have employed the concept of *han* as their theological lens for reinterpreting the experiences of oppression and suffering of the Korean *minjung*. They understand *han* in terms of three dimensions: feelings, social energy for change, and an interpretive event.

First, *minjung* theologians understand *han* as an underlying feeling of the Korean *minjung*, caused by and accumulated through experiences of suffering. *Han* is anger and sadness turned inward. It is a feeling of defeat, resignation, resentment, helplessness, and nothingness. Like these negative human feelings, *han* is primarily rooted in Korean cultural traditions such as folklore, shamanism, and literature. *Han* is not just a one-time psychological response to oppression and unjust treatment but an accumulation of such feelings and experiences. Suh Kwang-sun describes *han* in this way: "the feeling of *han* is not just an individual feeling of repression . . . this is a collective feeling of the oppressed. . . . [T]he feeling of *han* is an awareness both at an individual psychological level as well as at a social and political level."[26] Second, *minjung* theologians discover that the individual *han* manifest in the suppressed, amassed, and condensed experience of oppression can appear as a collective *han* that ultimately leads to a social movement. For example, Suh Nam-Dong, a prominent *minjung* theologian, does not see *han* just as dominant feelings, such as defeat, resignation, and nothingness, but rather "a feeling with a tenacity of will for life which comes to

---

minjung theologians regard this translation as inadequate. I expounded on its meaning in terms of Korean political and socio-economic background and analyzed its linguistic, cultural, and historical characteristics in my doctoral dissertation. See Ko, "Vulnerability of God," 50–62.

25. Yoo, *Korean Pentecostalism*, 221.
26. Suh, "Biographical Sketch," 25.

weaker being."²⁷ That is, collective *han* carries the energy for revolution and social transformation. In this sense, many rebellious movements in Korean history, such as the March First Movement in 1919 and the April Student Revolution of 1960, can be understood as manifestations of the social energy of *han*. Lastly, *minjung* theologians take on the concept of *han* as their hermeneutical lens for interpreting the experiences of *minjung* suffering. According to Moon Dong-Hwan, *han* not only provides communal energy for social change but also allows the *minjung* to anticipate a new history, bringing them to a mysterious encounter with God.²⁸ Through their *han*, the *minjung* can then experience God, who is transcendent over the *minjung* themselves and, at the same time, presents in *minjung* suffering.

For *minjung* theologians, the concept of *han* can be conceptualized as a method of theological reflection in the way that its three characteristics, as described above, integrate with the understanding of the *han* of Christ. The concept is thus primarily embedded in the experience of *han*, as I will now briefly articulate.²⁹ First, the theology of *han* arose and developed within the experience of *minjung* suffering. *Minjung* theologians, particularly Suh Nam-Dong, bring the concept into Christian theology by examining its meaning and implications for the *minjung* in light of the Christ event, more precisely the cross. In the theology of *han*, Christ's suffering points to Christ's *han*, which is linked to God's *han*. The experience of *han* is then related to soteriology. God's *han* revealed in Christ's *han* is with those who experience *han* for the sake of their liberation from *han*. Paradoxically, liberation from *han* does not come from the power of the omnipotent and omniscient God, but through the humble presence of the suffering and vulnerable God within the reality of *han*, since the *minjung* perceive the divine vulnerability through their own *han*. In this way, God's *han*ful presence is soteriological.

The theology of *han* primarily focuses on the *han* of Christ. Jesus' suffering and death on the cross caused his *han*. However, not only the crucifixion but also the entire life of Jesus Christ is full of *han*. His many years of suffering from humiliation, mockery, false accusations, and religious inquisitions are a profound source of *han*. In terms of the trinitarian relationship, we can say that God also experiences *han* through Jesus' *han*ful life

---

27. Suh, "Towards a Theology of *Han*," 58.
28. Moon, "Korean Minjung Theology," 5.
29. For the framework of *han* as a method of theological reflection, see Ko, "Vulnerability of God," 194–99.

and death. God's *han* expresses God's vulnerability to the creation in loving solidarity. For the *minjung*, this is perceivable. They understand the Christ event as an event of *han*. Through this event of *han*, the *minjung* recognize the divine vulnerability, as God voluntarily opens Godself to the world of *han* in love. This is a result of the vulnerable nature of divine love. Likewise, Christ's *han* leads us to a deeper understanding of the divine attribute of God's vulnerability. Therefore, by translating Christ's suffering as Christ's *han*, the theology of *han* shows us how God reveals God's vulnerability through God's *han*.

Likewise, these three lenses of theological reflection are linked to one another and function holistically. The characteristics of *han* can illuminate why and how the experience of *han* might be seen as the experience of Christians, whereas the experience of *han* brings specificity and actuality to the characteristics of *han*. Further, the experience of *han* can assist us in perceiving the experience of Christ's *han* as ours, while Christ's *han* can serve as a lens through which we can bind our human *han* to divine *han*. Therefore, this theology of *han* can provide a fresh lens through which we can read Fensham's theology anew.

*Han*ful Experience in Fensham's Theology

In this section, rather than assessing Fensham's theology critically, I will attempt to discover potential areas for constructive dialogue between his theology and the theology of *han*. Before moving on, it is important to clarify that, despite his understanding of the Korean concept of *han* that derives from his academic career, I do not think Fensham himself perceives or recognizes the *han* within him. Nevertheless, from my Korean perspective, *han* is embedded and perceivable in both Fensham's experience and theology.

As a gay person, Fensham experienced *han* throughout his life. The following description is his account of one tragic experience:

> This was not the first time I encountered a suicide of a gay person in my ministry. As a young pastor, one of my best friends, a brilliant philosophy professor at the local Roman Catholic seminary, committed suicide by jumping off a high-rise building. He could no longer live with the dissonance between what his church taught and his deep love for a man. Years later I would find myself standing at the edge of a lake in Northern Ontario contemplating a plan

to take my own life. I had been overcome by the same despair, inculcated by the teaching of my church, which became psychologically internalized as self-hatred.[30]

Although he does not use the term *han* when recounting his experience, Fensham appears to have experienced something similar to what many *han*-ridden individuals go through. Not only did he witness the horrific events of many of his LGBTQI2+ colleagues and friends committing suicide, but he himself was pushed to the point of almost following suit. Since Fensham was fully aware of the long-term existence of homophobia throughout Christian history, this was not a one-time event, and his feelings were not simply a one-time psychological response to a dreadful situation. As he clearly states, "this shared experience of homophobia and the way it becomes psychologically internalized, infecting society, including sexual and gender minority people, has a long history within Western Christianity that can be traced back to the journey of Christianity into Greco-Roman culture."[31] His suffering intensified over the course of his life, was internalized psychologically, and eventually developed into self-hared. I argue from my Korean perspective that this ultimately represents a *han* experience. Likewise, *han* as a negative feeling often drives the *han*-ridden to devastating outcomes, such as suicide.

However, Fensham's response was different. He realized that many sexual and gender minority people like him have suffered tremendously because of Christian doctrine, and, as an ordained minister and theologian, he has dedicated his life to standing in solidarity with them and to changing the Christian teaching that causes and justifies great harm. For Fensham, this is not a matter of theological debate but a matter of "Gospel witness to Jesus' teaching about the central interpretive principle of the scripture— Love God and neighbor."[32] Here, we have a glimpse of Fensham's *han* as social energy for transformation. His *han* as a negative feeling has been transformed into *han* as social energy to challenge and change homophobic Christian teachings and attitudes. During his twenty-five-year service as a member of the Committee on Church Doctrine of The Presbyterian Church in Canada, he has striven to change the denominational position that denies the rights of LGBTQI2+ people, and more importantly, he has challenged the objectification of people in theological debate, which,

30. Fensham, *Mission as Penance*, 36.
31. Fensham, *Mission as Penance*, 36.
32. Fensham, *Misguided Love*, 6.

by justifying harm done to fellow human beings, dehumanizes them.[33] In response, he published *Misguided Love: Christians and the Rupture of LGBTQI2+ People* in 2019. This book is the outcome of a long theological and spiritual journey of reflection on the suffering (*han*) of sexual and gender minority people, including himself, in Christian history. The most noteworthy thing that happened in his *han*-ful experience is that his *han* ultimately led him to seek the grace of God. In the very last section of *Misguided Love*, he states:

> When we deal with the affirmation of sexual and gender [minority] people, we are not dealing with a tension between justice, love and doctrine. We are dealing with a call to reflect the glory of God in pastoral grace extended to all in God's community of sinners in justice and love . . . If we are to glorify God in our faithful covenanted erotic relationships, we would have to find the grace to live out our relationships with suffering anguish and patience.[34]

From the *han* that drove him to utter despair, Fensham not only discovered a social energy that would transform that hopeless situation, but *han* also ultimately led him to seek the glory of God's grace. This is one of the most significant aspects of *han*, which is a revelatory event. *Minjung* theologians discover that the *minjung* perceive God through their *han*. They encounter a suffering and vulnerable God in their *han*. In the presence of the suffering and vulnerable God, the *minjung*, as *han*-ridden, experience liberation from their suffering and *han*.[35] Through the liberating event of *han*, they realize that they are accepted into God's gracious community, and, as Fensham rightly observes, find grace to live out their relationship with *han* (suffering anguish and patience). Likewise, Fensham demonstrates his deep empathy for the suffering (*han*) of the sexual and gender minorities through his own *han*ful experience and suggests how they might encounter the grace of the suffering and vulnerable God within their *han*.

Another crucial point where Fensham's theology resonates with the theology of *han* is in a Christian response to ecological crises. The theology of *han* not only addresses human *han* and the oppressive and exploitative systems that cause *han* in their lives, but it profoundly focuses on the *han* of the world and the destructive human involvement that causes ecological

---

33. Fensham, *Mission as Penance*, 37.
34. Fensham, *Misguided Love*, 248.
35. For an articulation of how the concept of *han* plays a role as a revelatory event that reveals a suffering and vulnerable God, see Ko, "Vulnerability of God," 82–86.

crises. In the theology of *han*, humankind and the natural world are mutually related and interdependent in God's creation. Like Suh's claim that everything in nature is woven into a web, the interrelatedness of God's creation shows that just as God's *han* is interconnected with human *han* in Christ, human *han* is inextricably linked to the *han* of the world.[36] The theology of *han*, for example, can interpret Romans 8:19–23, which describes the groaning of the whole creation, as the manifestation of the *han* of the creation, yearning for God's redemption in Christ alongside the children of God. Then, from the perspective of a theology of *han*, we can understand that as a result of the fall of humanity, the natural world suffers and accumulates *han* in the same way we do.

Fensham has engaged profoundly in the theological discourse on ecology. In his most recent work, *Mission as Penance*, he devotes one section to introducing his monographs on ecological issues in detail. He is well aware of the interrelatedness and interdependence of God's creation when he states, "in Gen 3 the brokenness of creation is introduced and it is clear that it is *human* brokenness."[37] Further, in an exploration of the relation of sin to ecology, he observes that our understanding of human sin is closely linked to our response to the suffering of the natural world.[38] In fact, human sin is essentially connected, not only to the cause of human *han* but also to the *han* of the world which has resulted from the global ecological crisis. Therefore, the way we understand human sin greatly affects our approach to the world's *han*. Fensham's emphasis on reframing the understanding of sin in terms of ecology points precisely to the possibility that we can engage with the ecological crisis in light of *han*.

Moreover, Fensham highlights that we need to reread and reimagine the biblical stories when engaging with the ecological issues in our present context. For instance, using Sally McFague's metaphor, he suggests that an image of creation as a child of God is one that may be used for the healing of creation.[39] Thus, rereading the biblical texts ecologically plays a crucial role in both understanding the creatures and the creation of God in order to respond to their suffering. In a similar way, rereading the stories of suffering in the Bible in light of *han* is crucial for understanding the *han* of

---

36. Suh, "자연에 관한 신학" ("Theology about Nature"), 91. Suh's theological interest in ecology began with his concern for the suffering of the *minjung*.

37. Fensham, *Mission as Penance*, 199.

38. Fensham, *Mission as Penance*, 174.

39. Fensham, *Mission as Penance*, 191.

the world and the groaning of the natural world. In other words, Fensham's eco-missiology and the theology of *han* have much in common in terms of rethinking and re-feeling our nature and destiny ecologically. Then, in order to build a constructive conversation between Fensham's eco-missiology and the theology of *han*, we might ask: What is eco-missiology, and how does it address the problem of the world's *han*? At the same time, in what way does the idea of *han* serve ecology, and what is the missional aspect of the theology of *han*?

As discussed above, Fensham's theology and experience can be read in light of *han* and thereby offer a credible way of unpacking the problem of the *han* of humanity and the world. More importantly, his *han*-like experience has led him to stand in solidarity with suffering people and pursue a theology of justice and love.

Concluding Remarks

Some may assess Fensham's work from a distance in a different way, both objectively and critically. However, that is not my job, for in the more-than-ten years I have been beside him I have witnessed his empathy for suffering people and his encompassing and tireless theological efforts on their behalf. In this chapter, I have simply attempted to display some characteristics of Fensham's theology through my Korean lens of *han*. Despite being a white South African and a North American theologian, Fensham has critically evaluated many of the shortcomings in Western theology and creatively reinterpreted and developed them within his own context, particularly in Canada and North America, for the mission of the church. More importantly, by carrying out his theological and pastoral work for the suffering, he has shown that his theology is deeply grounded in God's justice and love. His posture toward theology can be called precisely a bold humility, much as many say of his mentor, David Bosch.

My Korean theology of *han* is the fruit of Fensham's teaching and guidance. Fensham always encouraged me to conduct my doctoral research through the theological lens that I had grown up with and developed in my own soil. Many Korean theological students, including myself, have a tendency to uncritically follow the ideas of prominent Western theologians, such as Augustine, Calvin, and Barth, and apply them directly to our own context without taking their historical or cultural limitations into consideration. I was naturally imbued with this theological tendency. However,

Fensham's encouragement and his theological discipline challenged this tendency embedded in me and inspired me to see the beauty and creativity that God has infused in everyone, including myself. Fensham's experience and theology are full of *han*. He has not been frustrated by *han* as a negative feeling but has found communal and transforming energy therein. He has channeled that energy into invalidating the Christian teachings that harm many innocent people, including sexual and gender minorities and Canadian Indigenous peoples. Further, his theology points profoundly to the grace of the self-giving loving God who creates, transforms, and sustains all those *han*-ridden in Christ. Therefore, all I can say about him is that Fensham is indeed a person of *han*.

Bibliography

Bavinck, J.H. *Introduction to the Science of Missions*. Translated by David Hugh Freeman. Philadelphia: Presbyterian & Reformed Publishing, 1960.

Bosch, David. *Transforming Mission: Paradigm Shifts in Theology of Mission*. Maryknoll, NY: Orbis, 2011.

Effa, Allan. "Foreword." In *Mission as Penance: Essays on the Theology of Mission in a Canadian Context*, xi–xiii. Eugene, OR: Pickwick Publications, 2023.

Fensham, Charles. *Emerging from the Dark Age Ahead: The Future of the North American Church*. Toronto: Clements Academic, 2011.

———. *Misguided Love: Christians and the Rupture of LGBTQI2+ People*. Atlanta: Journal of Pastoral Care Publications, 2019.

———. *Mission as Penance: Essays on the Theology of Mission in a Canadian Context*. Eugene, OR: Pickwick Publications, 2023.

Ko, Bong-Chan. "The Vulnerability of God as Viewed from a Theology of *Han*: A Constructive Dialogue between Jürgen Moltmann and Suh Nam-Dong." PhD diss., Knox College and University of Toronto, 2024.

Moon, Dong-Hwan. "Korean Minjung Theology." Unpublished manuscript, 1980. Quoted in Jae Hoon Lee, *The Exploration of the Inner Wounds—Han*. Atlanta: Scholars, 1994.

Saayman, Willem, and Klippies Kritzinger. *Mission in Bold Humility: David Bosch's Work Considered*. Maryknoll, NY: Orbis, 1996.

Seitz, Jonathan A. "Mission as Penance: Essays on the Theology of Mission from a Canadian Context, Written by Charles J. Fensham." *Mission Studies* 40.3 (2023) 462–63. https://doi.org/10.1163/15733831-12341935.

Suh, David Kwang-Sun. "A Biographical Sketch of an Asian Theological Consultation." In *Minjung Theology: People as the Subjects of History*, edited by Commission on Theological Concerns of the Christian Conference of Asia, 15–37. Singapore: CTC-CCA, 1981.

Suh, Nam-Dong. "자연에 관한 신학" (Theology about Nature). *Theological Forum* 11 (June 1972) 85–96.

———. "Towards a Theology of *Han*." In *Minjung Theology: People as the Subjects of History*, edited by Commission on Theological Concerns of the Christian Conference of Asia, 47–69. Singapore: CTC-CCA, 1981.

Yoo, Boo-Woong. *Korean Pentecostalism: Its History and Theology*. Studies in the Intercultural History of Christianity. Frankfurt: Lang, 1988.

7

Charles Fensham

Missiologist as Poet[1]

Gregory P. Leffel

I ADMIRE CHARLES FENSHAM for being what I am not so much: empathetic, a world-affirming sensibility that appears to come to him without much effort at all. I must work at it. It helps me to reread his books now and again to restore a measure of empathy to my soul. Charles naturally intuits Creation's feel, the inner qualities of its existence. He catches the metaphysical music that blends the True, the Good, and the Beautiful, that, when arranged delicately by an artist of the soul, resonates with the values, the fullness, the *tremendum* and *fascinans* of Being. Charles's empathy penetrates to the heart of the heart of things. A sensibility that captures reality's resonant vibe. Captures it clearly enough to provide us all with a true sense of place in the cosmos; to sense the cosmos as a hospitable place to dwell

---

1. Charles, a warm congratulations on your retirement! I know that you are ready to move on—I am very happy for you to—but for the rest of us, well, your retirement comes too soon. We will miss you in this phase of your life. I am not sure what we will do without you. You have served the academy long and well, and have run the race with endurance, and I am certain that you will keep running the race to complete your vocation to serve Christ in your next phase. Thank you for your kind friendship over the years. And for being an exceptionally engaged, supportive, brilliant colleague! It has been an honor to write this piece for you—it has blessed me more than you can imagine.

in, and to dwell in it with some degree of confidence. Confident enough to build flourishing worlds and to fill our worlds with compassionate values.

Charles's empathetic art—to harmonize reality's reverberations and to turn the cosmos into a dwelling place for the soul—begins in what he calls *poiesis*: a truth-bearing science, as Aristotle understood it, a mode of human intelligence that draws its power from imagination, and that puts creativity to work to produce a decent world to live in. Charles writes about *poiesis* frequently, thinks about it deeply, marvels at its creative energies. It informs his theology and structures his missiology. *Poiesis* is the bright throughline in his written works. I've not thought much about *poiesis* in the past, especially philosophically. So, it is due time then to walk on the poietic throughline with Charles for a bit, to sort out what I think he means by *poiesis*, and to sort out my own thinking about it.

Not that I am entirely at sea regarding creativity and its power. Charles and I both studied architecture at university. I practiced it for many years in bi-vocational ministry. I *get* creativity: design, aesthetics, and the creative process come naturally to me. I know how to turn a vague idea into a concrete reality—I just never thought of it before as *poiesis*. My experiences give me a phenomenological rather than a philosophical place to start to imagine *poiesis*. But I will try to bring both together to round out my poietic sensibility. *Poiesis* is a productive power and among its powers to produce, Charles writes, is "the production of imagination."[2] My purpose here: To use imagination as creatively as I can to describe *poiesis;* to sketch out how Charles applies *poiesis* to the meaning and function of mission; finally, to draw out Charles's empathetic *poiesis,* and to celebrate, as Charles teaches us to do, the missiologist as poet, and the poetry of mission as doxology.

Poiesis and Imagination

Poiesis (from the ancient Greek root *poieo,* "to make"; the same root for *poetry*) is conceived traditionally as one leg in Aristotle's tripod of "right knowing"—of *science* broadly understood in three registers—alongside the concepts *theoria* and *praxis.*[3] *Poiesis,* the productive science, stands together with *theoria,* the theoretical science, and with *praxis,* the practical

---

2. Fensham, *Mission as Penance,* 119.

3. Fensham draws upon Bosch's treatment—and through him, Stackhouse—to develop the concept *poiesis* in relation to *theoria* and *praxis,* and to draw out its poetic and hermeneutical powers. Fensham, *Mission as Penance,* 118–22; *Emerging,* 24–35.

science: three distinct ways of human knowing that together form a unified whole of human understanding. "The principles of [Aristotle's] division are straightforward," writes Christopher Shields, "theoretical science seeks knowledge for its own sake; practical science concerns conduct and goodness in action, both individual and societal; and productive science aims at the creation of beautiful or useful objects."[4]

Listing these sciences, these three modes of human intelligence, all in a row—variously put historically as *theoria-praxis-poiesis,* reason-ethics-aesthetics, true-good-beautiful, thought-will-feeling—suggests a procession from most to least important. And misses the point: that by necessity we weave wisdom's broadcloth whole from all three sciences at once equally and together. Only the sum of the parts produces true, synoptic, and meaningful understanding. Each science interpenetrates, interrogates, and reinterprets the others, each equally judges the others' veracity.

The Western tradition does, in fact, privilege *theoria* (more on this problem later), fixated as the West is upon discovering theoretical truth and creating knowledge (epistemology). A close second in pride of place, *praxis* is consumed by the West's preoccupation with liberatory freedom (justice). A persistent Western prejudice gives *poiesis* short shrift at the end of the list. A prejudice that judges its products to be artificial, subjective, invented, poetic, ontologically unreal; they are simply made up things, not actual things that can be discovered in the empirical real world. This prejudice treats *poiesis* and its productions as derivative (parasitic) upon *theoria* and *praxis,* as mere applications of them, rather than as elements of their own generative science. Bluntly, that *poiesis'* fruit—its "beautiful or useful objects"—are well fit for the art museum or the workbench, but not for the objective rigor of the laboratory or the court of law.[5]

This is only a modern, Western prejudice, perhaps. It is also a categorical mistake that disparages the role of the unbounded, nonempirical, free, creative imagination in producing human understanding; and a mistake that denigrates the truth-revealing value—the right knowing, the science—embedded in what humans creatively produce. For Aristotle, Shields continues, "the *productive sciences* are mainly crafts aimed at the production of artefacts, or of human productions more broadly construed." A great range

---

4. Shields, "Aristotle." Citation from section 2, "The Aristotelian Corpus: Character and Primary Divisions."

5. On the biased dismissal of culture (civilization, *poiesis* in its widest sense) as artificiality by naturalizing scientific materialists (*theoria*), see Alan Wolfe's chapter, "In Praise of Artifice." Wolfe, *Future,* 30–61.

of productions: for example, "ship-building, agriculture, and medicine, but also the arts of music, theatre, and dance." Less tangible, though coming closer to Fensham's conception of the power of *poiesis*: "Another form of productive science is rhetoric, which treats the principles of speech-making appropriate to various forensic and persuasive settings, including centrally political assemblies."[6] In this last, I think, lies a hint of *poiesis'* function as science: To make a speech is to make a point. To make a point that is forensic and persuasive, is likewise to make it diagnostic and critical. To make such a point publicly reveals one's intention to change public perception, sensibility, consciousness—to change the public's reality itself—in what can be called not just a discursive, but a prophetic mode.

We can ask if political speech is *poiesis* at all, or if it is *praxis* in practice, or whether it flows logically from *theoria's* theories. Or all three: They overlap; that's the point of the tripod of right knowing. Though, each science addresses different objects of analysis from different angles: *Theoria* addresses empirical matters of fact (including ideas in the mind) accessed through physical sensation and mental cognition, disinterestedly described, explained in logical chains of causality, and modeled in logico-mathematical formulae; *praxis* addresses ethics produced from natural law, traditional virtues, or from rational calculation, especially their application to politics and political economy. Both delimit their rationality to their specific objects—epistemology and ethical action—and both reduce realities to what they can perceive or grasp within their given spheres ("sciences") of intelligence.

Poiesis, as I am trying to imagine it, overflows these reductionisms and delimitations on the scope of intelligence. It provides us with an "expanded rationality," a notion that Fensham takes from David Bosch.[7] A rationality that expands human understanding beyond the narrower scopes of *theoria* and *praxis*. Unchained from delimitation, I take *poiesis* to be nothing less than a fullhearted celebration of the *real*; a festival of comprehension that takes reality whole as its object of analysis; a carnival of intuition unbounded, of free-ranging imagination released to interpret the fullness of our sensations of reality as such. Including realities invisible to the other sciences—the quite real but intangible (unmeasurable) qualities of sentient experience: of consciousness, selfhood (the soul); of the sublime, numinous, ineffable, ecstatic; of grace; of love and fear, joy and

6. Shields, "Aristotle"; italics in the original.
7. Fensham, *Emerging*, 30.

happiness; of desire, interest, intention, thus of politics; of the capacity to project a desired future and to will it into existence; to produce something new *ex nihilo*. Imagination fertile enough to project into the mind an image of the cosmic whole—whole in *time* from the before of cosmic beginnings and after the cosmic end, and whole in *space* to the beyond of the boundaries of the outer edge of its cosmic event horizon.

Poiesis speaks in a scientific language all its own to express the otherwise inexpressible: a referential language, set in a universe of symbols, of metaphor and analogy, of dancing movement and musical sound, of textured and colored images—and of words, too, though never reducible to words alone, of drama, tragedy, story, myth. A language of all the things and symbols that point beyond themselves to illuminate the reality of our existence. *Poiesis*' scientific language arranges every symbol and interconnection of symbols in a meaningful order: It produces a semiotic system that renders the fullness of reality full in the fullness of human imagination. A language from which imagination draws to produce the beautiful or useful objects we need to produce a fully real world. A language that sounds like poetry and maybe something more.

It is tempting to conceive of *poiesis*' language and its creative products altogether as poetry itself. I might agree that this is true, but only if *poetry* is abstracted so expansively that it absorbs the meaning of *poiesis* entirely and severs the traditional meaning of *poetry* from its image of the poem. To be a bit technical, I prefer the term *semiotics*—"the semiotics of existence"—more familiar to linguistics and ontology, even urban planning, perhaps, and I would instead use *poetry* as a metaphor for *poiesis*. Though, not unlike poetry (which is itself a poietic production), the language of *poiesis* expresses itself in words and beyond words, in symbols and abstractions, connotations and juxtapositions, ideas and things—especially in concrete, physical things produced in the concrete world through the productive science to meet concrete needs.

Yet, poetry itself is a powerful language. Fensham applies it to the concrete production of meaning—to speak of God, of the gospel, of mission. To speak in a language of poetry, he tells us, means speaking not simply in poems, but in capturing "the music of language and how the creative themes, beat, and energy of language can help us remember, feel, see, dance, act and believe." It can speak, too, in a language without words: "communication that could be silent, graphic, plastic, or the expression of a human face and light in the eyes." Or of a bird's arc of flight, a hemlock's smell, a sand dune's blowing dust (these last, I infer from his sensitive writing on ecology). Poetic language is whole, inclusive, comprehensive; also, tender—indeed, empathetic. "Poetry is the way we grasp truth," Fensham says, "and is the way we live out of it." Importantly, "the gospel comes to us in poetry."[8]

The Integrative Science

Despite its poetic character, *poiesis* is quite concrete in the scope of its objects, constructive in its application. *Production* is the point of it—to turn ideas into materials and performances; to "enflesh" intuitions and sensibilities in beautiful or useful objects; to *integrate* thought into thing. *Poiesis'* symbolic universe provides the semiotic structure upon which our free imaginations draw to invent things that are not there, or not fully there yet and in need of refinement, be they ships, houses, statues, myths, or institutions. Ultimately, *poiesis* integrates its productive intelligence with *theoria* and *praxis* for the singular purpose of constructing a suitable, beautiful world to live in. To produce a "Cosmopolis," Stephen Toulmin called it; the perfect fusion of cosmic vision and the life of the city, the *polis*. The perfect city ancient Greeks labored to construct to make true, good, and beautiful their lives and communities.[9] For the writer of Hebrews, "the city that has foundations, whose architect and builder is God."[10]

Poiesis—as the aesthetic, the beautiful, science—is diagnostic, too. Aesthetics, which I take to be a virtue of *poiesis*, addresses all productions: material (e.g., paintings, buildings, food) and intangible (e.g., music, poetry, rhetoric). Aesthetic judgement assesses their quality of crafting; their fit (consonance) with their purpose; their quality of insight into the purpose of their purpose; the qualities of reality they reveal; and their capacity to resonate with the semiotic universe that *poiesis* renders visible. Beauty attaches to things done well; aesthetics judges how well they are done. To make an aesthetic judgement of a people's productions reveals the people themselves. Citizens may think their cosmopolis a peaceable place and a shining light, or else rotting muck in a cosmos "red in tooth and claw." Either way, their designs, their arts, if done seriously, will reveal their envisioned cosmic reality by how they emphasize production of, say, music or cuisine, or the production of guns and prisons. In this register, aesthetics

---

8. Fensham, *Emerging*, 10–11.
9. Toulmin, *Cosmopolis*; Fensham, *Mission as Penance*, 226.
10. Heb 11:10.

conducts a meta-criticism of the whole *oeuvre* of the people's imaginings, performances, and productions within the bounds of their cosmic reality. Herein, an aesthetic test, and indeed, a prophetic one: If *theoria, praxis,* and *poiesis* together fail to produce a beautiful way of life, then they likely have become *dis*-integrated, the "truth" of one or of all of them called into doubt. In the poetry of things, if it stinks, it's likely rotten.

Fensham says he acquired his appreciation for *poiesis* from David Bosch, his teacher in South Africa. Bosch, Fensham notes, was long troubled by the general reduction of human understanding in western society and church to *theoria* and *praxis* only. Not only this, but troubled by the poor fit between them—their *dis*-integration. Worse yet, by the polarization of *theoria* from *praxis,* epistemology from ethics, fact from value, *is* from *ought*. More to the point, of theology from mission. And Bosch, Fensham says, "considered the tension between practice and theory as best bridged in . . . *poiesis*."[11]

I take Fensham to mean that Bosch first identified and then desired to break up a false and rigorous binary wherein right knowing is reduced to just two of its three registers—to *theoria* and *praxis*. A crippling of the combined powers of the three registers of right knowing: right knowing reduced to a binary of "correct" (abstractly determined) theories/theologies and "correct" (motivationally pure) moral/ethical action. A death-grip on "right" theory and "right" practice not simply captivates the Western mind, but it also drains the world of its *poiesis;* of its human touch; of humanity's intuitive inner consciousness, sensibility, and wisdom; of its collective, creative imagination that is necessary to produce a wholesome, humane existence. "In some ways," Fensham adds, "the central protest of *Transforming Mission* [Bosch's *magnum opus*] is that both orthodoxy and orthopraxy, when made exclusive, miss something critical."[12] The world and the church suffer loss when *theoria, praxis,* and *poiesis* become *dis*-integrated, disconnected—or *poiesis* is effaced entirely as a competent, interpretive, integrative science. They come to "stink," and fail the aesthetic test. Christian mission, if anything, Fensham thinks, is called to *re*integrate the sources of right knowing in the semiotic fullness of the *poiesis* of Creation.

How did we, in the West anyway, manage over time to get to this bifurcated, *dis*-integrated, "poem-less" place? I do not wish to put words in Fensham's mouth (or Bosch's either), but I interpret the situation this way,

---

11. Fensham, *Emerging*, 10.
12. Fensham, *Mission as Penance*, 118.

and I imagine Fensham might agree: that since Nietzsche announced God's death and diagnosed the collapse of Christendom's metaphysical Cosmopolis in the 1880s, Western intellection gradually has reduced its scope to positivist science, to *scientism* (to a barren *theoria*), and to liberatory struggle for social justice (to *praxis*), and to these alone. The death of metaphysics (and of *poiesis*' illumining power along with it) has, as Nietzsche predicted it would, devalued the value of ultimate values and delimited the scope of imagination to the will to power. The West suffers a death of its own—a metaphysical death of transcendence that is memorialized in postmodernism's rejection of meta-narrative's transcendental vision and universal right knowing.[13] Functionally, we are left in a world stripped bare of its vital inner life and of a singular vision to guide it. Stuck in nothing more than a systematically rationalized, globalized, neo-imperialist, capitalist world system—and a failing one at that—and in the agon of globalized struggle for liberation from it.[14] (I will pick this up again, below, regarding Fensham's conception of the "dark age ahead.")

I think it important to note because it is so commonplace, that contemporary fascination with critical theory—with many critical theories addressing many subjects—nicely fits into this reductive, non-*poietic* global reality, though we might ask whether critical theory alone is enough to reintegrate the world. In Max Horkheimer's original conception, critical theory posits a systematic formation of power(s)—a totality, a structure—that overdetermines and distorts our lives, and from which we must liberate ourselves. Theory becomes genuinely *critical* when conscripted for service in the liberatory struggle, and when it is set into a dialectical feedback loop of thought and action to produce a *praxis* of liberation.[15] Horkheimer took industrial capitalism to be the structural totality. Totality—structure—applied in other frames is gendered (patriarchy), racialized (white supremacy), colonialized (Western hegemony). But in whichever direction

---

13. Consider Eagleton's summary of Nietzsche's influence on the postmodern generation: "A lot of postmodern types are Nietzscheans without being aware of it . . . [T]ruth is now a convenient fiction, the unity of the soul is an illusion, power rather than reason rules human affairs, history is a chapter of gruesome accidents and the world is a scene of flux and fluidity without inherent meaning or value." A state of affairs that produced "a culture in which freedom was boundless and thus vacuous, hierarchy was suspect and the very idea of an institution smacked of repression." A situation that produced a politics of fantasy whose "goal was to leap in one bound from a degraded present to a utopian future." Eagleton, "Seeds," 7.

14. Wallerstein, *World Systems*.

15. Horkheimer, "Traditional Theory."

critical theory is taken, it remains trapped in a reduced, two-dimensional, rationality/power, theory/practice model of the world. As such, it frames the world only negatively, as conflict and struggle over-against structural power.

Fensham, as I interpret him, rightly worries that, looking to the future, a singular, negative focus on "the struggle" leaves unresolved the condition of the world that will appear on the day *after* "the revolution"—too often disaster, as history teaches us—because the humane, generative, imaginative *positivity* and world-*producing* integrative power of *poiesis* is absent, forgotten, denigrated, and ignored. Think of revolutions (of France 1789, Russia 1917, China 1949 and the terrors that followed) and then of the poor dog that at last catches the car, never knowing quite what to do with it.

Western societies have managed to strangle the cosmic sublime imagination, disabled their capacity to formulate the common good or to integrate whatever disconnected notions they have of the common good.[16] Social critics call out for "the renewal of utopian energies."[17] Or for at least an approximate vision of a new Cosmopolis; even a foggy one is better than what we have. Not a utopia of mystics and armchair speculators, but of a schematic forward-looking vision that proceeds from *poiesis*, the *productive science*. One that begins with the concrete *now*; that imagines a vision of the possible; that sets it upon the future's horizon; and that grows from the worldly-wise experience that *poiesis* employs to turn human perception into imaginative ideas, into aesthetically coherent productions.

Throughout his work, Fensham gathers up these utopian energies from the gospel itself, from scriptural *poiesis,* from mission's historical engagements with real peoples and their suffering: his bright throughline. He combines them to pull the world back together; to make us comfortably at home again in the cosmos; and to integrate *poiesis* into *praxis* and *theoria* to produce a world scented beautifully enough to pass the "sniff test.

Mission and the Dark Age Ahead

Fensham of course swims confidently in *theoria*'s deep waters; after all, he is an accomplished systematic theologian. He theologizes in service to the creating, redeeming, consummating mission of God, and of God's own *poiesis* in speaking the cosmos into existence and judging the aesthetics

---

16. Sluga, *Politics*.
17. Kompridis, *Critique*, 277; Jameson, "American Utopia."

of the divine production to be very good—beautiful. And for Fensham, liberatory *praxis* is second nature. Early in his career, government agents ransacked his University of South Africa office to "politely invite" him to leave the country or face arrest for his anti-apartheid activism. Particularly, his resistance to conscripting young men into the S.A. Defense Forces to force them to enforce against their fellow citizens the very apartheid system they loathed. Though, I think of Fensham first as a pastor at heart, a scholar-practitioner second.

Fensham's pastoral sensitivity—his empathy—comes through in his recent book *Misguided Love: Christians and the Rupture of LGBTQI2+ People*.[18] His passion and motivation to write the book arose from his being *with* gender minority people; from *accompanying* them in their struggles (the same for his earlier anti-apartheid activism); from *empathizing* with their agony trying to fit together their Christian and gender identities while being othered and abused by their churches; and from their suicides. He writes professionally, politely; underneath it lies smoldering righteous anger at the church's long history of abusing gender minorities, its exclusions, tortures, mutilations, executions, psychological gaslighting, and conversion therapies. He researched thoroughly, argued rigorously *(theoria)*, and placed his book in service of activism, including his own *(praxis)*. But throughout, he hacked his way through a semiotic jungle of false images, twisted symbols, name-calling, manipulated disgust—in short, the dark, perverse poetry that reverses the gospel's life-giving *poiesis* and that turns imagination to the metanarrative production of death—and turns *poiesis* itself into a battleground.

Christian ministry never comes alive in the dark on the barren ice of frozen orthodoxy, of theoretical doctrines and moral policing, of faith and practice turned into already-made-up minds and coerced obligation. It comes alive when thawed out and illuminated among living people living real lives: When they freely imagine how life might work in the reign of God and apply genuine creativity to produce concrete realities that reflect it. To produce realities that reflect God's love beautifully enough to smell right. When Fensham says that *poiesis* is the missing ingredient between right belief and right action, I take him at his word and assume that he means it with deadly seriousness. Because without it, or when it is distorted, thought

---

18. Fensham, "Penace Before Those Who Are not Heterosexual or Cisgender," *Mission as Penance*, 35–48.

and action produce suffering and death—produce *real* traumatized and dying human beings and dying ecosystems.

"Our knowing and doing involve and evolve in the person," he says, "in relationship, empathy, awareness, and aesthetic grasp with others and God. That growth in insight, awareness, and motivation to action is facilitated by the integrative role of *poiesis*."[19] There always must be a morally-tender, intuitively sensitive, humane center to judge beliefs and ethics, especially when both are tightly bound up in traumatizing histories and oppressive traditions. "I would thus associate *poiesis*," Fensham writes,

> with all forms of imaginative production of the faith community that leads to wise action for the flourishing and liberation of God's people and creation. This use of *poiesis* . . . will allow faith communities to address the development of false binaries between thinking and doing, doctrine and justice, and obedience and love . . . thus to push further the idea that our knowing as Christians should be considered as an integrated cycle of imagining, doing, and thinking in growing motivation for action . . . facilitated by the integrative role of *poiesis*.[20]

Twice I have just quoted Fensham's phrase, "the integrative role of *poiesis*" to make the point, emphatically, that to restore *poiesis* restores *the one and only register* of human knowing that keeps human knowing humane. Humaneness, it appears, has gone into hiding these days or else died on the side of the road amid polarized politics, threatened identities, neo-nationalisms, neo-authoritarianisms, and the reduction of people to units of economic production. Or humaneness simply lost its lifeforce to the astringent soullessness of a West that has lost its feeling for the human, and in its absence has fallen irresistibly into the metaphysically frozen ditch of theoretical scientific materialism, intransigent contests for socio-political power, and data-driven, profit-obsessed, techno-corporate control. A frozen ditch wherein the West has created its own contemporary, modern, "advanced" tripod of right knowing to "update" Aristotle's ancient one: A new, skeletal tripod of physics (theory), power (practice), and property (production, reduced to capitalist production). It portrays a hard and harsh reality. In its bareness the modern tripod provides only a stripped-down science of human understanding; and this is all we have left to produce our

---

19. Fensham, *Mission as Penance*, 122.
20. Fensham, *Mission as Penance*, 121–22.

home in the cosmos. Physics-power-property leaves little poetry left over to make it beautiful.

I portray the situation darkly. Plainly, it troubles Fensham. He squares up against it in his book *Emerging from the Dark Age Ahead: The Future of the North American Church*. Fensham catches the gloom of our darkening age first in his reading of Jane Jacobs's *Dark Age Ahead* (he borrowed the title): "the possibility," he says, "that our global culture is entering a new dark age with a dramatic loss of knowledge and wisdom." Catches it once more in the gathering darkness of James Lovelock's "vision of the earth's environmental devastation." Then again in schizophrenic denial: "These pictures of cultural and ecological destruction stand in stark contrast to the optimism and entertainment-focused frivolity characterizing North American culture and media." To this dark amalgam Fensham adds global economic turmoil, pandemics, failing quality of life and health.[21] And in a long section at the center of his book, he details the deadening, darkening, vertiginous effect on consciousness produced by *technique*: the modern, technology-infused drive for rational, mathematical mastery of nature and society. Mastery that reduces value to the measurable, the managed, and the commercially mediated; that digitizes our life space and represents it back to us in forms amenable only to its digital logic; and that shrinks people down into passive observers looking at screens rather than free, creative, world-building actors.[22] All this darkness, too, "will profoundly affect the church in North America," and not for the good of it.

The dark age darkens, Fensham writes, having forgotten *poiesis*; society having lost the light of its humanizing *poietic* science along the way (or, worse, that society now generates a stunted, negative *poiesis* such as it is). Society and its church, the church and its society, entwine themselves in a common crisis of self-production that begins with their mutual forgetting and ends in nihilism.

> The metaphor of the Dark Age refers fundamentally to the loss of memory, wisdom, meaning, and moral ethic related to the reign of God and the vision of the restoration of God's creation . . . [D]arkness is not lodged in the loss of prosperity and the stimulation of infotainment, but rather in the loss of more basic things

---

21. Fensham, *Emerging*, 7–8.
22. Fensham, *Emerging*, 77–136.

that make us human, allow us to relate meaningfully and organize our relationships for the common good.²³

The dark age is only as dark as we make it. Christian mission, if it is to be a fit participant in God's mission to and for the world's sake, must learn to produce the arts of turning the lights back on to help us all emerge from the dark. Fensham is not stuck in crisis, and mission need not be either. Most of his writing in *Emerging* canvasses the missional resources embedded in scriptural *poiesis*—for example, the Social Trinity as model for community, *missio Dei* as inspiration to continue with God in the dual work of creation and redemption, *kenosis,* the self-emptying that binds individuals and communities in love. All are necessary to relight the symbolic universe of God's dealings with Creation. And to reopen the fullness of the life-giving sensibility inside of human beings created in the divine image. Not least, to restore *poiesis* to mission, hoping that its imaginative, integrative powers can produce a better map for making our way through the looming valley of the shadow of death and emerging alive on the other side of it. Or better, to produce a coherent, humane vision—a refreshed gospel, scraped clean of its historical barnacles—to reintegrate a fractured world.

Mission operates in the here and now, albeit nowadays in Fensham's present darkness. In the West at least, I suggest that mission must presently confront a central, existential dilemma whose solution has eluded the post-metaphysical West for well more than a century. A dilemma that allows nihilism to grow and to *dis*-integrate the world. Nietzsche (to return to the dark prophet of our darkening age) defined the problem for us: Nihilism results from the "devaluation of our highest values." Nihilism's deconstructive force follows forth from the death of God and the dismantling of a Christianly conceived existence. We ourselves in the West in our skepticism, rationalism, and scientism, Nietzsche says, have murdered Christendom's God and deflated Christendom's values. Will we then, he asks—*can* we even—take responsibility for our murderous deed and arrogate to ourselves the godlike powers needed to "revalue" our highest values and make them new?²⁴ Nietzsche, in Dionysian style, famously tried to and failed; so too did the postmoderns who followed him later in a deconstructive mood. Though, in fairness to Nietzsche, he also thought that the project to revaluate the world, to reintegrate it, and to overcome nihilism—the project he called "the revaluation"—might take two hundred years to complete if it

---

23. Fensham, *Emerging,* 8–9.
24. Nietzsche, *Portable Nietzsche,* 95–96; Sluga, *Politics,* 96–111.

can be done at all.²⁵ It might even exceed the capability of mere mortals to complete it and require the will-to-power of a new Jesus, a new Buddha, a Zarathustra, an Übermensch to accomplish it—should any of them ever appear on the scene (still the clock ticks).

Maybe I again risk putting words into Fensham's mouth, but I take his missiological project to help us "emerge from the dark age ahead" to be not unlike Nietzsche's: To revalue our highest values and to rescue value from the nihilism of the age. Though, *pace* Nietzsche (and obviously eschewing Nietzsche's gaudy, messianic Übermenschen!), Fensham draws forth his vitalized revaluation of value from the *poiesis* of the mission of the *living* God. And to advance his integrative reconstruction project, he begins by bringing *poiesis* back to the center to play once again its imaginative, humanizing, divinizing, *triangulating* role to reunite the triple sciences of right knowing.

Producing the World

Or should I say to bring back to missiology's center *poiesis' productive* energies? Fensham's *Emerging* puts on display a *poietic* cycle. Empathy: to sense public sensibility, to intuit our dark age's "future-present" threats. Poetry: to inventory Scripture's poetic resources that we need to relight the night. Invention: to render a beautiful and useful architectural design to produce a church to redeem the darkness. In other writing, especially his collected essays in *Mission as Penance*, Fensham presents his thoughts in more detail—*poietic* of course, and analytical and ethical—to produce a full, integrated vision for mission in North America. He sharpens his own identity, too, writing as a public missiologist to demonstrate how mission must serve the world not only to explain the world to itself, but also to serve the collective human project to produce the world in God's presence as the world travels forward into its future. (Here is where my own work has long converged with Charles's.)²⁶

---

25. Sluga, *Politics*, 98.

26. Fensham writes, "In some ways public missiology has been the theme of my missiological thinking since my 1991 doctoral dissertation with the title 'Missiology for the Future: A Missiology in the Light of the Emerging Systemic Paradigm.'" Fensham, *Mission as Penance*, 112. For a collection of his writing on public missiology, see *Mission as Penance*, 111–56, 203–15. Fensham is not alone in his desire to produce a world that resonates with the fullness, harmony, and beauty of Creation. Public missiology is a throughline that also aligns his work with my own—and with that of five others of us

Public missiologists, Fensham prominent among them, take as their object of analysis "modes of public order": the entire, varied ways and means by which human communities produce and assemble their shared beliefs, thoughts, knowledge, ethics, politics, economies, social structures, power structures, technologies, laws, sensibilities, and faith.[27] By another name, the "life worlds" that all peoples everywhere produce—*poiesis* in the world-production sense of its meaning—to imagine and to arrange everything they know about in the cosmos, every thought and thing, the human-to-human, the human-to-nonhuman (biological, ecological, technological). Assembling them all together in a semiotic constellation of meaning to produce a coherent vision for living well in the cosmos, even if it is an incomplete one.

Modes of public order always are in flux. They emerge and re-emerge in new forms, overlap, merge, or subdivide. Their centers, if indeed they have centers at all, never are fixed, their boundaries never clear. Public missiology captures (or tries to) the full life of public orders in their (re)emergence. Then it directs mission (public missiologists conceive mission, metaphorically, to be the yeast that leavens the emerging lump of dough from within) towards the constant process to produce human orders of life. Always and at Fensham's urging, public missiology directs mission towards *poiesis,* towards the productive science that connects thought and thing to make beautiful or useful objects to benefit the all-inclusive commonwealth (to use a sadly forgotten word), and to make of the commonwealth an object of beauty.

Public missiology imagines *the public* to be the entire space and time of collective life wherein such production happens.[28] Where living people assemble thoughts and things together, manage the relationships among them, and make of them a symbolic universe that makes the makers feel at home in the cosmos. The concept *public* captures collective human and other-than-human forms of living in their semiotic, *poietic,* flux, flex, and flow, locally, globally, cosmically. *The public*—when the concept *public* is

---

who, in 2014, first organized the public missiology "study group," and in 2023, jointly published the paper "What We Mean by Public Missiology" to explain it. All the way along, Fensham contributed his semiotic sensibility to our work as we developed our project; in some ways the paper itself can be read as a study in *poiesis*, the *productive science*. For the final, published document, see Leffel, "Public Missiology." An earlier draft of the paper is appended in Fensham, *Mission as Penance*, 219–29.

27. Fensham, *Mission as Penance*, 222–23.
28. Fensham, *Mission as Penance*, 223–26.

taken as a symbolic and symbolically interactive space, a semiotic space, a *poiesis* of cosmic vision and intimate friendship—is the space-time, the site of production from which the true, good, and beautiful Cosmopolis arises—if or when we let it.

For Fensham, who draws his vision first from the *poietic* treasures of Scripture's creation accounts, and for his fellow public missiologists, *poietic, integrative, productive* work is what people were in the very beginning created to do: To produce and to tend worlds, *the* world. This, because we all are reflections of God's image, reflections of God who produced the entire cosmos and made it beautifully. God, in God's own perpetual mission, produces and perfects the cosmic whole of it. Our human mission, finite and limited as it is, participates in God's mission to create as God creates, to produce as God produces—to tend to the world's life and to make it cohere beautifully. Beautifully enough to pass the aesthetic "sniff test"—indeed, to impart "the pleasing aroma of Christ"[29]—and finally, to return Creation to God in gratitude for God's gracious gift of life and beauty.

The Song of the Universe

I took my cue from Charles Fensham to think *poiesis* over; to imagine how *poiesis* might be considered in its imaginative fullness; to interpret its unique mode of human intelligence and its place in the tripod of right knowing. Now I will say what I think *poiesis* means: *Poiesis* as productive science is imagination, creativity in its fullness, a flight of intuition to round out the fullness of the sensibility of human understanding, of right knowing. I take *poiesis* to be an unhindered imagination of reality, of the cosmic whole of it: Reality made present-to-mind in symbols that point beyond themselves to project reality's wholeness onto the screens of our minds. *Poiesis* is the science that produces the semiotics of the cosmos to guide our production of a concrete world that is consonant with the real. I imagine *poiesis* to be *production in a poetic mode* (to use *poetic* in the expanded semiotic sense I noted earlier). It is *poetic production* to produce a beautifully useful world. To be a human being, I think, means to be a poet of the real and a producer of the world; to be a *poetic producer*. To come fully alive means to discover the joy of producing poetically, of making beautiful objects of our lives and worlds, of useful objects that enhance our joy of understanding.

---

29. 2 Cor 2:15.

Do No Harm

Why are we the way that we are? Curious poets, never dreaming to stop dreaming about what the cosmos is, what it means, what it should be like to live in it. Artists of the soul who never cease to produce the sublime. It just comes naturally to us, to creatures made in the image and shadow of Creator God. God, who by nature exists as the singular cosmic poetic producer. Poetic production, *poiesis,* it appears to me, flows forth out of the ground of our being. Maybe I stretch too far by imagining *poiesis* in cosmic terms that are anchored in the very being of Creation. But if this intuition is accurate, then it seems perfectly reasonable to me to imagine *poiesis* as a *fundamental science,* a science that springs up from Creation itself. A fundamental science that is indivisible from the tripod of human understanding—and just as real as *theoria* and *praxis* as fundamental sciences, even if its intuitive scientific method is harder to pin down. Yet *poiesis* is quite concrete in what it teaches us. Its contribution to truth telling is revealed in the worlds we humans produce with our theories, ethics, and imaginations. *Poiesis* judges the truthfulness and moral dignity of the entire scientific tripod of right knowing by its tangible, productive, aesthetic, worldly output. If we think we know all things, the proof is in the pudding we produce. If the pudding stinks, we know we got the recipe wrong.

I close by observing Charles's poetic imagination in free flight, his *poiesis* of Christian spirituality that he produced in his book *To the Nations for the Earth: A Missional Spirituality.* The book is of a distinctive type, designed to be a tapestry that weaves together, wraps up, and encapsulates nearly his entire *oeuvre* of thought. In its pages we meet Charles the professor, who puts the major themes of systematic theology to our service to unlock personal understanding and to confidently point us towards God. Meet Charles the pastor, who senses the sensibilities of faith, who empathizes with the soul's struggle to be faithful. Charles the poet, who lights the constellation of meaning that places us in the cosmos—Creation—and makes it our home. Charles the leader, who imagines the transformative vision for mission in and for the cosmos, and who imagines mission to be a vast social movement to produce the world, to tend to its life, to make of it a beautiful object.[30] A confident leader who steels the faithful's confidence in their God; likewise, who recognizes the world's stupefying complication, our limited grasp of it, the flimsiness of our explanations of it, and cautions overconfidence in them. A chastened leader, who leads in bold humility. Charles the liberating activist, who insists that our mission begins

---

30. "The Transformative Vision." Fensham, *Mission as Penance,* 114–27.

in penance for our history of world-changing arrogance; our history of authoritarian violence, of traumatizing, othering, and misjudging the missioned peoples on mission's receiving end; the abuse of human bodies and of nature's ecological body, too.[31]

Charles's book is lovely and rigorous and practical. His writing salvages Aristotle's tripod of right knowing, of complete human intelligence—of *poiesis, praxis,* and *theoria*—from the "dark age ahead," sets it upright on its feet, and reconnects its three sciences in a functional unity. He delineates his concepts clearly, keeps his arguments tight. Still, notice that my previous paragraph is but a list of certain features of Charles's book. I find it beyond me to summarize the book with conventional academic concision and still to portray its spirit. Charles's scope is cosmic, yet intimate, personal, his images both transcendental and concrete. The book's arrangement in five movements—Call, Listen, Journey, Sacrament, and Send—creates a rhythm, a tempo, a sequence, a direction to it that first picks us up as people at our lives' beginnings. By the end to have formed our souls in the image of our cosmic Creator and Sustainer—to have formed our spirituality in God and in the sweep of mission in and for the world. *To the Nations* reads more as story than pedagogy; more an epic poem even if written in simplified academic prose; more dance choreography than marching orders, music than rhetoric. Charles's book is poetry at work, a prose poem.

And a masterwork of *poiesis:* A delicate balance of the True, the Good, and the Beautiful that allows reason, ethics, and aesthetics to cohere in a singular vision for living at home in the cosmos. Right *thinking,* right *acting* blend with right *producing* to turn life into liturgy—turning the work of the people into a labor of love: of God, of our fellow creatures, of the earth, of the cosmos itself.[32] How do we know if Charles got his vision right? Well, if it passes the aesthetic "sniff test," of course. Charles himself, the missiologist as poet, provides the criterion for judgement: Does it produce an outflow of thanksgiving from the center of the soul? A centering of one's life in doxology?[33] A spontaneous overflow of thanks to the Cosmic poet and producer, our Creator, the One who sets our lives

---

31. Beginning with Johan Bavinck's exhortation to begin mission in penitence, Fensham develops his concept of "mission as penance" in Section 1 of *Mission as Penace,* 3–48.

32. "Liturgy," Fensham, *To the Nations,* 23–25; Fensham, *Mission as Penance,* 122–24.

33. "Doxology," Fensham, *Emerging,* 51–52, 161–68.

on the path of beauty? A people that sings the "Christian Song of the Universe"—in Charles's own verse:

> Hear all peoples your God is self-giving and faithful to God's promise to redeem all things through God's Messiah and in him through you all people and all creation.[34]

Bibliography

Eagleton, Terry. "Seeds of What Ought to Be." *London Review of Books,* February 22, 2024.

Fensham, Charles. *Emerging from the Dark Age Ahead: The Future of the North American Church.* Toronto: Novalis, 2008.

———. *Misguided Love: Christians and the Rupture of LBGTQI2+ People.* Atlanta: Journal of Pastoral Care Publications, 2019.

———. *Mission as Penance: Essays on the Theology of Mission from a Canadian Context.* Eugene, OR: Pickwick Publications, 2023.

———. *To the Nations for the Earth: A Missional Spirituality.* Toronto: Clements Academic, 2013.

Horkheimer, Max. "Traditional and Critical Theory." Translated by M. O'Connell, in *Critical Theory: Selected Essays,* edited by Michael O'Connell. Continuum, 1972.

Jameson, Frederic. "An American Utopia." In *An American Utopia: Dual Power and the Universal Army,* edited by Slavoj Žižek, 1–96. London: Verso, 2016.

Kompridis, Nikolas. *Critique and Disclosure: Critical Theory between Past and Future.* Cambridge: MIT Press, 2006.

Leffel, G, et al. "What We Mean by Public Missiology." *Missiology* 51.3 (2023) 268–81.

Nietzsche, Friedrich. *The Portable Nietzsche.* Translated and edited by Walter Kaufmann. New York: Penguin, 1954.

Shields, Christopher. "Aristotle." In *The Stanford Encyclopedia of Philosophy,* Winter 2023 edition, edited by Edward N. Zalta and Uri Nodelman. https://plato.stanford.edu/archives/win2023/entries/aristotle/.

Sluga, Hans D. *Politics and the Search for the Common Good.* Cambridge: Cambridge University Press, 2014.

Toulmin, Stephen. *Cosmopolis: The Hidden Agenda of Modernity.* 1990. Reprint, Chicago: University of Chicago, 1992.

Wallerstein, Immanuel. *World Systems Analysis: An Introduction.* Durham: Duke University Press, 2004.

Wolfe, Alan. *The Future of Liberalism.* New York: Knopf, 2009.

---

34. Fensham, *To the Nations,* 61.

8

A Different Kind of Congress

The Congress of Concern, 1968

Stuart Macdonald

IT ALL BEGAN AT the Charlottetown airport one month before. Three Presbyterian ministers, Walter McLean, Malcolm McCuaig, and Ian Glass, were returning from a World Missions Weekend. They began talking to a colleague, Stuart Coles, who worked at the denomination's national office, about an article he had recently published in the denomination's magazine, the *Presbyterian Record*. "Crisis = Danger + Opportunity" had laid out what Coles argued were the series of crises facing virtually every area of the life of The Presbyterian Church in Canada.[1] The idea of getting together and talking about it further was floated. Stuart Coles, who, according to a later article in the *Presbyterian Record*, "had hoped somehow, somewhere, people might be stirred to action" by the article, was delighted and immediately began to write (later revised with the assistance of others) a draft manifesto and prepare for a gathering.[2] The result was that one month later on June 4 and 5, 1968, one hundred and thirty Presbyterians from across Canada gathered at North Park Presbyterian Church in Toronto. The timing was carefully chosen—this was on the eve of the official gathering of the denomination, the General Assembly, and thus it was possible for interested

1. Coles, "Crisis," 10–11.
2. Dunn, "Congress of Concern," 16–17.

Presbyterians from across the country to be in Toronto a day early to participate in this "Congress of Concern."³

A Congress was not a novel idea. These gatherings had proven extremely useful over the years. The denomination's General Assembly, while it brought Presbyterians together from across the nation, was largely a business meeting concerned with receiving and approving official reports. It was also restricted in its membership: only a selected number of ministers and elders representing their particular presbyteries could attend and participate. It was also exclusively male, as women were not allowed—until 1966—-to be ordained as either elders or ministers. The 1967 General Assembly had seen the first two women elders. In 1968, one woman had just been ordained as a minister.⁴ While these very recent changes represented important steps forward, the nature and composition of a General Assembly was restrictive in terms of who could participate and what might be done. When the denomination felt there were larger issues that needed to be considered by a broader group, the idea of calling a Congress had evolved. There was a Congress in 1913 which met in Massey Hall, Toronto.⁵ A Pre-Assembly Congress had also been called to meet June 8 to June 10, 1925, by those who wished to continue as The Presbyterian Church in Canada after the creation of the United Church of Canada. The Pre-Assembly Congress in 1925 laid essential groundwork in preparing for the General Assembly that continued to meet after June 10, 1925, when the majority of Presbyterians had become part of the new denomination.⁶ Sometimes a Congress was attached to a General Assembly, while at other times it was a distinct event. The most recent Congress, held in Kingston in 1967 with the theme of Man in God's world, had become famous for the relative youth of its participants and the themes it addressed. One provocative address "Blueprint for a New

---

3. Very little exists in the secondary literature around the Congress of Concern. It is discussed briefly amidst a more general discussion on self-criticism within the denomination in Moir, *Enduring Witness*, 259–73. In a collection of photos celebrating The Presbyterian Church in Canada, although there are very contemporary pictures, including one of the 1967 Congress, of youth coffee houses, and of the Teen and Twenty Chapel, there are no photographs from the Congress of Concern; Bailey, *Covenant in Canada*, 149–51.

4. Shirley Jeffrey was the first woman ordained as a minister in The Presbyterian Church in Canada. Her picture appeared on the cover of the June 1968 *Presbyterian Record*, followed by a news item, 5.

5. A publication later emerged of the addresses. *Pre-Assembly Congress*.

6. PCC Archives, Pre-Assembly Congress file 1982–1003-3-18.

Model," given by Joseph C. McLelland had, been published verbatim in the *Presbyterian Record* to both applause and outrage.[7]

Calling the Congress of Concern

Calling a gathering together with one month's notice was a significant undertaking. While many Presbyterians would be in Toronto to attend the General Assembly, things still had to be organized. The need for another Congress, so soon after the 1967 Congress, must have struck some in the denomination as odd, even unnecessary. It is worth noting: this was not an officially sanctioned Congress. Calling this gathering was unusual and somewhat spontaneous. One senses in the documents created at the time a frustration that some of the issues raised at the 1967 Congress did not seem to have resulted in action. Invitations and material sent out for this gathering suggested that the Congress of Concern "should pick up some of the disturbance, insights and challenges of the 1967 Congress in Kingston," in particular because that event had "failed to make the leap from exciting talk into concrete action."[8]

An initial mailing attempted to discover what interest there might be in such a gathering. The top of the page began, "Warning this page must lead to some action."[9] This was handwritten in a balloon script, next to which there was a cartoon character who said, "Sock it to me!" The allusion was to a saying from the then popular TV show *Rowan and Martin's Laugh-In*: a conscious attempt was being made to be contemporary. Enclosed with this covering letter were two items, a copy of the article by Stuart Coles, "Crisis = Danger + Opportunity," that had appeared in the May 1968 *Presbyterian Record* and *The Congress of Concern—A Draft Manifesto*. Readers were encouraged to read the material, and, if they were committed to act, reply indicating they would be attending. They were also invited to indicate if they could billet anyone who might be coming. Travel would be covered for those attending the General Assembly. A travel pool was being established for others and all were invited to contribute to that travel pool. The letter

---

7. McLelland, "Blueprint for a New Model," 8–17. Responses to this article can be seen in the letters to the editor, *Presbyterian Record*, November 1967, notably by William Stanford Reid, 9.

8. The Presbyterian Church in Canada (PCC) Archives contain several files which include material on the Congress of Concern: 1988-1005-1-15, 1992-1076, registration form, 1988-1005-15. Much of the material is duplicated and included in each file.

9. PCC Archive, 1988-1005-1-15, "Warning."

noted that it was estimated that four sessions would be needed to consider the issues, and that "lukewarm commitment or casual attendance" would not be adequate. The manifesto, it was noted, was not a final document but a launching pad for a discussion and imagined a "revolutionary updating in our church's life but by evolutionary tactics."[10] One area for concern was specifically noted:

> One target of the shoot might be a massive reform of Assembly's procedure, so that the business could be accomplished in a far more intelligent and lively manner. The Assembly should steward its time so as to function much more in its early stages as a deliberative council of the church, and then out of this depth process shape up its legislative and policy-making actions in the closing two or three days.[11]

The letter continued that "our tactics must mobilize the energy, imagination and speed which our long-blocked and now belated beginnings makes imperative."[12] Thirty-one names followed, those who, from coast to coast, were supporting the call for this Congress.

The response to this letter was deemed to show enough interest that the Congress of Concern should proceed. North Park Presbyterian Church (near Keele and the 401) in Toronto was the location. The plan was for an event that began at noon on Tuesday (June 4) and continued until 4:00 p.m. on Wednesday. (General Assembly would open that evening at 8:00 p.m.)

The document began by noting who was *not* invited: those who wanted "things to remain substantially as they are"; those who wanted to defend the status quo in terms of doctrine, polity, ministry, and other aspects of church life; those who did not believe that there was any use "trying to liberate or renovate" the denomination; and those interested in reform but "not prepared to get into trouble, to be disturbed and to disturb the reactionaries, the timorous and the idolaters in our establishments" were told not to come.[13] On the other hand, the invitation to attend was extended to those with "a sense of urgency, and perhaps even of frustration and outrage, about the contrast between the pace of change in our world today and the pace of life" in the denomination, and those who had hope and who wanted to work with others with similar ideas were welcomed. An agenda for the

---

10. PCC Archive, 1988–1005–1–15, "Warning."
11. PCC Archive, 1988–1005–1–15, "Warning."
12. PCC Archive, 1988–1005–1–15, "Warning."
13. PCC Archive, 1988–1005–15, registration form.

day followed, as well as a tear-off registration form to provide the information needed by the registrar, the Rev. Doug Miles. Those interested were also asked to indicate their preferences (first, second, and third) for which of the eight task-force groups they wished to be a participant in.[14]

Alongside the invitation to attend were distributed the key documents. Again the "Crisis" article from the *Presbyterian Record* and the draft manifesto were distributed. The manifesto called for significant changes in the church. It began with a call for a "Recovery of Identity and Purpose" before moving on to call for a rethinking of the "intellectual content of the gospel" so it would better fit the contemporary situation, "restyling our ways of worship," the "scrapping of our medievil [sic] curricula and pedagogy" in theological education (particularly theological colleges), and different understandings of ordination that would provide more "freedom for ministry." Another section called for "Bridging the Gaps." It suggested there needed to be a greater awareness of the diversities in the denomination and the differences between those present. It spoke of the need to "take into account the gaps between young people and their seniors; between men and women; between the dreamers and the achievers; between the advantaged and the disadvantaged; between those of one color and another, between one creed an another, between one person and another." The issue was painted very broadly. What precisely the church should do about these gaps that had emerged was less clear. The manifesto was clearer when it spoke about the need to update the structures of the denomination. These, it argued, needed to be changed at all levels, from the congregational to the national and everything in between. Everything needed to be changed: "We desire the updating of our church courts, in terms of their scope, times and styles of meeting, membership, financing and vision, so as to shift their focus from the maintenance of a static religion to the nurture and empowerment of a missionary people." The church must become more creative, another paragraph urged. The need for action, it was also noted, was now: "We urgently ask for action by the 1968 General Assembly to break free from the customary clutter of its busyness and as its first priority to deal with the profound crisis that has generated this Congress of Concern and testament of hope."[15]

Perhaps the most important section of the manifesto, and certainly the one that was central at the actual Congress of Concern itself, was the opening section that spoke of recovering identity and purpose. This is

14. PCC Archive, 1988–1005–15, "Warning."
15. PCC Archive, 1988–1005–15, *Draft Manifesto*.

worth quoting at length, to see what was expressed and how extensive the concerns were:

> The world of this time faces unprecendented [sic] crises in the areas of affluence, poverty, social injustice, national tensions, inter-national and inter-racial hostilities. We seek a recovery of our church's sense of identity and purpose in mission for today and tomorrow. While our church is preoccupied with maintaining a traditional religion and a cumbersome institutional machine, men and women all around us are investing their lives in more authentic forms of service. The church must cleanse its mind of confusing and incapacitating fears arising from inherited notions of God and codes of behaviour. The biblical marks of the Christian koinonia must be recovered—freedom and interdependence, sensitivity and toughness, a sense of joy along with an awareness of the world's agony and monstrous evils, a passion for justice, truth and tenderness.[16]

The world was on fire. The church seemed unaware. People were turning away and committing their lives to other causes. There were indeed, the manifesto argued, reasons to gather and seek to reform the church. At least one group came to the Congress of Concern with a clear sense of one action that needed to be taken. Those from Montreal, led by Joseph McLelland, came to the gathering with a motion related to how the General Assembly could be reformed.[17]

What Happened at the Congress of Concern?

Those who arrived at North Park Presbyterian Church on June 4 would have witnessed a scene of some confusions as posters were still being tacked to the walls, name tags were being created "from psychedelic posters," and with informal discussions already taking place.[18] Looking at the posters on the wall, lunch and singing all took place before the gathering officially began at 1:30 p.m. The music throughout the event was provided by Warren McKinnon and Teen and Twenty Chapel, a Christian rock group based in Toronto.[19] The first block of time was given to discussing the idea of the congress,

---

16. PCC Archive, 1988-1005-15, *Draft Manifesto*.
17. Dunn, "Congress of Concern," 17.
18. Dunn, "Congress of Concern," 16.
19. Dunn, "Congress of Concern," 17. The program for the Congress of Concern also includes Jack Green and Wayne Smith as responsible for music at the event. PCC

and in particular the draft manifesto.[20] This was followed by responses from invited guests June Callwood, Wilson Head, Gregory Baum, In Ha Lee, and Ted Johnson. The program noted that these responses might be "supportive, interrogative, negative, provocative."[21] After these talks concluded, the congress was to break into seven task-force groups to explore the themes: Freedom and Courage to Think; Restyling Our Ways of Worship; The Education of the Church; Bridging the Gaps; Freedom For Ministry; Updating our Structures; and Creative Ways of Getting Things Done.[22]

Who came to this gathering? Valerie Dunn later reported in the *Presbyterian Record* that most of those present were "under 45, with a sprinkling of grey heads," then went on to note there were "71 ministers, 29 laymen and 30 women."[23] The list of those responsible for various aspects of this gathering were noted at the top of the program. The Congress of Concern was chaired by John C. Robson (then the minister at Queen Street East Presbyterian Church) and George I. Hopton. Those involved in planning and organizing the event were: Douglas Miles, Ron Mulchey, William Adamson, George Vais, David Diltz, Donald Warne, and Stuart Coles (all listed as the Secretariat); publicity was handled by Ed Oliverio and Valerie Dunn; as leaders of the various task-force force groups, Donald Collier, Paul McCarroll, Malcolm McQuaig, Warren MacKinnon, Wilfred McLeod, Bruce Miles, and Donald C. Smith; and leading music, Jack Green, Warren McKinnon, and Wayne Smith. Others listed in the program (and not noted already) included Walter McLean and Ian Glass.[24] Further insight into who participated in the congress can be gained by looking at who signed the *Declaration of Concern*.[25] What is noteworthy is that those leading the Congress of Concern and those present were a representative group within the denomination. They may have skewed younger (relatively) but, to import theological terms for divisions that developed in later debates, this was not a gathering of liberals or a gathering of conservatives: this was a gathering

Archive, 1988–1005–15, program.
  20. PCC Archive, 1988–1005–15, program.
  21. PCC Archive, 1988–1005–15, program.
  22. PCC Archive, 1988–1005–15, program. Although "Recovery of Identity and Purpose" was identified as one of the task-forces on the registration form, this work seems to have been done collectively as a plenary session.
  23. Dunn, "Congress of Concern," 16.
  24. PCC Archive, 1988–1005–15, program.
  25. PCC Archive. 1988–1005–15, *Declaration of Concern*, signed copy in the archive file 1988–1005–15.

that included both liberals and conservatives, as well as others who might not comfortably fit either of these labels. For all of the discussion of "rebels," what is striking is how establishment many of those at the Congress of Concern were. These were ministers from significant churches, or ministers who held significant positions within the national office. Indeed, two of the candidates for Moderator at the 1968 General Assembly, Ted Johnson and Stuart Coles, not only attended but played key roles at this gathering. In the end, neither succeeded in being elected that year with the Rev. C. J. MacKay being elected to serve as the Moderator for the Assembly that ran from June 5 to June 12.[26]

For all of the time slotted for listening to speakers and discussion, the organizers had set three specific tasks for the congress. The first was to look at the draft manifesto, specifically the first paragraph that spoke of identity and purpose, come to some sense of ownership of this, and to revise or produce an "other or further statement if desired." The second task was to look at the implications of the other parts of the manifesto, something that was naturally captured through the work of the task-force groups. Finally, the Congress was to "consider how best to bring our needs, concerns and proposals into the process of the General Assembly; other follow-up long and short range."[27]

The Declaration of Concern

One of the major tasks of the congress, and one of its most concrete achievements, was the revision of parts of the draft manifesto into a statement, entitled *Declaration of Concern*. This is worth quoting in its entirety, to give a sense of the issues facing the church as these were understood by the participants.

> Declaration of Concern
> We live today in a world which faces unprecedented crises manifest in poverty and affluence, blatant injustice between nations and within nations; loneliness, alienation, violence in our midst and around the globe. We who are members of the Church of Christ in this world seek a recovery of our sense of identity and purpose for a distraught generation.

26. "Assembly 1968," 9.

27. Three Tasks for Congress, mailed out to participants ahead of time. PCC Archive, 1988-1005-15.

We are starved for the Biblical marks of the Christian community, freedom and interdependence, sensitivity, toughness and joy. With these we need an awareness of the world's crying needs and monstrous evils, a passion for justice, truth and freedom.

We believe that our church at all levels tends to be ensnared by its own machinery; a situation for which we are as responsible as anyone else. We believe that God can liberate His people. His gifts are abundant. Our cash, property and people must be at His disposal. We can be an exciting part of Canada and of the Christian Church. And we further believe that the church can only find itself through the service of man's deepest needs.

We realize that we are not alone in our concern. With profound gratitude we recognize that many have said such things before and taken positive steps to implement reforms. But the church as a whole should be aware of the decisive importance of these problems. While claiming the traditional liberty of conscience of our church, we affix our names, pledging ourselves to do all in our power, within the Christian community, to bring about renewal and reform. Specific proposals are in the report to be released during the Assembly. (See document entitled GLEANINGS)

North Park Presbyterian Church,
June 5, 1968[28]

This document was then signed by those at the gathering. All but two participants signed. What is noteworthy is the breadth of the church reflected in these signatures. As already noted, these were leaders of the denomination who were not limited to one ecclesiastical or theological faction. There are the names one would expect to find (Joseph McLelland, John Robson, and Stuart Coles are obvious examples). There are also names from those not considered "rebels."

The answer to the broad acceptance may lie in the text itself, a subject we will return to after considering other items, including the work done in the task-force groups.

Task-Force Groups

Having grappled with the draft manifesto, having listened to provocative speeches, participants then turned to the task of working in their assigned

28. There are different versions of this in the archive file. This version spells "blatant" correctly and includes a note to Gleanings. PCC Archive, 1988-1005-15. There is no report from the group "Creative Ways of Getting Things Done."

task-force groups. As reported in the "Gleanings from the Task Forces" published subsequent to the gathering, those results were mixed, though the document hastened to explain this may have been the result of how matters were recorded as opposed to the interest shown in the topic.[29] "Gleanings" noted that most of the time spent at Congress was in these groups. The group focused on "Restyling our eays of Worship" was able to be practical, suggesting that in worship "contemporary language, music, graphic arts, dialogue, dance, should be explored and exploited."[30] It is worth pausing and remembering that in 1968 Canadian Presbyterians continued to use their *Book of Praise* (which included hymns and metrical psalms) first published in 1918. A revision was underway, but this would not appear until 1972. The King James Version of the Bible was in the pews, and ministers frequently used *Thee* and *Thou* as they spoke to God in the congregational prayers. Calls for a revision to how worship was being done thus seems reasonable and very practical. Similarly, the denomination had not been able to produce a contemporary statement of faith despite earlier attempts to do so. The lack of detail and specifics on the report from those working on "Thinking Out Our Faith" is thus surprising. They noted that "faith must find expression in language that people can understand." They also noted this process "must begin with the gut issues, the life and death situations that people face." What was not present was any specific calls on how these concerns might be addressed. There is no call, for example, for the relevant committee in the denomination, the Committee on Articles of Faith, to revive work on a contemporary confession. Similar comments in terms of a lack of concrete proposals could be made about the task-force group considering "The Education of the Church." The group assigned to discuss "Bridging the Gaps" articulated the challenges it saw but did not suggest any concrete actions until it came to the issue of women in the church. Here the task-force group went into detail, recognizing the recent changes which allowed ordination but arguing not enough change had happened. Indeed, the women present "hived off briefly" (to quote the report) in order to form a "separate caucus" which returned to the main group with this statement:

> We, the women of this Congress of Concern, as full members of the body of Christ, feel a rising dissatisfaction with the present structures for women within the church. Our gifts are many and

29. PCC Archive, 1988–1005–15.
30. PCC Archive, 1988–1005–15.

varied; our concern for service is real. We would ask the General Assembly to call a congress of women, based on all the women of the church, to consider a fresh approach . . . having in mind a re-assessment of our place and function in a serving church.

The women also indicated their support for the idea "that the purpose and function of the Order of Deaconesses be re-examined."[31]

Specifics were also raised in the reports of the remaining task-force groups. Those involved in looking at "Structures for Renewal and Action" began by noting it was "a symptom of our sickness that we can still become disturbed over such things as typewritten session minutes and term eldership." They continued to name other concerns and suggest specific changes (reduce the number of presbytery committees, open those committees to any interested party and not just ministers and elders). Various aspects of the structures needed to be changed and there was a call for that changed, noting,

> A proposal central to all other reforms of General Assembly lies in the direction of updating the style of Assembly agenda-handling by learning from such powerful demonstrations as the 1967 Congress held in Kingston, Ontario. We understand some of the commissioners to the Assembly this year intend to present [a] resolution on this matter, and we wish to communicate our whole-hearted support. The need for action is very urgent, in the lives and in the morale of our people.

Specific calls for change followed. Open the offices of Moderator and Clerk to lay people. There should be stated terms of service for those in denominational leadership. The group considering "Freedom for Ministry" also made specific suggestions. Indeed, some of the most radical and most quoted comments to come out of the Congress of Concern came from this task-force group. Amidst the usual commentary that the church was more than "a religious group that meets mainly on Sundays at 11 o'clock for worship," and that members of the church "serve not only when it is gathered but even more when it is scattered," one can see much more radical statements which called out specific faults that were being identified. The understanding of ordination must change. The distinction between clergy and laity was challenged: "the traditional distinction between clergy and laity is fallacious. Everyone must see themselves as servants, working together on the jobs confronting them." Different kinds of ministries needed to be recognized. The use of the word *Reverend* needed to be dropped. So,

31. PCC Archive, 1988–1005–15, 4.

too, "clerical and academic costume" needed to be abandoned. Ministers should "seriously consider freeing themselves and the community by no longer being on stipend salary, taking up other employment for their necessary income." A different kind of ministry was being imagined. Implicit was the suggestion (not always clearly defined or described) that things were not currently working. The report proclaimed: "Presbyteries must act as bishops in forming, nurturing, dissolving and re-forming pastoral ties, and not just rubber-stamping decisions made elsewhere."[32] What specific issues were behind this is not clear; indeed, this is the kind of statement that might be made (to applause) at many different times. What is noteworthy is how much space was given to the issue of ministers, and how radical some of the suggestions were.

As the "Gleanings" document shows, the Congress of Concern covered a wide variety of topics related to church life. Some of the calls to change were radical; indeed, so radical it was unlikely they had broad support or were ever likely to succeed. Calls for ministers to abandon their titles or dress differently, let alone go out and work at another job (while still seeing to all of the essential pastoral work and labor needed to write the kind of educated sermon that Canadian Presbyterians expected), were more reflective of the spirit of the times rather than any serious program of change. In contrast, calls to modernize hymns and the language of worship seem not only practical but reasonable. On the whole, however, the reports in "Gleanings" demonstrated more a general sense of uneasiness rather than specifics. Divisions were emerging within the church: but how were these to be addressed? The Congress of Concern provided few specific answers. Where the proposed actions of the Congress ended up focusing was on motions that were going to be moved at the 1968 General Assembly.

Publicity and Responses to the Congress of Concern

These more radical statements were (understandably) what was featured as Toronto's newspapers covered this gathering. "Church sick, says rebels," *The Toronto Telegram* proclaimed.[33] The frontpage headline on the *Toronto Daily Star* echoed that theme: "Presbyterians in rebellion for 'freedom' in

---

32. PCC Archive, 1988–1005-15, 7.

33. Clippings from these newspapers are in the archive file. PCC Archive, 1988–1005-15, *The Toronto Telegram*.

church music, prayer and preaching."[34] The *Star* provided the most detailed and extensive coverage. The concerns of various participants were quoted, as were sections of the manifesto.[35] The rebel theme was amplified with the inclusion of comments in the Star from the Clerk of the General Assembly, Louis Fowler. Fowler's letter to Stuart Coles was quoted extensively (though it is not clear if the Clerk was ever interviewed for the article). This effectively set up the theme of rebels versus authority figures (in this case, Louis Fowler, the Clerk of General Assembly). The *Star* also noted the presence of Stuart Coles and Ted Johnson, both candidates for moderator, as well as former moderator Deane Johnson, who was quoted as saying, "I am here because I want to hear what they have to say."[36] While all the Toronto papers stressed the theme of "rebels," different aspects were emphasized. The *Telegram* focused on the "Montreal group" and their call for a new kind of General Assembly.[37] The *Globe and Mail* focused primarily on the speeches given by the guests at the Congress of Concern. After noting the "radical caucus of reform-minded Presbyterian clergymen and laymen" and their willingness to be criticized, the *Globe* focused on the outside speakers. June Callwood blasted the congress because Olivet Presbyterian Church, near Yorkville, was not being used to house the hippies in the area. She castigated the church for its inaction, on not only this, but a variety of topics: "Were you there then? [the situation of homelessness in Yorkville] No. Where are you on abortion reform? Where are you when they build maximum security prisons with no windows and put people in them? Where are you with these damn downtown churches, big, empty museums when we need housing for the lower-income groups." Comments from Wilson Head, who worked for the Social Planning Council of Toronto, followed, as he argued the church needed to "undergo radical social reform if it wants to be relevant" and suggested the church needed to consider why they were "becoming irrelevant as a whole." In Ha Lee, general secretary of the National Christian Council of Japan who would also be attending the General Assembly, and Gregory Baum, a theologian at St. Michael's college, each of whom called the church to change and become more engaged, were also noted.[38] June Callwood's and Wilson Head's criticisms of the church were also carried in the Star.

34. PCC Archive, 1988–1005–15, *Toronto Daily Star*.
35. PCC Archive, 1988–1005–15, *Toronto Daily Star*, June 4, frontpage.
36. PCC Archive, 1988–1005–15, *Toronto Daily Star*, June 5.
37. PCC Archive, 1988–1005–15, *The Toronto Telegram*.
38. PCC Archive, 1988–1005–15, *Globe and Mail* (Toronto).

The message in the Toronto papers seemed to be that while the church was failing, there was a rebel group trying to bring change.

But was this true? How radical, or even rebellious, was the Congress of Concern? The Congress certainly met outside the normal processes and approvals of the denomination. But how radical was it? A much more nuanced portrait was given by Valerie Dunn in her coverage of the congress for the denominational magazine. She began by suggesting that while "the newspapers were quick to label them rebels," those who participated in the congress "were really reformers." She continued, "as their draft manifesto put it, they sought 'a recovery of our church's sense of identity and purpose and mission for today and tomorrow.'"[39] The article gave an overview of the congress and focused its attention as much on what the task-force groups had stated as it did the addresses given by outside speakers such as June Callwood and Wilson Head. Readers of the denomination's magazine heard about the work of the task-force group on Bridging the Gap, including the fact that woman participants had met separately at one point to voice their concerns and "dissatisfaction with the structures for women in the church, they pressed for a congress of all women to consider a fresh approach, including re-assessment of their place and function."[40] Valerie Dunn shared suggestions from some of the other task groups, including the possibility of the election of lay people as Moderator or Clerk of church courts and the suggestion that clerical garb and titles such as Reverend be abandoned. Her discussion of the suggestions from the task-force group on worship includes details that did not appear later in the "Gleanings" document that sought to capture the work of each of these groups. As well as suggesting modern translations, and even dance in worship, the group continued to imagine changes:

> And what about dialogue sermons even in the Communion service? Communion has become so holy we do not know what it means. Let's also admit that our style of building inhibits communication and burn the pews! And must we maintain large, useless churches? Then those hymnbooks—why not try loose-leaf ones so we can add new hymns and remove others when outdated?[41]

---

39. Dunn, "Congress of Concern," 16.
40. Dunn, "Congress of Concern," 17.
41. Dunn, "Congress of Concern," 17.

Readers of the denomination's magazine were given a full portrait of the Congress of Concern, what it had done, and what it suggested be done next. Whether they considered the results reform, or more than that, is unclear.[42]

Other responses to the congress can be seen in the comments submitted prior to its gathering. Some of these (as reported by Valerie Dunn) seem to have been used to decorate the room where the participants met, something that was a practice at the time. There is also some indication that the comments may have been read—but it is not clear from the program or reporting of the event when (or whether) this took place. The comments were generally thoughtful, both from those who supported and those who offered criticism of the event. Two Deaconesses who could not attend noted that "many of our concerns have already been expressed in the Draft Manifesto" and noted that the traditional ways of doing things were not working: "We feel stifled by the church."[43] Another individual expressed strong agreement with the issues being raised, in particular in Stuart Cole's "Crisis" article, but found that the manifesto seemed to be "a declaration of attitudes rather than a programme of action."[44] Other comments were more critical. A correspondent who identified himself as a member of the Assembly Council was critical of the way the gathering was called, not only the short notice but also the "semi-secret way," noting in the latter case no return address or signature. (It is unclear if this complaint was accurate: the material in the archives does have the address of the registrar and names attached to the various documents.) The concern here was that things be done properly and effectively: "I believe that if anything is worth doing, it is worth doing well." The correspondent went on to note that, were he able to attend he would want to participate in either the "Bridging the Gaps" group or the "Creative Ways of Getting Things Done" group, and if attention was paid to these items, most other things would fall into place. He concluded with a call for the need to "pull-together."[45] Another correspondent, identified as a Victoria Presbyter, sent in detailed comments, both of the "Crisis" article and the draft manifesto, along with a check in support. The comments indicate both an openness and willingness to change and a

---

42. Very few letters to the editor were printed in the *Presbyterian Record*. Whether this is indicative of how few were received, or the decision of the editor, is not clear.

43. In Absentia: PCC Archive, 1988-1005-15, Comments on the Congress of Concern, 5.

44. Dunn, "Congress of Concern," 4.

45. Dunn, "Congress of Concern," 2-3.

belief that the church needed to work to change. At the same time, the correspondent was critical of the language used in certain sections, including the section that spoke of "The Crisis": "may I suggest that the urgency of the present situation could be emphasized to better advantage by NOT (I repeat—not) using expressions which could be expected to antagonize and alienate many." Specific examples were provided, including later in the letter the description of our "medieval curriculum" in the theological colleges as "an unfortunate and non-factual statement."[46]

The comments that received the most attention were those by the Principal Clerk, Louis Fowler. Selections of his comments appeared in the press and the denominational magazine, most prominently his caution that participants could "get the reputation of being ecclesiastical hippies."[47] Less attention was paid to some of the substantive concerns raised by Fowler. One was his contention that the denomination, in the immediate years after 1925, had used the kind of structure that was being proposed: "I have been at gatherings—the first was in 1926—when the structure was your structure, and to question the findings of another group was the unpardonable sin." In Fowler's opinion, the current General Assembly that had "about eight full days of plenary sessions" was much more effective.[48] He was harshly critical of the suggestions for change being made in the manifesto:

> The matters outlined in your eight sections have been, at least 90% of them, before Assembly and special committees different times. Single phases of these problems have been given more time than you will have available in the total time of your congress. Many of you have been on these committees; you have had your say. You have rarely brought in a minority report, or rarely entered any meaningful dissent. Were you not satisfied? Men and women as good as yourselves have spoken. Have you no confidence in the most democratic Church in Christendom? What gives?[49]

Louis Fowler returns to this theme later in his letter, complaining that "there are men who deem themselves prophets and make a career out of making themselves obnoxious," and then added that these prophets "can

---

46. Dunn, "Congress of Concern," 6–7.

47. Dunn, "Congress of Concern," 16.

48. In Absentia: PCC Archive, 1988-1005-1-15, Comments on the Congress of Concern, 2.

49. In Absentia: PCC Archive, 1988-1005-1-15, Comments on the Congress of Concern, 1.

not submit themselves to the patient, Presbyterian way, and speak off the cuff on everything and expect to be heeded."[50] While he certainly raised questions about the legitimacy of calling such a gathering outside the official structures of the church, there was more to Louis Fowler's concerns than was expressed in media comments. Rather than portraying those involved as rebels, Fowler was suggesting they might indeed be those on the inside who has simply not won the debate on specific issues.

Accomplishments of the Congress of Concern

What, if anything, did the Congress of Concern achieve? Many of those who participated went from the congress to the 1968 General Assembly held at St. Andrew's Church, Toronto, which began at 8:00 that evening. In a document from the leadership of the Congress of Concern which circulated after Assembly, several key results of the gathering were highlighted. One was the resolution taken to Assembly calling for a change in format of the Assembly. Introduced as a notice of motion; this resolution was eventually passed.[51] A second achievement related to what was called the Cochrane Committee (officially The Special Committee on Recommendation No. 10 of the Administrative Council, 1965). The document took some credit for the continuation of this committee and the provision of funding for this committee. What is unclear is whether this would have happened without the impetus of the Congress of Concern. What does seem clear is that those who gathered at North Park Presbyterian Church and then went to Assembly were galvanized to push for action on the Cochrane Committee's work. The result was the Life and Mission Agency Project (LAMP) Report at the 1969 Assembly. Similarly, the success of the Committee on Recruitment and Vocations in receiving funding at the 1968 Assembly that allowed them to engage outside consultants was also celebrated. This resulted in the Ross Report (received in 1970). These were three major decisions made at the 1968 General Assembly. Each of these brought calls for change into the official decision-making processes of the denomination, something that should not be taken lightly. The organizers of the Congress

---

50. In Absentia: PCC Archive, 1988-1005-1-15, Comments on the Congress of Concern, 2.

51. There are various copies of this document in the archival file. PCC Archive, 1988-1005-15. The exact wording is not the same as what was presented or passed at the General Assembly. Acts and Proceedings, 1968, 16, 100-101.

of Concern met on June 25, 1968, to deal with some outstanding issues. For example, of the balance of funds left over after all expenses had been paid, a donation of $250 was made to the Hippie Hostel in downtown Toronto, an amount that covered one month's rent. This was done "as an expression of response to June Callwood's piercing of our conscience at the Congress.[52] An Ad hoc communications group was formed which distributed materials produced by the Congress of Concern, including a list of items under the title "What Can I Do?" which suggested a variety of actions, from circulating the documents to becoming more aware of issues: "Where I have a turn on [choosing the family's] radio or TV programs I can experiment a bit with controversial Christianity, rather than the bland trivialities that too often use up our TV and radio opportunities."[53] Most of the energy, however, seems to have been focused on the work of the LAMP committee, planning for the 1969 General Assembly with its new format, and what would eventually become the Ross Report. A group was formed in Toronto in March 1969, concerned that the upcoming General Assembly would not be as participatory as was hoped. The Assembly Caucus for Transformation (ACT) met at least twice, but it is not clear what came of their activities.[54] No obvious successor to the Congress of Concern emerged.

Did the Congress of Concern accomplish anything apart from what might have been achieved even if it had not met? This is a fair question to consider. If one were to look at the draft manifesto that circulated prior to the congress meeting, or the declaration signed by so many at the Congress, one might answer the question "no." The Presbyterian Church in Canada did not move in the direction, or directions, envisaged in these calls for action. One might even lament this failure, in particular given the numerical decline that has been the reality for The Presbyterian Church in Canada since the 1960s, and argue that this was a missed opportunity. At the same time, it is not apparent that either document provided a clear plan of action. Nor was the declaration produced by the Congress as radical as either the media reports concerning the Congress or the original manifesto. Indeed, it is worth pausing and noting how the texts differed, using one section of each to illustrate the point:

52. PCC Archive, 1988-1005-15, "What has resulted from the Congress of Concern and the 1968 General Assembly?"
53. PCC Archive, 1988-1005-1-15, "A Start into Action."
54. PCC Archive, 1988-1005-1-15, Correspondence, Janet Guilford, Act Worker, April 5, 1969.

> While our church is preoccupied with maintaining a traditional religion and a cumbersome institutional machine, men and women all around us are investing their lives in more authentic forms of service. The church must cleanse its mind of confusing and incapacitating fears arising from inherited notions of God and codes of behaviour. (Manifesto)
>
> We believe that our church at all levels tends to be ensnared by its own machinery; a situation for which we are as responsible as anyone else. We believe that God can liberate His people. His gifts are abundant. Our cash, property and people must be at His disposal. We can be an exciting part of Canada and of the Christian Church. And we further believe that the church can only find itself through the service of man's deepest needs. (Declaration)

The declaration pulled back from the more provocative—and alienating—language shown in the manifesto. The manifesto had little, if anything, good to say about the church. The action was happening in the world. In contrast, the declaration, while acknowledging there were issues and taking responsibility, still saw hope within the church. This contrast needs to be noted. The radical language of the manifesto, and some of the other statements made at the Congress of Concern, attract attention. The final text, however, was one that many people could agree with. It was a call for reform. The rebel label, however well it played in the media, was tempered by the actual documents themselves.

The accomplishments of the Congress of Concern may have been more modest than some had hoped but were nonetheless real. There does seem to have been a genuine concern across a wide theological and ecclesial perspective that things were not changing rapidly enough. People were willing to take a day and talk about the changes they wished to see. And changes did come. The 1969 and subsequent General Assemblies followed a different format that involved more participation through informal conversations at briefing groups. The 1968 General Assembly also took initiative on the Cochrane Report and out of this emerged one of the most significant reports produced by the denomination in the post-war period, the Life and Mission Agency Project (LAMP report). The calls of the Congress of Concern for greater representation, greater participation and greater voice are reflected not only in the text throughout the LAMP report, but also in how it proposed congregations should be organized with multiple committees meeting and feeding their work into the church session. This structure—for good and ill—shaped the next generation of the life of the denomination's congregations. The 1968 General Assembly also approved the funding of an outside consultant for the Committee on Recruitment and Vocations, which resulted in the Ross Report (1969). These changes—in how Assembly operated and in stimulating the two most significant reports of the late 1960s—might have happened without the Congress of Concern; nonetheless it seems clear that this gathering gave momentum to the call for these initiatives. It is telling that the next significant report produced within the denomination was the 1978 State of the Church report. This report was more grounded in the reality of the denomination's failure to grow, indeed its continuing loss of members, which came as a sobering reality so soon after the celebration of the denomination's centennial. The Congress of Concern sought to bring the Presbyterian church more into line with how other organizations were functioning and modernize it. While a noble goal, the results may not have been what was intended. Briefing sessions: did they allow for more participation from the average commissioner to General Assembly, or did they allow the denomination's committees and agencies a captive audience for presentations? A shorter Assembly: did it strengthen the power of the national office and provide less opportunity for debate? Did the average church member desire the level of participation that the Congress of Concern imagined? Was the average lay person as discontented as was assumed? And did the entire focus on "listening to the world"—as crucial as this was and is—mean less attention was paid to what the church had to say to the world? Looking back on the Congress of Concern raises all of these questions.

Bibliography

"Assembly 1968," *Presbyterian Record,* July-August 1968, 8–15.
Bailey, T.M. ed. *The Covenant in Canada.* Hamilton: McNab, 1975.
Coles, Stuart. "Crisis = Danger + Opportunity." *Presbyterian Record,* May 1968, 10–11.
Dunn, Valerie M. "A Congress of Concern," *Presbyterian Record,* July-August 1968, 16–17.
McLelland, Joseph. "Blueprint for a New Model," *Presbyterian Record,* September 1967, 8–17.
Moir, John S. *Enduring Witness: A History of the Presbyterian Church in Canada.* Toronto: Bryant, 1974.
Pre-Assembly Congress: Addresses Delivered at the Presbyterian Pre-Assembly Congress, held in Massey Hall, Toronto. Saturday, May 31 to June 6 with Reports of Committees. Toronto: Board of Foreign Missions, The Presbyterian Church in Canada, 1913.
The Presbyterian Church in Canada (PCC) Archives. Congress of Concern file 1988–1005–1–15.
———. Congress of Concern file 1992–1076.
———. Pre-Assembly Congress file 1982–1003–3–18.

9

The Inner Mission

Trauma, Extraversion, and Missiology

Glenn McCullough

THIS ESSAY HAS EMERGED from my work as a therapist, pastor, and teacher and also from a profound respect for Charles Fensham, who has been my own teacher and colleague at Knox College for over a decade now. I have always found Charles' life and work inspiring, not only in his concern for the social justice history and mission of Christian communities, but also in his concern for mental health and psychotherapy, which pervades his work in subtle and often unnoticed ways. In this essay, and in gratitude for Charles and his work, I want to consider the balance between these two concerns: the activist approach to social justice, and the contemplative approach to mental and spiritual health. This balance will be explored in the context of two related topics: the seeing and healing of trauma, both in ourselves and others, and the extraverted tendency in Christianity, and in the societies it has shaped.

Mark 1:40–45: Trauma and Extraversion

The word trauma has its roots in the word *wound*, and in the New Testament Jesus spends a good deal of his time healing wounds both physical and spiritual. Likewise, in the final scenes of the Gospel accounts Jesus is himself wounded, killed, entombed, and ultimately resurrected with the wounds still visible on his body. It was the seeing and touching of Jesus' wounds that allowed the famous doubting disciple, Thomas, to believe (John 20:24–29), and they remain as a powerful symbol in Christian faith, liturgy, and iconography. The power of this symbol is evident, for example, in psychosomatic experiences of stigmata, which have a good deal of historical evidence notwithstanding the dogmas of scientific materialism.[1] More broadly, the symbol of Jesus' wounds informs the wounded healer archetype, which is arguably the core metaphor in the history of Western psychotherapy.[2] A Jungian therapist once told me, in a cryptic statement that eventually became a kind of mantra for my own trauma healing, "the power is in the wound." But before there was power, there was also a great deal of pain and toxicity in my wounds—pain that I avoided for a long time. My journey from toxic wounds to powerful wounds was a journey of ego death and rebirth, a journey that involved a long process of showing my wounds to a few wise and sympathetic listeners who had made this journey before me.

In the Gospel of Mark, the first detailed description of Jesus healing a wound comes in the first chapter, when an unnamed man approaches him with a skin disease, traditionally identified as leprosy: "A man with leprosy came to him and begged him on his knees, 'If you are willing, you can make me clean.' Jesus was indignant. He reached out his hand and touched the man. 'I am willing,' he said. 'Be clean!' Immediately the skin disease left him

---

1. For a good summary see Krippner and Kirkwood, "Sacred Bleeding." By calling these phenomena *psychosomatic* I am not taking a position on whether they are supernatural. The latter is a word I would rather avoid because the history of science is a constant progression of the supernatural becoming natural. Further, and contra certain Thomist approaches, I do not posit a strict division between nature and grace, but an interpenetration of the two. With Augustine I would suggest that nature and its processes exist at every moment through a continuous infusion of grace.

2. See especially Ellenberger, *Discovery*. Ellenberger notes that most of the pioneers of psychotherapy were inspired by their own "creative illness." It was the exploration of their own psychological wounds that let both to the formulation of their theories, and to their effectiveness as clinicians. The "creative illness" can also be traced through the Existentialist and Humanist therapists (e.g., Viktor Frankl), and it continues with the more technique-oriented theories of today (e.g., Marsha Linehan's Dialectical Behavior Therapy [DBT] and Steven Hayes' Acceptance and Commitment Therapy [ACT]). The wounded healer archetype predates Christianity, for example, in the mythic figure of Chiron, and it was further elaborated in medieval Grail legends, for example, in the figure of the Fisher King. For an influential Christian rendering see Henri Nouwen, *Wounded Healer*. Nouwen traces the archetype to a story from the Talmud, which depicts a Messiah covered in wounds, which he "unbinds one at a time, and binds up again" (90).

and he was cleansed." This miracle will of course sound much too easy and much too clean for anyone who has struggled with psychological trauma, with all of its repetitive, volatile, and habitual patterning. Psychological trauma is usually healed in small steps and slow titrations, at times reappearing when we least expect it. Miracle cures are extremely rare these days and difficult for modern minds to imagine. One wonders if the miracle cure *itself* might have caused some difficulty for this man. According to the purity laws of the time, his life was instantly transformed from unclean outcast to accepted member of society when his skin wounds disappeared. Sudden changes, even positive ones, can often bring past traumas into bolder relief. From the vantage point of a new life or a new situation, the painful details of our old life often reveal themselves more clearly.

But after this radical transformation, something interesting happens in the text: "Jesus sent the man away at once with a strong warning: 'See that you do not tell this to anyone. But go, show yourself to a priest, and offer the sacrifices that Moses commanded for your cleansing, as a testimony to them.'" Jesus sternly prescribes a ritual of acknowledgement and self-awareness for this man. He orders him to perform the tender, vulnerable, and difficult work of showing himself—his whole body—to a priest, while also offering a ritual offering of thanks to God. Presumably, this ritual was in part a way of coming to terms with the transformation—letting go of the old and integrating the new.

Even more interesting, as the passage continues, we see that, while the man was undoubtedly grateful for the healing, he flagrantly disobeys Jesus' request: "Instead he went out and began to talk freely, spreading the news." Instead of the private and vulnerable act of showing himself to a priest and offering thanks, the man goes public. Instead of introverted contemplative awareness, the man chooses extreme extraversion and social action. The man in fact becomes one of the first missionaries, "spreading the news" of Jesus and his healing power. "As a result," the text concludes, "Jesus could no longer enter a town openly but stayed outside in lonely places" (Mark 1:40–45, NIV). One almost wonders if Jesus' forced introversion here is a kind of compensation or atonement for the man's extreme extraversion. It was certainly a result of it.[3]

---

3. My reading of this text is indebted to a sermon by Robert Dykstra I heard several decades ago. Biblical scholars tend to explain this passage in terms of the "Messianic Secret" in Mark. But this does not fully explain Jesus' ritual prescription for this man, nor the man's refusal to follow it.

Although our lives are separated by millennia, and my own miraculous experiences are much more modest, I do find myself resonating with this unnamed man, his wounds, and his impulsive extraversion. After a sudden and significant trauma in my own life—a car accident that took the lives of three close family members—I too found myself feeling suddenly and strangely extraverted. Rather than looking at my own wounds and dwelling on what had happened, I was suddenly taken by a strange desire to begin helping others and to make my life count in this way. In fact, it was at this point that I began thinking about becoming a minister and dedicating my life to this kind of service.

When I finally did begin to open up about the trauma I had suffered—to show myself—in this case to a therapist, I also felt a constant temptation to be diverted from this introspective path. The fantasy kept emerging that I should help others by becoming a therapist myself. Rather than explore my own trauma, it felt much more natural and helpful to explore the traumas of others. Eventually, a wise therapist told me that this fantasy is quite natural and that she had seen it in many of her clients: "When they start the work, they all want to become therapists," she said. "They catch this fantasy almost like catching a cold. I tell them that I caught it too when I started therapy. But I waited until the urge subsided before I began my own training as a therapist. Your own work is always the most important thing anyway, no matter what stage you are at."

Looking back, I am still surprised at how my strongly introverted personality, which had followed me from birth, shifted so quickly in the days after my sudden trauma, and how this extraversion reappeared as a potent fantasy later in therapy. Although I did not recognize it at the time, it was as if my trauma had deposited such a chaotic darkness in my unconscious that I could no longer look within for security and stability. I was forced, for the first time I can recall in my life, to look for an anchor in the outer world. I looked to friends, family, and my church community. I called old camp counsellors I had not seen in years. I even spoke very personally with the lawyer who was settling my family's affairs—an impromptu father figure of sorts. I was aware that all of this was out of character for me, but at the time it felt quite natural and necessary. In hindsight, I can see how this newborn extraversion served as a way both to conceal and to cope with the inner trauma. It served a valuable purpose, allowing me to postpone the full emotional impact and weight of the great loss I had suffered. And when

I did begin to explore these feelings in detail with a therapist, the extraversion remained as a tempting exit strategy.

C.G. Jung and Our Hyper-Extraverted World

Jung coined the now popular terms *introversion* and *extraversion* to describe two very different modes of adaptation, beginning in childhood, in which libido or life energy perpetually flows toward two very different concerns: the inner world or the outer world. Introverts find their sense of security and meaning within. The inner world is their safe harbor and walled garden, accessed in private rooms and private moments of silence and solitude.[4] Extraverts find their security and meaning in outer objects, people, and systems. They generally find the bustle and relational drama of social life quite energizing and intriguing. Solitude, without some driving task, is quite boring.[5] Jung acknowledged that the majority of people seem to evince some admixture of these dominant types: "There is, finally, a third group, and here it is hard to say whether the motivation comes chiefly from within or without. This group is the most numerous and includes the less differentiated normal person."[6] We might call this largest group the *ambiverts*. This Jungian theoretical picture becomes much more complex when we realize that an introverted ego is compensated by an extraverted unconscious, and vice versa. This means that each type, particularly in the second half of life, will be encouraged by the unconscious to find a kind of balance, middle way, or homeostasis, and the ego will be encouraged to give up its treasured habits and forge a new path.

---

4. "In a large gathering he feels lonely and lost. The more crowded it is, the greater becomes his resistance. He is not in the least 'with it,' and has no love of enthusiastic get-togethers. He is not a good mixer. What he does, he does in his own way, barricading himself against influences from outside . . . Under normal conditions he is pessimistic and worried, because the world and human beings are not in the least good but crush him . . . His own world is a safe harbour, a carefully tended and walled-in garden, closed to the public and hidden from prying eyes. His own company is the best." Jung, *Psychological Types*, 550–51.

5. Extraversion is characterized by interest in the external object, responsiveness, and a ready acceptance of external happenings, a desire to influence and be influenced by events, a need to join in and get "with it," the capacity to endure bustle and noise of every kind, and actually find them enjoyable, constant attention to the surrounding world, the cultivation of friends and acquaintances, none too carefully selected, and finally by the great importance attached to the figure one cuts." Jung, *Psychological Types*, 549.

6. Jung, *Psychological Types*, 515–16.

These types are also not fixed, and thus the large group of ambiverts can easily be swayed in one direction or the other by social structures and mores, particularly in the first half of life. In his day, Jung lamented that Western cultures were increasingly dominated by extraverts, who seemed to be imposing their noisy bustle on everyone else and drowning out the still small voice within (1 Kgs 19:12).[7] I am told that Jung even had strong feelings against phonographs and radios as purveyors of noise pollution and distraction. This seems almost laughable today, when so many of our living spaces, both public and private, are dominated by multiple beeping and blaring screens—televisions, computers, and cell phones. These devices are far from neutral.[8] They scream for our attention, and their addictive and harmful effects, on adults but particularly on children, are well documented.[9] Social media platforms not only encourage but behaviorally condition a strange and disconnected form of extraversion. On some platforms, participants compete for likes by posting the curated highlights of their personal lives. On others, social influencers, who seem to be incapable of an unpublished thought or experience, rise to novel form of social status. Meanwhile, in the physical world, even the architecture of public and private spaces has changed significantly, favoring open concept instead of private rooms. Solitude and silence are literally being designed out of our lives. And in our school and work environments, small group learning and team collaboration are championed as keys to creativity and productivity, when a good deal of empirical evidence shows just the opposite.[10]

This hyper-extraversion and constant distraction in our living spaces will of course be felt most deeply by introverts, who, if they cannot retreat to a quiet space, will retreat within their own thoughts. This retreat can easily go unnoticed by those extraverts who are continually pulled toward

---

7. On extraversion as a cultural ideal in the West, and on "the myth of charismatic leadership," see especially Cain, *Quiet*, 20–70.

8. Even today, the dominant approach one hears from technologists is that our myriad devices are value neutral, because it is humans who choose whether and how they are used. The fallacy of this view was noted many years ago, particularly by Jacques Ellul. See Ellul, *Technological Society*. See also McCullough, "Heidegger."

9. See for example Lissak, "Effects of Screen Time."

10. "Some forty years of research has reached the same startling conclusion. Studies have shown that performance gets worse as group size increases . . . The 'evidence from science suggests that business people must be insane to use brainstorming groups,' writes the organization psychologist Adrian Furnham. 'If you have talented and motivated people, they should be encouraged to work alone when creativity or efficiency is the highest priority.'" Cain, *Quiet*, 88–89.

urgent texts, emails, or social media posts on their phones. Most basically, the great loss in our screen-dominated spaces is the natural flow of human interaction and conversation, especially between introverts and extraverts, who have a natural tendency to misunderstand each other, even though they are frequently paired as romantic partners. We are now seeing the first generation come of age who have no previous standard of comparison. They never knew the natural flow of screen-free spaces.[11]

Likewise, for extraverts, most of the negative tone of everything I have said above will seem vastly overstated. Because they generally feel energized by this brave new world, they tend to see those who critique it as standing in the way of both enjoyment and progress.[12] This only furthers the natural misunderstanding between these two types, due to their fundamentally opposed modes of adaptation. But while extraverts generally embrace our over-stimulated world, they do not escape its deleterious effects, which encourage them to ignore the natural compensatory and corrective tendencies of the unconscious. The extravert's ego is growing increasingly out of joint not only with the introverts around them, but with their own introverted unconscious, and this lack of balance can only be ignored for so long. The spontaneous thoughts that emerge from the unconscious when we have a moment to ourselves are simply not being heard. The equanimity and stability provided by these thoughts is not being felt.

Jung was of course famous for his time spent in solitude. The remarkable stone tower he built at Bollingen on lake Zürich was designed as a medieval-era dwelling, with no electricity or running water. Jung retreated there to get in touch with the archaic tendencies of his own unconscious. His basic premise was that, for the vast swath of human history, we have lived as hunter gatherers. And while the conscious mind may be attracted by flashing screens and new gadgets, the majority of our nervous system and body are uncomfortable with these developments. Because the deepest parts of our unconscious are somatic, the modern ego is increasingly out

---

11. See especially Twenge, *iGen*.

12. The reference to Aldous Huxley's novel is an allusion to mass surveillance capabilities of our devices, which was revealed to the world by NSA whistleblower Edward Snowden and journalist Glenn Greenwald in June 2013. Snowden revealed that the NSA and the Five Eyes intelligence alliance are conducting illegal mass surveillance of their own populations via email accounts and cell phones. Three months earlier, when Director of National Intelligence James Clapper was questioned under oath by Congress, he claimed that the NSA does not collect any type of data on millions of Americans. Mass surveillance is likely having effects on mental health, particularly for introverts, and it is likely a significant reason for increasing mistrust of Western governments.

of touch with its own body and the natural ecosystems that support it. We have lost touch with the rhythm of nature in ourselves and our surroundings. Jung was acutely aware of these needs because of his own periods of introversion, especially a period that began in 1912 when he broke with Freud, from which all of his later theory emerged.[13] At eighty-two, Jung was still voicing his need for solitude to access the balancing effects of the unconscious: "I feel even more strongly the need to live in harmony with the inner demands of my old age. Solitude is for me a fount of healing which makes my life worth living. Talking is often torment for me, and I need many days of silence to recover from the futility of words."[14]

Extraversion as Concealment and Coping: Vignettes

Having noted the tendency to use extraversion as a means of concealing and coping with our inner wounds and having noted the way our society encourages this tendency, a few generic examples will help to flesh out the clinical picture. All of these examples are composites of individuals or groups I have known as a therapist or pastor, with details removed to protect anonymity. The first snapshot is of the late middle-aged man or woman who has climbed the career ladder to some kind of managerial or administrative role, but who begins to feel a deep sense of emptiness within, often accompanied by depression and/or anxiety. While the idea of a midlife crisis has entered popular consciousness, it still comes as a surprise for someone who is well-adapted, ambitious, and who has moved from success to success in the working world. If there have been some emotional traumas along the way, often these were not grieved sufficiently, and they may surface with the feelings of emptiness as a locus of fixation.

What is interesting for the therapist is that the growing emptiness is almost always compensated by an increasingly intense and extraverted workaholic tendency, often with continued career success, at least until the very final point of breakdown, if this ever comes. For many in this situation, tasks like responding to emails become a kind of unthinking compulsion or addiction. It feels quite impossible to take one's mind off work. The picture

---

13. "All my works, all my creative activity, has come from those initial fantasies and dreams which began in 1912, almost fifty years ago. Everything that I accomplished in later life was already contained in them, although at first only in the form of emotions and images." Jung, *Memories*, 192.

14. Letter to Gustav Schmaltz, May 30, 1957. Jung, *Letters*, 363.

emerges of someone who works with great efficiency and success, even appearing quite outwardly contented, and it may only be a romantic partner or therapist who is aware of the increasing void and absence of meaning within. If a breakdown comes, and a stress leave from work is possible, the situation is often exacerbated because the extraverted coping strategy is suddenly removed. There is no longer a constant stream of emails to hide the emptiness.

Moving from the working world to family life, it is still common to find parents, and particularly mothers, who invest so much of their time and energy in their children that they have nothing left for their own inner world. Social tropes of the sacrificial mother still encourage this tendency, particularly if these tropes are handed down unconsciously from mother to daughter. The results often prove tragic in that children, when they feel that a parent is controlling and overbearing, will often leave home quickly and decisively as soon as they have a taste of freedom. And with an empty nest, feeling betrayed and abandoned by their children, sacrificial parents are forced to look at the inner world they have neglected for so long. Having given up their inner life for their children, they often have very few skills and resources to cultivate a new sense of meaning and purpose apart from their children.

For women who have awakened to the injustice of the sacrificial mother trope, a fault they may identify in their own mother's generation, the working world can easily be coded in terms of meaning, purpose, freedom, and empowerment. But interestingly, I now see many such women in later life realizing that they have simply traded one extraversion for another. Those who managed to juggle children and a career often sacrifice dearly in terms their own inner world, and the growing awareness of this sacrifice often produces deep resentments against both individuals and social systems. Those who chose a career instead of children can likewise experience regrets, as the trope of female career empowerment runs aground on the fact that institutions generally care very little for the inner fulfillment of their employees. In general, the midlife crisis and quest for meaning, in both men and an increasing number of women, produces a fairly similar clinical picture revolving around questions of legacy. What have I accomplished with my life that really means something? What will people remember about me when I am gone? As these thoughts emerge, they are often accompanied initially by increasingly frantic extraverted attempts to make some kind of mark on the world, or to craft a more attractive persona that will be favorably remembered.

Families with highly ambitious and extraverted parents often produce similar patterns in their children, and thus extraversion as concealment and coping is often passed down unconsciously, but not always through career ambitions. A highly religious family, for example, might adopt a collective pattern of serving others and helping the disadvantaged, thus highlighting their extraordinary kindness. One should not underestimate the sense of meaning and fulfillment that can be generated by simple acts of kindness. But I have also known religious families where parents and children would almost compete against each other, outdoing one another in showing kindness, with the hidden secret that almost all of the family members were dealing with serious anxiety and depression. These inner feelings, and the reasons for them, were almost never discussed in the family system. Instead, the defense against them was the meaning and satisfaction gained from service. And the ability to help others in the midst of hidden internal suffering, the martyr trope, can actually increase the ego's secret pride in its virtuous disposition.

The above examples depict longstanding and habitual patterns of neglecting unconscious impulses, but as I noted at the beginning with my own experience, episodic events and traumas also frequently encourage extroversion as an initial coping mechanism. After the death of a spouse or a child, for example, some feel the desire to move to a new house and remove all traces of memory. Or after a divorce, for example, the fantasy might arise of travelling somewhere completely new, being totally unknown, and starting fresh with a completely new life. Some will actually follow these fantasies with varying degrees of success. But in many cases, the main thing people find in their new location is themselves, with familiar patterns of emotional turmoil and distress. The extraverted escape may in fact exacerbate loneliness, as they struggle to forge a support network in their new life. These generalized examples also presume largely middle-class experience. Working class people and families, who have usually confronted one or more traumas before middle age, are less susceptible to the mid-life crisis, and earlier confrontations with the unconscious produce a very different clinical picture.

By this point some of the more extraverted readers will likely be raising questions, or even feeling slightly annoyed. Why is extraversion so prone to unhealthy expressions? Cannot introverts also be unhealthy? The answer is yes, but unhealthy introversion has much less social support, and thus it is much less of a temptation. According to Western values, which have now been exported around the world, the unhealthy introvert is usually recognized as such, and even healthy introversion is seen as quite suspect. A common clinical picture of unhealthy introversion is found in young adults who are struggling to find their place in the world. They have an urgent need to make a difference, to make their mark, to express their spirit and creativity, and yet the entry-level jobs that appear before them seem totally intolerable: retail outlets, coffee shops, or cramped office cubicles with menial and boring routines. The common picture is of an introverted young adult living with their parents in a state of mild or even severe anxiety or depression, bemoaning the meaninglessness of the world and its lack of economic opportunities. Adults who are inured to meaningless work usually offer little in terms of support or wisdom. This clinical picture is well-known, and the difficulty for many therapists is that the problem seems to lie as much with the external world as with any introverted disposition in the client. To be well adjusted to a forty-hour work week with little or no meaning is a dubious accomplishment, and it is often the more gifted and creative clients who find this situation intolerable.

The picture is quite different with unhealthy extraversion because it can so easily appear to be healthy and adaptive. It easily cloaks itself in the form of the model employee or the compassionate altruist, with all of the attendant behavioral and social rewards and incentives. If the hidden sense of emptiness is accompanied by generalized anxiety, this anxiety in its initial phases can actually increase hard work and attention to detail on all fronts, thus increasing the behavioral rewards. The picture is very much like the one painted by Søren Kierkegaard in golden age Denmark:

> To be in despair does not mean, although it usually becomes apparent, that a person cannot go on living fairly well, seem to be a person, be occupied with temporal matters, marry, have children, be honoured and esteemed—and it may not be detected that in a deeper sense one lacks a self. Such things do not create much of a stir in the world, for a self is the last thing the world cares about and the most dangerous thing of all for a person to show signs of having. The greatest hazard of all, losing the self, can occur very quietly in the world, as if it were nothing at all. No other loss can occur so quietly.[15]

---

15. Kierkegaard, *Sickness unto Death*, 146.

Admittedly I am dealing in generalities here, which is always dangerous for a therapist. In the consulting room, everyone becomes completely unique, and this is as it should be. Nonetheless, I hope that these generalizations will help illuminate a pattern for the reader.

Caring for Care Workers

From these general snapshots, I want to move to a specific dynamic that affects those in the caring professions, and particularly those on the front lines of social justice work in religious communities, shelters, food banks, health care centers, and other social agencies, who work daily with people facing lack of housing, food insecurity, and the many physical and mental health issues that inevitably accompany the struggle for basic survival. In the past decade, I have seen several frontline justice organizations begin to experience difficulties; some have closed permanently. At first, I assumed it was because of swiftly increasing demands and lack of public support, but this was only part of the story. More heartfelt conversations with friends and colleagues revealed that much of the unrest in these organizations was due to staff conflict, itself emerging from the challenges of self-care in relation to the complex trauma they were seeing in clients on a daily basis. Complex trauma is very challenging to work with, and the vicarious trauma it engenders can be very difficult for care workers to see and process in themselves. Its dynamics, while specific, are also somewhat mysterious.

Before describing these dynamics, I want to be clear that I am not trying to place any blame on care workers. If blame is to be placed anywhere, it should likely be placed with the initiators of macro-economic forces that continue to eviscerate the North American middle class, increase billionaire fortunes, and leave an increasing number of people in desperate and traumatic circumstances.[16] The brutality of the age of realpolitik is evident in that even war and homelessness are seen as necessary instruments of

---

16. Oxfam Jan 2023 reports that "We are living through an unprecedented moment of multiple crises. Tens of millions more people are facing hunger. Hundreds of millions more face impossible rises in the cost of basic goods or heating their homes. Poverty has increased for the first time in 25 years. At the same time, these multiple crises all have winners. The very richest have become dramatically richer and corporate profits have hit record highs, driving an explosion of inequality" (1). "Since 2020, according to Oxfam analysis of Credit Suisse Data, this wealth grab by the super-rich has accelerated, and the richest 1% have captured almost two-thirds of all new wealth" (5). Oxfam International, *Survival of the Richest.*

economic policy.[17] And yet, as tent encampments become permanent fixtures in North American cityscapes, corporate media outlets and the public who follow them consistently cast those in desperate circumstances as the problem, seemingly unaware of the fact that many of the ultra-rich evade paying basic taxes.[18] The times are increasingly dark, and kicking against that darkness is increasingly difficult. Frontline care workers, and the people they serve, deserve our full attention. How is it possible to sustain a sense of hope, even as homelessness increases, and related overdose deaths skyrocket?

In the past decade, what was most noticeable in my conversations with frontline workers was that, although many of them were required to take time for self-care, and some were even required to see a therapist regularly, many reported that this inner work was at best unhelpful and at worst "useless." Many reported that they would much rather be doing the "real" work of helping vulnerable people, rather than the more intangible and nebulous work of looking within their own soul. This inner work often felt selfish and detached from the daily tragedies they were witnessing. Here the temptation of hyper-extraversion is increased by the fact that, on the frontlines, there is always someone who is suffering more than you are. And are not they more deserving of empathy and care? Are not their needs greater than yours?

This kind of extraversion can then be reinforced in potent ways. As stories are shared, and bonds of empathy are established with clients, the mysterious dynamics of vicarious trauma emerge, via transference and countertransference. As the care worker experiences the suffering of the client, a kind of invisible harmonic resonance is established, where the suffering of the care worker begins to seem indistinguishable from that of the

---

17. See McCullough, "Northrop Frye," especially quadrant four, which maps the dynamics of realpolitik in the modern age, 171–86.

18. ProPublica analyzed fifteen years of leaked confidential IRS data and found that the twenty-five richest Americans paid a true tax rate of just 3.4 percent on wealth growth of $401 billion between 2014 and 2018. "In 2007, Jeff Bezos, then a multibillionaire and now the world's richest man, did not pay a penny in federal income taxes. He achieved the feat again in 2011. In 2018, Tesla founder Elon Musk, the second-richest person in the world, also paid no federal income taxes. Michael Bloomberg managed to do the same in recent years. Billionaire investor Carl Icahn did it twice. George Soros paid no federal income tax three years in a row." Eisinger et al., "Secret IRS Files." See also Gibaud, *Whistleblowers*. Gibaud revealed a web of corruption linking UBS, the world's largest private bank, to tax evasion and laundering schemes. She has since been targeted by the French state and harassed by UBS via multiple lawsuits.

people they serve, *and to whom they are increasingly drawn as the only people who seem to understand this suffering.* The thought emerges in the care worker that the people they serve are the only ones who truly understand their inner feelings. A sentiment I heard regularly from frontline workers was something like this: "My friends and family, and even my therapist, just do not understand this work. They do not understand the suffering I am feeling. I cannot even talk to them about it. Only the people I care for really get it."

From here a dark cycle can emerge: as isolation, inner suffering, and burnout increases in the care worker, rather than looking within, they become drawn to increasingly intense outer suffering in the people they serve. In this way, helping those in crisis becomes the primary way the care worker feels alive in the midst of burnout, not only because of the adrenaline involved in confronting life and death on a daily basis, but also because it is the only way the care worker can connect to their own inner suffering, albeit indirectly.

The dangerous corollary is that, as this cycle continues, the actual people caregivers are helping can begin to recede from view. They become secondary characters in the drama of the caregiver's own inner struggle. In the end, the actual needs and feelings of clients can become completely occluded, even as the self of the caregiver becomes increasingly enlarged, even quite heroic, as it sees its own inner suffering everywhere except within. This enlarged self, rather than admitting its own needs and addressing them, projects its needs on the people it serves daily, and thus hides from them. Hyper-extraversion and activism conceal the inner struggle of the soul, and this concealment may appear in the form of a very heady heroism, even a kind of savior complex. Initially it offers huge behavioral rewards: you feel that you are alleviating in others the pain that you understand so well, and to some extent this may be true. You feel energized in your work. You feel such a close bond with those you are serving, as the only people who truly understand you. And you feel that you are one of the only people making a real difference in the world, while the rest of society remains oblivious.

We might call this the upswing phase. And if this dynamic is occurring in several staff members in the same organization, it can be accompanied by very buoyant and exuberant collective feelings. The organization itself may begin to feel that it is special, outdoing its sister organizations in altruistic zeal, and staff may even begin to silently compete with each other, working overtime and going the extra mile. More seasoned staff, who have already experienced the downturn phase that inevitably results, may offer advice for self-care that falls on deaf ears. If upswing staff are required to check in with a therapist, the therapist typically finds that they are not very engaged because they believe, secretly or openly, that their work is the only therapy they need. It provides excitement, satisfaction, and real meaning.

The shadow side is that organizations who function this way tend to create increasing dependency in the people they serve. The hint of narcissism in the heroic savior persona is easy to conceal because it is so obvious to the caregiver that they are spending all of their time serving others. The telltale sign is that organizations in this mode spend their time handing out fish, rather than teaching the skills of fishing. And at some point, the heroic and enlarged collective self of the organization will face a downturn, in which the tipping point often has a domino effect. As neglected inner needs and vicarious traumas break through and demand attention, often in the form of unmanageable anxiety and depression, two things are happening at once: As the extraverted coping strategy for avoiding the inner world fails, all of the behavioral and social rewards of the heroic personality also disappear. The ego simultaneously loses both a coping strategy and the many powerful rewards of meaning, purpose, and praise that enlarged it in the first place. This downturn can be very painful for organizations as several staff members may simultaneously begin to feel both overworked and undervalued. Conflict and blame usually ensue. Introverts are often the first to sense the problem, and if they do not raise their voice, or their voice is not listened to, they will often be the first to leave.

The generalized picture I am painting has a multitude of variations, and what Tolstoy said of families is also true here: Every happy organization is the same, and every unhappy organization is unique. But having observed various shades of discontent in frontline organization, I have noticed a commonality: The more difficult things get, the harder it becomes for individual members, let alone an entire organization, to look within at the traumas and pain points that are fomenting discord. An extraverted coping strategy that worked for so long is difficult to reevaluate and reversing course to deal with the inner traumas and griefs, particularly among several staff at the same time, is a difficult path to take. A much better strategy is to recognize the dynamics of the upswing-downturn cycle before it takes hold, and recognize the constant need for inner contemplative awareness, in order to temper the extremes of outer activist extraversion.

The Fractured Left and Class Consciousness

The dynamics of trauma in relation to extraverted coping and concealment also shed light on contemporary left-wing political movements in North America. A previous generation of left activists, emerging from the civil rights era, looked primarily at class and economic status as measures of equal rights, and thus social justice was generally understood in terms of wealth redistribution and socialist political structures. The goal of this previous generation was to galvanize a broad movement of working-class people and their allies, which crossed lines of race, gender, and sexuality. While combating discrimination based on race, gender, sexuality, and other factors was of course a significant aspect of this broad movement, the measure of emancipation was generally an economic measure.[19] Today, in what some are calling "boutique activism," the left seems to have fractured into various special interest groups who often struggle to understand each other.[20]

This fracturing was highlighted for me at a recent academic conference when a debate among the speakers erupted over which group had faced more trauma and discrimination. In a discussion about the meaning of the word *intersectional*, three speakers, representing the Jewish community, the LGBTQ2+ community, and the African American community respectively, began an increasingly heated exchange in an attempt to somehow rank the atrocities of the holocaust, the African slave trade, and the history of queerphobic violence. To many sympathetic onlookers the debate was difficult to watch, not only because any kind of moral calculus about such atrocities is

---

19. Martin Luther King, for example, understood that there would never be equal rights without economic justice. In 1964 he advocated a Bill of Rights for the Disadvantaged, which would include reparations for unpaid wages to victims of slavery and segregation, but importantly he also called for a broad coalition with working class whites and the labor movement. See King, *Why We Can Not Wait*, 137–38, 141–42. It was likely his push for socialist principles in his later years that led to his assassination by elements of the US intelligence agencies, including the FBI and CIA, while he was in Memphis to support a garbage worker's strike in 1968. See Pepper, *An Act of State*. Likewise, Fred Hampton's 1969 Rainbow Coalition was an attempt to build a working class movement that crossed racial lines and garnered support from various marginalized groups. It was the initial success of this movement that likely led to Hampton's assassination by the FBI in 1969. Hampton was shot while asleep in his bed, beside his pregnant fiancée. The point is that leftist movements are only threatening to the power elites when they build broad support based on class consciousness, which crosses lines of race, gender, sexuality, disability, education, etc.

20. On the importance of class consciousness, see Presbyterian Minister, Pulitzer Prize winner, and activist Chris Hedges, *Our Class*.

difficult, but because it was fairly apparent that each person was speaking from their own personal trauma wounds and crying out for a sympathetic listener. The fact that they were framing the discussion in terms of intellectual arguments and the scoring of academic points meant that the deep and historically continuous trauma behind all of their words was not being adequately heard, felt, or responded to.

This kind of fracturing and division in the left reflects the nature of trauma in at least two ways: First, trauma causes us to naturally identify with a group of people who have similar traumatic wounds; and second, the wounds of the group with which we identify always seem uniquely and singularly painful because we understand them from within, from direct personal experience. The therapeutic journey of working with our own wounds generally results in the slow realization that our wounds are not in fact unique, and that suffering of many and various kinds extends throughout the human family. But the ability to empathize deeply with suffering that does not bear a resemblance to our own is something that generally only comes with the introverted exploring of our own wounds. In short, at the beginning of trauma work, clients are inclined to say, "nobody understands me, except maybe those who have experienced what I have experienced." And by the end of the work, they generally begin to see, sense, and empathize with the many kinds of suffering that represent the human condition: "I now have compassion for all who suffer." Here again, it would seem that the current state of the fractured activist left reveals a form of extraverted concealment and coping with personal trauma wounds. Rather than championing the cause of one's own disadvantaged group over against others, inner attention to these deep wounds might allow greater awareness of the suffering endured by so many, and indeed the suffering of the biosphere itself. It might help create the kind of broad-based empathy that would empower a broad-based social movement.

Missiology and the Extraverted God

It strikes me that the patterns of trauma and extraversion I have mentioned above also illuminate certain aspects of the history of Christian mission. It may even be that societies shaped by Christianity have a certain proclivity toward extraverted concealment and coping. Beginning even with the Apostle Paul we find a remarkably driven personality, whose famous conversion on the Damascus Road marked a drastic shift from one extreme extraversion to another. From a radical persecutor of the fledgling Christian movement, Paul instantly became its chief defender, the apostle who "worked harder than all of them."[21] The remarkable dissonances and incongruities that plagued Paul's soul are evident enough in his writings. My point here is that he seems to have coped with these tensions and doubts through a remarkably activistic zeal, which at times put him at odds with the other apostles, particularly Peter and James.[22]

This Pauline pattern is reflected in missionary movements many centuries later. If trauma produces a kind of fracturing and division within the individual soul, we might also apply this principle by analogy to collective groups. In the case of Western Christianity, the fracture caused by the Reformation, itself the result of long periods of unrest, dissent, and persecution, seemed to ignite greater missionary fervor. The Jesuits, arguably the most prominent Roman Catholic missionary organization, emerged as the "shock troops" of the Counter-Reformation, and rather than attempting to settle the divisions in the collective Christian soul at home, they spread their partisan message abroad. Likewise, Protestants soon began spreading their partisan message in the modern missionary movement, which was itself born out of the growing factionalism of the Protestant churches. Given the traumas and divisions that sparked these fervent activist movements, it is not surprising that they accommodated themselves so easily to various forms of colonial violence. Trauma begets trauma, unless the cycle is broken through inner work. While such sweeping historical generalizations are vulnerable to critiques in any number of details, my point is simply that the fracturing of Christianity, rather than producing an increase in introspective soul-searching, seems to have produced an increase in competitive missionary fervor. Rather than looking within at the increasingly difficult paradoxes and contradictions of Christian self-understanding, missionaries went abroad to convince others that their faith was the pinnacle of religious understanding. The deep questions of a fracturing faith were seemingly concealed by an extraverted zeal to convert others.[23]

By way of conclusion, and with apologies for encroaching on a field in which I lack expertise, let me simply suggest that missiology, in order to be

21. E.g., 1 Cor 15:10.

22. See Gal 2:11–14. A balancing of Pauline and Petrine streams, as suggested by Hans Urs von Balthasar, amidst the full mandala of apostolic influences, might mitigate the extreme extraversion of the Pauline stream.

23. The wars of religion following the Reformation can also be seen, partly, as extraverted attempts at concealment.

balanced, might pay attention to the psychological dynamics of introversion and extraversion noted above. Whether mission is about spreading the news of Jesus, as we saw in Mark chapter one, or about a mission of social justice to heal the planet, both extraversions can be used to conceal inner doubts and fractures. If the inner fractures are traumatic, either personally or collectively, the resulting extraversion will likely perpetuate trauma rather than heal it. This may explain why so many well-meaning missionary activities have had negative consequences in cultures around the world. This balance between contemplative introspection and healing action is something that has attracted me to Professor Fensham's work.[24]

Professor Fensham's teacher, David Bosch, identified Karl Barth as "the Father of the modern theology of mission," and Barth's concept of the *missio Dei* may be one of contemporary missiology's most prolific concepts.[25] Barth's conception represents a significant reconfiguration of ancient Christian notions of the Trinity which, following Greek thought, conceived of God in a state of self-contained and self-sufficient perfection or aseity. For Barth, God is not a being who subsists in quiet introversion but a God who gives or sends Godself in radical extroversion. Or, more accurately, we might say that Barth attempted to include both concepts in his theology but emphasized the latter in his theology of mission.[26] Missiologists have since appropriated the concept of *missio Dei*, at times to justify a kind of radical extraversion. Given that both individuals and cultures tend to project their own desires on God, it is not surprising that our hyper-extraverted culture would prefer to worship an extraverted God. The recent popularity of the social Trinity conception might also reflect this tendency.

By contrast, the classical Western conception of the Trinity, coming from Augustine's *De Trinitate*, pictured the Trinity as a model for the *imago Dei* in the human soul, and particularly in the soul's movements

---

24. See especially Fensham, *To the Nations*.

25. Bosch, *Witness to the World*, 167. The spread of Barth's concept of *missio Dei* is usually traced to a paper he gave at the Brandenburg Mission Conference in 1932. The concept was popularized decisively at the International Missionary Council in Willingen, Germany, in 1952.

26. Barth's Christocentric formulation notes the remarkable confluence of activity and passivity in the life and work of Jesus Christ, which is a model for the fine and paradoxical balance I am hinting at here. We see in the Gospel accounts that Christ's inactivity often had remarkable effects, and likewise his actions often seem incomprehensible, at least in a worldly sense.

of memory, will/love, and understanding.[27] In this conception, a central goal of the Christian life was to search for God in the fields of memory, a project that Augustine himself pursued in the *Confessions*. In memory, a great many things are hidden, waiting to come to light. And I have argued elsewhere that Augustine's concept of memory was the historical prototype and precursor to the psychodynamic concept of the unconscious mind.[28] In memory we find past traumas and regrets, but for Augustine we also find eternal archetypes like love, goodness, truth, and beauty. And these archetypes allow hidden memories to be not only recovered but transformed—lit by a purer light—as they find their place in the larger narrative of God's love and forgiveness. The goal then of this inner mission of remembering past wounds, is to bring all that we have hidden in memory into the light and clarity of conscious understanding, surrounded by the love of God.[29] Only as we pursue this inner mission, I would suggest, will the appropriate actions of outer extraverted mission become clear. Only as we attend to our inner wounds will we learn how to heal the wounds around us.

My point is simply that if we would like to make God's extraverted sending—God's being for others—a model for the Christian life, we should also, and perhaps more fundamentally, remember that God's being was originally a model that spoke of deep inwardness, self-exploration, and self-awareness. We should be wary of promoting the outward and extraverted mission without at the same time recognizing the inner mission. When framed in relation to the history of Christian ethics, with its emphasis on dying to self and serving the other, this inner mission can easily sound self-indulgent and solipsistic. On the other hand, when we look at the history of Christian mission, and the many misguided and harmful actions done in the name of Christianity, we cannot help but think that more introspection and self-awareness are needed. I am suggesting here that, like the systole and diastole of the heart, like the inhalation and exhalation of the breath, mission ought to be understood as both an inward and an outward

---

27. Edmund Hill notes that Augustine's conception was not a "faculty psychology," as many have claimed, but rather a phenomenological approach to the soul's functioning. "In this respect," says Hill, "his approach has more in common with that of moderns like Freud and Jung than with the theories and speculations of ancient philosophers." Augustine, *Trinity*, 258–59.

28. McCullough, "Jacob Boehme," 30–45.

29. For Augustine, in trinitarian terms, this is analogous to the way that the Son interpenetrates with the Father, and knows the Father fully.

movement. Inward self-awareness wedded to outward acts of love speak of a God who draws us deeper both inwardly and outwardly.

Bibliography

Augustine of Hippo. *The Trinity*. Translated and edited by Edmund Hill. Brooklyn: New City Press, 1991.

Bosch, David. *Witness to the World: The Christian Mission in Theological Perspective*. London: Marshall, Morgan & Scott, 1980.

Cain, Susan. *Quiet: The Power of Introverts in a World that Can not Stop Talking*. New York: Broadway.

Eisinger, Jesse, et al. "The Secret IRS Files: Trove of Never-Before-Seen Records Reveal How the Wealthiest Avoid Income Tax." *Pro Publica*, June 8, 2021. https://www.propublica.org/article/the-secret-irs-files-trove-of-never-before-seen-records-reveal-how-the-wealthiest-avoid-income-tax.

Ellenberger, Henri. *The Discovery of the Unconscious: The History and Evolution of Dynamic Psychiatry*. New York: Basic, 1970.

Ellul, Jacques. *The Technological Society*. Translated John Wilkinson. New York: Knopf, 1964.

Fensham, Charles. *To the Nations for the Earth: A Missional Spirituality*. Toronto: Clements Academic, 2013.

Gibaud, Stéphanie. *Whistleblowers: The Man Hunt*. Foreword by Julian Assange. Paris: Max Milo, 2017.

Hedges, Chris. *Our Class: Trauma and Transformation in an American Prison*. New York: Simon & Schuster, 2021.

Jung, C.G. *Letters of C.G. Jung: Volume 2, 1951–1961*. London: Routledge, 1976.

———. *Memories, Dreams, Reflections*. Translated by Richard and Clara Winston. London: Collins, 1963.

———. *Psychological Types*, Vol. 6 of *The Collected Works of C.G. Jung*, edited by Gerhard Adler and R. F. C. Hull. Princeton: Princeton University Press, 2014.

Kierkegaard, Søren. *The Sickness unto Death: A Christian Psychological Exposition for Upbuilding and Awakening*. Kierkegaard's Writings 19. Edited by Edna and Howard Hong. Princeton: Princeton University Press, 1980.

King, Martin Luther. *Why We Can Not Wait*. New York: New American Library, 1964.

Krippner, Stanley, and Jeffrey Kirkwood. "Sacred Bleeding: The Language of Stigmata." In *Miracles: God, Science, and Psychology in the Paranormal*, Vol. 2: *Medical and Therapeutic Events*, edited by J. Harold Ellens. London: Praeger, 2008.

Lissak, Gadi. "Adverse Physiological and Psychological Effects of Screen Time on Children and Adolescents: Literature Review and Case Study." *Environmental Research* 164 (2018) 149–57.

McCullough, Glenn. "Heidegger, Augustine, and *Poiesis*: Renewing the Technological Mind." *Theology Today* 59.1 (2002) 21–38.

———. "Jacob Boehme and the Spiritual Roots of Psychodynamic Psychotherapy: Dreams, Ecstasy, and Wisdom." PhD diss., University of Toronto, 2019. https://hdl.handle.net/1807/99728.

———. "Northrop Frye, C.G. Jung, and the Grand Scheme of Things: Mapping the Psycho-Mythical Cosmos." *The Journal of Religion* 103.2 (2023) 145–86.

Nouwen, Henri. *The Wounded Healer: Ministry in Contemporary Society*. 1972. Reprint, New York: Image, 2024.

Oxfam International. *Survival of the Richest: How We Must Tax the Super-rich Now to Fight Inequality, Executive Summary*. Oxford: Oxfam House, 2023. https://www.oxfam.ca/wp-content/uploads/2023/01/davos-2023-summary-survival-of-the-richest.pdf.

Pepper, William F. *An Act of State: The Execution of Martin Luther King*. New York: Verso, 2003.

Twenge, Jean. *iGen: Why Today's Super-Connected Kids Are Growing Up Less Rebellious, More Tolerant, Less Happy—and Completely Unprepared for Adulthood (And What This Means for the Rest of Us)*. Toronto: Atria, 2017.

10

Radicalizing Women

The Abuse of Women by Radicals in the Reformation[1]

David Neelands

HOOKER'S ACCOUNT OF THE growth of fanaticism in the third chapter of the Preface to the *Lawes* includes the claim that "they" (the radicals) appeal to the emotions and make proselytes of weak women.[2]

Yet Hooker's close summary at the end of this chapter of the various stages in the growth of fanaticism, although it repeats the notion that "ye are by all means (i.e., even secret conferences and by appeal to the emotions), to nourish and witness your 'discipline' in yourselves, and to strengthen on every side your minds against whatsoever might be of force to withdraw you from it,"[3] makes no mention of women, weak or otherwise.

Elsewhere, we have seen how carefully Hooker considered the triumph of the Presbyterian program in Geneva, adopting the accounts of the "learned guides and pastors of Geneva," and how he used a noble source entirely sympathetic to Calvin and his allies, Theodore Beza's *Life of Calvin,* although

---

1. An earlier version of this paper was presented at the Sixteenth Century Studies Conference, Milwaukee, 28 October 2017.

2. Hooker, *Lawes*, Preface 3.13; 1:18.32—19.22.

3. Hooker, *Lawes*, Preface 3.16; 1:20.26—21.9.

sometimes with some subtle ironies.[4] In particular, I have noted that Hooker drew from Beza such details as that Calvin was censorious and difficult as a child, as his family noted; Calvin's preaching, although "the meanest of all other gifts in him" was so admired that it was said that one admirer would prefer to listen to a sermon of Calvin rather than one by St. Paul, if given the choice; Calvin is described as a "grave and wise man," a phrase Hooker adopts almost as a specific title to describe him and his close disciples; Beza's observation that wise men are men, and the truth is taken over directly, perhaps with some irony; and so on. And Hooker thought it useful to contrast the bearing and character of Calvin and Beza to illustrate points about their successive leadership. At the end of his life, in Hooker's notes in the margins of *A Christian Letter*, Hooker still has Calvin, as described by Beza, in mind.[5]

What has apparently not previously been noted, and which is relevant for considering the closeness of Hooker's attention to Beza and the other "learned guides and pastors of Geneva" is that the very title of Hooker's *magnum opus*, "Of the Lawes of Ecclesiasticall Politie," is found in Beza's *Life of Calvin*, which is probably the source of a slightly ironic borrowing by Hooker.[6] Beza twice uses the phrase *ecclesiasticae politiae leges* to describe the Presbyterian system drawn up by Calvin and accepted by the magistrates and people of Geneva:

> To resume our narrative, as soon as [Calvin] returned to the city, calling to mind the saying, (Matth. vi. 33) "Seek ye first. the kingdom of God, and his righteousness; and all other things will be added unto you," the first thing he did was to obtain the consent of the Senate to a form of ecclesiastical polity [Latin: *ecclesiasticae politiae leges*], which was agreeable to the Word of God, and from which neither ministers nor people should afterwards be permitted to depart.[7]
>
> Finally, he proved the difference between popish tyranny and the yoke of the Saviour, and thus easily succeeded in inducing the people to receive, with unanimous consent, the same laws of ecclesiastical polity [Latin: *ecclesiasticae politiae leges*] yet used by the church of Geneva, and which were written, read, and approved by the suffrages of the people on the 20th of November.[8]

4. See Neelands, "Use and Abuse."
5. See manuscript note on title page of *A Christian Letter*, Autograph Notes 4:3.7–14.
6. For a fuller account of this point, see Neelands, "Use and Abuse."
7. Beza, *Life of Calvin*.
8. Beveridge, "Preface," xli. See also "From a letter which Calvin himself addressed

But in his narrative of the progress of the fanaticism about "ecclesiastical polity" in Geneva, Hooker departs from Beza's account. In writing of the absorption of the Reformation, Beza describes many women in his *Life of Calvin:*

1. The Queen of Navarre, sister of Francis I (Jeanne III, 1528–72)—referred to four times: (1) patroness of Reformers (xxv), (2) "a woman of distinguished genius" but misled by Gerard Roussel (xxxi); (3) offended by Calvin's treatise against the Libertines (xlv); (4) ultimately seduced by the wiles of the papists (lxxxi).

2. Duchess of Ferrara (Renée of France, 1510–75; daughter of Louis XII; xxviii)—Calvin confirmed her in her "zeal for true religion"; she turned adrift Jerome Bolsec (lvii).

3. "Several ladies of the highest rank" among those arrested and imprisoned for attending the Eucharist in St. James' Street, Paris (lxxi).

4. Testimony of a matron whose daughters had been abused and who exposed the calumny of Sorbonists (lxxii).

5. A "lady of rank" burned at the stake in Paris (lxxii).

6. Queen Elizabeth—the singular piety and humanity of "Her Serene Majesty" (lxxix).

7. Two nieces mentioned in Calvin's will—received three quarters of amount two of their brothers received (lxxxviii).

8. Two female figures: (1) Sorbonne, "the mother who gave birth to [Peter Caroli] this most impudent sophist" (xxx); (2) Rome "the beast herself" (xxxi).

None of these, with the possible exception of Jeanne III, Queen of Navarre, who was offended by one of Calvin's writings and seduced by the wiles of the papists, could be called "weak women" proselytized by unscrupulous men with faulty reasoning.

---

in the same year to the Church of Montbelliard, any person may know what answer to give to those who complain of his excessive severity in enforcing the laws of ecclesiastical polity." Beveridge, xliv. The phrase "ecclesiastical polity" itself occurs once more: "No sooner was the republic thus freed from those pests, when, by another act of the Divine goodness, in consequence of the reply of the four Helvetian cities, (we mentioned that their opinion had on the previous year been asked by the Senate when making inquiry into the ecclesiastical discipline of Geneva,) all the ancient edicts relating to ecclesiastical polity were, contrary to the expectation of the factious, put to the vote, and carried by the common suffrages of the citizens." Beveridge, "Preface," lxviii.

Here is what Hooker says, with respect to "the people," in an elegant figure of repeated parallel phrases emphasizing, through the repetition of "this maketh," the conversion of mind, heart, and will involved:

> From hence, they are easilie drawne on to thinke it exceeding necessarie, for feare of quenching that good Spirit, to use all meanes whereby the same may be both strengthened in themselves, and made manifest unto others. This maketh them diligent hearers of such as are knowne that way to incline; this maketh them eager to take and to seeke all occasions of secret conference with such; this maketh them glad to use such as counsellors and directors in all their dealings which are of weight, as contractes, testaments, and the like; this maketh them, through an unweariable desire of receyving instruction from the maisters of that companie, to cast off the care of those very affayres which doe most concerne theyr estate, and to thinke that then they are lyke unto Marie, commendable for making choice of the better parte.[9]

Then, Hooker brings in the "weak women":

> In which respect it is also noted, that most labour hath bene bestowed to win and reteine towards this cause them whose judgments are commonlie weakest by reason of their sex. And although not *women loden with sinnes* [2 Tim. iii. 6.],[10] as the apostle S. Paule speaketh, but (as we verelie esteeme of them for the most part) women propense and inclinable to holines be otherwise edified in good things, rather then carried away as captives into any kinde of sinne and evill by such as enter into their houses, with purpose to plant there a zeale and a love towards this kind of discipline: yet some occasion is hereby ministred for men to thinke, that if the cause which is thus furthered did gaine by the soundnes of proofe, whereupon it doth build it selfe, it would not

---

9. Hooker, *Lawes*, Preface 3.12; 1:18.17–28.

10. The larger passage in 2 Timothy 3 is worth noting, as it comes in a set of epistles that has praised the work of Bernice and Chloe in the formation of Timothy and stress the wickedness of men who lead women into error: "[1]This know also, that in the last days perilous times shall come [2]For men shall be lovers of their own selves, covetous, boasters, proud, blasphemers, disobedient to parents, unthankful, unholy, [3]Without natural affection, trucebreakers, false accusers, incontinent, fierce, despisers of those that are good, [4]Traitors, heady, highminded, lovers of pleasures more than lovers of God; [5]Having a form of godliness, but denying the power thereof: from such turn away. [6]For of this sort are they which creep into houses, and lead captive silly women laden with sins, led away with divers lusts, [7]Ever learning, and never able to come to the knowledge of the truth." (2 Tim 3.1–7, KJV).

> most busilie endeavor to prevaile where least habilitie of judgement is: and therefore that this so eminent industrie in making proselytes more of that sex than of the other groweth, for that they are deemed apter to serve as instruments and helps in the cause. Apter they are through the eagerness of their affection, that maketh them, which way soever they take, diligent in drawing their husbands, children, servants, friends and allies the same waie; apter through that naturall inclination unto pittie which breedeth in them a greater readines then in men to be bountifull towards their Preachers who suffer want; apter through sundry opportunities, which they especially have, to procure encouragements for their brethren; finally, apter through a singular delight which they take in giving very large and particular intelligence how all near about them stand affected as concerning the same cause.[11]

It is fairly clear that, although the picture of the proselytized women may be patronizing, it is not otherwise negative. They are compared to the Virgin Mary in their personal (albeit mistaken) outlook. And women are thought generally to have qualities of ability (aptnesses) that would be admirable in anyone: These several aptnesses[12] of women include: (a) eagerness of their affection; (b) apter through natural inclination to pity—especially to preachers in want; (c) apter through their special opportunities to "procure encouragements" for their brethren; (d) apter for spreading "very large and particular intelligence" about those close to them.[13] And women we know can be numbered with God's saints, as Hooker's sermon "A Remedie against Sorrow and Feare, delivered in a funerall Sermon" (Sermon IV) suggests: Hooker invites friends grieving for the death of the woman to be silent and patient, since the death of his saints is precious in God's eyes.[14]

And the women are explicitly not "loaded with sin" as the women described in the New Testament are. They are the innocent victims of willful proselytizers who take advantage of their good qualities. In fact, appeal to women is evidence propagandists do not think their arguments are reasonable, that is, they use *ethos* and *pathos* rather than *logos* in their rhetoric:[15]

11. Hooker, *Lawes*, Preface 3.13; 1:18.32—19.22.

12. Compare *aptness* and *ability*: *aptness* being natural capacities that survive the Fall and come from our original created natures and *ability* being capacities we have lost through the Fall that require special elevating grace. Neelands, *Theology of Grace*, 166–71.

13. Hooker, *Lawes*, Preface 3.13.

14. *Remedie* [B1v]; 5:373.3–17.

15. For an extended treatment of Hooker's apparent analysis of the use of the modes

"if the cause which is thus furthered did gain by the soundness of proof whereupon it doth build itself, it would not most busily endeavor to prevail where least ability of judgment is." Significantly, this point, the whole of section 13, is one of the few points omitted in the careful and detailed summary of chapter 3 in section 16, as we have seen. We will return to the basis for Hooker's observation that in women there is "least ability of judgement."[16]

If Hooker did not get this critical reference to the exploitation of women by proselytizers using illegitimate means from Beza, where did it come from?

All parties to the Reformation seem to have resolved, with varying degrees of ambivalence, on the role of women in supporting whatever it was that they were against. From very different Reformation perspectives, but with conviction that they posed a danger because of their popularity, both Marjorie Kempe and Anne Askew were martyred under the watch of Thomas Cranmer.

Calvin himself had noted the problems of pious men and old women with respect to the idolatrous veneration of statues:

> If idolatry is just to transfer the honour of God to others can we deny that this is idolatry It is no excuse to say it is done through the excessive zeal of rude and ignorant men or old women. The extravagance is of wider extent It has everywhere prevailed and been approved even by those who sit holding the reins of government in the Church.[17]

In other words, idolatrous error is not to be blamed on the weak, including women, but on the authorities who tolerate and encourage their idolatrous piety. And, as is now recognized, Calvin himself, though not many of his successors, would have allowed women preachers in special circumstances.[18] Disrespect for women was also noted and criticized in the Catholic world. Thus, for instance, Elia Capriciolo blames those Dominicans involved in the Inquisition who torture confessions out of women heretics:

> you seize from the Valcamonica certain old women who are stupid and frozen in a kind of mental daze, and you interrogate them

---

of persuasion *ethos*, *pathos*, and *logos* in the consensus about the Presbyterian "discipline" in Geneva, see Neelands, "Deceit of the Evil Spirit."

16. See Eppley, "Contextualizing," 78–81.

17. Calvin, "An Admonition Showing the Advantages which Christendom might derive from an Inventory of Relics," in Beveridge, 291.

18. Neelands, "Defence of a Reformation."

about their faith, the Trinity, and other such topics. You bring in scribes and drag out proceedings; you conduct examinations under torture so that, by inflicting pain and torment on women who are admittedly little different from brutish beasts, you may appear as guardians of the Christian faith.[19]

This was an age when casual references to the intellectual weaknesses of women were commonplace. Consider, for instance Orsino's description of women in the first half of Shakespeare's *Twelfth Night*, or the better-known complaint of *Hamlet*, "Frailty thy name is woman." And, at the very beginning of Elizabeth's reign, pamphlets by John Knox and John Aylmer directly opposed on the question of the appropriateness of rule by a woman were agreed that women had inherent weaknesses with respect to exercising authority.[20]

Picking up on the words *brutish beasts* in the pamphlet of Elia Campanolo quoted just now, and remembering the reference in the service of *Matrimony* in the *Book of Common Prayer* that spoke of matrimony as

> not to be enterprised, nor taken in hand unadvisedly, lightly, or wantonly, to satisfy men's carnal lusts and appetites, like brute beasts that have no understanding; but reverently, discreetly, advisedly, soberly, and in the fear of God.

That is, brutishness in human beings (whether male or female) is there opposed to reverence, discretion, sobriety, and the fear of God, all engraced human capacities.[21] Hooker used the phrase "natural imbecility," nearly as a synonym for bestial brutishness, but with a clear and uniquely human reference.

It is important to note that Hooker used the archaic terminology of brutishness in connection with both respects in which human nature required God's grace to move to perfection, natural and spiritual, and that his theological assumptions are for a level equality between men and women. He occasionally uses the vocabulary to refer to human need for

---

19. 1505, with reference to the Dominican inquisitors in Brescia. Note that Elia Capriciolo, who wrote the pamphlet, assumes that women are notably inferior in intellect, though they are unfairly exhibited as bearing heresies, and cannot be blamed for their fanaticism. MacCulloch, *All Things Made New*, 84.

20. See Neelands, "Paul's Cross Sermon," 251–2.

21. Is there a connection with the use of the word *brute* in the marriage service? Animals follow the prescription to be fruitful and multiply, but this is somewhat regulated by the keepers among domestic animals, although it can be violent among the feral, as with deer in rutting season.

grace because of natural weakness, without respect to human sinfulness.²² Thus, when discussing the significance of the disputed use of the wedding ring (to be worn by the woman), he refers to "the verie imbecilitie of theire [women's] nature and sex."²³ Similarly, the phrase in the Preface that we are considering here clearly refers to a *natural* weakness in women, "whose judgements are commonlie weakest by reason of their sex."²⁴ But natural imbecility is not limited to female human beings: when Hooker argues for the need for Ministers, he notes that all human beings are infected by "mans imbecilitie and pronenesse to elation of minde," and therefore need officers to keep before them the truth of their innate weakness as well as the proneness to have too high an estimate of their own capacities.²⁵ And Hooker does not exclude himself in this estimate, humbly asserting that "wee in other mens offences doe behold the plaine image of our own imbecilitie."²⁶

Certainly Hooker does use *imbecility* in a way that makes clear the weakness is related to humanity considered as sinful (under which consideration there must be gender indifference):

> if Gods speciall grace did not aide our imbecilitie, whatsoever wee doe or imagine would be only and continuallie evill.²⁷

---

22. Some have failed to notice this double sense of human weakness. Paul Forte, for instance, seems to attribute "imbecility" simply to the inheritance of original guilt. He refers to I, xi, and to the discussion of "the end that all men seek but which they are prevented from discovering by reason due to the "imbecilitie" they have inherited through original sin. Forte, "Hooker's Theory of Law," 149. Forte confuses two things: the loss of the "natural" way of attaining the reward of bliss, which is no longer available as a result of the Fall, but which is still *known* to reason, and the present inability to discover the "supernatural way" of faith, which is unknown because it *exceeds* (even unfallen) human reason.

23. Hooker, *Lawes*, V.73.5; 2:403.26-27. This unscientific generalization is a commonplace of classical political philosophy and economics from Aristotle on.

24. Hooker, *Lawes*, Preface, 3.13; 1:19.1.

25. Hooker, *Lawes*, V.76.5; 2:418.16.

26. Hooker, *Lawes*, V.77.4; 2:426.25-26.

27. *Dublin Fragments* 1; 4:101.16-17. This idea, of course, was clear in the *Lawes*, but the word "imbecility" was not so clearly associated with the need for healing grace to restore fallen reason: "The search of knowledg is a thing painful and the painfulnes of knowledge is that which maketh the will so hardly inclinable thereunto. The root hereof divine malediction whereby the instruments being weakned wherewithall the soule (especially in reasoning) doth worke, it preferreth rest in ignorance before wearisome labour to knowe." Hooker, *Lawes*, I.7.7; 1:81.10-15.

Although we have the vocabulary of evil recognized, this passage might be considered as referring to a natural, innate, weakness. On the very next page, there is a passage that cannot be so considered:

> Which powers and faculties [of the human mind] notwithstanding retaine still their naturall manner of operation although their originall perfection be gone, Man hath still a reasonable understanding, and a will thereby framable to good things, butt is not thereunto now able to frame himselfe. Therefore God hath ordeyned grace, to counterveyle this our imbecillitie, and to serve as his hand.[28]

Thus, for Hooker, imbecility is not confined to women, in either the sense of natural weakness or in the sense of the inheritance of sin (even though each gender may have its own specific natural weakness).

Hooker comments ironically on the ecstatic expressions of women (and children) when held up as evidence of the Holy Spirit behind the vaunted novelties:

> If the Spirite by such revelation have discovered unto them the secrets of that discipline out of scripture, they must profess them all (even men, women, and children) Prophets.[29]

And in the Preface, Hooker follows this consideration of the abuse of women's weakness by the Radicals, a consideration that is not included in his summary of the steps outlined in the third chapter, by pointing that men and women stand in the same light in terms of being deceived and becoming fanatical, and therefore presumably being corrected by sound reason:

> But be they women or be they men,[30] if once they have tasted of that cup, let any man of contrarie opinion open his mouth to perswade them, they close up their eares, his reasons they waigh not, all is answered with rehearsall of the words of John 'We are of God; he that knoweth God heareth us:' as for the rest, ye are of the world; for this world's pomp and vanity it is that ye speak, and the world, whose ye are, heareth you.[31]

---

28. *Dublin* 2; 4:17–22.

29. Hooker, *Lawes*, Preface 3.10; 1:17.19–22.

30. In Book V, on the discussion of emergency baptism by women, a nearly identical phrase occurs: "For if want of callinge doe frustrate baptisme, they that baptize without callinge do nothinge be they women or men." Hooker, *Lawes*, V.62.1; 2:268.26—269.1.

31. *Lawes*, Preface 3.14; 1:19.22—20.3.

And so perhaps Hooker turned to the conclusion long before drawn by St. Augustine that men and women equally share, not just in the engraced life that comes from being in Christ, but in natural intellectual power and in the aptness for mental graces, despite actual differences in genders.[32] And Hooker (like Calvin) is criticizing not the weakness of women but the deceitfulness of those who abuse them.

Bibliography

Augustine. *Saint Augustine Confessions*. Translated by Henry Chadwick. Oxford, 1998.

Beveridge, Henry, ed. "Preface." In *Selected Works of John Calvin*, i–xii. Edinburgh: Calvin Translation Society, 1844.

Beza, Theodore. *Life of Calvin*. In *Selected Works of John Calvin*, edited by Henry Beveridge and Jules Bonet. Edinburgh: Calvin Translation Society, 1844.

Eppley, Daniel. "Contextualizing Richard Hooker's Hermeneutics." In *Richard Hooker: His Life, Work, and Legacy*, 7881. Toronto: St. Osmund, 2013.

Forte, Paul. "Hooker's Theory of Law." *Journal of Medieval and Renaissance Studies* 12 (1982).

Hooker, Richard. *The Folger Library Edition of the Works of Richard Hooker*. Cambridge: Belknap of Harvard University Press, 1977–1998. [All citations are from this edition, abbreviated as "FLE"; or volume, page, line, e.g., 2.22.25.]

MacCulloch, Diarmaid. *All Things Made New: The Reformation and Its Legacy*. New York: Oxford University Press, 2016.

Neelands, David. "The 'Deceit of the Evil Spirit' Among the Radicals, According to Richard Hooker." Toronto: Richard Hooker Society, Trinity College, May 18–19, 2017. Forthcoming.

———. "Richard Hooker, *adiaphora*, and the Defence of a Reformation *via media*." In *Richard Hooker and Reformed Orthodoxy*, edited by W. Bradford Littlejohn and Scott N. Kindred-Barnes, 3760. Reformed Historical Theology 40. Göttingen: Vandenhoeck & Ruprecht, 2017.

———. "Richard Hooker's Paul's Cross Sermon." In *Paul's Cross and the Culture of Persuasion in England, 1520–1640*, edited by Torrance Kirby and P. G. Stanwood, 245–61. Leiden: Brill, 2014.

———. "The Theology of Grace of Richard Hooker." ThD thesis, Trinity College and University of Toronto, 1988. http://hdl.handle.net/1807/99119.

———. "The Use and Abuse of John Calvin in Richard Hooker's Defence of the English Church." *Perichoresis* 10.1 (2012) 3–22. With appendix 2017. http://hdl.handle.net/1807/101842.

---

32. Augustine, *Confessions*, XIII.32.47, 302. Augustine acknowledges a partial actual subordination of women, yet "in mental power she has an equal capacity of rational intelligence."

11

Intercultural Theology as Ecumenical Theology

Hendrik R. Pieterse

THE ECUMENICAL MOVEMENT SEEMS to find itself at a point of stagnation, if not exhaustion. Phrases like "ecumenical crisis," "ecumenical winter," and "consensus fatigue" have become commonplace descriptions of the perceived current malaise. Even veteran ecumenists like Paul Avis have acknowledged the bleak situation: "Today institutional ecumenism is undergoing something approaching a crisis . . . Ecumenical endeavour, wherever it is found, is now shot through with doubt and uncertainty. Inertia and apathy confront ecumenism on every side. The movement is ripe for reform and—if possible—renewal."[1] This sense of confusion and uncertainty has prompted churches to become self-preoccupied, with the turn of the twenty-first century witnessing a resurgence of traditional and even traditionalist positions in the ecumenical movement.[2] German ecumenical scholars Karl-Heinz Dejung and Gert Rüppell agree, depicting this inward

1. Avis, "Ecumenical Theology," 32.

2. Vischer, "Major Trends," 48. He notes that the ecumenical picture at the turn of the twenty-first century "was contradictory. On the one hand, an urgency of a new commitment was recognized on all sides. On the other hand, uncertainty and confusion grew so strong that the churches were inclined to concentrate on themselves alone. Traditional and even traditionalist positions were in the ascendant."

turn as an attitude of confessional self-sufficiency (*Selbstgenügsamkeit*). For them, this attitude lies at the heart of the current ecumenical stagnation.[3]

For Dejung and Rüppell, the root cause of the current ecumenical lethargy is the failure on the part of the World Council of Churches (WCC) to come to terms with and prioritize in its work the implications of the unprecedented challenges posed by the catalytic social, political, religious, and cultural forces that have transformed world Christianity over the course of the twentieth century (accelerating markedly since the 1960s and 1970s), as nations and churches began to cast off the shackles of Western colonialism and assert their political and cultural autonomy. The postcolonial era has witnessed the emergence of an astonishing diversity of contexts, cultures, and languages in which churches now seek to witness to the one Gospel of Jesus Christ.

This emerging ecumenical context, aver Dejung and Rüppell, demands that the Council critically reevaluate and rethink its customary conceptions of church unity and the models employed to interpret it. Put simply, the WCC should more intentionally embrace and operationalize in its unity conversations a paradigm shift that has been underway in the ecumenical movement, including in the deliberations of the Council, already since the 1960s. They identify this paradigmatic shift as the transition from a guilt paradigm to a plurality paradigm. The guilt paradigm tended to consider confessional conflicts, cultural distinctions, contextual demands, and theological differences as signs of ecumenical guilt, failure, or scandal that needed to be overcome on the way to "organic union." In contrast, the plurality paradigm embraces this diversity as God-intended and God-willed. Indeed, far from being a problem to be solved, the world church's rich diversity today is precisely *the means by which the fullness of Christ's meaning for the church and the world can become manifest.*[4]

For Dejung and Rüppell, the chief obstacle to the full embrace of the plurality paradigm in the WCC (and perhaps especially in its Commission on Faith and Order) is the lingering persistence of totalizing thinking (*Einheitsdenken*), whose roots lie deep in the "Christian-European cultural synthesis" of the nineteenth and early twentieth centuries, with its presumptions of European cultural, scientific, and civilizational superiority and its proclivity for control and domination. The First World War exposed the cracks in this synthesis and World War II shattered it, but intentionally

---

3. Dejung and Rüppell, *Ökumenische Gemeinschaft*, 324.
4. Dejung and Rüppell, *Ökumenische Gemeinschaft*, 320-21.

cutting itself loose once and for all from this mindset has been difficult in the history of the Council. The meeting of the WCC in New Delhi (1961) has become a symbol of this tension-filled and conflict-ridden process of re-evaluation. It represents a search process about what can and must now be said theologically about culture and cultures after the death of the Christian-European cultural synthesis. Even so, observe Dejung and Rüppell, "the course of ecumenical debate has shown how arduous this process of dissolution from a fixation upon an absolute validity claim of European culture has been and still is." In many ways, this mindset continues to shape the Council's deliberations about unity and diversity in subtle ways, often by way of unacknowledged presuppositions and taken-for-granted patterns of thinking.[5] For example, World Christianity scholar Dale Irvin, in his detailed study of the history of the Commission on Faith and Order, discovers these lingering habits in the Commission's quest over the course of the twentieth century to identify *some single normative unifying origin or locus* in the history of the church, such as the World Missionary Conference (Edinburgh, Scotland, 1910), or the quest for the Tradition within the many traditions (Lund, Sweden, 1952), or identifying a common ecumenical past in the Nicene-Constantinople Creed of 381 (Montreal, Canada, 1963). Obscured in these efforts at visible convergence is the ambivalence of the church's historic entanglement with Western imperialism, thus risking ideological constructions of Christian unity and consensus. "To raise the ideological meaning of unity and consensus as articulated by Faith and Order," he says,

> is to recognize that formulations of doctrine and practice in the early centuries as well as today represent local theologies related to particular social and cultural contexts. To raise the question is at the same time to seek to discern the political processes of legitimation and suppression which went on then and now, concealing diversity and suppressing difference.[6]

That said, like Dejung and Rüppell, Irvin sees a new ecumenical paradigm struggling to be born. Emerging from the historical margins of the dominant discourse, this new paradigm does not seek to identify a new normative center, but instead advocates for decentered conceptions of Christian unity that embrace the contribution of the *ecumene*'s plurality of voices and cultural and theological traditions. While still largely marginal, this new

---

5. Dejung and Rüppell, *Ökumenische Gemeinschaft*, 326–27.
6. Irvin, *Hearing Many Voices*, 59.

paradigm is bearing fruit in Faith and Order's deliberations, evident, for example, in the recent prominence of the model of "unity in reconciled diversity,"[7] and, one might add, the growing impact of the spirituality and practice of receptive ecumenism.[8]

For Dejung and Rüppell, to break through the current ecumenical stagnation and to operationalize the plurality paradigm more comprehensively in the WCC's deliberations about church unity means adopting a different angle of vision (*Blickwinkel*)—one that is thoroughly *intercultural* in its orientation, theological convictions, and conciliar practice. Only such a robustly intercultural (and, by implication, interreligious) approach can help the WCC, where possible, to relativize and break up processes of conflict, stagnation, and paralysis. While interculturality has been part of the ecumenical movement—and of Christianity—from the start, in our day it has moved to center stage and can no longer be considered a marginal issue. Indeed, today, the necessity of an *intercultural* angle of vision touches the very center of an expanding Christian movement. The fact is, they note, this intercultural perspective has become the central challenge of a polycentric world Christianity, which manifests itself in its dizzying array of perspectives and practices in the context of multiple meaning systems and organizational structures. Therefore, it is imperative that ecumenical theology recognize its cultural embeddedness and thus its own contextuality. For this reason, *interculturality* should be embraced as a key conviction and practice in *all* ecumenical deliberations today. Such a move keeps us alert to the God-given right of Christians in different cultural settings to determine their own theological identities, and that such theological self-determination involves the contextual rethinking of the very core of the gospel, not just its outer expression.[9]

Current ecumenical experiences and encounters, Dejung and Rüppell conclude, make clear that the longer theology understands itself as an intercultural theology, the better it will serve the challenges of the new ecumenical situation. To make their case, they turn to the subdiscipline of intercultural theology, an emerging theological approach in European (and, more specifically, German) academic theology, with deep roots in missiology, ecumenics, and theology of religions. Intercultural theology, they claim, offers the resources needed to foreground the challenges and

---

7. Irvin, *Hearing Many Voices*, 74–75.
8. See, for example, Rusch, *Ecumenical Reception*.
9. Dejung and Rüppell, *Ökumenische Gemeinschaft*, 328.

demands of the fledgling plurality paradigm more robustly in Faith and Order and in the work of the WCC more broadly.[10]

While it should be clear, I want to reiterate that the focus of Dejung and Rüppell's critique and appeal is the churches in Europe (and, by implication, the West), since this is where they detect the most reluctance, and even resistance, to letting go of residual totalizing habits and to embracing the full theological, ecclesial, and practical consequences of the new plurality paradigm. Many of these churches, they say, have experienced the call to relinquish former theological and cultural dominance and to recognize the contextuality of their own theologies "as relativizing rather than enriching." Instead of stimulating a new ecumenical curiosity, Christianity's growing cultural and theological plurality has stoked attitudes of fear, anxiety, and loss. As such, it is crucial for the future of a polycentric ecumenism that the "churches of the North" address and change these attitudes.[11] Hence Dejung and Rüppell's enthusiasm for the potential of intercultural theology, given its location in the heart of European theology and its mission to expose and attack the remaining tendencies of European/Western theological normativity and privilege.

In the remaining pages, I evaluate Dejung and Rüppell's claims about the potential of intercultural theology to help overcome the obstacle that European/Western theology's residual totalizing tendencies and habits of theological privilege (however subtle) continue to pose for the fulsome embodiment of the plurality paradigm into the WCC's work. Given the historical (and, as Dejung and Rüppell rightly suggest, continuing) privileging of European/Western agendas and priorities in the history of the WCC (especially its Commission on Faith and Order), I agree that intercultural theology can offer fresh insights and correctives. However, I suggest, that intercultural theology's contribution also has distinct limitations, as I will point out.

I unpack my argument as follows. I begin with a brief overview of the origins, location, and aims of intercultural theology in European (more precisely, German) academic theology, as well as a look at the cognate field of World Christianity studies. The fact is the subject matter and research trajectories of these two disciplines are closely intertwined and scholars in both disciplines often draw on one another's work in their respective research projects. Then, I examine some of the questions and objections

---

10. Dejung and Rüppell, *Ökumenische Gemeinschaft*, 321–22.
11. Dejung and Rüppell, *Ökumenische Gemeinschaft*, 331.

intercultural theologians raise in their critique of current European/Western theology. These critical interventions, I submit, can indeed support the intercultural "turn" in the Council's work, as Dejung and Rüppell argue. However, and this is crucial, intercultural theology can do so only if we draw on *both* its good questions *and* its limitations. Those respects in which intercultural theology succeeds and those in which it falls short are equally valuable. *Both* are sources of insight as well as cautionary tales.

Intercultural Theology: A Brief Overview

It is important to note at the outset that intercultural theology is not a single, integrated movement or theological discipline in European academic theology. Rather, it is a loose concatenation of similar interests, presuppositions, and aims, which often leads to very different, at times even incompatible, proposals. That said, I agree with those who notice in this diversity enough conceptual, methodological, and theological coherence to warrant a shared designation as intercultural theology.[12]

Let me briefly outline the beginnings, orienting convictions, and aims of intercultural theology. German theologian Werner Ustorf's influential account of the movement reminds us that intercultural theology has very specific cultural origins. It traces its roots to the pioneering work of the Lutheran missiologist and ecumenist Hans Jochen Margull and his friend Walter Hollenweger (the latter rooted theologically in both the Reformed and Pentecostal traditions) in the 1960s and the two decades that followed. (They were later joined by a younger compatriot Richard Friedli, a Swiss Catholic missiologist.) Both Margull and Hollenweger were active in the reform movements within the World Council of Churches in the 1960s, advocating already then for the incorporation of the rising decolonial theologies in Asia, Africa, and Latin America into the Council's work.

Hollenweger was the first to use the term *intercultural theology* in his writings. He was also the one who gave systematic formulation to the basic principles of intercultural theology. These principles, it is important to note, remain orienting convictions in the vast majority of intercultural

---

12. Not everyone agrees. For example, in his recent introduction to the ecumenical movement, prominent German ecumenical theologian Ulrich Dehn claims that intercultural theology is too diffuse and uncoordinated to serve as a useful conversation partner in the ecumenical debates. Instead, he finds the cognate discipline of World Christianity studies much more suitable. See his *Weltweites Christentum*, 14–15.

theologies today. Intercultural theology, proposed Hollenweger (and here I quote Ustorf's summary):

1. Is "that scholarly theological discipline that operates within a particular cultural framework without absolutizing it."
2. Will select its methods appropriately. Western academic theology is not automatically privileged over others.
3. Has a duty to look for alternative forms of doing theology (such as non-Western and narrative forms).
4. Must be tested in social practice and measured by its capacity for bridge building between diverse groups.
5. Must not be confused with "pop-theology" that escapes from self-critical reflection.[13]

These principles imply, says Ustorf, that, for its pioneers, intercultural theology "does not think on behalf of others, but reflects its own premises in the presence of these others and, if things go well, together with them." These principles, he continues, give rise to attitudes, virtues, and perspectives that demonstrate intercultural theology's continuing value for opening up European theology to dialogue with non-Western theologies and religions.[14]

It is not difficult to recognize these principles in the projects of prominent contemporary intercultural theologians like Volker Küster, Henning Wrogemann, and Judith Gruber, among many others. Gruber, for example, argues that *interculturality* should become a *locus theologicus* for all theology, signaling theology's ineluctable cultural and contextual character. As such, intercultural theology foregrounds the fact that the relationship between culture and faith is "the very structural problem of Christianity," highlighting the enduring tension of "the mediation of universal truth [incarnated in Jesus Christ] in contingent times and places." For this reason, the tension between universality and particularity constitutes "the basic structure of Christian faith."[15] This makes intercultural theology inherently suspicious "of narratives that claim universality, essential truth or validity for themselves,"[16] as European/Western theologies have been wont to do.

---

13. Ustorf, "Cultural Origins," 237.
14. Ustorf, "Cultural Origins," 244–46.
15. Gruber, "Culture/s," 397–98.
16. Gruber, *Intercultural Theology*, 129.

Along similar lines, intercultural theologian Robert Schreiter notes that the contextual theologies emerging in the 1960s recognized

> that the universal [European/Western] theologies that had been presented to them were in fact *universalizing* theologies: that is to say, they extended the results of their reflections beyond their own contexts to other settings, usually without an awareness of the rootedness of their theologies within their own contexts.[17]

As a consequence, says Volker Küster, intercultural theologians do not aim to construct a new meta-theology (*theologia perennis*). Rather, they envision the role of intercultural theology as that of constituting a meeting platform (*Begegnungsplattform*), a space of mediation (*Vermittlungsinstanz*), where the various contextual theologies (including European/Western) within world Christianity can encounter one another and enter into theological dialogue and mutual learning. Intercultural theology, then, is primarily a hermeneutical project that seeks to interpret the dynamics of theological transformation processes in the *inter* between the various culturally mediated theologies. As such, it hopes to create a third space (Homi Bhabba) in which these theologies can meet in a spirit of mutual respect, humility, and vulnerability (*Verwundbarkeit*) to explore similarities, differences, and mutual learning opportunities. That said, however, Küster is clear that it is European/Western theology that stands most in need of this radical shift in perspective. In many ways, they remain *the* obstacle. Therefore, intercultural theology's main objective is to coax European/Western theology out of its current insularity and open it to the riches of world Christianity.[18] This resolute focus on European/Western theology is widely shared among intercultural theologians, regardless of the often-deep differences between their various formulations.

Intercultural theology thus sees itself as a subversive movement within European/Western theology, seeking to expose and critique remaining habits of dogmatic, methodological, and epistemological privilege, often manifesting themselves in attitudes of confessional self-sufficiency and insularity. They attack the tendency in European academic theology to proceed as if the cultural-religious pluralism now characterizing Christian theology, not to mention the increasing proximity and encounter between different world religions (also in Europe), does not demand a radical reconception

---

17. Schreiter, *New Catholicity*, 2.
18. Küster, *Einführung*, 15, 110, 132, 209, 291.

of the way it plies its trade. Finnish missiologist and ecumenical theologian Mika Vähäkangas speaks of the need for European theologians to break out of the "confessional-national bubbles" that have heretofore shaped European theology's social and intellectual frame of reference and to become open, vulnerable, and receptive to substantive and lasting dialogue with theologies and religious orientations outside the West.[19] This fundamental commitment to exploring the significance of today's cultural-religious pluralism for the future of Christian theology and the mission of the church has prompted intercultural theologians to insist that European theologies should incorporate not just the intercultural and the interconfessional but also *the interreligious* as basic dimensions of their theological projects.[20]

For its part, World Christianity studies emerged and developed roughly in tandem with intercultural theology, getting its start in the 1980s and gaining momentum in the 1990s onward. These two disciplines evince many intersections and overlaps in subject matter, methodology, and interests. Australian missiologist John Flett puts the relationship succinctly: "Intercultural theology is a method shaped in response to world Christianity as a phenomenon."[21] As such, all intercultural theologians consider dialogue with World Christianity studies as essential to their work, and many incorporate it as an orienting framework for their approaches.[22] Yet, while intimately related, the two disciplines heretofore have had somewhat different emphases. World Christianity studies have thus far focused predominantly on interventions in the field of church history and Christian historiography. As such, it sets out to correct the rather parochial and Eurocentric accounts of church history in the past. These accounts often followed a similar trajectory, in which Christianity began

> as a religious movement which, though born in (Southwest) Asia or the Middle East, from its very beginnings, moved to the eastern part of the Roman Empire through Asia Minor and ended in Rome where Peter and Paul completed their apostolic careers. Subsequently, from Rome, and later from other European countries, the narrative goes on, the Christian Church, both Roman Catholic and Protestant, dispatched its missionaries to all corners of the globe. In this account Christianity is perceived as a Western

---

19. Vähäkangas, *Context*, 57.
20. Küster, *Einführung*, 27.
21. Flett, "Method in Mission Studies," 719.
22. Vähäkangas, *Context*, 50–58.

religion, as distinct from Eastern ones such as Hinduism and Buddhism, whose goal is to evangelize and civilize the pagan and barbarian non-Western world.[23]

In countering such jaundiced accounts of Christian origins and subsequent missionary expansion, World Christianity scholars seek to construct histories of Christianity that reflect the intercultural, multidimensional, and multidirectional nature of the Christian movement from its beginnings. From the start, they argue, Christianity has spread west, east, north, and south simultaneously, with Africa and Asia hosting flourishing Christian communities and dominant centers of theological scholarship for centuries, long before the faith's subsequent Western turn. In doing so, they seek to recover and give voice to forgotten, neglected, or even ignored Christian stories in the many locales in which the faith had (and still has) a presence. As a result, more comprehensive and more representative accounts of the Christian story can be constructed—tellings that demonstrate that the Christian faith has had a *polycentric* nature and shape from its inception. This means that World Christianity as we experience it today should not be seen as a *novum*, but rather as an (admittedly unprecedented) flowering of an intercultural and transnational logic that is inherent in the faith as such. What is desperately needed, then, and what many scholars of World Christianity see as their principal task, is to construct new and enlarged conceptual, historical, and methodological "maps" that can do justice to these historical and contemporary dynamics.[24]

Not surprisingly, World Christianity studies overwhelmingly focus on non-Western manifestations of Christianity. This predilection is driven by resistance to previous Eurocentrism and an interest in showing that "non-Western Christians [are not] merely an extension of 'missionary history' [but] are an important expression of the Christian faith in its own right." Thus, World Christianity scholars seek to emphasize "decentralized local expressions of the faith autonomous of Western control." However, a growing number of World Christianity scholars in recent years have begun to see behind this obsession with the particular "moral commentary" that, in their opinion, unduly maintains the West–non-West binary and so "obscures larger-scale connections and networks as well as cross-cultural

---

23. Phan, "Doing Theology," 27–28.

24. See, for example, Koschorke, "Transcontinental Links," 28–56. See also González, "Beyond Christendom," 189–202.

continuities" in the world Christian movement.[25] As a corrective, they encourage renewed attention to the universal—those transnational and transcontinental connections, relationships, and networks that have, both historically and now, given the world's Christians a sense of belonging to something larger than themselves. David Maxwell refers to this sense as "a global Christian consciousness" that "transcend[s] the dualism between the West and the rest, and metropole and colony . . . [and] remind[s] us that Christians of all hues have co-operated to fashion shared identities and institutions."[26]

A number of scholars have begun to point out the dramatic significance of World Christianity studies for the renewal of the ecumenical movement. Raimundo Barreto, in an essay titled "How World Christianity Saved the Ecumenical Movement," argues that world Christianity studies has enabled ecumenism, especially through the agency of global South scholars, to critique and abandon "centuries of Eurocentric epistemic hegemony," and thus to advocate for a broader vision of the ecumenical and of ecumenical relationships.[27] In similar vein, noted North American World Christianity scholar Dana Robert, in reflecting on the 1910 Edinburgh Conference from the vantage point of its centennial commemoration in 2010 observes:

> Rather than beginning with the western missionary movement and moving towards 'World Christianity," Edinburgh 2010 proceeded from the diversity of Christianity as multi-cultural, worldwide movement towards mission . . . The difference between now and a century ago is that theological, ethnic, and cultural diversity is the starting-point rather than the goal of Christian mission . . . Relational networks define a world in which there are multiple centres of Christian life, and peripheries extend in every direction.[28]

Intercultural Theology and Quest for Ecumenical Unity

My brief surveys of intercultural theology and World Christianity studies above have hopefully revealed the ready intersections and overlaps with Dejung and Ruppell's concerns. Indeed, the "new ecumenism," which both

25. Cabrita and Maxwell, "Relocating," 3–4.
26. Maxwell, "Historical Perspectives," 62.
27. Barreto, " World Christianity," 225, 227, 231, 235. For another perspective, see Jathanna, *Decolonizing Oikoumene*.
28. Robert, "Co-Operation," 57–58.

intercultural theology and World Christianity scholars embrace, is just Dejung and Rüppell's plurality paradigm made concrete. Thus, intercultural theologians and scholars of World Christianity readily affirm Dejung and Rüppell's project, agreeing fully with the challenge posed by continued European/Western self-preoccupation. They are unanimous in their critique of the self-sufficiency and insularity of European/Western theologies. Volker Küster's definition of intercultural theology can stand proxy for this unanimity among intercultural theologians:

> Intercultural theology aims to break through the self-referentiality of Eurocentric-Western, as well as conservative evangelical, theology by way of a radical paradigm shift. Insofar as it substantiates respect for the other, recognizes difference, and renders itself vulnerable, intercultural theology creates room for dialogue. This relational approach enables each position to acknowledge its contextuality [*Kontextgebundenheit*] and opens up ecumenical learning opportunities that can stimulate the formulation of reflexive theologies also in the West.[29]

In this final section, I open a brief conversation around shared concerns between intercultural theology/World Christianity studies and the unity conversations in the WCC. The intent is not for intercultural theologians and World Christianity scholars to instruct or lecture their WCC compatriots. Rather, it is to invite Council members to listen in on intercultural theologians' debates about the radical ways in which a postcolonial perspective on plurality, difference, interculturality, and especially power reshapes perceptions, definitions, and possible models of ecumenical unity and theological authority. I identify and briefly discuss two areas in which intercultural theologians and World Christianity scholars might have a contribution to make.

Culture, Identity, and the Dynamics of Power

The first point to note is that intercultural theologians would advise their Council colleagues to pay deeper attention to the way definitions of *culture* and *identity* shape perceptions of plurality and its uses in Christian unity. Traditionally, European/Western theologies and cultures have been tethered to what Robert Schreiter calls integrated concepts of culture. Such concepts "depict culture as patterned systems in which the various elements

---

29. Küster, *Einführung*, 209.

are coordinated in such a fashion as to create a unified whole." As such, they can serve the need for "greater organic unity" and firm identities.[30] Intercultural theologians would urge their WCC colleagues to ask whether such integrated concepts of culture may help explain, at least in part, the complacency in the Council that Dejung and Rüppell decry. After all, an integrated understanding of culture easily stimulates centripetal tendencies and a sense of cultural and theological self-sufficiency. Ironically, observe Dejung and Rüppell, the current model of "unity in reconciled diversity" might unwittingly embolden this self-sufficiency. They fear that *reconciled* here might easily be (and often is) "understood as completed," thus discouraging the ongoing "challenging task of 'learning,' 'correction,' and 'cleansing'" among the churches.[31] In similar vein, British Methodist ecumenical scholar David Carter worries about "the possibility that the concept might be taken to validate an easy-going acceptance of variety without any real spiritual wrestling with truth."[32]

A second deleterious effect of integrated concepts of culture, says Schreiter, is that these integrated concepts asily fall prey to totalizing and essentializing tendencies: "They exclude or suppress that which cannot be assimilated and integrated into the whole." It is not hard to see how such exclusionary tendencies could abet the *Einheitsdenken* we discussed earlier and obscure the imperialist connotations that Irvin highlighted.

What is needed for fitting construals of plurality and identity today are what Schreiter calls globalized concepts of culture. In such a conception, culture is not understood

> in terms of ideas and objects, but as a ground of contest in relations ... Culture is something to be constructed rather than discovered, and it is constructed on the stage of struggle amid the asymmetries of power. [Under these conditions, identity is not something uniform and easily demarcated but is] always viewed as fragmentary or multiple, constructed and imagined.[33]

Scholars who employ a globalized concept of culture—and this would include the vast majority of intercultural theologians and students of World Christianity—find postcolonial and decolonial theories, with their careful analyses of *alterity* and *difference* more fitting for examining the complex

---

30. Schreiter, *New Catholicity*, 49–50.
31. Dejung and Rüppell, *Ökumenische Gemeinschaft*, 163.
32. Carter, "Unity," 413.
33. Schreiter, *New Catholicity*, 53–54.

dynamics of identity formation today, including Christian identity. In this respect, Volker Küster views intercultural theology as a "hermeneutics of the stranger" and asserts that in the encounter with the (Christian and religious) stranger, Christian identity has to be continually renegotiated. It is never settled but increasingly hybrid and fluid.[34] In recent years, intercultural theologian Judith Gruber has shed fresh light on the ubiquitous role of *power* in Christian identity formation. Read through a postcolonial lens, the mediation of the Christian message "is not a one-dimensional, continuous process, but a plural and fragmented constellation of identity constructions."[35] Intercultural theologians would invite their Faith and Order colleagues to ask whether they should not include in their deliberations more thorough attention to postcolonial studies and its astute analyses of power. For example, what might the postcolonial emphasis on alterity, difference, and power reveal about operative definitions of identity in conciliar deliberations, perhaps especially the understanding of confessional identities? Do these definitions reflect integrated or a globalized perspectives on culture? Do they adequately reflect the fragmented, volatile, and hybrid nature of Christian identity today? For example, the WCC's latest convergence document, *The Church: Towards a Common Vision*, shows no evidence of having struggled with these postcolonial perspectives on the dynamics of power. This is all the more distressing, since it had at its disposal—and, in fact, makes use of—the landmark Faith and Order paper on ecumenical hermeneutics, *A Treasure in Earthen Vessels: An Instrument for an Ecumenical Reflection on Hermeneutics*. This fine statement calls for a "hermeneutics of suspicion" in which dialogue partners apply to themselves "an approach which perceives how self-interest, power, national or ethnic or class or gender perspectives can affect the reading of texts and the understanding of symbols and practices."[36] While *The Church* affirms that "cultural and historical factors contribute to the rich diversity within the Church," a hermeneutics of suspicion makes no appearance in thematizing of this rich diversity.[37] For intercultural and World Christianity scholars, this is a great opportunity missed, especially since the plurality paradigm

---

34. In this respect, Küster views intercultural theology as a "hermeneutics of the stranger." In the encounter with the (Christian and religious) stranger, Christian identity is never static or settled; it is increasingly hybrid and fluid and has to be continually renegotiated in the course of the ensuing dialogue. See his *Einführung*, 118–29.

35. Gruber, "Culture/s," 409–10.

36. WCC, A Treasure in Earthen Vessels, 11.

37. WCC, *The Church*, 16. For specific references to *Earthen Vessels*, see 9 and 23.

of the new ecumenism takes such postcolonial and decolonial perspectives for granted in their construal of Christian identity, difference, and unity (cf. Barreto's essay above).

Cultural-Religious Pluralism and the Search for a "Wider Ecumenism"

Intercultural theologians can assist their WCC colleagues with a further set of helpful reflections about the meaning, depth, and scope of *plurality*, this time regarding the controversies surrounding the import of interreligious engagement for the integrity of Christian witness, often referred to as the *wider ecumenism*. Incidentally, to me, this conversation could be enriched when linked to the calls for an expanded definition of *ecumenical*, spearheaded primarily by theologians from the global South. For these scholars, the diversity of theologies, rationalities, and cultural and contextual demands evident in the new ecumenism makes such a redefinition absolutely essential. While these two conversations clearly have different (though, in my view, not incompatible) aims, their concerns nevertheless overlap in important respects. Here, I merely note the benefit of such a conversation and not pursue it further. Instead, I will point to two other reasons why an expanded definition of *ecumenical* is crucial for the new ecumenism taking form before us.

As we saw, Barreto has already set out the need for reconceiving the meaning and scope of *ecumenical*. For him, such an expanded reconception is necessary to do justice to the "liberating interculturality" within the emerging new ecumenism "[that] privileges the interweaving of different rationalities, emphasizing respect, solidarity, conviviality, dialogue, and collaboration, without overlooking matters of cultural asymmetry and injustice."[38] Intercultural theologian Henning Wrogemann agrees, but adds that an expanded definition of the ecumenical also requires an expanded perception of the subjects, the forms, and the media of Christian theological expression found within today's polycentric Christianity. While valuing the work of the World Council of Churches, Wrogemann argues that its continued tethering to European/Western priorities, stereotypes, and theological preferences means that it fails to—or chooses not to—include within its orbit of the *ecumenical*, churches, people, movements, and theological persuasions that did not comport with its theological interests. Thus, in

38. Barreto, "World Christianity," 235.

the 1980s, the WCC, because of its particular liberationist agenda at the time, foregrounded movements like Korean *minjung* theology, but downplayed or even ignored emerging Pentecostal, charismatic, and evangelical movements. *"That which is different, otherwise, or offensive (such as fundamentalist movements, congregations, or churches)"* should also be among the *subjects* of the ecumenical movement.[39] Doing so, he says, means that the WCC's heretofore preoccupation with theology as *written text* means they tend to miss the crucial fact that in the global Christian *ecumene*, theology is constructed, employed, and lived *through many forms and media*. For millions of Christians, theology expresses itself through art, proverbs, rituals, festivals, and various forms of meditation.[40] Ignoring this rich tapestry of forms and media risks missing ways of doing theology and formulations of doctrine, belief, and practice that are increasingly characterizing the ecumenical movement today. Commenting on the current restrictive definitions of ecumenism, missiologist and ecumenical theologian Veli-Matti Kärkkäinen asks the following searching question: "Is there really any theological justification for denying the true churchliness of hundreds of millions of Christian communities from Pentecostals to other Free Churches . . . Is not such denial yet another form of colonialism, a form of exercising power by the 'Old World' (i.e., Old Christendom) over the 'New World?'"[41] In my view, it is essential and urgent that our WCC colleagues attend to these criticisms.

I now turn to the question of interreligious ecumenism. Here I want to explore the crucial decision on the part of intercultural theologians to include the *interreligious* as a fundamental dimension of the task of intercultural theology. They recognize that engaging theologically with religious pluralism *dare not be considered incidental or optional for theology today*. They understand that for many Christians, especially in Africa and Asia, living in contexts where another religion or other ancestral religious traditions are dominant, the task of determining clearly where the cultural ends and the religious begins is not so easy. These ancient religious traditions have shaped these cultures indelibly over many centuries, so that making sharp distinctions between ecumenism and interreligious dialogue often distorts the reality on the ground.[42] In this respect, Vähäkangas urges

---

39. Wrogemann, *Intercultural Hermeneutics*, 20.
40. Wrogemann, *Intercultural Hermeneutics*, 19.
41. Kärkkäinen, "Growing Together," 67–68.
42. Küster observes that in such contexts, interreligious contact is always already

his theological colleagues to acknowledge that all religions, including Christianity, are syncretistic in the sense of building on prior religious traditions. No religion "can ever begin from a *tabula rasa*."[43] Therefore, for intercultural theologians, failing to incorporate the question of interreligious relationships as an indispensable aspect of the theological task risks practicing theologies that lack credibility and persuasive power amid the cultural-religious pluralism that characterizes our world (and, increasingly, also Christian existence) today.

I begin by noting that the question of Christianity's relationship to the other world religions has a long and venerable history in the World Council of Churches. The arguments and rationale for a wider ecumenism make little sense when viewed apart from this history.[44] Veteran ecumenical theologian Wesley Ariarajah finds the fact that arguments for an expansion of the meaning of *ecumenical* originated in Asia, and elsewhere outside the West, significant. Many theologians in these contexts grew frustrated with the "church-oriented" character of European-North American ecumenism—a consequence of Europe's almost complete Christianization over the centuries and thus its relative lack of contact with other religions (with the exception, perhaps, of Islam). The domination of the church in Western Christendom made unity among the warring confessions ecumenism's primary object. For proponents of the wider ecumenism, Ariarajah argues, the meaning of the word *ecumenical* simply must break free from this North Atlantic definition. It is too restrictive, leaving

> no room in it for the 92.5 percent of the people of my country [India] who live by other faith traditions. Unless what is "ecumenical" is not simply *about,* but in some measure *constitutes,* the whole inhabited earth, it has too little to say to, and much less to do with, the majority of the world's population. Hence the call for a "wider ecumenism."[45]

This wider ecumenism requires a radical revision in theologies of religion. Such revised theologies should no longer view conversion as the primary goal of interreligious engagement but, rather, emphasizes mutual respect, dialogue, and collaboration. Regrettably, says Ariarajah, many theologians still see this wider ecumenism as a threat to the urgency for inner-Christian

---

cultural contact. See his essay "Who, With Whom."

43. Vähäkangas, *Context,* 120.
44. For an excellent survey, see Ariarajah, "Interfaith Dialogue," 614–27.
45. Ariarajah, "Wider Ecumenism," 326; emphasis added.

ecumenism, thus perpetuating the either/or logic that still characterizes many Christian theologies of religion.[46]

What significance might these conversations in intercultural theology (as well as among non-Western theologies) have for WCC debates about religious pluralism? I will point out just one instance, the vexed debates around "syncretism." If the line between culture and religion is fuzzy, as intercultural theologians suggest, and if all religions are in some sense syncretistic, as Vähäkangas argues, what are the implications for the meaning and continued plausibility of the notion of syncretism? Should it be radically revised, or perhaps even abandoned as a relic of earlier Western missionary arrogance? If so, what are the implications for the ongoing need to discern between "legitimate" and "illegitimate" diversity, as *The Church: Towards a Common Vision* rightly points out?[47]

I do not have room here, of course, for an in-depth analysis of syncretism and its complicated history in the WCC.[48] Instead, let me note a couple of insights from intercultural theologian Henning Wrogemann's reflections on the topic. It would at least highlight some of the issues in play when viewed through an intercultural lens. He begins by pointing out that in recent years uses of the term *syncretism* has been become more nuanced; they denote both positive and negative connotations, depending on the theologian's theological perspective. As we noted above, intercultural theologians are suspicious of too easy hard-and-fast distinctions between religion and culture. For Wrogemann, instead of abstract definitions of *syncretism*, theologians should turn to how the term functions in practice. This means acknowledging that syncretism is a *contextual* affair. This means paying close attention to the actors involved and their intentions in employing the term. This allows us to observe that the use of the concept always involves conflicts about Christian identity *in concrete contexts and debates about*

---

46. Ariarajah, "Wider Ecumenism," 328. In this respect, it is disappointing that intercultural theology continues to employ rather conventional theologies of religion. The various proposals on offer run the gambit of the exclusivism-inclusivism-pluralism options, with many theologians rejecting the pluralist approach a viable theological option. A few, such as Schmidt-Leukel, do make the pluralist perspective their operative framework. Schmidt-Leukel argues that intercultural theology should transition to what he calls "interreligious theology" (which he claims is truer to the intent of these pioneers). See his essay "Interkulturelle Theologie," 4-16.

47. WCC, *The Church*, 16-17.

48. The fault lines in this discussion were laid bare most dramatically during the WCC's gathering in Canberra (1991), where the Korean theologian Hyun Kyung Chung drew on Korean shamanistic and other ancestral traditions in her plenary address.

who has the authority to define it. Thus, Wrogemann concludes: "the term is quite obviously self-referential, which means that it says less about the phenomenon as such and more about the position of the particular individual or group using the term."[49] This is a helpful perspective, because it clarifies that syncretism is a *relational* matter, which calls for careful attention to the identity claims at stake in the particular context and the actors' concrete purposes in advancing these claims. Dogmatic claims imposed from the outside (including launched from the perch of academic theology and ecumenical councils!) inevitably fall short, because they overlook these contextual and relational dynamics.

Conclusion: A Tribute

I conclude this essay with a word of deep appreciation to Dr. Charles Fensham. I have had the privilege of striking up a lasting friendship with Charles over many years of encounter and collaboration in the American Society of Missiology. With a few other colleagues, we conceived of the idea of public missiology as a framework for missiology today. Charles played a leading role in the years of intense conversation and collaboration, which led to the publication of our "manifesto."[50] You are an excellent scholar and dear friend, Charles.

Bibliography

Ariarajah, S. Wesley. "Interfaith Dialogue: Milestones of the Past and Prospects for the Future," *Current Dialogue* 71.5 (2019) 614–27.

———. "Wider Ecumenism: A Threat or a Promise?" *The Ecumenical Review* 50.3 (1998) 321–29.

Avis, Paul. "Ecumenical Theology 1910–2010: Does It Have A Future?" *Modern Believing* 51.3 (2010) 30–38.

Barreto, Raimundo C. Jr. "How World Christianity Saved the Ecumenical Movement." *Protestantismo em Revista* 46.2 (2020) 222–42.

Briggs, John, et al., eds. *A History of the Ecumenical Movement—1968–2000*, vol. 3. Geneva: World Council of Churches, 2004.

Cabrita, Joel, and David Maxwell. "Introduction: Relocating World Christianity." In *Relocating World Christianity: Interdisciplinary Studies in Universal and Local Expressions of the Christian Faith*, edited by Joel Cabrita et al., 1–44. Theology and Mission in World Christianity 7. Leiden: Brill, 2017.

---

49. Wrogemann, *Intercultural Hermeneutics*, 345.
50. Leffel et al., "Public Missiology," 268–81.

Carter, David. "Unity in Reconciled Diversity: Cop-Out or Rainbow Church?" *Theology* 113/876 (2010) 411–20.

Dehn, Ulrich. *Weltweites Christentum und Ökumenische Bewegung*. Berlin: EB Verlag, 2013.

Dejung, Karl-Heinz, and Gert Rüppell. *Ökumenische Gemeinschaft im Wandel der Zeiten: Interkulturelle und interreligiöse Perspektiven der Ökumenische Bewegung*. Berlin: EB Verlag, 2016.

Flett, John G. "Method in Mission Studies: Comparing World Christianity and Intercultural Theology." *Theologische Literaturzeitung* 143 (2018) 718–31.

Gibaut, John, and Knut Jørgensen, eds. *Called to Unity: For the Sake of Mission*. Regnum Edinburgh Centenary Series 25. Eugene, OR: Wipf & Stock, 2015.

González, Justo L. "Beyond Christendom: New Maps." *Toronto Journal of Theology* 27.2 (2011) 189–201.

Gruber, Judith. "Culture/s as a Theological Challenge: Towards a Systematic Approach to Intercultural Theology." In *Interreligious Hermeneutics in Pluralistic Europe: Between Texts and People*, edited by David Cheetham et al., 397–413. Currents of Encounter. Amsterdam: Rodopi, 2011.

———. *Intercultural Theology: Exploring World Christianity after the Cultural Turn*. Research in Contemporary Religion 25. Göttingen: Vandenhoek & Ruprecht, 2018.

Hock, Klaus. *Einführung in die Interkulturelle Theologie*. Darmstadt: Wissenschaftliche Buchgesellschaft, 2011.

Irvin, Dale T. *Hearing Many Voices: Dialogue and Diversity in the Ecumenical Movement*. Lanham, MD: University Press of America, 1994.

Jathanna, Gladson. *Decolonizing Oikoumene*. Delhi: Indian SPCK, 2020.

Kärkkäinen, Veli-Matti. "Growing Together in Unity and Mission." In *Called to Unity: For the Sake of Mission*, edited by John Gibaut and Knut Jørgensen, 67–68. Regnum Edinburgh Centenary Series, vol. 25. Eugene, OR: Wipf & Stock, 2015..

Koschorke, Klaus. "Transcontinental Links, Enlarged Maps, and Polycentric Structures in the History of World Christianity." *Journal of World Christianity* 6.1 (2016) 28–56.

Küster, Volker. *Einführung in die Interkulturelle Theologie*. Göttingen: Vanderhoeck & Ruprecht, 2011.

———. "Who, With Whom, About What? Exploring the Landscape of Interreligious Dialogue." *Exchange* 33.11 (2004) 73–92.

Leffel, Gregory P., et al. "What We Mean by Public Missiology." *Missiology: An International Review* 51.3 (2023) 268–81.

Maxwell, David. "Historical Perspectives on Christianity Worldwide: Connections, Comparisons, and Consciousness." In *Relocating World Christianity: Interdisciplinary Studies in Universal and Local Expressions of the Christian Faith*, edited by Joel Cabrita, David Maxwell, and Emma Wild-Wood, 47–69. Theology and Mission in World Christianity 7. Leiden: Brill, 2017.

Phan, Peter C. "Doing Theology in World Christianity: Different Resources and New Methods." *Journal of World Christianity* 1.1 (2008) 27–28.

Robert, Dana. "From Co-Operation to Common Witness: Mission and Unity, 1910–2010." In *Called to Unity: For the Sake of Mission*, edited by John Gibaut and Knud Jørgensen, 46–58. Regnum Edinburgh Centenary Series 25. Eugene, OR: Wipf & Stock, 2015.

Rusch, William G. *Ecumenical Reception: Its Challenge and Opportunity*. Grand Rapids: Eerdmans, 2007.

Schmidt-Leukel, Perry. "Interkulturelle Theologie als Interreligiöse Theologie." *Evangelische Theologie* 71.1 (2011) 4–16.

Schreiter, Robert J. *The New Catholicity: Theology Between the Global and the Local.* Maryknoll, NY: Orbis, 1997.

Vähäkangas, Mika. *Context, Plurality and Truth: Theology in World Christianities.* Eugene, OR: Pickwick Publications, 2020.

Vischer, Lukas. "Major Trends in the Life of the Churches." In *A History of the Ecumenical Movement—1968-2000*, vol. 3, edited by John Briggs et al., 23–49. Geneva: World Council of Churches Publications, 2004.

Wimmer, Franz Martin. *Interkulturelle Philosophie: Eine Einführung.* Vienna: Facultas Verlags-und Buchhandels AG, 2004.

World Council of Churches (WCC). *A Treasure in Earthen Vessels: An Instrument for an Ecumenical Reflection on Hermeneutics.* Faith and Order Paper 182. Geneva: WCC Commission on Faith and Order, 1998.

———. *The Church: A Common Vision.* Faith and Order Paper 214. Geneva: World Council of Churches Publications, 2013.

Wrogemann, Henning. *Intercultural Hermeneutics.* Intercultural Theology, vol. 1. Downers Grove, IL: IVP Academic, 2016.

Ustorf, Werner. "The Cultural Origins of 'Intercultural Theology.'" *Mission Studies* 25 (2008) 81–103.

12

Sinister Soldiers and Single Women

Billie Anne Robinson

SECURITY PEOPLE ON THEIR appointed rounds in the British Museum kept coming across *une femme d'un certain âge*, complete with backpack, camera, notepad, and spreadsheet, working in front of the Lachish relief in Room 10B.[1] Near the end of her second day *in situ*, a guard approached her and asked her what she was doing.

"I am counting left-handed warriors."

Unsurprisingly, his comment was: "Why?"

At the time, she answered with a suitably erudite comment about the sociological, psychological, artistic and theological implications of warriors' behavior and the disguised humor within the wall relief structure.

He went away shaking his head, muttering.[2]

---

1. Carved from gypsum, among other activities, the relief panels portray Sennacherib's triumphal military parade after the conquest of Lachish in 700 BCE. See https://www.britishmuseum.org/collection/galleries/assyria-lion-hunts (British Museum, "Assyria: Lion hunts, Siege of Lachish and Khorsabad," 710–635 BCE).

2. Something that I am convinced Charles Fensham did often over the extended period of time that he was my dissertation advisor, although he was far more gracious and subtle. He also asked "Why?" regularly and *he* expected detailed answers. He was a stalwart, supportive presence during the entire process, for which I am grateful. I respect

Premise

The dust has settled, the dissertation has been accepted and the framed doctoral sheepskin hangs on my office wall, and that question came to mind again. Why had I been counting left-handed warriors on a wall carved in Nineveh between 700 and 681 BCE? Why had I spent hours investigating the behaviors of characters portrayed in two short pericopes in the Hebrew Bible written more than twenty-five hundred years ago?

"The foremost and perhaps the only aim of the Bible is the moral improvement of the world, essentially an educational undertaking" resounds for me.[3] Further, David Bosch's contention that Biblical hermeneutics is never-ending[4] encourages the investigative mind to posit a multitude of valid theological interpretations for any specific text and encourages diversity of thought and the use of alternate methods of analysis and imagination.

Text and Provisos

The book of Judges is a collection of narratives, composed over hundreds of years with a number of redactions.[5] Theological meanings are presented obliquely within the storylines rather than as a catalogue or lists of expectations. It is plausible to suggest that at least some of these stories were based on historical fact and were sufficiently theologically important to be retained during the rewriting processes although most commentaries agree that they likely became fictionalized and romanticized over time.[6]

By their individual skills and creativity, Ehud and Ja'el,[7] characters in the book of Judges, ensured the survival of the Israelite people. I originally perceived Ehud's left-handedness and Ja'el's gender/sex as incongruous and atypical within the status quo of the era in which these stories were shaped

---

his scholarship tremendously, while, even today, I mourn his adamant stance that the zombie apocalypse had to be eradicated from my footnotes. Welcome to my world, Charles. Remember: it's not "retirement." *They* pay you to stay away.

3. Radday, "On Missing the Humour," 32.

4. Bosch, "Towards a Hermeneutic," 25.

5. There is a mainstream understanding that Judges was composed over a period of about six hundred years and came into its final redacted form around 588± BCE. Walton, "Deuteronomistic History," 169–70, quoting Noth. See also Boling, *Judges*, xxi, 30–31 and Soggin, *Judges*, 7–8.

6. See Boling, *Judges*, xxi, 30–31; Soggin, *Judges*, 7–8, for two examples.

7. Ehud and Eglon (Judg 3:12–30); Ja'el and Sisera (Judg 4 only).

and I saw within North American society today the same categorization of women and left-handedness as limiting factors.[8] I was intrigued by the success of these seemingly disadvantaged protagonists and the overlay of humor that was subtle but identifiable. I consider the pericopes to be heavily fictionalized because there is currently very little evidence outside the biblical canon that these tales have any identifiable historical basis. I propose, therefore, that they should be regarded as *märchen* rather than fact-based portrayals of a true event.[9]

I posit two exceptions to the general *märchen* categorization of *unreality* for the stories. The ramifications and nuances of the portrayal of the left-handed warrior in the Ehud-Eglon pericope have a distinctive historical and scientific foundation. Scientific research has established that, within every human population, between 2 and 12 percent of the people are genetically disposed to be left-handed.[10] There are identifiable warriors within the Lachish triumphal relief who appear to be left-handed. This artistic interpretation within a distinctly provable historical event rooted in the same era as the final version of the book of Judges provides further evidence of the possibility of a left-handed warrior.[11]

Secondly, Ja'el's use of a tent peg and hammer is physically possible for a woman. The use of the peg as a weapon further meets the societal/

---

8. There *has* been a tremendous positive change in Canadian society's perception of, and attention to, these two issues within my lifetime but I contend that the intentional, deliberate bias against women and left-handedness continues.

9. "A *märchen* is a tale of some length involving a succession of motifs or episodes. It moves in an unreal world . . . and is filled with the marvelous. In this never-never land humble heroes kill adversaries, succeed to kingdoms and marry princesses." Thompson, *The Folktale*, 8. *Märchen* widens the audience and expectations beyond the "fairy tale/folk tale" labelling.

10. Harris, "Cultural Influences, 205. Other scientists consider this percentage constant in all cultures. Bloom and Lazerson, *Brain, Mind and Behaviour*, 294. In other areas and times of the fighting world, the Scottish Clan Kerr were considered to be elite left-handed swordsmen, in the 1600s. Lawson, *Kerrs of Ferniehirst*, 24.

11. There are a number of warriors who are carrying their shields on their right arm, with evidence of a spear/javelin in the background on their left side. The action of the relief moves from left to right. The reliefs themselves have been dated to 700–681 BCE, 100± years before the final redaction of Judges of 588± BCE. Sennacherib's historical identity has been validated through these reliefs and three cuneiform prisms found in the British Museum, London, the Oriental Institute, Chicago, and the Israel Museum, Jerusalem, that supply information about him. In the Hebrew Bible, Sennacherib as a character is mentioned as a malevolent presence: 2 Kgs 18:13, 19:8, 19:16, 19:20, 19:35, 19:36; 2 Chr 32:1, 32:2, 32:9–10, 32:20–22; Isa 36:1, 37:17, 37:21, 37:36, 37:27, etc.

religious mandates of the Israelite culture and did not violate Israelite expectations of gender differentiation at that time.[12]

These scientific truths ground the pericopes in physical reality, provide a complementary foil to the *märchen* qualities of each pericope and make their entirety more believable and palpable.

Overall Structure

Each pericope is similar to a modern murder mystery with an introduction, a complete *märchen* plot, and an epilogue. There is blood, gore and violent death, deception, deceit, sexual innuendo, and potential eroticism, which culminate in a surprising *märchen* climax. The presence of so many *hapax legomena* allows an interpreter considerable flexibility of thought and the further potential of a humorous interpretation and further encourages and strengthens Bosch's premise.[13]

Plot and Setting

Within Judges 1–16, in which these pericopes are found, each plot is similar, cyclical and repetitive: Israel misbehaves and is overrun by an evil ruler; a heroic figure, designated by YHWH, steps up to vanquish the oppressor; Israel behaves for a while; the cycle continues.[14] The settings and time structures are ambiguous in twenty-first century terms, much in the pattern

---

12. Women were forbidden battle weapons. Hammer, tent pegs (and the millstone used by A Certain Woman in Judg 9) were not considered men's weapons or implements of war so their use by women was acceptable. See Matthews, *Judges and Ruth*, 72, referring to Pitt-Rivers, "Stranger," 27. The viability and methodology of Sisera's tent peg death is discussed in Feinsod, "Three Head Injuries," 320–24.

13. Halpern, *First Historians*, 58. "Bound of the right hand" is almost a *hapax*, found only twice, in 3:15 and 20:16. Other *hapax*, whose proposed meanings greatly influence the meanings within the pericopes include *misderonah'* (3:23), *prsdn* (3:22), and *rqqh* (4:21, 22).

14. The structure is actually more complex, but the above model remains valid. There are ten distinct components of the structure of Judges 1–16, most elements of which Ehud's and Ja'el's stories contain. 1, apostasy; 2, YHWH abandonment; 3, an oppressor arises; 4, Israelites remonstrate to YHWH; 5, a deliverer/savior is designated, 6, YHWH's spirit descends on the deliverer; 7, the word *judge* is used; 8 the deliverer receives YHWH's special endorsement; 9, the evil influence is eradicated and 10, peace is established. Then the cycle repeats, with new protagonists and antagonists.

of, "once upon a time in a country far away," reenforcing the *märchen* designation, but these details are less important to the present day reader.[15]

Characterization

Each character is unique. The rhetorical portrayal of their personalities and the nuances of their eccentricities and actions create the emotional core of each pericope and enrich the impact of these tales.

It is emphasized that Ehud is left-handed. Within the Hebrew Bible, there is no specific negativity toward left-handedness, other than for Temple officials, so that the term *disadvantaged* is a twenty-first century misnomer.[16] Plot manifestations suggest that the label should be instead employed to refer to Eglon's security people, who, in their assumptions that everyone is right-handed and their acquiescence to Eglon's commands, fail to protect him. The innuendo of the possibility of a homoerotic encounter adds another layer of understanding and intensity to any interpretation of Eglon's naivety and acquiescence.[17] One can question *how* he retained power for so long with such an inept army.

Ja'el is another commanding, though contradictory, personality. Initially she appears to be a threat to Israelite autonomy. Her (absent) husband is clearly identified as Sisera's ally (Judg 4:11, 17). She is not directly established as Hebrew or Israelite, so she must be considered an alien, suspect within the Israelite honor system, especially in her status as a solitary female.[18] Her behavior within the plot as a self-determining, assertive

---

15. All geographic locations lack twenty-first century exactitude. Neither Ehud's City of Palms nor Ja'el's Hazor and Kedesh is definitively identifiable, although the City of Palms is often considered to be Jericho. (refer to Deut 34:2.) See Mays, *Bible Commentary*, 407, 563, 1132. The settings, nonetheless, provided a textual richness for the original reader, for whom such details were relevant. Time is similarly oblique. Othniel reigns for forty years; Jabin rules for twenty years. The numbers are too neat for "reality." These two classifications may well have also indicated some humorous intonations to which we have no access.

16. See also Gen 48:13. If left-handedness for the reader means "disability and an inability to use the right hand effectively," the author/redactor instantly corrects that notion with verse 3:16, and the construction of the sword.

17. One of the many *hapax* is important to this aspect of the story. For interpretations of the small room and the possibilities of a sexual tryst, see Jull, " *chrqm* in Judges 3," 63–75, and Barré, "Meaning of *prsdn*," 1–11.

18. As a descendant of Moses' father-in-law, Ja'el's husband Heber *should* be considered within the Israelite sphere of influence, however obliquely one might suggest, but

woman who acts within a situation of personal adversity, seems to be in direct conflict to the expectations of a passive presence as many Israelite women are in other narratives.[19]

Jaël's determination, creativity, and physical strength together kill Sisera. She initially enacts Israelite norms by offering (upgraded) hospitality and comfort and later employs a culturally appropriate *female* tool as a killing device. She has rejected female gender norms of passivity, becoming a woman-warrior, in a category similar to Deborah, working without any direct male influence. Jaël also reverses several important story elements, firstly contradicting the expectation that the predictive Deborah will be Sisera's nemesis.[20] Secondly, in in the wider context of worldly military tactics, she repudiates the normative battle strategy of rape as an instrument of male-dominated war if one accepts the suggestion that Jaël seduces Sisera prior to killing him. The language is ambiguous and abstruse enough that this is an appropriate suggestion.[21] Thirdly, in contradiction to preconceived notions that only Israelites can save Israel, the non-Israelite, Jaël, becomes a liberator.[22]

---

it is clearly stated in 4:11 that "Heber the Kenite has separated from the other Kenites": that precludes that supposition or at the least, makes his loyalties to his clan paradoxical and suspect.

19. My choice of the word *assertive* rather than *aggressive* is culturally loaded. Non-active women include Rachel who serves as an-almost mute cameo foil in Gen 29. As well, Sarah is passive throughout her narrative, remaining in her tent with the visitors as a cook and servant (Gen 18:1–10), and has no narrative presence when Isaac is about to be sacrificed (Gen 22).

20. Judg 4:9: And she [Deborah] said [to Barak], "I will surely go with you; nevertheless, the road on which you are going will not lead to your glory, for the Lord will sell Sisera into the hand of a woman." At this stage in the pericope, the reader is led to expect Deborah's involvement in this part of the action.

21. One proponent of this behavior is Niditch, *Judges*, 58ff. The historical confirmation of rape as a military strategy and a tool of intimidation continues today. Consider the ongoing conflicts in Gaza, Ukraine, and Nigeria.

22. Even the proposition that only Israelites can save Israel from apostasy or foreign conquest is faulty. Non-Israelites often facilitated Israelite survival: e.g., the Egyptian princess saves Moses/Israel (Exod 2); the Moabite Ruth becomes the clearly identified and lauded ancestor of David/Jesus (Ruth).

Violence

To consider *violence* as "any action which contravenes the rights of others, injury to life, property or person,"[23] requires one to include non-physical elements such as emotional, spiritual, verbal, intellectual, and psychological actions. This broadens and emphasizes the all-encompassing impact of violence. The physical violence of each plot is easily identifiable: Ehud kills Eglon with a sword in his stomach, and Jaël pegs Sisera's head to the ground. These methods are unusual and creative in structure, setting, and implementation, unlike deaths as imagined/realized on an active battlefield, where swords, javelins, bows, arrows, and knives predominate.[24]

Ehud and Jaël also display evidence of symbolic and oral violence shown as misdirection, threats, and blatant verbal falsehoods.[25] Behaving as the perfect hostess, Jaël placates Sisera and is able to kill him, and Ehud, as the perfect gift-bearing guest, is equally as successful.[26]

Humor

All scholars must firstly accept that humor is in the eye of the beholder; perspectives that bear consideration can easily become contentious.[27] As in all academic ventures, it is essential that readers scrutinizing biblical texts for humor be able to identify their own personal prejudices.[28]

It may seem incongruous and contradictory to suggest that a sacred or holy text could contain hints of humor, but in the past sixty years

---

23. Burt, Friendship and Society, 162.

24. Not to mention slingshots, for which the Benjaminites were famous. Judg 9:28.

25. Ehud: "I have a secret message for you, O king" (3:18) and "I have a message from God for you" (3:20). Jaël: "Turn aside, my lord, turn aside to me; have no fear." (4:18) and her misdirection in 4:21: He said to her, "Stand at the entrance of the tent, and if anybody comes and asks you, 'Is anyone here?' say, 'No.'" Jaël appears to acquiesce to Sisera's request, knowing she can fulfil it because Sisera will be dead (and therefore "not here") before anyone approaches the tent. She disobeys Sisera when she welcomes Barak with "Come, and I will show you the man whom you are seeking" (4:22).

26. Jaël upgrades the offers of food and drink; Ehud's gift is a message.

27. Many scholars and philosophers have written extensively about humor beyond the biblical realm: Northrop Frye, Robert R. Provine, Stephen Leacock, Ron Jenkins, for example. A reader's lack of personal empathy for and involvement in the scenario often increases the impact of the humor. Bergson, *Laughter*, 111–2, 118.

28. The contention that one must have a sense of humor to see humor bears consideration.

particularly, it has become accepted that the scholarly exploration of humor is important to augment Biblical interpretation.[29] Such luminaries as C.S. Lewis wrote that laughter was a positive indication of God's presence,[30] and Radday concurred: "humour is indispensable [to comprehend the rich shadings of biblical texts]."[31]

The original storytellers' presentations would have included nuanced tone, innuendo, and personal demeanor to enrich their story, emphasizing particular elements like humor in their productions.[32] Their intention was *always* to use these stories as a device to build a sense of community and commonality within the audience. Beyond the entertainment factor, the overall purpose of each story was to define theological boundaries while excluding non-believers from a thorough appreciation. Supplemented by the humor, these tales encouraged separation and exclusivity as a subversive expression of superiority.[33]

Humor within writing, speech or incident evokes a response but that response need *not* presume laughter or positive feelings.[34] Biblical humor is sophisticated and specialized while also subversive and covert.[35] The following components are evident in these specific pericopes.

Surprise and incongruity are intrinsic to all humor: surprise occurs where previously determined expectations or appreciations of a situation are

---

29. Substantive works include Good, *Irony in the Old Testament*; Aichele, *Theology as Comedy*; Exum, *Tragedy and Comedy*; Radday and Brenner, *On Humor*. While these tomes have been instrumental in encouraging present day humor-related studies, humor itself is not a new topic. There is an interesting book copyrighted in 1892, *Wit and Humour of the Bible* by Marion D. Shutter.

30. In *The Screwtape Letters*, Screwtape instructs his acolyte devil that Christianity without laughter is considered the Devil's work and should be used to Hell's advantage. Lewis, Letter XI, 50–55.

31. Radday, "On Missing the Humour," 32. The first part of this quote is cited earlier: "The foremost and perhaps the only aim of the Bible is the moral improvement of the world, essentially an educational undertaking."

32. Perception of humor within the written word is imposed by the reader and is ambiguous. With the spoken word, the speaker injects the emotion, and the observer interprets, an equally ambiguous process.

33. "We get the joke and you do not. Therefore, we are distinct and separate from you and better."

34. "Humor and Laughter are not necessarily the same thing." Chittister, *Rule of Benedict*, 72. Laughter may reflect feelings of unease, discomfort, and/or panic.

35. Landy, "Humour as a Tool," 13.

invalidated.[36] Surprise and incongruity can be found in the misuses of words, contradictions of characterizations, ambiguities of relationships, and the confusion of gender classification, where societal rules are ignored or overturned. Ehud's and Ja'el's initial portrayals as potentially disadvantaged influences the beginning of each pericope, initiating the confusion and setting the stage for a humorous outcome. The two deliverers proceed to deceive their victims with words that placate, mislead, and are contradictory in intent. Red herrings distract and divert readers, encouraging incorrect assumptions and expectations. Again and again, the readers are faced with unfolding actions that contradict their expectations. Ehud and Ja'el successfully discombobulate both reader and plot with their repudiation of gender stereotypes and military strategies. The equivocation of the possibility of sexual trysts in each story further casts aspersions on the efficacy of the Israelite standard of sexual exclusivity and injects additional tension into the plot.[37]

Preconceived expectations of plot development are upended and discarded. Ehud and Ja'el are successful in their actions where, at the beginning of the narrative, a reader might be loath to predict their success because each operates as an independent agent, seemingly without other human and/or Godly support. Although Ehud is designated a savior (3:15), Ja'el has no such official label and seems an adjunct to the primary storyline of Barak's and Deborah's adventures. Ehud is permitted close physical contact with an abusive king. Ja'el invites a stranger into her tent. These behaviors are unusual when compared to other biblical narratives.[38] They are precursors of subsequent atypical actions.

Language is manipulated with puns, *double entendres*, and other linguistic devices. The *hapax* particularly encourages humorous consideration of alternative plot developments. Ehud's escape has been widely debated, and at least one possible meaning of the *hapax* within that segment gives rise to situational fecal humor.[39] Because of the *hapax*, it seems that many of these nuances are apparent more obviously in the Masoretic Hebrew.

36. Ja'el is the instrument of Sisera's downfall, not Deborah. Ehud is unexpectedly granted unfettered access to an oppressive monarch. See Brenner, "On the Semantic Field," 41.

37. Another reasonable question is whether the expectation of sexual exclusivity is a reader's twenty-first century imposed value or whether it is within the gender normatives of the redactors and the societies within which the pericope was created.

38. One example: Sarah stays in her tent while Abraham entertains the three visitors. There are clear indications that the men remain outside. (Gen 18:1–10).

39. Jull proposes that the *hapax hrqm* should be translated as "toilet" so that Ehud potentially makes his escape through the external opening. If so, this is a humor that

Names are used as predictive, descriptive devices to signal divine approval and ethnic origins, to enrich the narratives with their ingenious nuances that ridicule the antagonists, a further overlay of subtle humor and innuendo. George B. Gray argues that *Ehud* was originally compounded from one form of the Hebrew, "Father," which reinforces his divine mandate.[40] Ja'el's name clearly includes one honorific for YHWH; *El* Sisera's name alone identifies him as non-Israelite, thereby rendering him an alien and beyond lawful Hebrew consideration and respect.[41] Recognized in the text as Moabite/non-Israelite, *Eglon* is likely a nickname because it is most often translated as "young bullock" or "fat calf." This designation accentuates his physical demeanor and pokes fun at his corpulence.[42]

Hyperbole is a common indicator of humor that is readily apparent. Pre-knowledge of biblical details is important to identify this disguised humor. Ehud is introduced as "Ehud son of Gera, the Benjaminite, a left-handed man" (3:15), an important linguistic alert. The literal Hebrew translation is: "Ehud, son of (the clan) Gera, (from the tribe called) Son of the Right Hand, (who is) A man bound with respect to his right hand."[43] The term *Gera* is *only* associated with the tribe of Benjamin, as a small, relatively insignificant presence[44] *and* the tribe of Benjamin is considered one of the lower ranked tribes of Israel.[45] Ehud's introductory identification, therefore, becomes "Ehud, son of Benjamin, the Benjaminite, the *non-Benjaminite*," which evolves, in vernacular, to: "Ehud, a minor member of a small group within a lesser Israelite tribe, whose physical demeanor contradicts the

---

evokes discomfort and perhaps revulsion, true toilet humor.

40. Gray, *Studies in Hebrew*, 26 n4. Scholars have had great fun with Ehud's name. It has variously been translated as "majesty,"(Soggin, *Judges*, 49); "splendour," (Lindars, *Judges 1–5*, 140); "God of Praise," (Comay and Brownrigg, *Who's Who*, 106); and "Loner," (Boling, *Judges*, 85), among others.

41. Boling sees him as one of the Sea People or Philistines (*Judges*, 94). Soggin has several suggestions from Luvian to northern Anatolian (*Judges*, 63).

42. Radday notes the humor of Eglon's name in "Humour in Names," 63. Gray translates it as "calf," (Gray, *Hebrew Proper Names*, 92), as do Boling (*Judges*, 85) and Soggin, (*Judges*, 49). Soggin considers Eglon to be a caricature. The implications of body shaming as humor should be noted.

43. The precise translation of the Masoretic Hebrew, the latter phrase, is a *hapax*, found only in Judges.

44. Each of the nine times *Gera* occurs in the Bible, it is linked to *Benjamin*. Gera is posited as a subgroup or clan of the tribe of Benjamin. See Soggin, (*Judges*, 50); Boling, (*Judges*, 86); Halpern ("Ehud," 414).

45. As a tribe, they were almost decimated later in the book of Judges (22:1).

status quo of his tribe," the repetitive irony of a left-handed person who is part of a group identified as "of the right hand."

Mark. E. Biddle, in particular, considers another element of humor, irony, to be crucial to understanding faith and theological truth. "[Irony] is the most theological form of humor because it calls for one to look deeply into the obvious for signs of a somewhat veiled but more fundamental truth."[46] Situational and spoken irony abound and are critical to the plots. Pre-knowledge is again necessary to recall that many other Israelite saviors successfully fulfilled YHWH's plans, while beginning their narrative lives as less advantaged members of the family/clan and society.[47] This provides further tension to the plot. Ehud's presence is a major, subliminal insult directed at Eglon. Instead of sending a high ranking tribal elder or chief with the tribute, the Israelites have sent the maintenance man, dishonoring Eglon by their lack of respect to the hierarchical power scale. As a member of a low-ranking clan of a low-ranking Israelite tribe, Ehud's ultimate success becomes satirically and ironically humorous because that rank is used as a supplementary cudgel. Ehud triumphs *in spite of* his social status.

There is other situational incongruity, as Ehud uses a non-traditional weapon. The Benjaminites were respected as slingers (*à la* David) and bowmen,[48] yet Ehud uses a sword. A knowledgeable reader's query would begin: "How is Ehud going to accomplish his mission using a sling or a bow and arrow in a confined space?" that amends to "Why is he constructing a *sword*?" and "Where did he learn *that* skill?," questions that instantly encourage more detailed thought. These surprises again upend readers' expectations and ongoing hypotheses. Within speaker irony, Ehud invokes God's name to entice Eglon to a private meeting, but he uses the more general *El'ohim* rather than the specifically Hebrew-oriented YHWH, within the Hebrew, denigrating Eglon's intelligence and understanding yet again.[49]

Irony abounds with Ja'el as well. As a predictive narrative device, Deborah's affirmation that "The Lord will sell Sisera into the hand of a

46. Biddle, *A Time to Laugh*, 53.

47. Jacob (Gen 28), Joseph (Gen 23), and David (1 Sam), for example, were similarly considered to be disadvantaged at some stage in their narratives.

48. Judg 20:16 clarifies: "Of all this force [of Benjaminites], there were seven hundred picked men who were left-handed; every one could sling a stone at a hair, and not miss." This analysis is, of course, ironic as well. Who but YHWH can "not miss"? The archers are found in 1 Chr 12:2 "They were archers, and could shoot arrows and sling stones with either the right hand or the left; they were Benjaminites."

49. This is most obvious in the Hebrew.

woman" (Judg 4:9) implies that she, Deborah, will be the instrument of Sisera's downfall. It is easy for such a reader to forget that Deborah is a prophet, and prophets make predictions that do not necessarily involve themselves personally. Ja'el's actions contradict this prediction, upending another expectation. She is an isolated, seemingly defenseless, woman, far from a battle scene and other people, with a husband ostensively an ally of Sisera. Both situational and speaker irony are engaged.[50]

Ja'el and Ehud deceive, lie, and distract their adversaries in the fulfillment of their objectives, using trickery, deception, prevarication, and wit, all of which may be components of humor.

External Implications

Within the wider context of the entire book of Judges, it is evident that there is a tenuous and flexible dynamic within YHWH's involvement with the Chosen People. Israelites appear to have free will, and when they misbehave, YHWH gets involved to punish them by facilitating the overthrow of their political system by an individual tyrant, who in the Ehud-Ja'el pericopes are non-Israelites. Only when the Israelites entreat YHWH's help does the deity become re-involved, sending individual saviors, who were men *and* women, to somehow displace the despot. It is the individual God and the individual agent working together who free the body of guilty Israelites from their anguish and subjugations that they instigated through their own theological and cultural misbehavior. The savior's persistence, creativity and physical abilities are emphasized. Although they have YHWH's mandate, whatever support is offered is hidden and not directly apparent. All manner of behavior is considered appropriate in the overthrow of the tyrant, and within the horrific details, these stories teem with disguised comic relief.

YHWH seemingly chooses lower-ranking, divergent people as agents of change. Their "weaknesses" are narratively negated almost immediately by their God-given mandate and their clever, charming, and resourceful behaviors.[51]

---

50. Ja'el upgrades the offers of food and drink (4:18–20). She lulls Sisera, with an attitude that seems to acquiesce to his wishes, all contradictory actions considering her succeeding actions.

51. Whether or not they do have knowledge of their responsibilities. Ehud is clearly designated by YHWH, but there is no textual indication that Ja'el is aware of her godly commission.

Do No Harm

Protecting their compatriots and achieving their goals independently seem important to both deliverers: Ehud dismisses his fellow tribute bearers before he returns to kill Eglon, and Ja'el's location emphasizes her isolation and separateness from tribe and family.

To resolve the conflict, all is fair when Israelites are at war. Individual behavior is based on expediency and opportunity. All types of physical violence are acceptable to protect, defend, or re-establish Israelite autonomy, as is non-physical (verbal) violence like clever repartee, outright lies, and sexual entrapment.

There appears to be no Hebrew equivalent of the Geneva Conventions, and the saviors have great theological latitude. They treat the Israelite cultural and sexual expectations with impunity. They pay no attention to the strictures of "You shall not murder" and "You shalt not commit adultery."[52] In direct contradiction, the limitations of cultural demands are honored when Ja'el uses a "woman's" tool to accomplish her deed, so she does not violate war and male-specific mandates, while Ehud employs a specifically-designed male weapon, a sword.

The actions of the plot and the characters were not deliberately choosing to be humorous. The authors and redactors have imposed the humor with their linguistic choices in an effort to influence the readers. The humor moderates the impact and horror of the graphic portrayal of the murders and is meant to validate the protagonists' actions, while making the violence palatable and acceptable. The humor hopes to depict Ehud and Ja'el as positive characters rather than the cold-blooded killers that their premeditated actions would suggest. YHWH-based names reinforce this impression of acceptability and further exploit their divine mandate. In contrast, the antagonists are given derisive nicknames and circumstances to perpetuate and strengthen their negative position. Eglon and Sisera are introduced as established, seemingly competent, long-serving rulers, yet they are quickly duped and defeated by characters who are strangers to them. Eglon is killed in an ignominious location, and his death is described in a detailed, lascivious manner.[53] The details of Sisera's death are similarly graphic and startling. He lets down his guard and is conned by a woman when he accepts all her ministrations at face value, rather than questioning

---

52. Exod 12:13–14. The questions here would be how widespread the awareness of was, and acceptance of the Commandments for the Israelites of that time.

53. If one accepts Jull's hypothesis. Jull, "*chrqm* in Judges 3," 63–75, and see also Barré, "The Meaning of *prsdn*," 1–11.

everything, which he should have been doing, considering he was on the losing side of a major battle, fleeing for his life.[54]

Thoughts

I believe the Bible in its entirety to be the source of salvific, not scientific, truth, contained in a complex, multidimensional text that encompasses a variety of theological mandates and guidelines. The Bible is a clever manifestation of human discourse with God that attempts to explain the unexplainable.

It is a reality that people remember detailed stories when the contents and order of the any list are beyond their ken.[55] Narratives are easy to remember because their plots are sequential and have identifiable structures. From that recall, readers construct whatever philosophical/theological lessons they choose that validate their appraisals, long after they have forgotten the real and implied morals and motivations of the original storytellers. The structures, themselves, encourage latitude for a variety of interpretations.

Stories are a clever, almost nefarious, way in which writers can inculcate the reader with their agendas, attitudes, philosophies, and theologies. From my very first academic introduction to the Hebrew Bible, I was intrigued by the stories in the book of Judges. What could they tell *me* about the Hebrew faith and how could I apply that to my Christianity?

The overall sense of Ehud's and Ja'el's assumed weaknesses and the ambiguity of their victories appealed to my Baby Boomer sensibilities. Although I am right-hand dominant, I understood the dynamics and difficulties of left-handedness among my friends. Deborah, as a power broker and authority figure, along with Ja'el's success over an experienced male leader, provided me with role models.

What is the relevance of these stories for twenty-first century Christian theology in general? I can propose a limited scope of suggestions.

The stories of Ehud and Ja'el do contain several almost-universal Christian theological truths beyond the following caveat.

---

54. Judg 4:17–21.

55. This unscientific evaluation is based on personal anecdotal experience. I have often enquired of churchgoers: "Tell me about today's homily." Without exception, the pew-person will recount and evaluate an anecdote, often with the comment, "But I do not recall much else."

Canadian democracy and the rule of law together have a three-thousand or so year evolutionary history, the latter five-hundred years of which has been influenced by the Judaeo-Christian beliefs of the British Empire and aristocracy, who were primarily Church of England, after the English Reformation.[56] It is too simplistic to baldly state that Canadian federal democracy is completely Christian in composition, but laws and statutes generally reflect Christian tenets, including at least some of the Ten Commandments.[57]

In Canada, murder/homicide[58] and lesser acts of violence are not considered appropriate means of political displacement, except within actions prompted by a federal declaration of war. Canadians further have an understanding that an individual person might be permitted to use violence to defend self and property, but it is not automatically deemed appropriate. It must be validated through the justice system. At all times, Parliament, the rule of law, and the courts prevail.[59]

In twenty-first century terms, these factors limit the acceptability of Ehud's and Ja'el's climatic actions. Ehud's behavior cannot be fitted into the realm of reasonable, battle/war related aggression because it does not take place on the "legitimate" battlefield, nor has there been a lawful or stated declaration of war. Eglon's death must be considered suspect. Ja'el's actions are slightly more justifiable because she was hypothetically protecting hearth and home, although Sisera was asleep when she kills him. The understanding of women's roles in violent encounters has evolved over the past fifty or so years in North American society, as have their roles within society.[60] I suggest that a similar transformation might well have been taking place over the six hundred or so years in which these stories were

---

56. From Greek democracy to beyond the English Reformation triggered by Henry VIII (1491–1547), democracy continues to evolve.

57. Including, in Exod 20:13–16: 13 You shall not murder. 14 You shall not commit adultery. 15 You shall not steal. 16 You shall not bear false witness against your neighbour (NRSV). These are within the Canadian criminal and civil codes at all three levels (municipal; provincial; federal).

58. *Homicide* is the legal term, with various gradations. *Murder* is the popular vernacular.

59. Lethal force against a home intruder is legal only when a court of law considers it to be reasonable and proportional to the threat faced. Among other factors, there must be a *reasonable* fear of imminent harm. Sections 34 and 35 of the *Canadian Criminal Code*.

60. Within media at least. In the 1997 movie *G.I. Jane*, the heroine is not permitted to kill. By 2024, in the Marvel movie series and mainstream television programs (e.g., *The Equalizer*), female characters fight, torture, and kill as a regular facet of plot development.

redacted, with Ehud's and Ja'el's behavior posited as exemplars of acceptable behavior in the final redactions. The redactors cleverly encouraged such a shift in reader perception when they cloaked the scenarios in a humorous overlay to endorse, yet downplay, the results. Nevertheless, I would hesitate to be the defense counsel were either situation to be presented in a Canadian court of law. Examples of Christian theological truths can be noted:

1. God is a living, though occasionally quiet, presence in human lives and has an active commitment and involvement to ensure the wellbeing of God's people.[61]

2. God uses the skills of all peoples to achieve prescribed aims, regardless of individual attributes that might seem to be disadvantages. Social rank and other limitations are irrelevant to God.[62]

3. A solitary savior supported by a singular God saves the large body of followers.

4. An individual person's initiative, creativity, perseverance, and endurance are attributes that can effectively contribute to the fulfillment of God's commands.[63]

5. Deliverers have a loyalty to the larger group, whom they actively protect. They put the welfare of the group above their own personal safety and ignore the possibility that it was the group itself that triggered the upheaval.[64]

6. God makes use of all committed people. It is not necessary for the deliverers to be believers or involved in ritual worship for them to serve as God's agents.[65]

7. Ours is not a humorless deity. I accept that the Bible was written by humans directed by God and conclude that the humor we find in the texts is another indication of the Almighty's vast grasp of our reality.

---

61. YHWH anoints Ehud directly (3:15) and is present very clearly with Deborah (4:4+) but is only implied in the Ja'el segment.

62. The various protagonists, including Ehud, Ja'el, Barak and Deborah, although the latter two are not active agents in the Ja'el chapter but serve as triggers for Ja'el's behavior. Ehud as the lowest of the low (3:15); Ja'el as a single woman (4:11, 17).

63. The general behavior of both protagonists throughout the pericopes.

64. Ehud sends his fellows away (3:18); Ja'el lives alone (4:17).

65. Nowhere in either selection is there any mention of worship. Indeed, in the entire section, chapters 1–16, worship is seldom, if ever, mentioned.

I concur with Doris Donnelly that, without humor "we rob ourselves of the lightness and freedom necessary to notice and then to adore God."[66] Without humor, these stories become aberrations rather than cautionary, expository tales. Reinhold Niebuhr has an important insight, which I espouse:

> Humour is . . . a prelude to faith; and laughter is the beginning of prayer . . . The intimate relation between humour and faith is derived from the fact that both deal with the incongruities of our existence . . . Laughter is our reaction to immediate incongruities . . . faith is the only possible response to the ultimate incongruities of existence.[67]

These stories may not cause the readers to laugh out loud, but their incongruities should lead them to evaluate the texts with fresh perspectives and insights.

More to Ponder

Every book and narrative of the Bible is worthy of study to assist congregants to deepen their faith and develop further theological understanding and insight. The book of Judges is not prominently featured in survey texts on Old Testament/Hebrew Bible theology or in the Revised Common Lectionary.[68] The book is yet another victim of "lectionary gymnastics," a theological tendency to ignore or negate those parts of the Bible that are contentious or ambiguous in theme or content.[69] Many pew-Christians have no knowledge of the book because they never hear them in church.

John Dominic Crossan offers the ultimate conclusion that encourages further evaluation, prayer, and study:

---

66. Donnelly, "Divine Folly," 388.
67. Niebuhr, *Discerning the Signs*, 111–13.
68. Brueggemann, *Old Testament Theology*, has one reference to Judges (173). There is only one selection from Judges that is found in the three-year cycle of the Revised Common Lectionary: Judg 4:1–7, Year A, Proper 28.
69. *Lectionary gymnastics* is an appropriate term to refer to texts that are ignored, avoided or negated during the religious year. The phrase was coined by Nelson-Pallmeyer, *Is Religion Killing Us?*, xiv. I personally suspect that "professional theologians," those who make such decisions, do not know the texts intimately or are afraid of them. It may well be that they feel there is not enough time to adequately explore these texts.

> My point once again is not that the ancient people told literal stories and we are now smart enough to take them symbolically but that they told them symbolically and we are now dumb enough to take them literally. They knew what they were doing, we do not . . . The Bible always forces us to choose because the Bible is ambiguous, and ambiguity requires us to make a choice.[70]

In every element of our religious faith, we have choices. There are always myriad possibilities. That should not stop us from doing what is most important to continue our theological learning: reading, pondering, evaluating, praying.

Bibliography

Aichele, George, Jr. *Theology as Comedy*. Lanham, MD: University Press of America, 1980.
Barré, Michael. "The Meaning of *prsdn* in Judges III 22." *Vetus Testamentum* 41.1 (1991) 1–11.
Bergson, Henri. *Laughter, An Essay on the Meaning of the Comic*. Translated by Cloudesley Brereton and Fred Rothwell. New York: Macmillian, 1991.
Biddle, Mark E. *A Time to Laugh: Humor in the Bible*. Macon, GA: Smyth & Helwys, 2013.
Bloom, F., and A. Lazerson. *Brain, Mind and Behaviour*. 2nd ed. New York: Freeman, 1985.
Boling, Robert G. *Judges: Introduction, Translation, and Commentary*. Anchor Bible 7. Garden City, NY: Doubleday, 1975.
Bosch, D.J. "Towards a Hermeneutic for 'Biblical Studies in Mission.'" *Mission Studies* 3, no. 2 (1985), quoted in *Emerging from the Dark Age Ahead: The Future of the North American Church* by Charles Fensham. Ottawa: Novalis, 2008.
Brenner, A. "On the Semantic Field." In *On Humor and the Comic in the Hebrew Bible*, edited by Yehuda T. Radday and Athalya Brenner. Sheffield: Almond, 1990.
Brueggemann, Walter. *Old Testament Theology: An Introduction*. Nashville: Abingdon, 2008.
Burth, Donald X. *Friendship and Society: An Introduction to Augustine's Practical Philosophy*. Grand Rapids: Eerdmans, 1999.
Chittister, Joan. *The Rule of Benedict*. New York: Crossroad, 1993.
Comay, Joan, and Ronald Brownrigg. *Who's Who in the Bible: Two Volumes in One*. New York: Bonanza, 1980.
Criminal Code. Revised Statutes of Canada 1985, c. C-46. Ottawa: Department of Justice Canada.
Crossan, John Dominic, and Richard G. Watts. *Who Is Jesus: Answers to Your Questions about the Historical Jesus*. Louisville: Westminster John Knox, 1996.
Donnelly, Doris. "Divine Folly: Being Religious and the Exercise of Power." *Theology Today* 48.4 (1992) 388.
Exum, Cheryl J., ed. *Semeia* 32: *Tragedy and Comedy in the Bible*. Atlanta: Scholars, 1984.

---

70. Crossan and Watts, *Who Is Jesus*, 79.

Feinsod, M. "Three Head Injuries: The Biblical Account of the Deaths of Sisera, Abimelech and Goliath." *Journal of the History of the Neurosciences* 6.3 (1997) 320–24.
Good, Edwin M. *Irony in the Old Testament*. 2nd ed. Bible and Literature Series 3. Sheffield: Almond, 1981.
Gray, George Buchanan. *Studies in Hebrew Proper Names*. London: Black, 1986.
Halpern, Baruch. "Ehud." In *Anchor Bible Dictionary*, vol. 2, edited by David Noel Freedman, 414. New York: Doubleday, 1992.
———. *The First Historians*. San Francisco: Harper & Row, 1988.
Harris, L.J. "Cultural Influences on Handedness: Historical and Contemporary Theory and Evidence." In *Left-Handedness: Behavioral Implications and Anomalies*. Edited by S. Coren. Advances in Psychology 67. Amsterdam: North-Holland/Elsevier Science, 1990.
Jull, Tom A. "*chrqm* in Judges 3: A Scatological Reading." *Journal for the Study of the Old Testament* 23 (1998) 63–75.
Landy, Francis. "Humour as a Tool for Biblical Exegesis." In *On Humor and the Comic in the Hebrew Bible*, edited by Yehuda T. Radday and Athalya Brenner. Journal for the Study of the Old Testament Supplements 92. Sheffield: Almond, 1990.
Lawson, Bob. *The Kerrs of Ferniehirst 1205–1692*. Quoted in "Clan Kerr," Wikipedia. https://en.wikipedia.org/wiki/Clan_Kerr.
Lewis, C.S. *The Screwtape Letters*. Toronto: Saunders, 1945.
Lindars, Barnabas. *Judges 1–5: A New Translation and Commentary*. Edited by A. D. H. Mayes. London: T. & T. Clark, 1995.
Matthews, Victor H. *Judges and Ruth*. New Cambridge Bible Commentary. Cambridge: Cambridge University Press, 2004.
Mays, James L., ed. *The HarperCollins Bible Commentary*. Rev. ed. San Francisco: HarperSanFrancisco, 2000.
Nelson-Pallmeyer, Jack. *Is Religion Killing Us? Violence in the Bible and the Qur'an*. New York: Continuum, 2003.
Niditch, Susan. *War in the Hebrew Bible: A Study in the Ethics of Violence*. New York: Oxford University Press, 1993.
———. *Judges: A Commentary*. Louisville: Westminster John Knox, 2008.
Niebuhr, Reinhold. *Discerning the Signs of the Times: Sermons for Today*. New York: Scribner, 1946.
Pitt-Rivers, J. "The Stranger, the Guest, and the Hostile Host." In *Contributions to Mediterranean Sociology: Mediterranean Rural Communities and Social Change*, edited by J. G. Peristiany. Paris: Mouton, 1968.
Rad, Gerhard von. *Holy War in Ancient Israel*. Translated and edited by Marva J. Dawn. Grand Rapids: Eerdmans, 1991.
Radday, Yehuda T. "Humour in Names." In *On Humor and the Comic in the Hebrew Bible*, edited by Yehuda T. Radday and Athalya Brenner. Journal for the Study of the Old Testament Supplements 92. Sheffield: Almond, 1990.
———. "On Missing the Humour." In *On Humor and the Comic in the Hebrew Bible*, edited by Yehuda T. Radday and Athalya Brenner. Journal for the Study of the Old Testament Supplements 92. Sheffield: Almond, 1990.
Radday, Yehuda T. and Athalya Brenner, eds. *On Humor and the Comic in the Hebrew Bible*. Journal for the Study of the Old Testament Supplements 92. Sheffield: Almond, 1990.
Robinson, Billie Anne. "Laughing in the Face of Violence: Theological Implications of the Inter-relationships between Violence and Humour in the Book of Judges." ThD diss.,

Toronto School of Theology, University of Trinity College, University of Toronto, 2019.

Shutter, Marion D. *Wit and Humour of the Bible*. Gutenberg Ebooks, 1892. https://archive.org/details/withumorofbiblooshut.

Soggin, J. Alberto. *Judges*. Translated by John Bowden. Old Testament Library. London: SCM, 1987.

Thompson, Stith. *The Folktale*. New York: Dryden, 1951.

Walton, John. H. "The Deuteronomistic History." In *A Survey of the Old Testament*, edited by Andrew E. Hill and John H. Walton. Zondervan, 2009.

13

Naming Human and Divine

Expansive and Inclusive Liturgy in The Presbyterian Church in Canada

Sarah Travis

Introduction

CONFESSION SHOULD LEAD TO transformed lives. When we confess our sins, we are invited into a fresh space of being in which we are forgiven by God and made ready to live in a more just and loving manner. In 2022, my denomination, The Presbyterian Church in Canada (PCC), made a confession to God regarding its behavior and attitudes surrounding the LGBTQI community.[1] This confession acknowledges the church's sin toward LGBTQI peoples and urges the PCC toward renewed relationship, within and beyond the space of public worship.

One of the sins the church confesses is its failure of the language we use to describe each other and God. The confession to God and to LGBTQI

---

1. I am using the acronym LGBTQI to be consistent with the language used in the PCC Confession. In this context, the letters stand for lesbian, gay, bisexual, trans/transitioning, queer/questioning, and intersex. A full acronym would include A (Asexual) and 2S (2 spirited).

people carries significant weight within the denomination—it guides and binds the denomination's actions. While the confession has been adopted by the whole denomination, there is tremendous work to be done in terms of bringing it to life in the worship and relationships of the denomination. In short, although the denomination has decided to welcome LGBTQI ministers to preside at pulpit, font, and table, not all agree with these decisions.[2] Furthermore, even those churches which desire to be more inclusive and expansive in their ethics and attitudes may struggle to enact inclusivity and expansiveness, especially in their liturgical language. Choosing different language requires making a commitment to a challenging task. It is a task, however, that leads to a stronger and more faithful community.

Specifically, this essay wonders what changes are needed liturgically if the PCC is to live out the implications of the 2022 Confession to God and to LGBTQI people. How might expanded language aid the community in naming a deeper truth about itself and the Divine? I explore the language and imagery used for the human and Divine in worship and ask how language and imagery might be transformed to enhance hospitality for both divine and human participants. The PCC Confession requires a transformation of previously held ethics and attitudes, and I seek to continue this transformation as we reach out toward God in hopes of uttering more truthful and faithful words to describe the community in which we dwell, at the center of divine love.[3]

Liturgically, we are shaped and formed by language. Not only by language—also by melody and silence, embodied action, and water, bread, and wine. More embodied ways of worshipping are often undervalued in reformed worship settings that tend to value the head over the heart. Yet language remains one of the most powerful ways of knowing God and defining humanity. How must our language change as our communities change? To what extent does language drive continued change within communities? As I tell my students, it is important that we say what we mean—about God and about people. If we are talking about male beings, then absolutely we should use the term *men*. If we are talking about male and female beings

---

2. For more on the decision made by the PCC regarding sexuality, see PCC, "Gender and Sexuality."

3. This essay is intended to celebrate an aspect of Charles Fensham's contribution to scholarship. Charles has influenced me tremendously to think about just and loving language for people and for God. In his always gentle way, he models the life of one who has thought deeply about such matters. I am grateful for his influence on my work and ministry.

then it is appropriate to use language that includes both, such as *humankind* or *people*. If we speak of a God who transcends human categories, why then would we restrict ourselves to male pronouns and titles for God? The God we worship cannot be contained by human language but must be represented by human language all the same. Our words are always inadequate, and yet, somehow, we must find the words to express the inexpressible. Kimberley Bracken Long writes: "the language used in worship ought to be biblical, creative, eloquent, imaginative, and expansive—language that says that something is happening here that happens nowhere else—language that invites us into an event, a way of being, and the expectation that we will encounter the holy."[4] I would add that our worship language should be pastoral—it should take into account the needs of the gathered body. Worship language should help us to encounter God—not leave us feeling unwanted or excluded. While I focus on LGBTQI inclusive language in this article, it is important to consider the inclusiveness of our language concerning race, class, and disability, as well as gender and sexual orientation.

Language in the PCC

There is tremendous diversity within Presbyterian churches in Canada. While there is no set liturgy, most follow reformed fourfold structure that begins with a gathering, moves on to the Word, then the response to the Word, and the sending. Within each of these sections, worship leaders are free to include a variety of worship elements, always including prayer and song, scripture, and sermon, but not necessarily in a particular order or employing a particular style. There is also diversity in terms of theological perspective—some churches are more progressive; others are more traditional. What they have in common is that all worship leaders attempt to use language and imagery to describe both God and the human community. While we have a Book of Common Order, it is optional—we do not have set prayers or liturgies, so worship leaders are free to choose words and images that speak to the community and its social location. Many Presbyterian worship leaders turn to the PCC's website, where the most recent version of the Book of Common Worship is available with revisions to make it more inclusive and expansive. Thus, such language is available for all worship

---

4. Long, "Beyond Merely Adequate," 3–11.

leaders, and it constitutes a choice to use a non-inclusive version of the liturgies within that book.[5]

While the PCC does not have an all-encompassing language policy, it has guidelines for using inclusive language. In 2021, the General Assembly passed the following motion related to its Rainbow Communion report: "That with the support of the resources from the Life and Mission Agency, the courts of the church, agencies, colleges and camps review and update their policies, procedures and practices, including the language used, by June 2022, to ensure they reflect the full inclusion of all people."[6] A style guide for writing from one department reads: "Great care should be taken to avoid language that is demeaning or that stereotypes others on the basis of sex, race, ethnicity, sexual orientation, class, income, geography, mental and physical characteristics, and age. The language we use not only reflects our thinking but also shapes it."[7] It is the policy of the national office of The Presbyterian Church in Canada that inclusive language is to be used in reports, presentations, worship resources, and official communications. Language should be used in ways that express "the dignity and worth of God's beloved people and creation and the grace and hope of Jesus Christ."[8]

How might worship leaders and congregations be encouraged to enact the policy within the worship setting? How does the 2022 Confession lead to a change in practice? The following sections explore the possibilities and limitations of inclusive and expansive language for congregational use. While the PCC is the focus of this essay, any denomination that is making decisions about the inclusion of all sexualities will benefit from this exploration.

The Confession

The 2022 Confession addresses a variety of actions and attitudes that have negatively influenced the treatment of LGBTQI people in the church. It is

---

5. It has been a very different experience for denominations that use a common prayer book as their normative guide for worship. For example, the Anglican Communion has employed inclusive and expansive language in its Book of Common Prayer since 1985. See Oliver, "Containing the Uncontainable," 27–43.

6. A&P 2021, 661.

7. PCC, "Guidelines": This style guide is detailed and provides guidance for worship leaders who wish to make their language more inclusive/expansive.

8. PCC, "Guidelines," 40.

addressed to God and to LGBTQI people, and it presumes a breach in relationship that is contrary to God's desires for humanity. It calls the church "to acknowledge harms done; to seek forgiveness from God and those who have been harmed; to stop causing harm; to repent of wrongdoing; and to begin a new journey of reparation, restoration, and reconciliation within the community of believers."[9] Even in the courts of the church, those who are not cisgender or straight have been "attacked, shunned and belittled."[10] People have been forced to choose between their sexuality and the church, and the church has often perpetuated lies about LGBTQI people that put them at risk of abuse. "The church has no higher calling than to offer the worship that belongs to God. In worship, we find strength and hope for proclaiming God's reign in the world. Yet often our language in worship is not inclusive and renders many people and their families invisible. This makes worship a wounding and alienating experience."[11] The church has not nurtured or supported LGBTQI people, making them vulnerable to "internalized homophobia, self-loathing, depression, substance abuse, self-harm, homelessness, and suicide."[12] The church confesses that it has embraced ideologies and narratives that have harmed LGBTQI people in many ways. It seeks the restoration of relationships both among human beings and between the Divine and human.

While this confession marks a significant step forward for the PCC, it is only the beginning of the work that needs to be done. Much more difficult are the tasks of righting wrongs, changing behavior, and creating lasting reconciliation. It is, of course, the individual LGBTQI person who must decide whether they will accept the plea for forgiveness. Human beings are slower to forgive than God. Theologically, we are assured of pardon if we truly and humbly repent of our actions and attitudes. Unfortunately, homophobic and transphobic attitudes and actions continue within the PCC. Even though the whole church accepted the Confession and thus made the confession, not all ministers and congregations have taken it to heart.[13]

---

9. PCC, "Confession," 1.
10. PCC, "Confession," 2.
11. PCC, "Confession," 2.
12. PCC, "Confession," 3.

13. While liberty of conscience is granted in the case of participating in weddings and ordinations involving LGBTQI individuals, there is no such liberty of conscience in participating in the Confession. It is the confession of the whole church.

My argument here is that the enactment of this confession will require effort and intentionality on the part of the church. Implicit in the Confession is a promise to repent—to think and act differently. In confessing a variety of sins committed against LGBTQI people, the 2022 Confession looks for an alternate pathway into the future, in which relationships can be reconciled. *Reconciliation* is not an abstract term but one rooted in real relationships. There is a need for reconciliation among many parties. In the space of God's grace, there is room for reconciliation among those who have caused harm and those who have been harmed. There is room for reconciliation among those who are theologically affirming and those who are not. The whole denomination has been damaged by the experience of wrestling the theology of sexuality and thus there is a sense in which the PCC needs to find healing within itself.

The PCC will need to decide how it will live out its confession as it seeks to repair broken relationship. For example, the church will need to begin to formulate a new expression of care and commitment to LGBTQI people. I am proposing that inclusive and expansive language are one pathway of repentance—a commitment to change liturgical language in response to the harm that has been done in the past. The confession, as described above, addresses specifically the ways that language has fallen short or caused damage to LGBTQI individuals and communities. Inadequate language for human beings has caused alienation and woundedness in its exclusivity, resulting in a sense that LGBTQI people do not belong in liturgical spaces, as they are not named properly in such spaces. While the confession does not specifically refer to language for God, the way we name God will have consequences for how we perceive each other and our varied callings. Such change will not be easy to accomplish, and this essay will address the resistance and challenges to changing the language and imagery that is familiar.

Implications for Language about Human Beings—Inclusivity

The need for confession to God regarding human sexuality implies that our previous attitudes and actions have been inadequate. Certainly, our language has been inadequate. In the spirit of the PCC Confession, it is incumbent on the church to stop causing harm. Exclusive language for people is a continuation of harm. It is harmful to use language that implies the existence of only two genders—male and female—or language that implies that sexual relationships occur only between men and women. LGBTQI inclusive language refers to positive word choices that acknowledge and respect the differences and diversity of people in the church, including their bodies, genders, and relationships. This will involve a careful examination of the language we use to describe the members of our congregations and those beyond its walls.

All language that represents people within the liturgy should be evaluated for its inclusiveness. For example, the common greeting "Brothers and Sisters" is not inclusive of nonbinary folk and is easily replaced with "Siblings." To use such terminology is to honor the differences among the worshippers—some will identify as male, some as female, and some as something in-between. We should also, for example, refer to people using the names and pronouns they prefer. This is partially about getting away from heteronormative assumptions which hold that heterosexual relationships are normative, and all other relationships are derivative. Instead, the language of worship should embrace the wideness of identity present in the sanctuary.

Implications for Language about God—Expansive

In order to discover the link between the 2022 Confession and the need for expansive language, it is helpful to think about the ways that our language for God shapes who we are as individuals and as a body. Social reality, to a certain extent, is constructed on our human perception of Divine nature. The way we name God shapes our ethics and our actions. Exclusive or narrow understandings of the Divine contribute to exclusive and narrow understandings of human community. For example, Ruth Myers said in an interview: when "we have a strongly masculine image of God," a patriarchal and hierarchical worldview is created that "allows for abuse of women, sexual harassment, sexual exploitation, and a sense of entitlement by men to women's bodies."[14] This is a serious claim, that our language for God can shape our human relationships.

As I have argued elsewhere, God's life in Trinity opens up a new pathway for human beings to perceive themselves in relation to God and in relation to one another. If the Trinity is characterized by freedom, self-giving, diversity, and openness, then the way people approach the world may also

---

14. Quoted in Gabriel, "Episcopal Church."

be characterized by these things.[15] If the Divine nature is characterized by domination, selfishness, homogeneity, and fixedness, Christians who attempt to mirror God in their living will enact these characteristics. Perhaps the most interesting aspect of the Trinity for this study is the implication that the Trinity may be conceived as diverse or homogenous. In order to preserve monotheism, the Trinity has been historically understood to be intensely unified. Yet the persons of the Trinity maintain difference—they exist with essential unity but difference in function and role. Thus, the persons of the Trinity are self-differentiated—they do not merely dissolve into one another. As distinct yet unified beings, the Creator, Son, and Holy Spirit preserve plurality rather than erasing it.[16] Unity, then, comes from the interaction of the persons rather than some sort of sameness. *Perichoretic unity* describes the ways that the persons of the Trinity are bound together in a dance of love. While human beings cannot hope to achieve such a level of unity, we may find that this concept of a differentiated Trinity opens the possibility of relationships that are characterized by difference and diversity rather than enforced homogeneity.

Also relevant is the idea that the Trinity is a dynamic relationship that is not closed or fixed but open to all of creation. "In perichoretic fashion, each Person is open to the other and makes space for the other. The Trinity opens to creation as the created other is drawn into fellowship. Each is affected by the other."[17] As a dynamic entity, the Trinity is a space of change and transformation—the future is not defined by what has happened in the past. The Trinity opens itself to creation, and human communities in the image of the Trinity are more likely to be available to change, transformation, and expansion.

What does all this have to do with the language we use for God? If God is fixed and unchanging, Christians may feel compelled to be similarly fixed and unchanging when it comes to the language used for God, as well as other people. If the Trinity compels us toward homogeneity, then we will be unlikely to view diversity and difference as gift rather than curse. Rather, a God who is open to all of creation, who leads the circulation of divine love throughout the human community, is more likely to inspire a sense of playful creativity in which our language can be expanded. Similarly, a Trinity

---

15. See Travis, *Decolonizing Preaching*, chapter 3. These ideas are drawn from Jürgen Moltmann's social trinity.

16. Travis, Decolonizing Preaching, loc 1145.

17. Travis, Decolonizing Preaching, loc 1151.

that enjoys diversity within itself opens to us the possibility of enjoying, even celebrating, difference in the human community. How we name God matters. According to the national office of the PCC, "while the term 'Father' is often employed as a metaphor and title for God in worship, it is not the most frequently used image of God in the Bible. Among the other frequently used images for God in the Bible are Creator, Light, Strength, Power, Healing One, Tower of Strength, Shepherd, Deliverer, Loving Kindness, Potter, Dwelling Place, Redeemer, Radiant, God of Peace, Living God, Lawgiver, Consuming Fire, Almighty."[18] The purpose of using multiple names for God and avoiding the exclusive use of male pronouns for God is to avoid cultivating an exclusively male image of God.

Implications for Preaching

An essay about worship language in the reformed tradition must address the preaching of the church. The Word proclaimed lies at the heart of Presbyterian worship. The 2022 Confession requires a change in the language and imagery used in sermons. This is primarily an act of careful representation. What language do we use to describe the LGBTQI members of our faith community and the larger community beyond the church? The preacher can begin by becoming knowledgeable about what constitutes inclusive language. Preachers can then ask themselves: How does the language of my preaching include or exclude those who are listening to me? Do I include sermon illustrations that reflect a variety of sexualities and genders? Most preachers are accustomed to this process because we naturally think about those things that are especially relevant for our listeners—we know that Miss Jones is a gardener, and Mr. Singh is worried about his daughter. We will search scripture and our environment to find illustrations that will speak to those individuals. In the same way, we are invited to search scripture and our environments for illustrations that include LGBTQI people in truthful ways. Some preachers will argue that they do not have LGBTQI folks within their communities. Preachers must remember that they are not privy to every aspect of identity within their congregations. There are things that we do not know—burdens carried by our parishioners and those they love. A word of graceful inclusion can go a long way to repairing harm that has been done to individuals and churches.

---

18. PCC, "Guidelines," 46.

Implications for Sacramental Language

In the sacraments of Baptism and the Lord's Supper, we receive the embodied truth of God's love. Both sacraments are opportunities to speak about God's welcome to all people. Perhaps the wideness of Christ's table is most abundantly obvious in our "Invitation to the Table." Presbyterian congregations have a long history of fencing the table—determining who is worthy and who is unworthy to participate in the eucharistic meal. We still fence the table when we invite particular individuals to participate (i.e., all those who are baptized; all those who love the Lord.). The invitation to the table that we include in the communion liturgy will determine who is welcome at the table. Preachers and church leaders must come to a deep understanding of the theology that undergirds this invitation. If it is Christ's table, do we get to decide who does not get fed? How can my words open a space of hospitality that explicitly names and welcomes those who are here to participate?[19] If the leaders do not want to explicitly welcome LGBTQI individuals, why not? What is the theological impetus behind that decision?

In baptism, Christian children and adults are brought into the life of the church in the name of the *Father, Son and Holy Spirit*. There is considerable debate about the inclusiveness of this term, and many theological reasons for keeping it. Whether clergy choose to use *Father* or a more inclusive *Creator*, the important thing is to use a variety of terms for God in the baptismal liturgy beyond the threefold formula. The use of inclusive/expansive language does not mean that we must let go of everything familiar. "At other times, we may choose to continue to use traditional and cherished terms alongside other words and terms so that a clearing can be created that allows more of the congregation to find themselves and their God named in community."[20] Those who are being baptized are created in the image of God, and thus our imagining of God should leave room for a variety of identities.

Our baptism binds us to the church. It is a graceful initiation to community life, in which we are joined together in one Body—the Body of Christ. The 2022 Confession is, in essence, an opportunity to repair and build the Body of Christ. As baptized Christians, we are invited to seek always the good of the other. Sometimes we must sing songs which we do not

---

19. Worship leaders are often addressing individuals that they do not know and cannot see, if they are livestreaming or recording their services.

20. MCC, Inclusive Language Guidelines.

like because others find meaningful encounter with God in singing them. Sometimes we must use language that feels strange on our tongue because it makes the person next to us feel welcomed and included.

Resistance

When I was a teenager, I encountered the concept of inclusive language for the first time. I had a negative reaction to the very idea, immediately dismissing it as "political correctness," that is, something done purely to appear virtuous. I did not understand how powerfully language shapes perceptions of self and others. Gradually, as I personally felt the sting of being excluded by language in the liturgy because of my gender, I realized how important it is to include everyone who gathers in the worship space in the language we choose. It was an upsetting experience to be in worship, listening to a scripture being read, and realizing that the language did not include my gender. In that specific case, the worship leader had chosen a version of scripture that used *men* instead of *men and women*. I felt that I, as a woman, was being removed from the story, erased from the narrative. When I engaged the male worship leader in conversation, he was shocked and offended that I would raise such an issue. He had never felt the sting of being excluded because of gender.

If I was resistant to changing my language for people—how much more difficult it is to change our language for God? I suspect that my argument here is deeply contentious within The Presbyterian Church in Canada. There is considerable debate about language, just as there is considerable debate about the full inclusion of LGBTQI ministers and parishioners. Some will argue that God is Father because God is named as such by Jesus himself. I have no issue with naming God as Father as long as Father is not the only term we use to describe God. To limit ourselves to one term goes against the biblical witness which uses a variety of terms to describe the Divine.

Truthfully, even as I lead worship in more conservative congregations, I have never had anyone complain about my use of a variety of terms for God. Neither has there been resistance about using inclusive language for people. The change can appear seamless to the congregation. People do vehemently resist changing the language of familiar hymns, for example. In Canada, there is considerable debate about our national anthem, "O Canada." For the past several decades, it has been customary to sing "true patriot love in all our sons command." It is relatively easy to change this to a more inclusive lyric—"in all of us command" or "in all thine own command," and yet many are resistant to such change. The irony is that the words of the anthem have changed over the years—the version we sing today is not the original. Even more alarming to some people is the idea of changing familiar Christmas carols which use non-inclusive language. Some will argue that traditional pieces of music should not be changed but preserved in their original forms. I would argue that the community of people that listens to our words is of more significance than the intentions of the original author. In other words, our language affects real people who are struggling to know that they are loved and belong. Worship participants are of more importance than our resistance to change.

One of the commonly expressed concerns about inclusive language is that it is grammatically incorrect. It is generally very easy to transform exclusive text into inclusive text without making it grammatically incorrect. It is concerning, however, that people are more worried about grammar than they are worried about the feelings and experiences of the people in front of them. For example, while it may be grammatically questionable and offensive to our sensibilities, it makes a world of difference to refer to nonbinary individuals as *they* rather than *he* or *she*. Using a person's chosen pronouns is an act of respect, an acknowledgement of their desire to be known as they are—not according to any conventions of language, but because the person in front of you wishes to be named in a particular way. It would be comparable to insisting on calling William by his full name instead of his chosen nickname, Bill. Few of us would deny a person the right to be called by a particular name, but many of us would resist using a person's chosen pronouns.

My childhood was spent in the Anglican church. I can still recall the words of the Book of Common Prayer—they are rooted deep in my memory and are connect to experiences and emotions. Familiarity is another barrier to using inclusive language for people. It is disorienting when familiar liturgical texts are changed—especially those which live in our hearts and our memories. The question is whether we are willing to relearn a way of speaking and praying that can more adequately name the reality around us. Language, especially around sexuality and gender, is changing rapidly. How do we encourage people to be flexible and nimble with language—even playful—so that we as a Christian culture are not tied to particular words but to their meaning and the degree to which they adequately represent reality?

A clergy friend was recently recounting her experience in a local congregation. As minister, she changed the language of the Lord's Prayer from *debts* to *sins*. There was an uproar within the congregation, and many were reluctant to make the change. What lies behind this fixedness on particular words in the liturgy?

While changing language is difficult for parishioners, it is also difficult for worship leaders. We too are wedded to our familiar ways of speaking and describing. It can feel clumsy to use new words and we may stumble over unfamiliar images. As we often know these liturgies by heart, it will take some effort to learn a new way of speaking.

Overcoming Resistance

Liturgy as a whole is intended to disrupt our familiar frameworks. We worship a God who frequently turns our expectations upside down. The liturgy tells the story of a God who interrupted time to send a child to lead us out of sin and shame. Liturgy should surprise and disconcert us—it is not intended to be comfortable or to maintain the status quo.

One of the challenges facing the PCC is the need for the 2022 Confession to be made at the local as well as the national level. It is designed for liturgical use and should be used broadly within the church. An astute worship leader will use the opportunity to explain the need for confession and describe the ways that repentance—changed behavior and attitudes—results from the making of the confession. There are some congregations that will refuse to make such a confession because they do not believe that they have contributed to harm within the LGBTQI community. The congregations that are willing to make such a confession will already recognize that harm has been done, and that there is a need for change and repentance. They can be encouraged to think through the implications for their own liturgical and social space.

One of the ways we can change the language of liturgy is for worship leaders simply begin to speak differently. As I noted above, I have rarely encountered resistance to expansive or inclusive language when I have employed it in the liturgy or in a sermon. That is, unless it challenged familiar words of prayers or hymns.

The congregation may require education about what words mean and how they are experienced by others, especially LGBTQI individuals. After preaching a sermon which used the acronym LGBTQI, a member of the congregation asked me to explain what all the letters mean. I assumed that my listeners grasped the meaning of my acronym, but some do not understand and have not had it explained in a coherent manner. Sermons can be excellent opportunities to describe and explain various concepts and ideas that are not widely understood.

Worship leaders can encourage the congregation toward a broader, more playful perspective on God and God's identity. As worship leaders and preachers, we are tasked with continually encouraging openness toward God by casting an image of God that is larger, more expansive than narrow ways of thinking about the Divine. The goal is to enlarge our imaginations so that we may image God more adequately as a being beyond our knowing but also knowable, in the strange logic of faith. Jesus is more than the gospels can communicate, the Creator is beyond what we can express, the Holy Spirit is mysterious and transformative. To expand our language and imagery is to express faith in a God who will always exceed our human limitations of language and imagination.

Transgender theologian Austin Hartke relates the openness of language to the ways that human beings understand one another. He discusses the categories of creation which appear in binaries in Genesis 1—the light and darkness, earth and water. However, as Hartke argues, these categories do not account for the whole of reality. There is dusk, and dawn, and marshes. Hartke argues for expanded categories for human beings:

> Just as we would not expect astronomers to cram things like comets and black holes into the categories of sun or moon, we should not expect all humans to fit into the categories of male and female. Instead of asking the text to define and label all that is, we can ask God to speak into the space between the words, between biblical times and our time, and between categories we see as opposites.[21]

Conclusion

This essay has argued that a liturgical turn toward more inclusive language for people and expansive language for God is an appropriate response to the 2022 Confession of the PCC. The Confession requires repentance—a change in attitudes and behaviors toward LGBTQI communities. This repentance can be partially enacted by changing liturgical language so that

---

21. Hartke, "Nonbinary Gender."

it more adequately reflects human experience and our experience of the Divine. While there is considerable resistance to such change, worship leaders can ease the situation by using inclusive/expansive language naturally and well; by educating their congregations about the meaning of such language; and by encouraging congregants toward a more playful image of God. Having made our confession, we are invited into a new way of being that includes everyone and points to the mystery and magnificence of God, who will not be confined to our faltering words.

Bibliography

Gabriel, Dani. "Why The Episcopal Church Is Changing the Book of Common Prayer." *Sojourners*, August 6, 2018.

Hartke, Austen. "Nonbinary Gender and the Diverse beauty of Creation." *The Christian Century*, April 25, 2018.

Long, Kimberly Bracken. "Beyond Merely Adequate: Poetic Sensibility in Liturgical Language." *Liturgy (Washington)* 25.2 (2009) 3–11.

Metropolitan Community Church of Toronto (MCC). "Inclusive Language Guidelines." https://www.mccchurch.org/files/2018/12/MCC-Inclusive-Language-Guidelines_Updated-2017.edit_2018.pdf.

Oliver, Matthew S.C. "Containing the Uncontainable: An Analysis of Expansive Language in The Episcopal Church, 1987–2018." *Anglican Theological Review* 103.1 (2021) 27–43.

Rainbow Communion Report. Presbyterian Church in Canada, 2021. Available at www.pcc.ca.

The Presbyterian Church in Canada (PCC). "Confession to God and LGBTQI People." https://presbyterian.ca/2022/06/07/confession-to-god-and-lgbtqi-people/.

———. "Gender and Sexuality Inclusion." https://presbyterian.ca/justice/social-action/gender-sexuality-inclusion/.

———. "Guidelines for Use of Inclusive Language." https://presbyterian.ca/resources/resource-finder/download-info/canadian-ministries-guidelines-use-inclusive-language/.

Travis, Sarah. *Decolonizing Preaching: The Pulpit as Postcolonial Space*. Eugene, OR: Cascade Books, 2014.

14

A Prophet of Old

Jesus the "Public Theologian"[1]

Ernest van Eck

Introductory Remarks

WHO WAS JESUS, THE Galilean from Nazareth? Since Reimarus's (1694–1768) answer to this question in 1778,[2] scholars interested in the historical Jesus have answered this question in many different ways. According to

---

1. This essay is a reworked version of a paper presented at a conference titled "Prophetic Witness: An appropriate mode of public discourse in democratic societies?" held at the University of Pretoria on October 26–27, 2009. The paper was initially published as E. van Eck, "A Prophet of Old: Jesus the "Public Theologian,"" in H. B. Bedford-Strohm and E. de Villiers, eds., *Prophetic Witness: An Appropriate Contemporary Mode of Public Discourse?*, 47–74, Zürich: Lit Verlag, 2012 (Theology in the Public Square/Theologie in der Öffentlichkeit Band 1), and a reworked version was published as E. van Eck, "A Prophet of Old: Jesus the "Public Theologian,"" *HTS Teologiese Studies/Theological Studies* 66.1 (2010), Art. #771. DOI: 10.4102/hts/v66i1.771.

2. According to Reimarus (in his *Fragments* published after his death by Lessing [1729–1781]), Jesus saw himself as a (political) kingly messiah and had the intention to establish an earthly kingdom during his lifetime by delivering his people from the bondage of Rome. Jesus thus was not the "spiritual" messiah who died for the sins of humankind, was resurrected and will return in glory. This picture of Jesus, according to Reimarus, was an invention of his disciples after his death.

Schweitzer, Jesus was the direct opposite of Reimarus's Jesus: Jesus was a typical Jewish apocalyptic who proclaimed a futuristic (heavenly) kingdom.[3] Vermes, on the other hand, sees Jesus as a Galilean Hasid (a holy man or rabbi in the charismatic tradition of Galilee).[4] Brandon understands him as a zealot-like Jewish revolutionary who had political aims,[5] while Smith describes him as a miracle-worker (magician).[6] Since 1985, an abundance of divergent profiles of Jesus have been suggested by scholars.[7] In these varied profiles, the Jesus that emerges is understood as anything from an itinerant cynic-like philosopher,[8] a Jewish Mediterranean peasant,[9] a Spirit-filled person or charismatic holy man,[10] an eschatological prophet who announced the restoration of Israel in terms of a non-apocalyptical kingdom within space-time history,[11] a prophet of social change,[12] a prophet and child of Sophia,[13] a marginal Jew,[14] a Jewish Messiah of sorts,[15] a fatherless Jew,[16] to a Galilean shamanic figure.[17]

This essay argues that the understanding of Jesus as an (ethical-eschatological) social prophet should be taken seriously.[18] First of all, it is clear

3. Schweitzer, *Quest*. See also Bornkamm, *Jesus of Nazareth*.
4. Vermes, *Jesus the Jew*.
5. Brandon, *Jesus and the Zealots*.
6. Smith, *Jesus the Magician*.
7. 1985 is seen as the year in which the so-called Third Quest or Renewed New Quest (depending on the approach taken) to the historical Jesus started. This renewed interest in who the historical Jesus was gave rise to many (and varied) profiles of Jesus.
8. Mack, *Myth of Innocence*; Downing, *Christ and the Cynics*.
9. Crossan, *Historical Jesus*.
10. Borg, *Meeting Jesus Again*; Twelftree, *Jesus the Exorcist*.
11. Sanders, *Historical Figure*; Casey, *From Jewish Prophet*; Wright, *New Testament*; Wright, *Victory of God*; Allison, *Jesus of Nazareth*.
12. Theissen, *Shadow of the Galilean*; Horsley and Hanson, *Bandits*; Horsley and Silberman, *Message*; Kaylor, *Jesus the Prophet*; Oakman, *Political Aims*; Oakman, *Economic Questions*; Oakman, *Jesus and the Peasants*; Van Eck, *Parables of Jesus*.
13. Schüssler Fiorenza, *Jesus: Miriam's Child*.
14. Meier, *Marginal Jew*.
15. Stuhlmacher, *Jesus of Nazareth*; De Jonge, *Jesus, the Servant-Messiah*; Dunn, "Messianic Ideas," 365–81; Bockmuehl, *This Jesus*.
16. Van Aarde, *Fatherless in Galilee*.
17. Craffert, *Life of a Galilean Shaman*.
18. This statement does not exclude the possibility that Jesus most probably was, for example, a healer and an exorcist. It simply emphasizes that at least one of Jesus' attributes was that of being a social prophet.

that some of Jesus' contemporaries saw him as one of the "ancient prophets" (Luke 9:19) like John the Baptist, Elijah, or Jeremiah (Mark 8:28 and *par.*). Simon the Pharisee assumes that Jesus is popularly held to be a prophet (Luke 7:39). When Jesus enters Jerusalem, he is greeted as the "prophet from Nazareth of Galilee" (Matt 21:11), and while Jesus is in Jerusalem the religious leaders cautiously plot his arrest because they fear the crowd who holds Jesus to be a prophet (Matt 21:46). Even members of Antipas's court thought that Jesus was one of the prophets of old (Mark 6:15 and *par.*). In the Emmaus narrative, Jesus is referred to as a "prophet mighty in word and deed" (Luke 24:19).[19] Second, the parables in the Synoptic Gospels and the *Gospel of Thomas* paint a picture of Jesus as a prophet of old. Many of the issues and themes addressed by Old Testament prophets like Isaiah, Jeremiah, Amos, and Hosea can be indicated in Jesus' parables. Two of these common themes, inclusivism (accommodation) and social injustice, will be attended to in this essay. It will also be argued that Jesus, as a social prophet during his public ministry, can be depicted as a "public theologian" *par excellence*. This also holds for the life and work of Charles Fensham.

Jesus As Social Prophet in his Parables

The understanding of Jesus as a social prophet in his parables is based on a specific approach to the parables that operates from the following points of departure: First, Jesus told his parables in first-century Roman Palestine (circa 27–30 CE), an advanced (aristocratic) agrarian society under the combined control of the Roman Empire and the Jewish aristocracy[20] (Judaea). Advanced agrarian societies were aristocratic, with the working of the land (agriculture) as the main economic activity. Society was divided into the *haves* (the ruling elite) and the *have-nots* (the ruled peasantry). Although comprising only 2 percent of the population, the elite controlled most of the wealth (up to 65 percent)—by controlling and exploiting the

---

19. All these materials take it for granted "that Jesus was popularly acclaimed as a prophet or called a prophet by his opponents" (see Herzog, *Prophet and Teacher*, 99), thus making it quite likely that Jesus was called a prophet during his lifetime. According to Wright, the early church unlikely invented the many sayings which call Jesus a prophet. The reason for this is that it is simply risky theologically to do so since it might have appeared "that he was simply being put on a level with all the other prophets" See Wright, *Victory of God*, 162.

20. The Roman Empire favored traditional forms of rule (indirect rule) and allowed the use of local temples or cults/religions.

land and sea; its produce and its cultivators (the peasantry and fishermen whose labor created the produce). Local, regional, and imperial elites imposed tributes, taxes, rents (e.g., Herod in Galilee), and tithes (e.g., the Jewish elite in Judaea), extracting wealth from non-elites by taxing the production, distribution, and consumption of goods. In short: the elite lived at the expense of the non-elite. The elite did not rule because of democratic elections, but rather through the use and abuse of power and hereditary control of land. The rulers treated controlled (conquered) land as their personal estate to confiscate, distribute, redistribute, and disperse as they deemed fit. The elite thus shaped the social experience of the peasantry— social control was built on fear, and the relationship between the ruling elite and the ruled non-elite was one of power and exploitation.[21]

Because the elite exploited the non-elite, the peasantry in first-century Roman Palestine lived at the edge of destitution. Palestine in the first century was part of the Roman Empire. Rome claimed sovereignty over land and sea—its yield, the distribution of its yield, and its cultivators (the peasantry). This was done through a tributary system. The Roman tribute consisted of two basic forms: the *tributum soli* (land tax) and the *tributum capitis* (poll tax), and non-payment of these taxes was seen as a rebellion against Rome. Rome ruled Palestine through native collaborators from the elite who had the responsibility of paying the annual tribute, extracted from the peasantry to Rome. During Jesus' public ministry, this was the responsibility of Herod Antipas in Galilee and the temple authorities in Judaea and Samaria. The wealth required to support Herod's lavish lifestyle and his many building projects came from the peasantry through a second level of tribute and taxes: Antipas and the Herodian elite first claimed the so-called "surplus of the harvest"; to which further tribute and taxes were added. This left the peasantry of Galilee in a situation where their level of subsistence functioned within a very narrow margin. The only way to survive was to borrow from the elite, who were always willing to invest in these loans (with interest rates of up to 48 percent)[22]—knowing that their

---

21. For the salient features of advanced agrarian societies see *inter alia* Polanyi, *Great Transformation*; Lenski, *Power and Privilege*; Carney, *Shape of the Past*; Finley, *Ancient Economy*; Oakman, *Economic Questions*; Hanson and Oakman, *Palestine*; Fiensy, *Jesus the Galilean*; Fiensy, *Social History*; Freyne, "Urban-Rural Relations," 75–91; Rohrbaugh, "Agrarian Society," 4–7; Stegemann and Stegemann, *Jesus Movement*; Herzog, *Prophet and Teacher*; Carter, *Roman Empire*; Carter, "Matthew's Gospel," 181–201.

22. Interest rates up to 48 percent are attested (Brutus' loan to Salamis; Cicero, *Letters to Atticus*, 5.21.10–12). In general, however, interest was limited to 12 percent by edict,

debtors would likely be unable to repay, thus allowing them to foreclose and add that peasant's land to their estates.[23] Peasants thus lost their land and, in a downward spiral, first became first tenants, then day laborers, and then beggars.

The situation of the peasantry in Judaea was similar. In 6 CE, Augustus deposed Archelaus, declared Judaea and Samaria a Roman province (administered by Syria), and appointed the priestly aristocracy (centered in the temple in Jerusalem)—under the control of a prefect (Pilate in the time of Jesus)—to maintain order and collect the Roman tribute. The temple elite in Judaea were no different from those in Galilee. To maintain their power base (the temple system), they added tithes, offerings, and contributions during religious festivals to the Roman tribute. Even the peasants of Galilee were subject to this demand, despite living outside the jurisdiction of Judaea. Peasants who could not pay were labelled unclean. Although the land (ideologically speaking) belonged to peasant smallholders who inherited their ancestral plots, the priestly elite also acquired peasants land by investing in loans. The elite in Galilee and Judaea thus became the dominant force in land ownership. Small peasant farmers were increasingly displaced by large estates owned by the powerful and exploiting elite. All this left the peasantry "on the edge of destitution, and often over the edge."[24]

---

although rates of 20 percent are also attested (see P. Mur. 114; P. Mur. 18; also see Kloppenborg, "Response").

23. Goodman, "First Jewish Revolt."

24. See Borg, *Jesus*, 227. Chancey provides the following summary of a social-contextual reading of economic pressures on the peasantry in first-century Palestine, which is worth noting: "These economic pressures are, in turn, often associated with the actions of Herod Antipas, particularly his rebuilding of Sepphoris and his foundation of Tiberias . . . Antipas' creation of new cities placed new strains on the peasant majority of Galilee. The cities required a reorientation of the distribution of agricultural products; whereas farmers had once focused on growing crops for their own subsistence, they now had to produce surplus crops to feed the cities. Taxes and rents imposed by the parasitic cities and their elites combined to facilitate this transfer of foodstuffs. But taxes served not only to feed the cities; tax increases would have been necessary just to build them. The cities served as focal points for the collection of taxes not only for Antipas but also for Rome. To pay their taxes, peasants had to sell off their surplus for coins, and Antipas minted bronze coinage for just this purpose, to facilitate payment of taxes. These intertwining policies of taxation and monetization pushed family farmers beyond what they were able to produce, causing them to seek loans from city-based lenders and to sell their lands to city-dwelling estate owners. Some farmers became tenants on what had been their own lands, others were forced to become day laborers, others became artisans and craftsmen, others resorted to begging, and still others turned to social banditry. It is within this context of a debilitating economic crisis that we must place the historical Jesus, with his

In this exploitative situation, caused by the kingdom of Rome and the "kingdom of the temple," the central message of Jesus was the kingdom of God.[25] This kingdom was not a futuristic-apocalyptic reality (a position recently defended by Allison[26]), but ethical-eschatological in content.[27] It was a kingdom here and now, a transformed world; a kingdom "that challenged the kingdoms of this world,"[28] a kingdom that challenged the exploitative social and economic relations in Jesus' society.[29] This kingdom was "the immediate reign of God that is now present in the potential of the human imagination to see the world differently and to act accordingly."[30] This is also the point of view of Cupitt, Borg, and Funk:

> Jesus' Kingdom had been ethical and this-worldly. It was about committing oneself ethically to life and to one's neighbour here and now, in this world, and in the present.[31]

The kingdom was for the earth, political and religious and involved a transformed world.[32]

> [T]he kingdom of God was a kingdom of this world. Jesus always talked about God's reign in everyday, mundane terms—dinner parties, travellers being mugged, truant sons, laborers in a vineyard, the hungry and tearful.[33]

---

call for a different type of kingdom." See Chancey, "Disputed Issues," 1–2.

25. See, for example, Borg, *Jesus*, 165: "God and God's kingdom were at the center of Jesus' life and mission" and Hoover, "Art of Gaining," 18: "The central idea or symbol of Jesus' teaching was the kingdom of God . . . The kingdom is what Jesus' teaching is and is also the goal he was aiming for."

26. Allison, Jesus of Nazareth.

27. For the sake of clarity, I follow Crossan's definition of eschatology. According to Crossan, Jesus was eschatological, but not apocalyptic. This "odd" statement is clarified by Crossan's understanding of eschatology, either being apocalyptic or ethical in character: ethical eschatology can be defined as transformative, social, active and durative; while apocalyptic eschatology refers to an eschatology that is destructive, material, passive and instantive (see Crossan, *Birth of Christianity*, 257–92, and Crossan in Miller, *Apocalyptic Jesus*, 69).

28. Borg, *Jesus*, 186.
29. Moxnes, *Economy*.
30. Patterson in Miller, *Apocalyptic Jesus*, 71.
31. Cupitt, "Reforming Christianity," 51–64.
32. Borg, *Jesus*, 186.
33. Funk, "Jesus of Nazareth," 90.

From the above, it is clear that Jesus' parables are not to be read for a view on the future or the end of time.[34] The parables should rather be interpreted as an imagined kingdom (reality) where different social relations and power structures operate.

As such, Jesus' parables were "dangerous speech." In a society where politics and kinship were the only exclusive arenas of life,[35] any religious statement was, in essence, political.[36] The aristocratic kingdom of Rome dealt with the non-elite through social institutions characterized by power and resource inequities (political economy). Jesus' parables, conversely, "were underwritten by culturally informed values that envisioned alternate institutions."[37] For Jesus, this institution was the kingdom of God.

Moreover, when Jesus spoke in his parables about the presence of a new kingdom other than the aristocratic kingdom of the Roman Empire, it was a political statement. When Jesus urged his hearers to be a community where God's presence, and not Rome's presence, was fully established, a community where there was justice for everyone (including one's enemy), a community that welcomed strangers,[38] it was a political statement. When Jesus spoke of God's rule as a power opposed to the social order established

---

34. One should also remember that Mediterranean people were rather markedly present-orientated, with past second and future third. Matthew 6:34 can serve here as a good example. See Malina, "Christ and Time." See also Kloppenborg, "Response," 5: "For peasants, the future is tomorrow or the next harvest, not some distant *parousía*."

35. Malina, *Social Gospel*, 15–16.

36. All societies might be viewed as consisting of at least four social institutions: kinship, politics, economics and religion. See Parsons, *Structure and Process*. While modern societies generally attend to these four institutions as separate spheres of life, first-century Mediterranean people treated politics and kinship as the only exclusive arenas of life. See Malina, *Social Gospel*, 15–16. In the political sphere, therefore, there was political religion and political economy, but no separate religion and economy. In the kinship sphere, there was domestic (kinship) religion and domestic (kinship) economy, but no separate religion and economy. See Malina, "'World of Paul"; Malina, *New Testament World*.

37. Oakman, *Jesus and the Peasants*, 253. See also Oakman, *Jesus and the Peasants*, 105: "For Jesus God's rule was a power opposed to the social order established in Rome." Jesus made use of kinship religion and kinship economy to address the exploitative political economy and political religion of Rome. See also Oakman, *Jesus and the Peasants*, 97, 105: In Jesus' parables, he favored a fictive family in which relations were modelled on those of close kin, with exchanges taking place through arrangements of generalized reciprocity, taking no account of exchanges or debt. Jesus' parables urging for an alternative kinship economy that can be called the kingdom of God, therefore were political.

38. Bessler-Northcutt, "Learning to See God," 55.

in Rome,[39] it was a political statement. When Jesus told stories that applauded the elite who practiced generalized reciprocity (taking no account of exchanges or debt),[40] it was a political statement. And when Jesus told stories that transgressed the purity rules of the temple, making impure leaven and mustard seed positive symbols for God's presence, it was also a political statement. As a matter of fact, any talk about values that envisioned an alternative for the power and privilege of Rome and the temple was political. Jesus' parables, therefore, were political. They were stories of social critique on the first century's oppressive political, religious, and social context. They did not, to use the words of Schottroff, describe "a specific historical event, but a political structure."[41] Jesus' parables, however, did not only grind "against the temple elite (the kingdom is impure) and the Roman Empire" (divide and conquer).[42] Criticism was also levelled at peasant interests[43]—peasant villagers also had to overcome some of their prejudices and interests (e.g., the unforgiving slave [Matt 18:23–34]; the older brother in the prodigal son [Luke 15:11–32]; the victim in the Samaritan [Luke 10:30–35]). Herzog is therefore correct when he describes Jesus' parables as "a form of social analysis."[44] Or, in the words of Oakman: "The kingdom represents social challenge and transformation. Jesus' historical activity was essentially about politics and the restructuring of society, and not about religion or theology."[45]

Finally, the parables of Jesus are not stories about God, but stories about God's kingdom. There is a general tendency amongst parable scholars to identify the actors or characters in the parables with God,[46] or even Jesus

39. Oakman, *Jesus and the Peasants*, 105.
40. Oakman, *Jesus and the Peasants*, 105.
41. Schottroff, *Parables of Jesus*, 103.
42. Scott, "Reappearance of Parables," 113–14.
43. Oakman, *Jesus and the Peasants*, 180.
44. Herzog, *Parables*, 3.
45. Oakman, *Jesus and the Peasants*, 296. See also Carter, "Matthew's Gospel," 199: "In the . . . first-century world, religion and politics did mix. Imperial politics, economics, societal structures, and religion were interwoven, each playing an interconnected part in the societal fabric and maintaining of elite control. Thus, to engage the gospels as religious texts concerned only with religious issues is a-historical and anachronistic. Our world is shaped by our Western attempts to separate religion from the rest of life, and therefore we, when reading the gospels, arbitrarily select, detach, isolate, and elevate a religious aspect of the . . . first-century world, while ignoring political, economic, and cultural factors and their interconnectedness."
46. See, for example, Snodgrass, *Stories with Intent*, 20: "Many parables are

himself.[47] To read the parables from this perspective is to depict a Jesus that made theological statements and told stories about heaven. Jesus had no doctrine of God, made no theological statements, and never used abstract language. "His parables are not stories of God—they are stories about God's estate."[48] Or, in the words of Herzog: "the parables were not earthly stories with heavenly meanings, but earthly stories with heavy meanings."[49] They are stories about "the gory details of how oppression served the interests of the ruling class," exploring how human beings could respond to an exploitative and oppressed society created by the power and privilege of the elite (including the temple authorities).

From this perspective, the father in the parable of the Prodigal is a father who subverts the patriarchal system of his day; it is a story of how fathers—who are part of the kingdom—should treat their prodigal sons; it is a story that pictures a totally new understanding of what family entails. In the same way, the owner in the parable of the Tenants is not God, but rather a patron who treats his clients in a totally different way than is normally the case in the kingdom of Rome. In the parable of the Workers in the Vineyard, the owner is someone who depicts a non-violent kingdom;[50] and in the parable of the Unforgiving Servant the king is not God the "heavy," but a king that exercises authority in a way befitting the kingdom of God.[51] The

---

'monarchic'; i.e., they are dominated by the figure of a father, master, or king, who is generally an archetype for God. Some deny that these monarchic figures reference God . . . and render Jesus' parables lame and ineffective."

47. A few examples: in the parable of the unforgiving servant (Matt 18:23–34), the king who shows compassion towards a hugely indebted slave is a symbol for God (see, e.g., Hultgren, *Parables of Jesus*, 27; Borg, *Jesus*, 177); in the parable of the prodigal son (Luke 15:11–32), the father symbolizes a compassionate God (see, e.g., Hultgren, *Parables of Jesus*, 86; Borg, *Jesus*, 17; Snodgrass, *Stories with Intent*, 128); in the parable of the leased vineyard (*Gos. Thom.* 65:1–7 and Mark 12:1–8 and *par.*), the owner is interpreted as God and his son as Jesus (see Bailey, *Middle Eastern Eyes*, 425); and in the parable of the workers in the vineyard (Matt 20:1–15), the owner again is a symbol for God, and the steward a symbol for Jesus (see Hultgren, *Parables of Jesus*, 36; Bailey, *Middle Eastern Eyes*, 364; Snodgrass, *Stories with Intent*, 20, 377).

48. Funk, "Jesus of Nazareth," 90.

49. Herzog, *Parables as Subversive Speech*, 3.

50. Van Eck, "Tenants in the Vineyard."

51. See Beutner, "Mercy Unextended," 33–39: "In this parable God is not the 'heavy'. The moment God is cast outside the parable 'we are in a fresh position to understand the irony of Jesus when he speaks of God's domain in terms of a kingdom'. If Jesus speaks ironically of the activity of God as kingdom, he may well mean 'whatever else you think of, do not think of kingdom; think instead of its exact opposite'. When this happens, the

characters in the parables do not point to God. The parables point to the kingdom of God, in that "there is something about the parable as a whole that is like the kingdom of God."[52]

To summarize: The parables picture Jesus as a social prophet. In first-century Palestine (circa 27–30 CE) the elite (Roman and Jewish) shaped the social experience of the peasantry, social control was built on fear, and the relationship between the ruling elite and the ruled non-elite was one of power and exploitation. Because of this, the peasantry lived at the edge of destitution. In this exploitative situation, Jesus spoke in his parables of a new and different world—the (ethical-eschatological) kingdom of God. His parables were political stories about God's kingdom, "not earthly stories with heavenly meanings, but earthly stories with heavy meanings,"[53] exploring how human beings could respond to an exploitative and oppressed society created by the power and privilege of the elite. In short, the parables of Jesus the social prophet were the kingdom, a kingdom that posed a real threat to Rome's rule and put him in conflict with the religious authorities.

Inclusivism and Critique of Social Injustice

Jesus and Inclusivism

In his parables Jesus frequently addressed two "social illnesses" of his day—religious exclusivism (as advocated by the Jewish temple elite in their understanding of God in terms of his holiness)[54] and social injustice (as

---

king in the story has no longer divine attributes, he is a mere mortal like the hearers, and we and the hearers no longer feel compelled to automatically defend his every action as wise, reliable and irreversible. Think then of this king as an elite that usurped their land, much despised by the peasantry. Think then what Jesus wants to say about the way authority should be exercised in the kingdom of God. See also Verhoefen, "First Will Be First," 49, on the workers in the vineyard (Matt 20:1–15): "Through many centuries scholars have identified the owner as a God figure. The parable is not about God, but about God's kingdom. The parable is a clear response to a question Jesus' audience might have asked regularly: what is the kingdom of God like? Not: what is God like!" According to Verhoefen, this is also the case in the parables of the Prodigal and the Samaritan: the figures of the father and the Samaritan are all human beings whose behavior is an example of human behavior in God's kingdom. "It is about the breaking down of conventional wisdom, the tearing apart of social boundaries and barriers, the display of unconditional love for the righteous and sinners alike, it is the breaking in of the kingdom of God!"

52. McGaughy, "Jesus' Parables," 11.
53. Herzog, *Parables as Subversive Speech*, 3.
54. Van Eck, *Galilee and Jerusalem*.

practiced by the Roman and Jewish elite). Contrary to the Jewish temple elite's "politics of holiness," Jesus advocated a "politics of compassion,"[55] a kingdom that also included the socially "impure" (e.g., the lame, the blind, cripples, lepers, and women). This message of Jesus is found *inter alia* in the parables of the mustard seed (Mark 4:30–32 and par.; *Gos. Thom.* 20:1–4), the leaven (Matt 13:33; Luke 13:20–21; *Gos. Thom.* 96:1–3), and the great banquet or dinner party (Luke 14:16–24; Matt 22:2-14; *Gos. Thom.* 64).

In the parable of the Mustard Seed, Jesus compares the kingdom of God with a man sowing a mustard seed in prepared soil,[56] which grows into a tree (or large bush) that becomes the nesting place (shelter) for the birds of the sky. This comparison of Jesus was, to say the least, shocking. It meant that the kingdom was impure and inclusive. Moreover, it implied that the kingdom of God had taken over the kingdom of the temple. How does one get to this conclusion?

First of all, the kingdom is described as being present in the activity of a peasant in a rural area and not in the activities of the temple elite in Jerusalem. The kingdom thus has shifted from the center to the periphery; from the most holy (holy of the holies) to the least holy, the land of Israel.[57]

Secondly, the mustard seed figures prominently in discussions of "diverse kinds" regarding purity.[58] Fundamental to the purity code of Leviticus is the principle that dissimilar things are not to be mixed (see Lev 19:19).[59] Thus, planting a mustard seed in a garden[60] or prepared soil with

---

55. Borg, *Conflict*.

56. According to Luke 13:19, the mustard seed is planted in a garden. In the *Gospel of Thomas* 20:4, it falls on prepared soil. In Mark 4:31, it is sown on the ground, and in Matthew 13:31 it is sown in a field. Much has been said in parable scholarship on these differences, especially concerning the possible "original reading" of this aspect of the parable (see e.g., Scott, *Hear Then the Parable*, 374–77). Although this question is indeed important, our interest here lies in the simple fact that the sower consciously plants the seed in prepared soil, either a cultivated field (Oakman, *Jesus and the Peasants*, 11) or a garden (Scott, *Hear Then the Parable*, 377) with other seed.

57. *Kelim* I, 6–9.

58. Scott, Hear Then the Parable, 374.

59. "Keep my decrees. Do not mate different kinds of animals. Do not plant your field with two kinds of seed. Do not wear clothing woven of two kinds of material (NIV; see also Deut 22:9–11).

60. *Kilayim* 3.2 is clear on the fact that a mustard seed could not be planted in a garden: "Not every kind of seed may be sown in a garden, but any kind of vegetable may be sown therein. Mustard and small beans are deemed a kind of seed and large beans a kind of vegetable" (*m Kil* 3.2, in Scott, *Hear Then the Parable*, 375).

other weeds (clearly prohibited) signifies impurity. The kingdom of God is mixed and therefore impure. Regarding impurity, the small size of the mustard seed also plays a role. In Jewish sources (e.g., the Talmud), smallness is sometimes associated with unclean things.[61] But this is not all. The comparison of the kingdom with a mustard seed goes even further. The mustard plant is an annual plant, a weed, and grows wild.[62] After it has been planted, it spreads rapidly and cannot be stopped; it cannot be gotten rid of easily. So, it becomes a nuisance.

It also takes over. This aspect of the mustard seed is evoked by the described outcome of its planting: it grows into a tree where the birds of the sky build their nests. This imagery, according to Scott, "conjures up the mighty cedar of Lebanon"[63] (see Ezek 17:22–23; 31:2–6; Dan 4:10–12; Ps 104:16–17). In these verses, the powerful kingdoms of Egypt, Assyria, Babylonia, and Israel are compared to the majestic and formidable cedar. It is, however, in the mustard "tree" that the birds of the sky come to nest. The comparison is evident: the mighty cedar has been supplanted by something impure.[64] In its branches, the birds of the sky, including the Gentiles,[65] will find shelter.

The comparison of the kingdom with a mustard seed has one final connotation. The mustard seed was also used for medicinal purposes, to cure illnesses such as serpent bites, scorpion stings, fungi, inflammation, toothaches, stomach problems, and to promote menstruation and

---

61. "The Daughters of Israel have undertaken to be so strict with themselves that if they see a drop of blood no bigger than a mustard seed they wait seven days after it" (b. Ber. 31a, in Scott, *Hear Then the Parable*, 377).

62. See Pliny, *Natural History*, 29.54.170, in Scott, *Re-Imagine the World*, 37: "It grows entirely wild, though it is improved by being transplanted: but on the other hand when it has once been sown it is scarcely possible to get the place free of it, as the seed when it falls germinates at once."

63. Scott, *Re-Imagine the World*, 38–39.

64. "[F]or Jesus... God's empire is more pervasive than dominant. It is like a pungent weed that takes over everything and in which the birds of the sky can nest; it bears little if any resemblance to the mighty, majestic, and noble symbol of the empire of Israel or Caesar." Scott, *Re-Imagine the World*, 39.

65. Jeremias, *Parables of Jesus*, 147. According to Jeremias, κατασκηνοῦν—used in Mark 4:32, Matthew 13:32 and Luke 13:19—is a technical term for the incorporation of the Gentiles into the people of God. See *Joseph and Asenath* 15:7; see also Manson, *Sayings of Jesus*, 133.

urination.⁶⁶ As such, the mustard seed, symbolizing the kingdom of God, will cure the "illnesses" of the kingdoms of Rome and the temple.

In the parable of the leaven (Q 13:20–21; *Gos. Thom.* 96:1–3), the kingdom of God is also depicted as unclean and inclusive. The parable is only a short one-liner but explosive: The kingdom is like a woman that leavens flour until it is all leavened. Why is this explosive? Because the kingdom is blasphemously juxtaposed with leaven that is impure and unclean, and, above all, this is all described as the doing of a woman. In essence, the divine is identified with the unclean, the impure.⁶⁷

Like the parable of the mustard seed, the parable of the leaven begins with a jolt. "The very fact that the woman is making the bread herself indicates a rural, peasant background."⁶⁸ Once again, the kingdom is portrayed as being active within the realm of a peasant in a rural setting rather than within the sphere of influence of the temple elite in Jerusalem.

Furthermore, the presence of the kingdom is depicted through the actions of a peasant woman. In the first-century Mediterranean world, males were associated with purity, while women were associated with religious impurity. First-century Palestine was a patriarchal society where women were often regarded as the mere property of the men to whom they belonged or were embedded in.

> [In a] culture, where the principal symbolization of social relations was in terms of kinship the social structure was patriarchal. The father was the head of the family, in no uncertain terms; . . . in such traditional patriarchal societies . . . wives and children . . . are treated as the property of the male head of the household.⁶⁹

This status of the husband was based on the conviction that life was contained in the seed of the male, and that "the female provided nothing beyond a place for the seed's growth until birth."⁷⁰ Subsequently, women needed men to be whole, and inherently possessed the possibility to shame their husbands:

---

66. See Pliny, *Natural History*, 20.87.236–237, in Scott, *Hear Then the Parable*, 380.
67. Scott, "Reappearance of Parables," 99–101.
68. In urban areas, bread was typically purchased from a bakery. For instance, significant remnants of bakeries exist in places like Ostia Antica and Pompeii. However, in the parable, we encounter a scene where a woman in a rural village is preparing to bake bread. See Scott, *Re-Imagine the World*, 25.
69. Horsley, *Jesus and the Spiral*, 232. See also van Aarde, *Fatherless in Galilee*, 226.
70. Malina-Jacobs, *Beyond Patriarchy*, 1.

> Unlike the male whose gender made him whole and complete, the female was raised with a sense of shame which made her as dependent on the male for her own "completeness" as she was dependent on him for children, support and honor. The woman whose modesty and strictly controlled behavior in public manifested this sense of shame brought honor on the males to whom she was attached.[71]

Clearly, the presence of the kingdom in the activity of a peasant woman, who was not even allowed into the temple (holy space) and who served as a symbol of impurity, was a shocking image. This kingdom was in the "wrong place" and included the "wrong people." God's active location has shifted from purity to impurity, a "scandalous relocation of the divine presence."[72]

Moreover, leaven, like a mustard seed, is surely no correct symbol of the kingdom of God. According to the kingdom of the temple, with its politics of holiness, unleavened was the symbol for purity and the divine, as can be deduced, for example, from Exodus 12:19–20: "For seven days (during Passover—EvE) no yeast[73] (leaven—EvE) is to be found in your houses. And whoever eats anything with yeast in it must be cut off from the community of Israel, whether he is an alien or native-born. Eat nothing made with yeast. Wherever you live, you must eat unleavened bread."[74]

Unleavened was seen as the proper symbol for the divine, while leaven was a symbol for moral evil and the unclean.[75] In the ancient world, ac-

---

71. Malina-Jacobs, *Beyond Patriarchy*, 1. The patriarchal relationship between males and females was understood analogous to God's creation: "God is to man as man is to woman; man is to nature what man is to woman; the master is to slave as man is to woman, the emperor is to his people as man is to woman, the teacher is to his pupil as man is to woman." See Malina-Jacobs, *Beyond Patriarchy*, 2.

72. Bessler-Northcutt, "Learning to See God," 59.

73. The translation of ζύμη as "yeast" in the New International Version (see also, e.g., the NEB and NRSV) is anachronistic. Yeast is a leavening agent, but "not all leaven is yeast in the modern sense, that is, a leavening agent that can be purchased in refrigerated cubes or as a dried substance in a package." See Hultgren, *Parables of Jesus*, 406. In antiquity, leaven consisted simply of fermenting dough, and therefore should not be equated with yeast. See also Scott, *Hear Then the Parable*, 324: "Leaven is made by taking a piece of bread and storing it in a damp, dark place until mould forms. The bread rots and decays, unlike modern yeast, which is domesticated."

74. From Exodus 12:19–20 it is clear that in the Old Testament unleavened bread is seen as a symbol of that which is holy and pure. Leavened, on the other hand, is seen as unholy and impure. In the New Testament we have several examples of leaven as something negative (see Mark 8:15 and par.; 1 Cor 5:6–8; Gal 5:9).

75. Scott, "Reappearance of Parables," 99. See also Boucher, *Parables*, 75.

cording to Scott, the process of leavening stood as a metaphor for moral corruption. "Just as a decomposing corpse swells up, so does a leavened loaf. A modern example is the swollen corpse of roadkill. That corpse swells up for the same reason that bread swells up—fermentation."[76] Leaven is a product of fermentation (rotten bread) and is associated with a corpse, thus impure.[77] As such, the juxtaposing of kingdom and leaven was blasphemous: the divine is identified with that which is unclean and unacceptable—the impure.[78] Moreover, the leavening process only stops when everything is leavened, when everything is corrupted. Scott summarizes this shocking one-liner of Jesus as follows:

> This one sentence parable redefines the divine. The divine is identified with the unclean, the impure. The involvement of the divine with the unclean does not result in the unclean becoming clean. The parable does not end with "until it was all unleavened." Rather the divine becomes unclean or to restate this insight even more provocatively, God becomes unclean.[79]

The parable of the leaven must have been shocking to those, like the temple elite, who understood God in terms of his holiness (that is, "unleavened"). For the "leavened," however, the parable was good news. In the kingdom there was a place for women and the socially impure (i.e., the so-called sinners like the lame, the blind, cripples, and lepers). God's kingdom indeed was inclusive. God's holiness was not as understood and defined by the temple. His holiness was compassion. God was not like unleavened bread but leavened, which means that the boundaries of the sacred, as established by the understanding of God in terms of his holiness, were eliminated.[80]

Inclusivism is also one of the topics in the parable of the Great Banquet or Dinner Party (Q 14:16–24; *Gos. Thom.* 64). Before we turn to the aspect of the parable that is of interest here, two remarks need to be made for the sake of clarity. In the first-century Mediterranean world, a man was known by the company he kept. Read this statement literally. This was especially the case where meals were concerned. Likes only ate with likes. Elliott

---

76. Scott, *Re-Imagine the World*, 25.

77. "That leaven in the ancient world was a symbol for moral corruption has long been recognized . . . panary fermentation represented a process of corruption and putrefaction in the mass of dough." See Scott, *Hear Then the Parable*, 324.

78. Scott, "Reappearance of Parables," 100.

79. Scott, "Reappearance of Parables," 100.

80. Scott, *Re-Imagine the World*, 34.

describes this relation between food codes and social codes in the time of Jesus as follows:

> In any society or sub-group thereof, there is generally a correlation of the rules and boundaries concerning what one eats, *with whom one eats*, when one eats, how one eats, where one eats, *to what community, group, or kinship network one belongs*, and what constitutes the groups *traditions, values, norms, and worldview*.[81]

With whom one ate thus was an indication of the group one belonged to (e.g., the elite, the Pharisees). It was also, very importantly, an indication of one's status and honor (the pivotal social value in the world of Jesus). Therefore, people, for example, the elite, regularly invited people with the same or higher status to a meal to enhance their status and honor. The parable of the Great Banquet or Dinner Party is an example of such an effort to enhance status and to gain honor. However, it is also a good example of Jesus' attitude towards this ever-present desire for the enhancement of status and honor (and an exclusive and stratified society as a product thereof). Let us consider the Lukan version of the parable (Luke 14:16–24): A man (most probably an elite, since he can prepare a δεῖπνον μέγα ["great" supper]) invited guests (probably also elite since they can buy fields and as many as five pairs of oxen[82]) to supper. On the day the supper was to take place, the guests were invited again.[83] They, however, make excuses to not attend. When one takes their lame excuses[84] into consideration it is clear

---

81. Elliott, *Home for the Homeless*, 103 (emphasis mine).

82. In general, a farmer in first-century Palestine would have been in possession of as much land as one or two oxen can plough (more or less ten to twenty hectares). A person who wanted to buy five yokes of oxen thus gives an indication of his material abilities, thus most probably an estate holder and part of the elite class. A farmer, who has just bought five pairs of oxen, will own at least forty-five hectares. Therefore, the farmer is a very wealthy man. Jeremias, *Parables of Jesus*, 177.

83. The double invite was a special courtesy which was part of the way the upper circles (elite) in the first-century Mediterranean did things. The first invite was sent out prior to the banquet and the second one was brought by servants on the actual day of the event.

84. Issuing an invitation was an art because the host had to know which people, those on the same level or/and above his social location, would be likely to accept the invitation. If they did not accept the invitation, he would face rejection and shaming. The host in the parable most probably invited people who were slightly above him in the social scheme of things. If the invited guests accepted the invitation, they were obligated to extend a future invitation in return, which would mean an enhancement of his honor and status. By doing this, he could court wealthier elites as patrons. However, the invited guests most probably decided that by attending the supper, there was nothing to gain;

that the invited guests, between the first and second invitation, have come to realize that their attendance will do nothing to enhance their status and honor; it may even be to their detriment.[85] This information most probably came their way by means of the "gossiping-channel"[86] that was part and parcel of nonliterate societies like that of Jesus.[87]

Clearly, the host was shamed, but he reacted in a totally unacceptable way. He first sent his servant to the πλατείας (wide street within a city)[88] and ῥύμας (city thoroughfares)[89] to fetch the socially ostracized and unclean/impure (like the poor, the crippled, the lame, and the blind; i.e., those excluded from the temple). Because there was still room left, he then again sent his servant, this time to the ὁδοὺς (road between two centers)[90] and the φραγμοὺς (path or area along a fence [where desperately poor people might stay]).[91] The latter most probably was the place outside the city where the impure had to stay during the night because of their social impurities.

This was Jesus' kingdom. Everyone was accommodated, especially the impure ones who were not welcome in the kingdom of the temple.

---

rather, a possible loss of honor and status. Therefore, they denied the invitation. Herzog, *Prophet and Teacher*, 205.

85. The procedure of purchasing land in the ancient Middle East was a very time-consuming and extensive process. There was not a lot of available cropland in the Middle East, and for this reason, the buyer would study and inspect the land for months (or even years). The quality of the soil was of utmost importance, drainage was vital, and it was crucial to determine whether it faced winter sun. The terraces needed to be inspected, and it had to be verified whether there were any fruit trees on the property. This highlights how lame the excuse of the first guest was, having first bought a field and then only wanting to inspect it. Bailey, *Middle Eastern Eyes*, 314. Considering the above, it becomes evident just how weak the guest's excuse is, and it is clearly a public insult because no one would buy a field before inspecting it. The same applies to the second excuse. A pair of oxen has to tire at the same speed and have the ability to pull together. Therefore, nobody would buy a pair of oxen before they had been tested, as two oxen that cannot work together are useless and definitely not an asset. Jeremias, *Parables of Jesus*, 177. The third excuse is just as offensive, since the man invited does not even ask to be excused.

86. "Among nonliterate people (only 2–4 percent could read or write in agrarian societies), communication was basically by word of mouth. Where reputation (honor status) is concerned, gossip informed the community about (and validated) ongoing gains and losses, thereby providing a guide to proper social interaction." Malina and Rohrbaugh, *Social-Science Commentary*, 367.

87. Malina and Rohrbaugh, *Social-Science Commentary*, 366–68.

88. Louw and Nida, *Greek-English Lexicon*, 19, 1.103.

89. Louw and Nida, *Greek-English Lexicon*, 1:19, 1.104.

90. Louw and Nida, *Greek-English Lexicon*, 1:18, 99.

91. Louw and Nida, *Greek-English Lexicon*, 1:19, 105.

Moreover, the honorable man was the one that was willing to receive these outcasts at his table—like Jesus did (see, e.g., Mark 2:16).

Jesus and Social Injustice

Several parables of Jesus addressed the many social injustices experienced especially by the peasantry in first-century Palestine. One of these parables is the parable of the Rich Man and Lazarus (Luke 16:19–26). The backdrop of the parable is that of the advanced agrarian (aristocratic) society of first-century Palestine, in which the ruling class controlled most of the wealth by controlling the land, its produce, and the peasants whose labor created the produce.[92] Because of the heavy tax burden, most peasants struggled to live above the level of subsistence, accruing heavy debts ("investments" from the elite) that they could not repay.[93] The result of this rising indebtedness was the forming of ever larger estates, tenancy, and a landless class.[94] The peasantry was constantly threatened with downward mobility and a loss of subsistence—being displaced from smallholder to tenant, then from tenant to dependent day laborer, and eventually ending up as part of the expendables of society (e.g., beggars like Lazarus).

In the parable, the elite is represented by the rich man, who shows his status by flaunting his wealth through the clothes he wears. To enhance his honor and status, he feasted every day, most probably with other elites who stood in patron-client relationships with him. Being part of the elite, he also competed for clients amongst the poor and the peasantry. These patron-client relationships put him in the position to control more and more land, produce, and labor.

At his gate, one of the products of his exploitation, Lazarus (who represents the exploited peasantry), spends his days.[95] Lazarus had become

---

92. Carter, *Roman Empire*, 3; Hanson and Oakman, *Palestine*, 96; Horsley, *Spiral of Violence*, 11; Horsley, *Jesus and Empire*, 34.

93. Goodman, "First Jewish Revolt," 426.

94. Kloppenborg, *Tenants in the Vineyard*.

95. The reason why Lazarus ended up at the gate of the rich man can only be speculated upon. Maybe he was the second or third son of a peasant farmer who only had enough land for the eldest son to inherit; maybe he had to leave the family plot and seek work elsewhere because there were too many mouths to feed in a household living below, or just at, the level of subsistence; or maybe his father had lost his land because of rising indebtedness and eventual foreclosure on his mortgage by one of the exploiting urban elite. Herzog, *Parables as Subversive Speech*, 119. He may even have been a smallholder of

one of the expendables of the society the rich man and the other elite created. Lazarus was no longer of any use to the rich man. Since it is said that he was put there every day,[96] it means that he could not beg or take part in the daily *salutation* of the patron. Thus, he was no occasion for almsgiving or the enhancement of honor. Nothing could be gained by making Lazarus a client, even in terms of negative reciprocity, and to show *hospitium* to him (e.g., looking after his sores) would have made Lazarus his equal. This, of course, would have meant a loss of honor for the rich man. To him, Lazarus was expendable in every sense of the word—but also a result of the social and economic injustices of the elite in first-century Palestine. Lazarus had no honor left: he was economically poor;[97] poor in the sense that he could not maintain his status as a peasant smallholder;[98] he had no family ties left; and, above all, he was considered socially and ritually impure. His name says it all: only God can help.

In the parable, the name Lazarus (only God can help) is not accidental. It typifies how Jesus sided with the poor, the expendables, and the socially impure of his day.[99] This, however, was not how the rich man acted, even though nothing prevented him from doing otherwise. The gate was there; it even belonged to him. But he did not cross it—simply because there was nothing in it for him. He could only lose some honor.

When the rich man dies, he is confronted with the kind of patronage towards, and solidarity with, the poor and destitute that Jesus advocated. Abraham, the example *par excellence* of hospitality in the Old Testament,

---

inherited land who, because of among other things, the excessive tax burden imposed by the ruling elite, lost his land. Whatever the case may have been, the road that led to the gate of the rich man was a one-way street: first tenant; then day laborer; eventually drifting to the city where work was scarce, meaning he did not find work and had to become a beggar. The parable describes the final stretch of the road he travelled: he has become malnourished and covered with sores, not even able to beg anymore.

96. Fitzmyer, *Gospel According to Luke*, 1131.

97. Hollenbach, "Defining Rich and Poor," 58.

98. Malina, "Wealth and Poverty," 355.

99. In a situation where Jesus knew very well that the exploiting rich were only becoming richer and the poor poorer, Jesus' concern for the poor is not surprising. He congratulated the poor (Q 6:20; *Gos. Thom.* 54) and the hungry (Q 6:21; *Gos. Thom.* 69:2), condemned the rich and those who were well-fed at the cost of the poor (Luke 6:24–25), and exhorted the rich to sell their possessions and give to the poor (see Matt 13:44, 45–46; *Gos. Thom.* 76:1–2, 109:1–3). He also criticized patronage and clientism, based on the principle of negative reciprocity, by modelling all personal relations on those of closed kin—that is, generalized reciprocity. Oakman, *Jesus and the Peasants*, 103–7.

clearly embodies Jesus' attitude towards the poor. Lazarus is sitting at the table (bosom) of Abraham. *Hospitium* has been extended to him. And then the surprise in Jesus' parable! Abraham is not willing to help the rich man. This is indeed an oxymoron—Abraham not being hospitable?! This simply cannot happen where Abraham is involved. But it does happen—Abraham does not show hospitality. And then the big and final shock: this gate between the rich man and Abraham cannot be opened. It cannot be crossed. It has been closed forever.

This is the gist of the parable. When patrons (e.g., the rich) who have in abundance do not cross the gate to the poor, a society is created wherein a chasm so great is brought into existence between the rich (elite) and the poor (peasantry) that it cannot be crossed. The worlds of the urban elite and the peasantry drift so far apart that the gap between them eventually cannot be closed. Go through the gate while you can. Just as unthinkable as it is for Abraham not to do what he can, it is also unthinkable for those who can help not to do so. Abraham, being the example of hospitality, had no reason to turn his back on the rich man. The same holds for the rich man—nothing stood in the way of him helping Lazarus. It was not impossible to help Lazarus. The protection of his status and honor, however, made it impossible. And when this happens, nobody can become part of the kingdom—neither Lazarus nor the rich man. This is the result of patrons not being patrons. Real patrons are children of Abraham, and they take care of the poor (Luke 19:8-9).

In the Thomasine version of the parable of the Tenants (*Gos. Thom.* 65),[100] Jesus addressed another social injustice—the systemic violence that

---

100. The parable of the tenants in the *Gospel of Thomas* 65 is translated by Funk, Hoover and the Jesus Seminar as follows: "1An [userer] owned a vineyard and rented it to some farmers, so that they could work it and he could collect its crop from them. 2He sent his slave so the farmers would give him the vineyard's crop. 3They grabbed him, beat him, and almost killed him, and the slave returned and told his master. 4His master said, 'Perhaps he did not know them.' 5He sent another slave, and the farmers beat that one as well. 6Then the master sent his son and said, 'Perhaps they'll show my son some respect'. Because the farmers knew that he was the heir to the vineyard, they grabbed him and killed him." See Funk et al, *Five Gospels*, 510. When one compares Mark's version of the Tenants with the version in the *Gospel of Thomas* 65, three major differences can be indicated. First, there is an intimate connection between the parable and Mark's plot. See Kloppenborg, *Tenants in the Vineyard*, 219-20. Mark's framing of the Tenants by Mark 12:1a, 6a, 7c and 12 integrates the parable into his plot, highlighting the hostility of Jesus' opponents that started in Mark 3:6 and is ever present in the narrative (see e.g., Mark 7:1-5; 8:11-13; 12:13-17; 12:18-27; 12:35-37). Of special importance is Mark 12:6a (ἀγαπητόν), a Markan addition to the original parable that integrates the parable into Mark's Christology (see e.g., Mark 1:1, 1:9-11; 8:31-32; 9:7; 9:31; 10:33-34; 15:39). The second distinguishing feature of

was also part and parcel of first-century Palestine. Jesus was born and carried out his public ministry in an advanced agrarian Palestine that was in a situation of colonial occupation—described by Malina as a "ruralized society,"[101] or, in the words of Horsley, an "imperial situation" maintained by a "politics of violence" that subjected, pacified, and exploited the occupied land and its people.[102] This pacification and domination, without exception, furthered the interests of the imperial (and the Jerusalem) elite.[103] Domination by the ruling elite was not only material in content (the appropriating of produce and labor) but also influenced personal well-being and feelings. It deprived the ruled of their dignity and was degrading and humiliating. As Carter says, "It exacts not only agricultural production but an enormous personal toll of anger, resentment, and learned inferiority."[104]

Horsley calls this total domination a "politics of violence" or, more precisely, "institutional" or "structural" violence—the illegitimate or unauthorized use of power against the will or desire of others.[105] Also, as the illegitimate use of power, violence can be physical, psychological, or spiritual, applied directly or indirectly, overtly or covertly. Following these distinctions, Horsley argues that first-century Palestine was in a situation of institutional or structural violence: people were dominated and pacified with the use of extensive and widespread violence done largely in indirect ways (e.g., indirect rule and taxation), both covertly and overtly. In short, Roman rule was institutional or structural violence.

Violence perpetrated by the Roman aristocracy consisted of taking land by force, a legal system biased towards the elite, clamping down on any resistance with excessive force (direct overt); controlling both land and sea, its yield, and the bodies that worked the land and sea through taxation, cheap labor and census (direct covert); patron-client relationships to enhance

---

the parable is Mark's close relationship to texts of the Tanak (Isa 5:2, 5; Gen 37:20, 24). The third distinguishing feature of Mark's version of the parable is the allusion to the Deuteronomistic pattern of God's repeated sending of the prophets to Israel and their repeated and violent rejection (Mark 12:5b); the only trace of the Deuteronomistic schema in Mark. The parable of the Tenants in Mark is thus not only closely linked to Mark's plot and theology, but also contains features that are neither typical of Mark's other parables nor of parables in general. See Kloppenborg, *Tenants in the Vineyard*, 223–41.

101. Malina, *Social Gospel*, 19–22.

102. Horsley, *Spiral of Violence*, 3–19. See also Carter, *Roman Empire*, 1–3.

103. Horsley, *Spiral of Violence*, 5; Herzog, *Prophet and Teacher*, 3.

104. Carter, *Roman Empire*, 11.

105. Horsley, *Spiral of Violence*, 21.

honor and status, displaying wealth and power, and building dependency (indirect overt); and controlling various forms of communication (political propaganda) in the form of coins, buildings, and temples (indirect covert).

This imperial ideology was based on claiming the favor of the gods. Rome proclaimed that they were chosen by the gods (especially Jupiter) to manifest their rule, will, and blessings, to show their presence and favor throughout the world, and to rule an "empire without end." As such, they claimed sovereignty over sea and land and all its inhabitants. This ideology, logically, included the right to domination and power and a belief in Rome's superiority.

Jesus' stance on this structural violence can be deduced from the *Gospel of Thomas* 65.[106] In this parable, Jesus first of all challenges indirect violence, that is, the first-century values of wealth and status. The owner, in using his status and power, does not succeed in getting his vineyard back. All self-evident or ordinary/normal expediencies like the connection between status and social power, the privileges of ownership, and the normalcy of status displays are unsuccessful and ineffective. Put differently, the normal elite values of status, honor, and power (as indirect overt violence) are questioned by Jesus.[107]

---

106. A reading of Mark 12:1–12 (and *par.*) suggests that Jesus condoned, even instigated, physical or direct overt violent behavior. In the Markan version of the Tenants Jesus, after describing the violent behavior of the tenants, asks a rhetorical question on what the owner of the vineyard will do with his violent tenants. His answer is simple: violence will be answered with violence—the owner will kill the tenants and give the vineyard to others. In the Matthean version the question asked by Jesus is not rhetorical and is answered by those present in the temple (see Matt 21:23) in more or less the same way, but with one exception: the tenants will be killed (as in Mark) *so that* the vineyard can be given to others that will render the owner his "rightful" part of the crop—an answer that is positively received by Jesus. Simply stated, this can be understood as Jesus not only condoning violence but also the expropriation of peasant land by the aristocratic elite with the view of accumulating wealth and status. This, however, is not the end of the story, since the Lukan Jesus goes even further. After telling the parable and putting the same rhetorical question and answer forward as in the Markan version, those present vehemently oppose Jesus' answer of fighting fire with fire. Jesus, however, dismisses their reaction by quoting Psalm 118:22 and adding a Midrash-like interpretation with an overt violent implication (see Luke 20:18). In the Markan version of the Tenants (and therefore also Matthew and Luke in terms of the two-source theory) it is most probably not Jesus speaking, but Mark's Jesus. Mark most probably reworked an original parable into an allegory of salvation history that features Jesus' death as the climactic moment of God's relationship with Israel. Mark's Tenants is a piece of theology, "a reading of salvation history in allegorical dress." Kloppenborg, *Tenants in the Vineyard*, 111. As a result, Jesus' stance on violence cannot be inferred from Mark 12:1–12 and its parallels—an analysis of the *Gospel of Thomas* 65 most probably will bring us closer.

107. Kloppenborg, 352.

In the parable, Jesus also criticizes the use of direct physical violence. In *Gospel of Thomas* 65, the tenants' resort to physical violence (with its climax in the killing of the owner's son) reaps no gains. Their violence leads to nothing, and in the end, the owner is the one who has honor—not because he tries to protect his honor through status and power, but because he does nothing after his son is killed. Lintott has indicated that in the Roman Empire, possession normally was a function "of the ability to take, hold, and exploit land. Possession involved force."[108] The possession of land, by using force, was seen by the aristocracy as a right. Moreover, "possessions which were originally acquired by force will therefore, in the end, have to be defended by force."[109] In the *Gospel of Thomas*, the owner refrains from using violence to regain his possession. In other words, honor is gained by acting in precisely the opposite way to that which was regarded as normal. Status and honor are not retained or gained by using violence—the honorable person is the one who refrains from using violence.

Let us finally turn to the parable of the talents (Q 19:11–27). Ethnocentric capitalist readings of this parable, in which the first two slaves (who respectively increase the monies entrusted to them ten- and fivefold) are seen as the heroes of the story and the third slave (who hides the money in the ground [Matt 25:25] or ties it in a cloth [Luke 19:20]) is seen as the villain, are abundant. But in a world where all goods were perceived as available only in limited quantities,[110] and people (like the elite) who enriched themselves were seen as morally corrupt thieves,[111] this parable—if this is indeed its meaning—would have been heard by a peasant as a "text of terror."[112]

In a brilliant reading of the parable, Rohrbaugh has shown that the meaning of the parable is just the opposite.[113] The third servant, who gained nothing, can only be seen as a villain from an elitist point of view. From the

---

108. Lintott, *Violence*, 30.

109. Lintott, *Violence*, 30.

110. Foster, "Peasant Society"; Malina, *New Testament World*; Malina, "Wealth and Poverty."

111. "[I]n the eastern Mediterranean in New Testament times, 'rich' or 'wealthy' as a rule meant 'avaricious, greedy,' while 'poor' referred to persons scarcely able to maintain their honor or dignity." Malina, "Wealth and Poverty," 355. Traditional peasant societies (like that of the first-century Mediterranean) perceived all resources in terms of "limited goods," and therefore saw wealthy persons as "thieves" who had benefited at the expense of the poor. Malina, *New Testament World*, 71–93; Malina, "Wealth and Poverty."

112. Rohrbaugh, "Text of Terror," 33.

113. Rohrbaugh, "Text of Terror," 32–39.

point of view of Jesus (and the peasantry), however, he is the hero. The third slave is the only one in the parable that acted responsibly and in an honorable way: by hiding the money that was entrusted to him in the ground, he refuses to be part of the exploitative practices of the elite investing in loans at such a high-interest rate they knew their debtors would not be able to repay—which in turn gave them, for example, the opportunity to foreclose and add the debtor's land onto their own estates.[114] If this is indeed the meaning of the parable, it was bad news for the elite (like the one in the parable) who "prey upon the weak, take additional shares of the limited pie and thereby amass what is not rightfully theirs."[115] In the parable, Jesus thus was putting his finger on a social injustice of which the peasantry was on the receiving end.

Inclusivism and Critique of Social Injustice in the Old Testament

Universalism: Prophetic Traditions in the Old Testament

Jesus' accommodation of the social outcasts of his day and people from different ethnic backgrounds than Judeanism was not a novel concept. This inclusive approach is rooted in the prophetic traditions of the Old Testament. Like Jesus, Second Isaiah lived during the Second Temple period, characterized by its politics of holiness. Moreover, Second Isaiah, like Jesus, demonstrated openness towards the Gentile world.[116] According to Blenkinsopp, Second Isaiah provides evidence that Israel was already a confessional community—a community that welcomed proselytes.[117] For example, in Isaiah 44:3–5, the Abrahamic tradition (Gen 12:1–3) is interpreted to suggest that the blessing of the nations is realized through their adherence to the religion of Abraham's descendants. This adherence is achieved by personal decision, without the requirement of circumcision. Similarly, Isaiah 45:20–25 conveys the same message: Gentiles are invited

---

114. Goodman, "First Jewish Revolt."

115. Rohrbaugh, "Text of Terror," 34.

116. Some scholars go as far as to argue that Second Isaiah provided the model for Jesus' and early Christianity's openness to the Gentile world *vis-à-vis* the religious particularism of the Second Temple. See Blenkinsopp, "Prophet of Universalism," 99; Gelston, "Universalism," 112. There are, however, also scholars that argue the direct opposite. See Gelston, "Universalism," 378–9.

117. Blenkinsopp, "Prophet of Universalism," 86. See also Lohfink and Zenger, *God of Israel*, 47–49.

to turn to Yahweh to accept salvation, which entails a confession of faith in Yahweh (Isa 45:23; see also Isa 45:14; Exod 18:8–12; Josh 2:9–11; 2 Kgs 5:15). Blenkinsopp also notes that this universalistic approach of Second Isaiah extends to Trito Isaiah.[118] In Isaiah 56:1–8, Yahweh promises salvation not only to foreigners but even to eunuchs, who were considered socially impure. Here, incorporation and membership are "determined not by ethnic or national considerations but by a profession of faith." In the future, Israel will include Gentiles as well.[119]

Gelston shares a similar perspective to Blenkinsopp regarding Second Isaiah.[120] According to Gelston, passages such as Isaiah 43:8–13, 44:3–5, and 44:6–8 (with Isaiah 43:21 to a lesser extent) reflect Second Isaiah's universalistic tendencies. These texts suggest that Gentiles will come to recognize Yahweh as the sole God and supreme power of the world—"surely a form of universalism."[121] Like Blenkinsopp, Gelston interprets Isaiah 44:3–5 as evidence of Second Isaiah's universalistic outlook: "individuals who are not Israelites by birth will become adherents of YHWH."[122] Furthermore, Isaiah 45:22 reinforces this message even more explicitly: Gentiles are invited to partake in the salvation offered by God[123]—the same salvation Jesus referenced when he spoke about the kingdom of God.

Old Testament Prophecy and Social Injustice

Jesus' stance on social injustice was not unprecedented. His concern for the poor aligns with the priestly,[124] Deuteronomic,[125] wisdom,[126] and prophetic traditions in the Old Testament, which emphasize protecting the poor from the exploitative practices and systemic violence of the rich (e.g., Isa 3:14–15).[127]

---

118. Blenkinsopp, "Prophet of Universalism," 93. See also Lohfink and Zenger, *God of Israel*, 47–49, 53–57.

119. Blenkinsopp, "Prophet of Universalism," 95.

120. Gelston, "Universalism," 377–97.

121. Gelston, "Universalism," 385.

122. Gelston, "Universalism," 386.

123. Gelston, "Universalism," 391.

124. See, for example, Exod 22:25 and Lev 19:10.

125. See, for example, Deut 15:4–11.

126. See, for example, Prov 14:31; 22:9, 22.

127. Fiensy, *Jesus the Galilean*, 96, 132.

The Old Testament prophets vehemently opposed the exploitative practices of the elite at the expense of the common peasants, with Amos and Hosea serving as prominent examples. Their prophetic activity occurred in the eighth century BCE, during the reign of Jeroboam II in Israel (the north) and Uzziah in Judah (the south).[128] This historical period bears striking similarities to first-century occupied Palestine. Under the leadership of Jeroboam II and Uzziah, Israel and Judah experienced unprecedented economic growth and political stability.[129] They colonized vast amounts of territories to the east, west, and south (see 2 Chr 26:6–8). As is often the case, colonization resulted in economic benefits that almost exclusively favored the rich (the elite ruling class) at the expense of the majority—the peasantry.[130]

Using the urban centers, which grew significantly during this period, as political and administrative hubs, the elite established a taxation system that effectively extracted surplus from the rural areas. Agricultural activities were commercialized, enabling the elite to import horses and chariots in exchange for local specialty items like wine and oil. This acquisition of military resources afforded the elite the power and political control needed to dominate the peasantry.[131] To sustain their lifestyle of leisure and luxury—including conspicuous consumption of items such as fine linen, expensive ornaments, and perfume—the elite sought extensive trade relations, which necessitated extracting the maximum economic surplus.

To maximize their economic advantage, more land was converted for the production of commercial crops, resulting in a shortage of staples essential for the peasantry's survival.[132] Consequently, peasants had to rely on local markets to purchase food they previously produced themselves, where merchants exploited them. This led to widespread debt and dire economic conditions among the peasantry. In times of drought, they were forced to borrow money to survive. Failure to repay these loans resulted in the foreclosure of their lands, facilitating the elite's creation of large estates and further commercialization of agriculture. Seeking redress in the courts proved futile; controlled by the elite, the courts were biased and served as tools to subvert justice.[133]

128. Mays, "Justice," 4.
129. Premnath, "Amos and Hosea," 126.
130. Escobar, "Social Justice," 170; Premnath, "Amos and Hosea," 127.
131. Premnath, "Amos and Hosea," 129.
132. Premnath, "Amos and Hosea," 130.
133. Premnath, "Amos and Hosea," 131.

Amos and Hosea criticized this situation in very sharp terms. Amos condemned the elite for hoarding plunder and loot in their palaces (Amos 3:10) and summoned them from their palaces in Ashdod to witness the oppression in Samaria (Amos 3:9). He further warned them that their strongholds and fortresses would be plundered (Amos 3:11). Hosea similarly criticized the exploitative urban centers: Israel had forgotten its Maker and built palaces, while Judah had multiplied fortified cities, which Yahweh would devour (Hos 8:14; see also Hos 6:1–3). Hosea condemned the elite's reliance on military power (Hos 10:13–14) and their treaties with Assyria and Egypt that allowed them to procure military equipment (Hos 12:1).[134]

Amos had stern words regarding the excessive extraction of surplus. He accused the elite of exploiting the poor by exacting taxes on wheat (Amos 5:11), trampling the heads of the poor into the dust (Amos 2:7), and oppressing and crushing the needy (Amos 4:1). Hosea also criticized the elite's excessive lifestyle (Hos 7:5) and condemned their drunkenness to the point of sickness. Amos denounced the corrupt practices of market merchants (Amos 8:5–6) and critiqued the interest on loans (Amos 2:6), the taking of collateral for loans (Amos 2:8), and the exacting of payment in kind (Amos 2:8). He also condemned the subversion of justice (Amos 5:7, 10). Hosea, in turn, criticized the sociopolitical and economic policies of the elite (Hos 1:2–9, 7:7, 8:4).[135]

Amos and Hosea condemned the exploitative kingdoms of Jeroboam II and Uzziah,[136] just as Jesus spoke against the kingdoms of Rome and the temple elite. The exploitative practices of these kingdoms were similar, as were the social critiques of the prophets Amos and Hosea and the social prophet Jesus.

Concluding Remarks

In colonial situations, such as those witnessed during the times of Amos, Hosea, and Jesus, the elite always had a significant stake in maintaining the status quo.[137] Their interests needed protection. Even the middle strata

---

134. Premnath, "Amos and Hosea," 129.

135. Premnath, "Amos and Hosea," 129–32; Mays, *Hosea*, 12–13.

136. In the same century Micah's message was the same as that of Amos and Hosea. He criticized the elite for their ruthless acquisition of peasant land (Mic 2:2), their failure to serve the cause of justice (Mic 3:1–2) and condemned the cities the elite lived in (Mic 1:5).

137. Horsley, *Spiral of Violence*, 16.

(e.g., scribes and scholar-teachers like the Pharisees and Sadducees in Jesus' time) made adjustments to secure a role in the colonial system.[138] However, there were also individuals from the ordinary ranks of society who assumed the role of prophetic spokespersons for God and leaders of the people.[139] Jesus embraced this role and, following in the footsteps of his predecessors such as Isaiah, Jeremiah, Amos, and Hosea, proclaimed an inclusive God who condemns exploitation and structural violence against the marginalized in society. Like Isaiah, Amos, and Hosea, Jesus chose to tread "the dangerous path of justice and righteousness," to borrow Berquist's term.[140] It is, therefore, understandable that some of his contemporaries regarded him as "one of the prophets of old."

Therefore, Jesus can be regarded as a "public theologian." Public theology, as defined by Van Aarde, does not involve professional theologians or pastors (referred to as the *theological elite*) conducting theology in the public sphere.[141] Instead, it involves public theologians—individuals from various walks of life such as neighborhood saints, strangers, and fellow citizens[142]—engaging in theological discourse in public settings. These public theologians represent diverse backgrounds, including film directors, novelists, scientists, philosophers, poets, artists, technicians, salespersons, and administrative officials. Their theological reflections manifest in various forms, including movies, songs, poems, novels, art, architecture, protest marches, clothing, newspaper and magazine articles, personal blogs, and graffiti.[143] Moreover, the content of their theological reflections often encompasses political and social issues.

Jesus was such a public theologian. As an artist (τέκτων) from Nazareth, he reflected on God. His reflection manifested, among other things, in vivid imagery conveyed through words. These images, his parables, depicted a distinct and novel kingdom with a Ruler who is compassionate and inclusive, a kingdom devoid of exploitation and systemic injustice. As such, his parables served as a form of social analysis, presenting a challenge to prevailing social norms and advocating for societal transformation;

---

138. Horsley, *Spiral of Violence*, 16.
139. Horsley, *Jesus and Empire*, 103.
140. Berquist, "Dangerous Waters," 54.
141. Van Aarde, "What Is 'Theology.'"
142. Storrar, "Kairos Moment," 7–8.
143. Van Aarde, "What Is 'Theology,'" 1216.

fundamentally, they addressed political issues and advocated for the restructuring of society.

Charles Fensham embodies the spirit of a public theologian. While he is a professional theologian, Charles also functions as a neighborhood saint and a fellow citizen, always ready to engage in theological discourse, particularly in public settings, especially on issues of social justice and the rights and protection of LGBTQIA2S+ people. Early in his academic career in South Africa, Charles experienced significant challenges because of his staunch opposition to apartheid. I believe this experience, in some way, prepared Charles to advocate fearlessly for the rights of the LGBTQIA2S+ community. Despite facing adversity, he consistently stood up for the marginalized and exploited members of society, all while maintaining his typical gentle demeanor. In his message and manner, one can discern glimpses of a compassionate and inclusive kingdom free from discrimination and systemic injustice. We are forever in his debt.

Bibliography

Allison, Dale C. *Jesus of Nazareth: Millenarian Prophet*. Minneapolis: Fortress, 1998.

Bailey, Kenneth E. *Jesus through Middle Eastern Eyes: Cultural Studies in the Gospels*. Downers Grove, IL: IVP Academic, 2008.

Berquist, Jon L. "Dangerous Waters of Justice and Righteousness: Amos 5:18–27." *Biblical Theology Bulletin* 23.3 (1993) 54–63.

Bessler-Northcutt, Joe. "Learning to See God: Prayer and Practice in the Wake of the Jesus Seminar." In *The Historical Jesus Goes to Church*, edited by The Jesus Seminar, 51–63. Santa Rosa, CA: Polebridge, 2004.

Beutner, Edward F. "A Mercy Unextended: Matthew 18:23–43." In *Listening to the Parables of Jesus*, edited by Edward F. Beutner, 2:33–39. Jesus Seminar Guides. Santa Rosa: Polebridge, 2007.

Blenkinsopp, Joseph. "Second Isaiah—Prophet of Universalism." *Journal for the Study of the Old Testament* 42 (1988) 83–103.

Bockmuehl, Markus. *This Jesus, Martyr, Lord, Messiah*. Edinburgh: T. & T. Clark, 1994.

Borg, Marcus J. *Conflict, Holiness and Politics in the Teaching of Jesus*. New York: Mellen, 1984.

———. *Jesus: Uncovering the Life, Teachings, and Relevance of a Religious Revolutionary*. New York: HarperCollins, 2006.

———. *Meeting Jesus Again for the First Time: The Historical Jesus and the Heart of Contemporary Faith*. San Francisco: HarperOne, 1994.

Bornkamm, Günther. *Jesus of Nazareth*. New York: Harper & Row, 1960.

Boucher, Madeleine I. *The Parables*. New Testament Message 7. Wilmington, DE: Glazier, 1981.

Brandon, Samuel G. F. *Jesus and the Zealots: A Study of the Political Factor in Primitive Christianity*. Manchester: Manchester University Press, 1967.

Carney, Thomas F. *The Shape of the Past: Models and Antiquity*. Lawrence, KS: Coronado, 1975.

Carter, Warren. "Matthew's Gospel, Rome's Empire, and the Parable of the Mustard Seed (Matt 13:31–32)." In *Hermeneutik Der Gleichnisse Jesus: Methodische Neuansätze Zum Verstehen Urchristlicher Parabeltexte*, edited by Ruben Zimmerman and Gabi Kern, 181–201. Wissenschaftliche Untersuchungen zum Neuen Testament 231. Tübingen: Mohr Siebeck, 2008.

———. *The Roman Empire and the New Testament: An Essential Guide*. Nashville: Abingdon, 2006.

Casey, Maurice. *From Jewish Prophet to Gentile God: The Origins and Development of New Testament Christology*. Louisville: Westminster John Knox, 1991.

Chancey, Martin A. "Disputed Issues in the Study of Cities, Villages, and the Economy in Jesus' Galilee." Boston, 2008.

Craffert, Pieter F. *The Life of a Galilean Shaman: Jesus of Nazareth in Anthropological-Historical Perspective*. Matrix: The Bible in Mediterranean Context 3. Eugene, OR: Cascade Books, 2008.

Crossan, John D. *The Birth of Christianity: Discovering What Happened in the Years Immediately after the Execution of Jesus*. San Francisco: HarperCollins, 1999.

———. *The Historical Jesus: The Life of a Mediterranean Jewish Peasant*. San Francisco: HarperCollins, 1991.

Cupitt, Don. "Reforming Christianity." In *The Once and Future Faith*, edited by Karen Armstrong et al., 51–64. Santa Rosa, CA: Polebridge, 2001.

De Jonge, Marinus. *Jesus, the Servant-Messiah*. New Haven: Yale University Press, 1991.

Downing, Francis G. *Christ and the Cynics: Jesus and Other Radical Preachers in First Century Tradition*. Sheffield: Sheffield Academic, 1988.

Dunn, James D. G. "Messianic Ideas and Their Influence on the Jesus of History." In *The Messiah: Developments in Earliest Judaism and Christianity*, edited by James H. Charlesworth, 365–81. Minneapolis: Fortress, 1992.

Elliott, John H. *A Home for the Homeless: A Social-Scientific Criticism of 1 Peter, Its Situation and Strategy*. 2nd ed. Minneapolis: Fortress, 1991.

Escobar, Donoso S. "Social Justice in the Book of Amos." *Review and Expositor: A Baptist Theological Journal* 92.2 (1995) 169–74.

Fiensy, David A. *Jesus the Galilean: Soundings in a First Century Life*. Piscataway: Gorgias, 2007.

———. *The Social History of Palestine in the Herodian Period: The Land Is Mine*. Lewiston, NY: Mellen, 1991.

Finley, Moses I. *The Ancient Economy*. Sather Classical Lectures 43. Berkeley: University of California Press, 1973.

Fitzmyer, Joseph A. *The Gospel According to Luke X–XXIV: Introduction, Translation, and Notes*. Anchor Bible 28A. New York: Doubleday, 1985.

Foster, George M. "Peasant Society and the Image of Limited Good." *American Anthropologist* 67.2 (1965) 293–315.

Freyne, Seán. "Urban-Rural Relations in First-Century Galilee: Some Suggestions from the Literary Sources." In *The Galilee in Late Antiquity*, edited by Lee. I. Levine, 75–91. New York: Jewish Theological Seminary of America, 1992.

Funk, Robert W. "Jesus of Nazareth: A Glimpse." In *Listening to the Parables of Jesus*, edited by Edward F. Beutner, 89–93. Jesus Seminar Guides 2. Santa Rosa, CA: Polebridge, 2007.

Funk, Robert W., et al. *The Five Gospels: What Did Jesus Really Say? The Search for the Authentic Words of Jesus: New Translation and Commentary*. New York: Macmillan, 1993.
Gelston, Anthony. "Universalism in Second Isaiah." *Journal of Theological Studies* 43.2 (1992) 377–98.
Goodman, Martin. "The First Jewish Revolt: Social Conflict and the Problem of Debt." *Journal of Jewish Studies* 33.1–2 (1982) 402–29.
Hanson, K. C., and Douglas E. Oakman. *Palestine in the Time of Jesus: Social Structures and Social Conflicts*. 2nd ed. Minneapolis: Fortress, 2008.
Herzog, William R. *Parables as Subversive Speech: Jesus as Pedagogue of the Oppressed*. Louisville: Westminster John Knox, 1994.
———. *Prophet and Teacher: An Introduction to the Historical Jesus*. Louisville: Westminster John Knox, 2005.
Hollenbach, Paul. "Defining Rich and Poor Using the Social Sciences." In *SBL 1987 Seminar Papers*, edited by Kent Richards, 50–63. Atlanta: Scholars, 1987.
Hoover, Roy W. "The Art of Gaining and Losing Everything." In *The Historical Jesus Goes to Church*, edited by The Jesus Seminar, 11–30. Santa Rosa, CA: Polebridge, 2004.
Horsley, Richard A. *Jesus and Empire: The Kingdom of God and the New World Disorder*. Minneapolis: Fortress, 2003.
———. *Jesus and the Spiral of Violence: Popular Jewish Resistance in Roman Palestine*. San Francisco: Harper & Row, 1993.
Horsley, Richard A., and John S. Hanson. *Bandits, Prophets, and Messiahs: Popular Movements at the Time of Jesus*. Minneapolis: Winston, 1985.
Horsley, Richard A., and Neil A. Silberman. *The Message and the Kingdom: How Jesus and Paul Ignited a Revolution and Transformed the Ancient World*. Minneapolis: Fortress, 1997.
Hultgren, Arland J. *The Parables of Jesus: A Commentary*. The Bible in Its World. Grand Rapids: Eerdmans, 2000.
Jeremias, Joachim. *The Parables of Jesus*. Translated by S. H. Hooke. 2nd ed. London: SCM, 1972.
Kaylor, R. David. *Jesus the Prophet: His Vision of the Kingdom on Earth*. Louisville: Westminster John Knox, 1994.
Kloppenborg, John S. "Response to Ernest van Eck: The Parables of the Galilean Jesus: A Social-Scientific Approach." Presented at the 2009 annual meeting of the Context Group, Buffalo, 2009.
———. *The Tenants in the Vineyard: Ideology, Economics, and Agrarian Conflict in Jewish Palestine*. Wissenschaftliche Untersuchungen zum Neuen Testament 195. Tübingen: Mohr Siebeck, 2006.
Lenski, Gerhard E. *Power and Privilege: A Theory of Social Stratification*. New York: McGraw-Hill, 1966.
Lintott, Andrew W. *Violence in Republican Rome*. Oxford: Oxford University Press, 1999.
Lohfink, Norbert, and Erich Zenger. *The God of Israel and the Nations: Studies in Isaiah and the Psalms*. Translated by Everett R. Kalin. Collegeville, MN: Liturgical, 2000.
Louw, Johannes, and Eugene A. Nida, eds. *Greek-English Lexicon of the New Testament Based on Semantic Domains*. Vol. 1. Goodwood: National Book Printers, 1988.
Mack, Burton L. *A Myth of Innocence: Mark and Christian Origins*. Philadelphia: Fortress, 1998.

Malina, Bruce J. "Christ and Time: Swiss or Mediterranean?" *Catholic Biblical Quarterly* 51.1 (1989) 1–31.

———. *The New Testament World: Insights from Cultural Anthropology*. 1st ed, Louisville: Westminster John Knox, 1981.

———. "Religion in the Imagined New Testament World: More Social Science Lenses." *Scriptura: International Journal of Bible, Religion and Theology in Southern Africa* 51 (1994) 1–26.

———. "'Religion' in the World of Paul." *Biblical Theology Bulletin* 16.3 (1986) 92–101.

———. *The Social Gospel of Jesus: The Kingdom of God in Mediterranean Perspective*. Minneapolis: Fortress, 2001.

———. "Wealth and Poverty in the New Testament and Its World." *Interpretation* 41.4 (1987) 354–67.

Malina, Bruce J., and Richard L. Rohrbaugh. *Social-Science Commentary on the Synoptic Gospels*. 2nd ed. Minneapolis: Fortress, 2003.

Malina-Jacobs, Diane. *Beyond Patriarchy: The Images of Family in Jesus*. New York: Paulist, 1993.

Manson, T. W. *The Sayings of Jesus*. Cambridge: Cambridge University Press, 1951.

Mays, James L. *Hosea: A Commentary*. Old Testament Library. Louisville: Westminster John Knox, 1969.

———. "Justice: Perspectives from the Prophetic Tradition." In *Prophesy in Israel*. Philadelphia: Fortress, 1987.

McGaughy, Lane C. "Jesus' Parables and the Fiction of the Kingdom." In *Listening to the Parables of Jesus*, edited by Edward F. Beutner, 7–13. Jesus Seminar Guides 2. Santa Rosa, CA: Polebridge, 2007.

Meier, John P. *A Marginal Jew—Rethinking the Historical Jesus: The Roots of the Problem and the Person*. Vol. 1. New York: Doubleday, 1991.

Miller, Robert J., ed. *The Apocalyptic Jesus: A Debate*. Santa Rosa, CA: Polebridge, 2001.

Moxnes, Halvor. *The Economy of the Kingdom: Social Conflict and Economic Relations in Luke's Gospel*. Overtures to Biblical Theology. 1988. Reprint, Eugene, OR: Wipf & Stock, 2004.

Oakman, Douglas E. *Jesus and the Economic Questions of His Day*. Studies in the Bible and Early Christianity 8. Lewiston, NY: Mellen, 1986.

———. *Jesus and the Peasants*. Matrix: The Bible in Mediterranean Context 4. Eugene, OR: Cascade Books, 2008.

———. *The Political Aims of Jesus*. Minneapolis: Fortress, 2012.

Parsons, Talcott. *Structure and Process in Modern Societies*. New York: Free, 1960.

Polanyi, Karl. *The Great Transformation: The Political and Economic Origins of Our Time*. Calvin and Calvinism 6. Boston: Beacon, 1957.

Premnath, D. N. "Amos and Hosea: Sociohistorical Background and Prophetic Critique." *Word and World* 28 (2008) 125–32.

Rohrbaugh, Richard L. "Agrarian Society." In *Biblical Social Values and Their Meaning: A Handbook*, edited by Bruce J. Malina and John J. Pilch, 4–7. Peabody, MA: Hendrickson, 1998.

———. "A Peasant Reading of the Talents/Pounds: A Text of Terror." *Biblical Theology Bulletin* 23 (1993) 32–39.

Sanders, E. P. *The Historical Figure of Jesus*. New York: Penguin, 1993.

Schottroff, Luise. *The Parables of Jesus*. Translated by Linda M. Maloney. Minneapolis: Fortress, 2006.

Schüssler Fiorenza, Elisabeth. *Jesus: Miriam's Child, Sophia's Prophet—Critical Issues in Feminist Theology*. New York: Continuum, 1994.

Schweitzer, Albert. *The Quest of the Historical Jesus: A Critical Study of Its Progress from Reimarus to Wrede*. Translated by William Montgomery. London: A & C Black, 1910.

Scott, Bernard B. *Hear Then the Parable: A Commentary on the Parables of Jesus*. Minneapolis: Fortress, 1989.

———. "The Reappearance of Parables." In *Listening to the Parables of Jesus*, edited by Edward F. Beutner, 95–119. Jesus Seminar Guides 2. Santa Rosa, CA: Polebridge, 2007.

———. *Re-Imagine the World: An Introduction to the Parables of Jesus*. Santa Rosa, CA: Polebridge, 2001.

Smith, Morton. *Jesus the Magician*. New York: Harper & Row, 1978.

Snodgrass, Klyne R. *Stories with Intent: A Comprehensive Guide to the Parables of Jesus*. Grand Rapids: Eerdmans, 2008.

Stegemann, Ekkehard W., and Wolfgang Stegemann. *The Jesus Movement: A Social History of Its First Century*. Translated by O. C. Dean Jr. Minneapolis: Fortress, 1999.

Storrar, Willaim. "A Kairos Moment for Public Theology." *International Journal of Public Theology* 1.1 (2008) 5–25.

Stuhlmacher, Peter. *Jesus of Nazareth—Christ of Faith*. Peabody, MA: Hendrickson, 1993.

Theissen, Gerd. *The Shadow of the Galilean: The Quest of the Historical Jesus in Narrative Form*. Minneapolis: Fortress, 1987.

Twelftree, Graham H. *Jesus the Exorcist: A Contribution to the Study of the Historical Jesus*. Tübingen: Mohr Siebeck, 1993.

Van Aarde, Andries G. *Fatherless in Galilee: Jesus as Child of God*. Harrisburg, PA: Trinity Press International, 2001.

———. "What Is 'Theology' in 'Public Theology' and 'Public' about 'Public Theology'?" *HTS Teologiese Studies/Theological Studies* 64.3 (2008) 1213–34.

Van Eck, Ernest. *Galilee and Jerusalem in Mark's Story of Jesus: A Narratological and Social-Scientific Reading*. Hervormde Teologiese Studies Supplementum 7. Pretoria: Kital, 1995.

———. *The Parables of Jesus the Galilean: Stories of a Social Prophet*. Matrix: The Bible in Mediterranean Context 9. Eugene, OR: Cascade Books, 2016.

———. "The Tenants in the Vineyard (GThom 65/Mark 12:1–12): A Realistic and Social-Scientific Reading." *HTS Teologiese Studies/Theological Studies* 63 (2007) 909–36.

Verhoefen, Paul. "The First Will Be First: The Labourers in the Vineyard." In *Listening to the Parables of Jesus*, edited by Edward F. Beutner, 41–50. Jesus Seminar Guides 2. Santa Rosa, CA: Polebridge, 2007.

Vermes, Géza. *Jesus the Jew: A Historian's Reading of the Gospel*. New York: Macmillan, 1973.

Wright, N. T. *Jesus and the Victory of God*. Christian Origins and the Question of God 2. SPCK, 1996.

———. *The New Testament and the People of God*. Christian Origins and the Question of God 1. Minneapolis: Fortress, 1992.

15

The Threefold Office of Christ (Munus Triplex) in Canadian Presbyterian Theology

John A. Vissers

SINCE COMING TO CANADA from South Africa in the late 1980s, Charles Fensham has been actively engaged as a minister and professor of theology in the work of the Committee on Church Doctrine of the General Assembly of The Presbyterian Church in Canada. This national committee "considers and reports on all matters of faith and order which the General Assembly may from time-to-time refer to it and makes recommendations to the General Assembly for the furtherance of the church's continuing ministry of determining and declaring the church's confessional position."[1] As a member of this committee for over twenty-five years, the Rev. Dr. Fensham has worked tirelessly and written reports on matters of faith and order such as the mission of the church, the nature of confessional standards, 2SLGBTQI+ inclusion, and the ordination questions for ministers and elders.

As Professor of Systematic Theology at Knox College from 2002 to 2023, Fensham followed in the footsteps of his predecessors Iain G. Nicol and David W. Hay, who also made significant contributions to the

---

1. Mandate of the Committee on Church Doctrine, the General Assembly of The Presbyterian Church in Canada. The Committee was originally called the Articles of Faith Committee (until 1970).

theological identity of Canadian Presbyterianism through their work on the Committee on Church Doctrine.[2] To illustrate the importance of such work, this essay examines how the historic Reformed doctrine of the threefold office of Christ was applied to the church's doctrine of ministry in the 1960s, and the role played by Professor David W. Hay in that development.[3]

The Preamble to the Ordination and Induction Questions for ministers and elders within The Presbyterian Church in Canada, adopted by the General Assembly in 1970, contains the following statement: "All ministries proceed from and are sustained by the ministry of the Lord Jesus Christ. He is our Prophet, Priest, and King, the Minister of the covenant of grace."[4] What is the significance of this reference to Jesus Christ as Prophet, Priest, and King? What is its origin, and what role has it played in the theology and practice of Canadian Presbyterianism?

The description of Jesus as Prophet, Priest, and King is called the "Threefold Office of Christ" (Latin, *munus triplex*). The *munus triplex* is found in five official documents of The Presbyterian Church in Canada: *The Westminster Confession of Faith* (1646); *The Westminster Larger Catechism* (1647–1649); *The Westminster Shorter Catechism* (1647–1649);[5] *The Preamble to the Ordination and Induction Questions* (1970); and *A Catechism for Today* (2004). It does not appear in *The Declaration of Faith Concerning Church and Nation* (1955), and it is absent from *Living Faith* (1984). Of the four confessional statements adopted by The Presbyterian Church in Canada as "Parallel Standards" in 1962, only the Heidelberg Catechism (1563) contains it.[6]

---

2. David W. Hay was Professor of Systematic Theology from 1944–1976. He was succeeded by Iain G. Nicol who served from 1976–2002.

3. An earlier version of this essay was delivered as a paper to the annual meeting of the Canadian Society for Presbyterian History at Knox College, University of Toronto on September 23, 2023.

4. Preamble to Ordination Questions, PCC, *Book of Forms*, "Standards and Subscription."

5. The Westminster Confession of Faith, 8.1; The Larger Catechism, Questions 42–45; The Shorter Catechism, Questions 23–26. The Westminster Standards were adopted by The Presbyterian Church in Canada in 1875, 1889. It is not explicitly in the Westminster *Presbyterial Form of Church Government*.

6. The Heidelberg Catechism, Lord's Day 12; Question 31. The Belgic Confession (Guido de Brès, 1559) refers to Jesus Christ as Priest and King but does not employ the threefold office. The Second Helvetic Confession (Bullinger, 1562–1566) also calls Jesus Christ King and High Priest, emphasizing the royal priesthood of Jesus, but does not use the threefold office. The Gallican Confession does not use the threefold office

The doctrine of the Threefold Office of Christ originated with the Protestant Reformer John Calvin in the sixteenth century, and after Calvin the *munus triplex* became a staple of European and British Reformed theology. Calvin argued that in the Old Testament the covenant between God and Israel was mediated by prophets, priests, and kings, chosen by God, and anointed with oil and by the Spirit. In his person and work *(officium)* as the Messiah, Jesus fulfilled these three offices.[7] As a prophet, Jesus fulfilled Old Testament prophecy; he is the prophet par excellence, the mediator of revelation, himself the Word of God, who proclaimed God's love, the one through whom we come to know God. As a priest, Jesus Christ secured salvation through his ministry of reconciliation and intercession by way of his vicarious suffering and saving atonement. He continues this ministry of intercession through his ascension at the right hand of God the Father.[8] As a king, the reign of Jesus Christ is spiritual and eternal. Through his royal office the Messiah accompanies and aids his people in the vicissitudes of this mortal life and prepares them for the life everlasting.[9]

Calvin was not the first theologian to speak of the threefold office, but he was the first to develop it into a robust account of the redemptive work of Christ. In early and mediaeval theology, examples of a triple office can be found.[10] During the Reformation, Erasmus referred to Christ as Prophet, Priest, and King in his *Commentary on the Second Psalm* (1522). In 1530, the Lutheran theologian Osiander—with whom Calvin quarreled extensively in the *Institutes*—used the threefold office in a written submission

---

of Christ or refer to Christ as Priest or King. The Scots Confession (John Knox, 1560) does not mention the threefold office explicitly. It expresses a similar idea when it speaks about Jesus Christ "our Head and only Mediator . . . whom we confess and avow to be the Messiah promised, the only Head of his Kirk, our just Lawgiver, our only High Priest, Advocate, and Mediator" in whose "honours and offices no one should presume to intrude themselves."

7. Calvin, *Institutes*, Book II, Chapter XV, 1–6. For Calvin, Jesus is the Mediator of the *one* covenant of grace in the *one* threefold office *(munus)*, under the two dispensations of law and gospel.

8. Calvin, *Institutes*, Book II, Chapter XV, 3–5.

9. Calvin, *Institutes*, Book II. Chapter XV, 3–5.

10. Eusebius (d. 339) connected the anointing of priests, kings, and prophets with the Messianic office of Jesus. Chrysostom (d. 407) argued that Christ surpassed Abraham (prophet and priest) and David (king and prophet) by possessing all three dignities. Thomas Aquinas (d. 1274) believed that Christ, as the Head of all, possessed the perfection of all graces, including those that belong to lawgivers, priests, or kings. Thomas Aquinas, *Summa Theol.* III. Q.22, art. 1–2. Cf. Jansen, *Calvin's Doctrine*, 30–32.

to the Diet of Augsburg to emphasize that righteousness and holiness do not rest in meritorious works, but solely in Christ's work as king, prophet, and priest. Calvin's adoption of the *munus triplex* was influenced by Martin Bucer with whom Calvin worked from 1538 to 1541 in Strasbourg. Bucer referred to the three offices in his exegesis of John 1 and Psalm 45.

The first extended use by Calvin of the *munus triplex* was in the French Genevan Catechism (1541–1542),[11] and he included a chapter on the threefold office in Book II of the 1559 *Institutes*. For the sixteenth century Protestant Reformation, the *munus triplex* found its finished form in the Heidelburg Catechism.[12] Most of what followed in the Reformed tradition from the sixteenth to the nineteenth centuries was theological commentary on the threefold office in relation to the redemptive work of Christ as set out by Calvin and Heidelberg. The inclusion of the *munus triplex* in the seventeenth century Westminster Standards as a description of Christ's redemptive work was decisive for Scottish Presbyterianism—and therefore for Presbyterians in Canada.

By the eighteenth century, the first serious cracks in the soteriological edifice built upon the doctrine of the threefold office in Protestant theology began to appear, initially among Lutherans. Johann August Ernesti (1707–1781) complained that the metaphorical phrases of the threefold office obscured rather than clarified Christ's work of satisfaction.[13] Furthermore, he argued, the three offices were insufficiently distinguished and therefore one title might justly cover them all.[14] In the late nineteenth century, Albrecht Ritschl levelled similar criticisms.[15]

J.F. Jansen's 1956 book *Calvin's Doctrine of the Work of Christ* summarized two criticisms of Calvin's use of the threefold office and its subsequent development in the Reformed tradition. First, it is not explicitly biblical. The twofold office of Jesus Christ as Priest and King has an explicit basis in Scripture (Heb 7). So too does the idea that followers of Jesus are members of a royal priesthood (1 Pet 2:9; Rev 1:6). It is also true that one can see in the New Testament the idea that Jesus is a prophet; but there is no explicit threefold office. Second, the development of the threefold office

---

11. The Genevan Catechism (French 1541–1542, Latin 1545), Questions 34–45.

12. Zacharius Ursinus, Heidelberg Catechism (1563), Questions 31 and 32.

13. J. A. Ernesti, *De Officio Christi Triplici* (Opuscula Theologica), 1773, 371–96. Cited by Jansen, Calvin's Doctrine, 18.

14. Muller, "Threefold Office."

15. Ritschl, Christian Doctrine.

in the Reformed tradition represented what Jansen called an accretion of doctrine, i.e., it grew with the addition of layers of theological meaning beyond what Calvin had intended. By the time The Presbyterian Church in Canada was trying to find its theological way after church union in 1925, the *munus triplex* was an unlikely candidate to serve as a basis for a doctrine of ministry. But it did. Why?

First, Roman Catholicism had adapted the *munus triplex* for the doctrine of the church. In the nineteenth century, John Henry Newman suggested that the threefold office of Christ extended to the body of Christ, i.e., the church. This aligned with the Tübingen Catholic theologians of the day, such as J.A. Mohler, who saw the church as an extension of the incarnation.[16] Pope Pius XII in his encyclicals *Mystici Corporis* (1943) and *Mediator Dei* (1947) restricted the application of the threefold office to the ecclesial hierarchy and the sacerdotal system on the basis that these designations had been extended from Christ to the apostles.[17] In all this, the *munus triplex* was extended beyond the work of Christ (soteriology) to include the doctrine of the church and its ministry (ecclesiology).

Second, the influence of the theological renewal from the 1920s to the 1950s associated with Brunner and Barth was important. Emil Brunner employed the threefold office in his *Christian Dogmatics* to ground his Christology in salvation-history which he interpreted through Christ's work in revelation, atonement, and divine sovereignty. Karl Barth adapted the threefold office in the dynamic tripartite structure of Volume IV ("The Doctrine of Reconciliation") of his *Church Dogmatics*.[18] Through the influence of Walter Bryden and his students, the theologies of Barth and Brunner

---

16. Wainwright, *For Our Salvation*, 115–17.

17. The Second Vatican Council followed this approach. The 1994 *Catechism of the Catholic Church* describes the church and its pastors as "a priestly, prophetic, and royal people" who participate "in these three offices of Christ and bear responsibilities for mission and service that flow from them." 783 (Part One, Section Two, Chapter Three, Article 9, Paragraph 2, Number I, 206).

18. Initially, in *The Mediator*, Brunner did not employ the *munus triplex* because it had become so identified with Reformed scholastic orthodoxy. However, he changed his mind on this and used it in his Christian Dogmatics as the basis for an exposition of the redemptive work of Christ. Barth used the *munus triplex* as the overall structure for his three volumes in *The Doctrine of Reconciliation*. In his descent and humiliation (volume IV.1), Jesus Christ as Lord is Servant (*munus sacerdotale*—office of priest). In his ascent and exaltation (volume IV.2), Jesus Christ as Servant is Lord (*munus regium*—royal office). In volumes IV.3.1 and IV.3.2, corresponding to the *munus propheticum*, Jesus Christ is the True Witness.

played a significant role in Canadian Presbyterian theology from the 1930s to the 1970s.[19]

Third, Presbyterians were influenced by the emergence of the ecumenical movement in the twentieth century. As already noted, the threefold office is not uniquely Reformed. The *munus triplex* was embraced by the Lutheran and Roman Catholic traditions. It was also adopted by Eastern Orthodox theologians. In his Warfield Lectures at Princeton Theological Seminary in 1948, the General Secretary of the World Council of Churches, Willem Visser t' Hooft, expounded the Kingship of Christ within the context of the *munus triplex* as the basis for church unity.[20] Methodist theologian Geoffrey Wainwright has argued that throughout the twentieth century the threefold office of Christ provided a rich resource for ecumenical theology, especially in ecumenical dialogues concerning the church, ministry, and sacraments.[21]

This was the historical-theological context within which the Articles of Faith Committee met in the 1950s and 1960s. Following the adoption of the "Declaration of Faith Concerning Church and Nation" by the General Assembly as a subordinate standard in 1955, the General Assembly directed the Articles of Faith Committee to begin work on "The Church's Relation to Her Standards." In 1963, the inclusion of the *munus triplex* appeared in the report to the General Assembly in the proposed "Short Preamble."[22] The subcommittee working on this included David Hay, Professor of Systematic Theology at Knox College. From 1944 until 1975 he taught most of the ministers of The Presbyterian Church in Canada. He was an influential teacher at the College and a significant voice in the Committee.

In lectures on "The Divine Institution of the Holy Ministry" at Knox College and Ewart College, Professor Hay argued for a robustly theological account of ministry grounded in the redemptive work of Christ. He did so by appealing to the Reformed tradition itself, namely the *Form of Presbyterial Church Government* (Westminster, 1645) and *The Westminster Larger Catechism* (Q.45). He noted that both documents grounded the order and government of the church in Jesus Christ as the King and Head, and that

---

19. Walter Bryden (1883–1952) taught history and theology at Knox College from 1925 to 1952 and served as Principal from 1945 to 1952. He was instrumental in the reception of the theologies of Brunner and Barth in Canada. Many of Bryden's students served on the Articles of Faith Committee in the 1950s and 1960s.

20. Visser 't Hooft, *Kingship of Christ*.

21. Wainright, *For Our Salvation*, 103–9.

22. PCC Archives, Minutes, 1973–1014–15.

Christ exercises his office as King through the church and its officers.[23] He argued, however, that the *kingly* concept by itself was inadequate, and he proposed the *munus triplex* as the basis for a Reformed doctrine of ministry:

> We should amplify, qualify, and enrich the doctrine of the Westminster Divines by speaking of the ministerial office in connection not only with Christ's kingly office, but also in connection with his prophetic role (which obviously relates at once to preaching), and to his priestly role (which again, obviously relates to the administration of sacraments.[24]

To support this argument, Hay pointed out that the Westminster Divines described pastors as prophets who have charge of the word and as priests who have charge of the ordinances. Simply put, while the *Presbyterial Form of Church Government* did not explicitly name the threefold office, Hay believed that in practice it should be extended to the order of the church and the doctrine of ministry. Moreover, he saw a deep convergence between the Reformed tradition and the Roman Catholic tradition on this point.[25]

Following the introduction of the "Short Preamble" with the *munus triplex* to the General Assembly in 1963, it was finally adopted in 1970 along with the new ordination vows. Since 1970, the doctrine of the threefold office of Christ has been declared as the basis of the church's doctrine of ministry at every ordination and induction service of a minister and elder. As noted earlier, the *munus triplex* is not in *Living Faith*,[26] but it is included in *A Catechism for Today*.[27] In the new catechism it returned to its

---

23. "The Preface," *The Presbyterial Form of Church Government*. *The Larger Catechism*, A. 45. "Christ executeth the office of a king, in calling out of the world a people for himself, and giving them officers, laws, and censures, by which he visibly governs them."

24. Hay, "Sign and Word."

25. David Hay also argued for the apostolic succession of ministry and emphasized the priestly dimension of the threefold office in its application to the ministry of Word and Sacraments within The Presbyterian Church in Canada.

26. One might expect to see the *munus triplex* in *Living Faith* in Chapter 3.4, "Jesus is Saviour," where Jesus is named as the Mediator, or in Chapter 7.2 "Ministry," where Jesus is named as King and Head.

27. William Klempa was the convenor of the Articles of Faith Committee when the final report on the Preamble and Ordination questions was presented in 1969. As a Calvin scholar, Klempa knew the tradition of the threefold office in Reformed theology well and he had written about it in his doctoral dissertation on Calvin's doctrine of the covenant under Professor Thomas F. Torrance at Edinburgh in the late 1950s. It is worth noting that Klempa was also a member of the committee which drafted the new catechism but that he was not a member of committee which drafted *Living Faith*. But further work is

former place, as an explanatory doctrine of the redemptive work of Jesus Christ as Messiah and Mediator.

This brief essay is an origin story. It explains why a sixteenth century European Reformed doctrine reemerged with force in twentieth century Canadian Presbyterianism. It also illustrates the important role played by professors of Systematic Theology at Knox College in The Presbyterian Church in Canada's task of reformulating the Reformed faith through the work of the Committee on Church Doctrine. The task of a theologian is to examine how doctrine originates and develops; how it functions, flourishes, and fades. Christian doctrines are sites where excavation and interrogation occur. They are meeting places for conversation and interpretation about what the faith has meant in the past, and what it means now for the people of God. For Canadian Presbyterians in the 1960s, the doctrine of the threefold office of Christ was such a meeting place, and Knox's professor of Systematic Theology at the time was at the center of the discussion. My colleague, Professor Charles Fensham, stands in this noble tradition. For the first quarter of the twenty-first century, Charles has been at the center of many of the theological issues with which The Presbyterian Church in Canada has wrestled, including a proposed revision of the Preamble to the Ordination Questions, which is currently before the General Assembly for study and comment. For this important work, and all his contributions, we honor and thank him.

Bibliography

Barth, Karl. *Church Dogmatics.* IV: *The Doctrine of Reconciliation.* Edited by T. F. Torrance. Translated by G. W. Bromiley. Edinburgh: T. & T. Clark.
Brunner, Emil. *The Mediator: A Study of the Central Doctrine of the Christian Faith.* Translated by Olive Wyon. London: Lutterworth, 1934.
———. *The Christian Doctrine of Creation and Redemption.* Dogmatics 2. London: Lutterworth, 1950.
Calvin, John. *Institutes of the Christian Religion.* Library of Christian Classics 20. Edited by John T. McNeill. Translated and indexed by Ford Lewis Battles. Philadelphia: Westminster, 1960.
Catechism of the Catholic Church, Second Edition. Revised in accordance with the official Latin text promulgated by Pope John Paul II. Libreria Editrice Vaticana, 1997.

---

required to understand the place of the threefold office in The Presbyterian Church in Canada after 1970. Further research is also required to explore whether the *munus triplex* played any significant role in nineteenth-century Canadian Presbyterianism, whether in official statements, or in preaching and teaching.

Hay, David. "Sign and Word." Lectures on the Reformed Doctrine of Ministry, 1999–5001-2-6. David Hay fonds, The Presbyterian Church in Canada Archives, Toronto, Ontario.

Jansen, J. F. *Calvin's Doctrine of the Work of Christ*. Cambridge: James Clarke, 1956.

Muller, E. F Karl. "Jesus Christ, Threefold Office of." *Christian Classics Ethereal Library*, Calvin College. https://ccel.org/s/schaff/encyc.

The Presbyterian Church in Canada (PCC). *Book of Forms*. Toronto: The General Assembly Office.

The Presbyterian Church in Canada (PCC) Archives. Minutes of the Articles of Faith Committee, 1973–1014-15. Articles of Faith/Church Doctrine Committee fonds. Toronto, Ontario.

The Presbyterian Church, United States of America. *Book of Confessions*. Louisville: Office of the General Assembly.

Ritschl, Albrecht. *The Christian Doctrine of Justification and Reconciliation: Positive Development of the Doctrine*. Translated by H. R. Mackintosh and A. B. Macaulay. Edinburgh: T. & T. Clark, 1900.

Visser 't Hooft, Willem. *The Kingship of Christ: An Interpretation of Recent European Theology*. Stone Lectures 1947. Harper, 1948.

Vissers, John. *The Neo-Orthodox Theology of W.W. Bryden*. Princeton Theological Monograph Series 56. Eugene, OR: Pickwick Publications, 2011.

Wainwright, Geoffrey. *For Our Salvation: Two Approaches to the Work of Christ*. Grand Rapids: Eerdmans, 1997.